MAP
OF THE
NEW RIVER
from its Source near the
TOWN OF WARE TO LONDON,
and part of the
RIVER LEA.

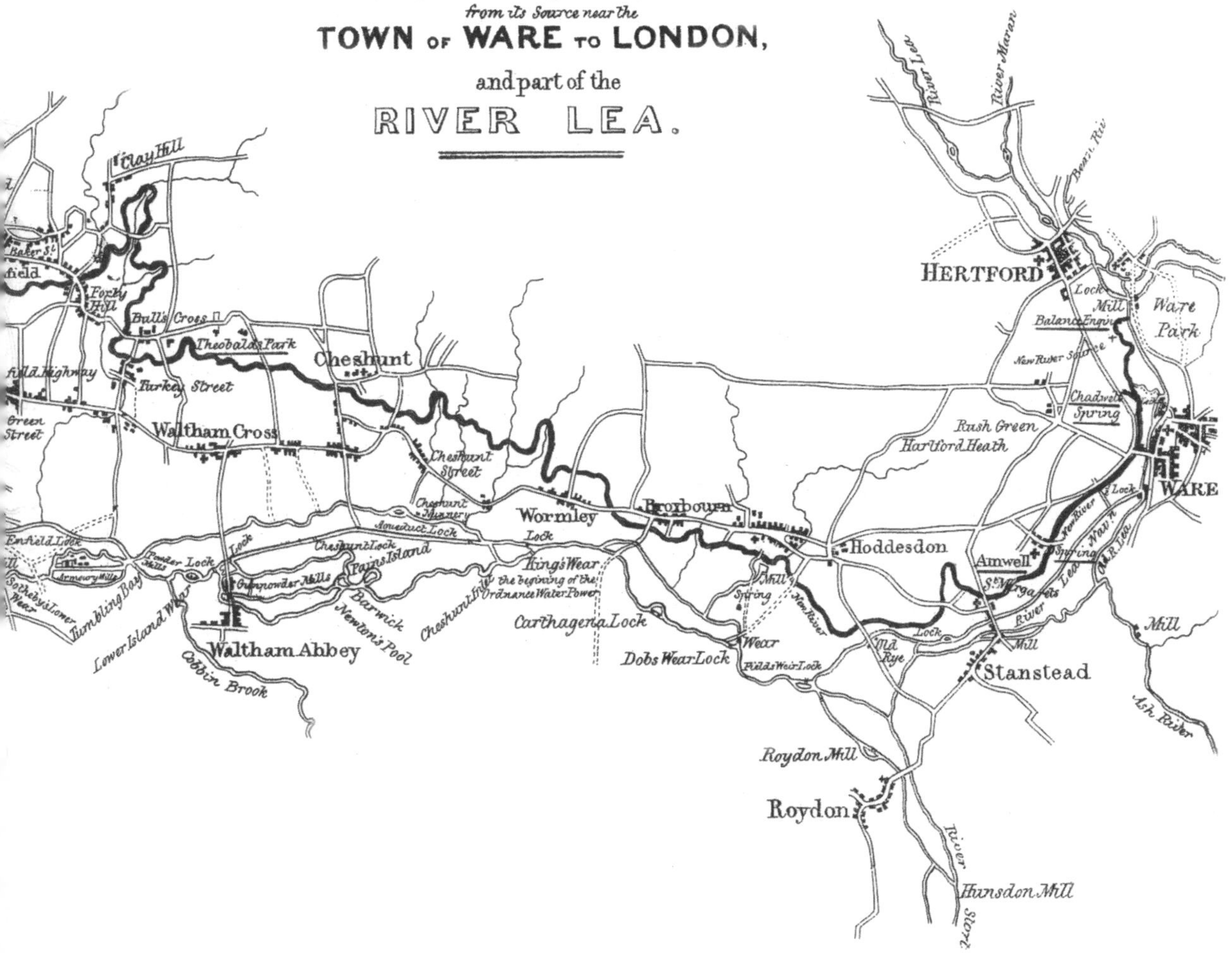

London's
NEW RIVER

First published 2003
by Historical Publications Ltd
32 Ellington Street, London N7 8PL
(Tel: 020 7607 1628)

ISBN 0 948667 84 2
British Library Cataloguing-in-Publication Data
A catalogue record for this book is available from the British Library
Printed by Edelvives in Zaragoza, Spain

The Illustrations

The following illustrations were reproduced by kind permission of:
British Library: *23, 24*
British Museum: *31, 32*
Roger Cline: *13, 33*
Peter Garland: *80*
Guildhall Library, London: *16*
London Borough of Hackney: *78*
Historical Publications: *1, 2, 3, 4, 5, 6, 12, 14, 15, 18, 21, 22, 25, 29, 35, 43, 44, 45, 46, 50, 53, 60, 64, 65, 67, 68, 69, 70, 75, 76, 77, 79*
London Metropolitan Archives: *20, 26, 37, 38, 42, 52, 55, 56, 57, 58*
Stewart Johnson: *dustjacket and back endpaper*
© Royal Society: *36*
Science Museum Library, Berry Collection; Trustees Science Museum: *9*
Robert Ward: *8, 11, 34, 39, 40, 41, 47, 48, 51, 54, 63, 65, 81, 82, 83, 84, 85, 86*
Thames Water: *10, 27, 71, 72, 74*

London's NEW RIVER

Robert Ward

HISTORICAL PUBLICATIONS

For Theya

Contents

List of illustrations

Preface

No city can prosper without good water, and London owes much to the New River. This book sets out to tell the story of a man-made waterway over forty miles long, conceived in the time of Queen Elizabeth I and a major part of London's water supply ever since. It is gleaned from masses of records that extend over four centuries, and as a result has to be selective.

Many of the places mentioned in the text can be found on the front endpaper map, while the maps on pages 215-7 show further detail. The Bowles engraving on pages 14-15 gives a good over-view of the works on Islington Hill as they were in 1752, and the surveys and maps at pages 131, 177 and 186 cover the same area. There is a chronology of principal events at pages 237-8.

Spelling

The spelling used in original documents has usually been retained. The exceptions are that some abbreviations have been expanded for clarity, such as *majesties* for *m'ties,* and *ye* is printed as *the,* the way it was always pronounced.

The Myddelton family name can be found spelt in many different ways, but when Hugh Myddelton signed his name he put the *e* before the *l*, and that is the spelling used here. The River can be spelt Lee or Lea, but Lea has been preferred here except in direct quotes.

Dates, money, weights and distances

Until 1752 the English calendar year began on 25 March. So, 31 December 1708 was followed by 1 January 1708, and so on until 24 March 1708, which was immediately followed by 25 March 1709. To avoid confusion, all dates in this book are in the modern form. This means that all old-style dates between 1 January and 24 March have had one year added to them.

Sums of money are shown in the pre-1971 form of pounds, shillings and pence, abbreviated as £ s. d. One pound was equal to twenty shillings, and each shilling was equal to twelve pence, so there were two hundred and forty pence in a pound. The New River was designed, built, upgraded and described in terms of miles, yards, feet and inches, and it seemed preferable not to attempt any conversions. Approximate metric equivalents are as follows:

1 mile = 1.6 km. 1 yard = 0.91 m. 1 foot = 0.3m. 1 inch = 2.54 cm. 1 acre = 0.4 hectares. 1 rod, or pole = 5½ yards. 1 pound = 454 g.

Thanks

My personal thanks are due to Dr Denis Smith for suggesting the New River as a line of research, to Howard Usher, archivist to Lord Ralph Kerr at Melbourne Hall, to Maxwell Craven of Derby, to Ronald Bennett, formerly Company Secretary to the New River Company Limited, to Emma Stephenson-Smith, to Ian Sutton, to Robin Winters and others at Thames Water, to members of the Greater London Industrial Archaeology Society and to many others who have offered help and advice along the way.

This book owes much to the invariably helpful staff of many libraries, archives and organisations, including Berkshire Record Office, Birkbeck College, University of London (Department of Extra-mural Studies), Birmingham City Archives, British Library, the Department of Prints and Drawings at the British Museum, British Architectural Library (Royal Institute of British Architects), Bruce Castle Museum, Cambridge Central Library, City of London Record Office, Derby Industrial Museum, Emmanuel College, Cambridge, Family Records Centre, Fortress Study Group, Oxford, Goldsmiths' Company, Guildhall Library, Hampshire Record Office, Historical Manuscripts Commission, Honourable Artillery Company, Hunterian Library at Glasgow University, Institution of Civil Engineers, Islington Local History Collection, Kew Steam Museum (Bryce Caller), Lambeth Palace Library, London Borough of Camden Archives, London Metropolitan Archive, Museum of London, National Monuments Record, Orkney Library, Public Record Office (National Archive), Rijksmuseum, Amsterdam, Royal Society of London, Royal Society of Arts, Scottish Records Office, St Paul's Cathedral Library, Science Museum Library, Suffolk Records Office, University of Nottingham (Hallward Library), Westminster City Archives.

Robert Ward
London, 2003

CHAPTER ONE

On Islington Hill

On Islington Hill – Water supply in Roman and Elizabethan London – The London Bridge Waterworks – London's need for water – Colthurst's plan for a New River – Colthurst's Charter – The role of the City – Hugh Myddelton of Denbigh – Raising the money.

On Islington Hill

It is almost two thousand years since London began to be a city. Its location on the tidal part of the Thames at a point where the river could easily be crossed, and where it was possible to use the ebb and flow of the tide to help to convey seagoing vessels in and out made it, from very early times, a trading city. The size of its population can only be guessed, but it had a protective wall eight miles long. When the Romans left there was a period of decline before others came in their place – invaders, merchants and settlers.

Centuries passed and London still flourished as a centre for trade, especially after William the Conqueror built his Tower at its eastern edge, although the city was still small when Elizabeth came to the throne in 1558. It nowhere reached as far as a mile inland from the waterside. Beyond its walls and the nearby settlement at Westminster open fields lay on every side. Queen Elizabeth wanted it to stay that way, and decreed that there should be no new building within three miles of the city, so London stayed small for a few more decades.

Any visitor in search of a vantage point from which to see it all headed north. Starting from old St Paul's Cathedral, which stood on the same site as the present one from 1280 until the Great Fire destroyed it in 1666, a twenty-minute walk on steadily rising ground led to the summit of what was then called Islington Hill. Looking back from that hilltop the whole city could be seen – houses, churches, towers and cathedral, all in a haze of wood-smoke, and behind them the sinuous curves of a river that was then far wider than it is today. Over to the right, across open fields could be seen another settlement – the little city of Westminster, with its abbey church and the Palace of Whitehall where the Queen held court.

This view that pleased so many has vanished. Attempts to stop the spread of building were in vain, and by 1700, the population was over half a million and the suburbs had reached the lower slopes of Islington Hill. By 1830, the hilltop itself had been engulfed by squares and terraces of houses. It was what the artist George Cruikshank attacked as 'The March of Bricks and Mortar' in a drawing that showed how the fields were vanishing under rows of cheaply-built brick houses. Ironically, Cruikshank lived in one of the very houses in Amwell Street, just below the summit of Islington Hill, which blocked – and still blocks – the wonderful view.

Because it has lost its view, the hill has today lost much of its significance. Its name disappeared long ago and does not appear in indexes to London streets. But from the summit of the hill now – it is called Claremont Square

– a walk back down towards the city is rewarded by tantalising fragments of the unrestricted panorama that once could be admired. A side turning to the west shows how steeply the ground falls to the valley of the Fleet river – long since channelled underground – and there is a prospect over rooftops to Senate House, the Telecom Tower and endless tracts of London to the west. Where the street bends there is a sudden glimpse of the dome of St Paul's, but only these fragmentary views are now possible from ground level.

Many artists recorded the earlier panorama. Perhaps the best known was the Venetian Antonio de Canale, or Canaletto. He came to London in 1746 and stayed for ten years, apart from two short trips to Venice. A pen and ink drawing he made from the hilltop, now in the British Museum, resulted in an engraving that shows it all. The drum and dome of Wren's Cathedral is dominant, silhouetted against the Surrey hills and surrounded by the spires and towers of all the other churches rebuilt since the fire eighty years before, perhaps some fifty of them also to Wren's designs. By Canaletto's time the two cities of London and Westminster had expanded along the Strand until they had met, so the vista of rooftops stretches unbroken from left to right. Even on the south bank, much of it marshy ground ill suited to building, the borough of Southwark was quickly spreading.

Only in the foreground of Canaletto's scene (shown on the jacket and rear endpaper of this book) do the fields remain, stretching a few hundred yards downhill towards the suburbs of Finsbury, Clerkenwell and Holborn. But they are not empty fields. As well as grazing animals, there are groups of strollers, and the foreground is suddenly striking. In the centre of his landscape Canaletto has placed a tapering round tower, its top capped with a shapely ogee dome. It looks like a windmill, but without arms or sails. Next to it is a small square building, with a pyramidal roof and some sheds, and a high fence surrounds them all. Just to the left is a round pond with a colonnaded house on its far side. Another pond is nearer the hilltop, seen in the lower right hand corner of the picture. This one is square, with a cistern house on the far bank where spouts of water pour into the pond.

To a Londoner of that time the subject matter was obvious. What Canaletto had drawn was the New River waterworks, with London in the background. It is interesting to compare his drawing with others done from the same spot before and after, because an odd fact emerges. Canaletto, admired above all for the meticulous, almost photographic quality of his work, has rearranged the landscape. The square pond with its cistern house and gushing spouts, which he has banished to the right hand corner, really belongs in the very centre of the foreground as can be confirmed from numerous maps and drawings, before and since. It is not a matter of perspective or viewpoint – he has just moved it to one side, a hundred yards or more, to a place it never was, for the sake of his composition (*ill.1, p.14, and ill.26, p.131*).

The New River waterworks is only one aspect of the story of Islington Hill, but it provides the theme for this book. A waterworks sounds as dull as could be, but this one can be linked not only to artists and engravers such as Canaletto, Cruikshank and Wenceslaus Hollar but also to the forgotten fortifications that were hurriedly built to protect London during the Civil War. It is linked to Sir Christopher Wren, and Robert Mylne who followed Wren as surveyor of St Paul's and was also surveyor to the New River Company. There are links to Elizabeth I, James I and Charles I and Charles II, to Robert Harley – Queen Annes's secretary of state and later Earl of Oxford – to Daniel Defoe, to the scientist and engineer John Smeaton, to Matthew Boulton and James Watt of steam engine fame, and to the obscure but fascinating George Sorocold – the builder of the tower Canaletto put at the centre of his drawing – a man whose death remains a mystery to this day.

As for the tower, its base is still there to be seen. The stump of the massive walls, three feet six inches thick, stands nine feet high and has been neatly capped with a tiled roof. What it was, and how it came to be there, will become clear as the book proceeds.

1 View of London and the New River works at Clerkenwell; Thomas Bowles, 1752. Unlike the Canaletto engraving used on the jacket of this book, the upper pond (now the site of the Claremont Square reservoir) is in the correct position, in the centre foreground of the illustration.

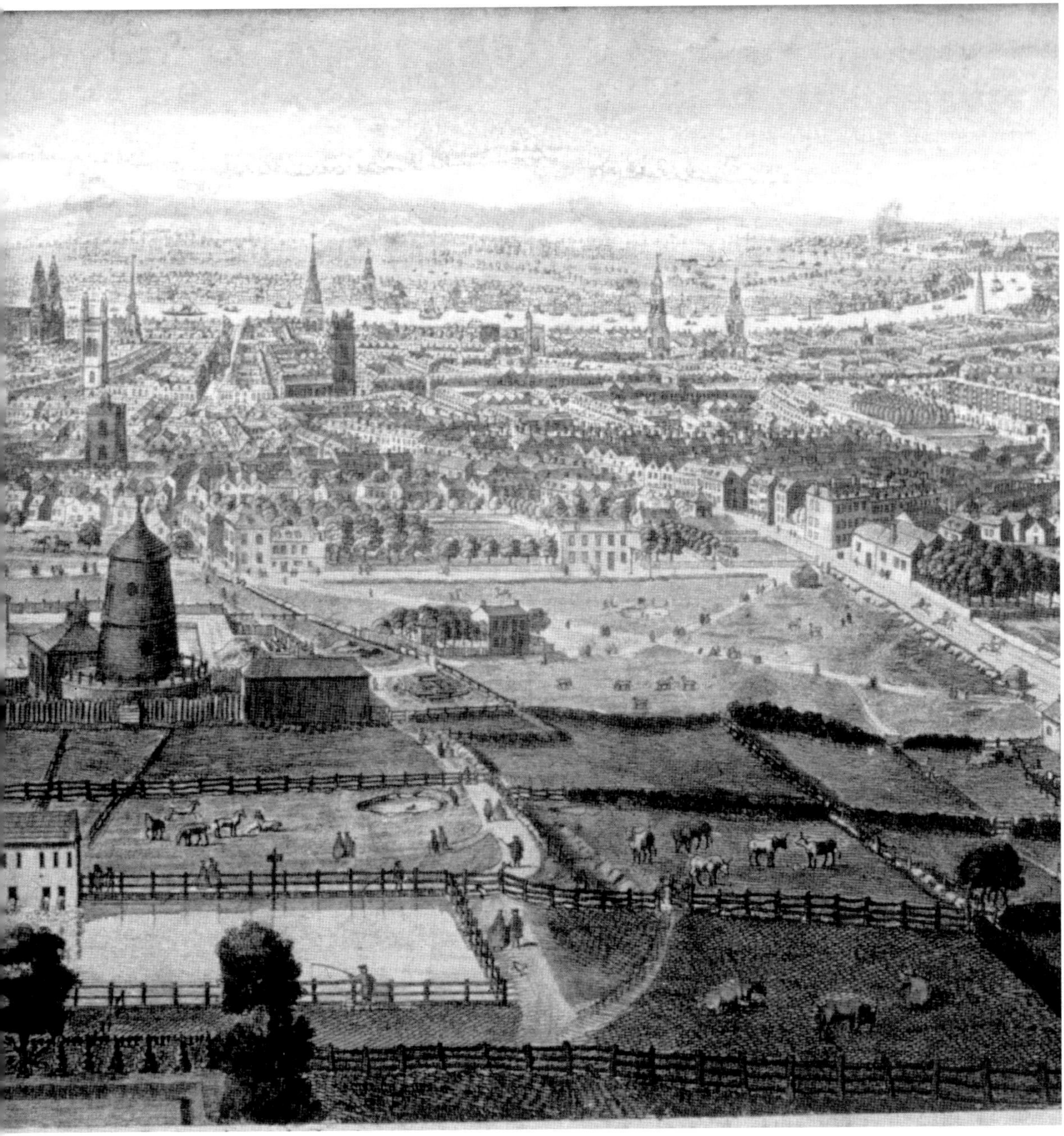

Water supply in Roman and Elizabethan London

Water mattered to the Romans, and they sited London where water-bearing gravel beds made for easy well digging. After long speculation about their methods, no less than three of their wells have been found in London since 2000, with evidence that they raised water with endless iron chains of wooden buckets, powered either by men or animals. After the Romans, such methods were forgotten and when Queen Elizabeth I came to the throne, London had nothing resembling a modern water supply. In part, this was because water was not seen as a necessity. For one thing, plain water was not generally regarded as a sensible drink. Perhaps because of the risks of contamination, beer was the usual drink for most households. It was not a strong beer, either in terms of alcohol or flavour. It was 'small beer,' a simple drink fermented from malt and boiling water, drunk by young and old. Neither was much water needed for personal hygiene, which was less of a preoccupation then. Most people's bodies remained unwashed from season to season, as did their clothes. Clothes were woollen, and wool stays cleaner than cotton.

Some water was needed for household purposes and preparing food. In London, it came from a variety of sources. Some districts had wells – like the Clerks' Well, which gave its name to Clerkenwell and still exists down a flight of steps behind a door just off Clerkenwell Green. Elsewhere there were hand-operated pumps to raise water from underground springs, or water could be fetched from the Thames or one of the lesser streams that still ran above ground, like the Fleet, the Tyburn and the Walbrook. Water carriers plied the streets selling water from casks they carried from a yoke across their shoulders or long wooden barrels carried aslant their backs, for a farthing a gallon. Above all, benefactors down the centuries had given or bequeathed funds to build conduits that brought water in lead pipes and troughs from springs in the nearby countryside, at Marylebone and elsewhere, to public fountains, known as conduits, in the City. There were several of these, in Fleet Street, Threadneedle Street, Dowgate, Cripplegate, Aldgate, Aldersgate, and Aldermanbury. There was a great conduit in Cheapside and a small one in Stocks Market. The cistern of the great conduit of Cheapside was rediscovered in recent excavations – a vaulted stone room down a flight of steps from the street, built in 1286.[1]

2 A 17th-century water carrier

The London Bridge Waterworks

It was the ingenuity of a man called Peter Morice, or Morris as the family later spelt its name, that gave London its first regular water supply direct to private houses in 1582. He was Dutch, or by some accounts German, and his idea was to harness the flow of the Thames to drive pumping machinery.

London Bridge at that time had nineteen separate arches, and most of the width of the

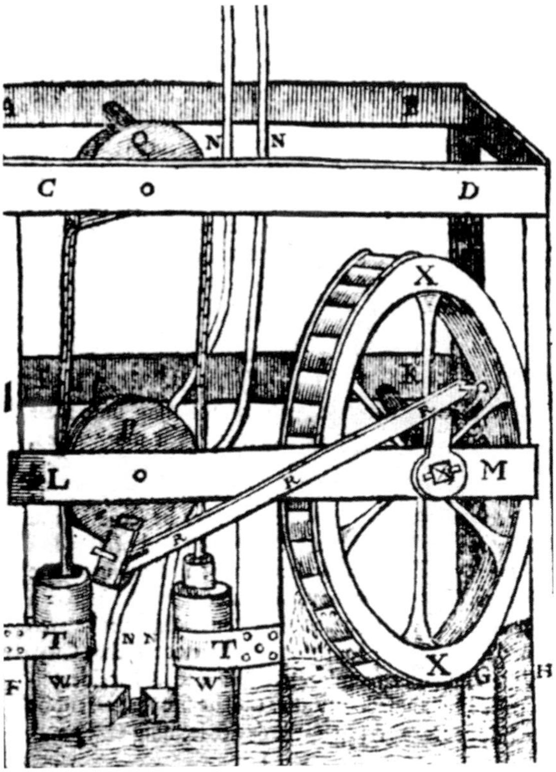

3 Morice left no drawings of his pumping machine at the London Bridge Waterworks, but fifty years later an engineer called John Bate drew this picture of it, which appeared as a woodcut in his book The Mysteries of Nature and Art, published in 1635.

river was blocked by 'starlings', stone footings that supported them. These held the water back and caused strong currents through the arches at most states of the tide – good conditions for a waterwheel.

Morice planned that as the current flowed, so his wheel would turn, and crankshafts could harness this movement to work the plungers of pumps up and down. By this means, river water would effortlessly be pumped into a high tank, and from there it could be piped by gravity wherever it was needed. This was an imaginative scheme for the time and some of the City fathers whose approval was needed may have doubted its feasibility. To allay such fears and to display his command of water, Morice set up one of his pumps by the river and worked it until it projected a jet of water over the nearby church of St Magnus Martyr. This must have been an impressive feat in 1582 and fully persuaded his audience of his abilities. Not only did the mayor and aldermen agree to give Morice a lease of the first arch of the bridge for the modest rent of ten shillings a year, but he somehow persuaded them that the lease should run for no less than 500 years. Morice accordingly built his waterwheel and pumps, and began to supply the immediate neighbourhood, charging those householders who wished to be connected to his mains. The scheme was a success, and within two years he was granted a lease of the second arch – again for 500 years – where he installed another wheel and pumps. He died a wealthy man, and his successors continued to receive the profits until they finally sold their interest more than a century later, as described in chapter 10.

Despite its profitability, the London Bridge Waterworks was not a complete solution to London's need for water. First, the water in the Thames rises and falls greatly twice a day with the tides, which vary in their power according to the phases of the moon and the direction and strength of the wind. A constantly fluctuating water level does not make for an efficient water wheel.

Then again the quality of the water was sometimes very poor, as it might contain sewage or the effluents of all the noxious trades whose waste found its way into the river – complaints were being made about pollution in the river as early as the 1300s. Additionally the waterwheels could not pump anything like sufficient water for the City's needs, and endless waterwheels could not be replicated under all the arches of the bridge because the watermen would never have allowed it. Above all there were practical difficulties in raising the Thames water high enough to supply the higher parts of the City. To squirt a single jet over a church is one thing; to maintain a constant supply for a whole city quite another.

Perhaps worst of all, the waterwheels were under the arches nearest the shore, where the water was at its shallowest. The Thames was much wider at that time, before later wharves and embankments confined it in a narrower channel, and the river was very shallow at the sides. On 13 December 1718 a long dry spell combined with a strong westerly wind to lower the river 'so that the people walked across it in different parts, as also through most of the arches of London Bridge.'[2] Because of such variations, Morice's showpiece supply can never have been more than a partial solution.

All this time London continued to grow. By 1600 the population was about 250,000 – one twentieth of the entire population of England and Wales. As it grew, so its need for water became ever more pressing.

London's need for water

Peter Morice's works at London Bridge only supplied water irregularly and to the southern parts of the City, while the supply from the ancient conduits was inadequate and unreliable. New waterworks occasionally appeared, but always on a small scale. In 1593 the City had granted a lease to Bevis Bulmer of Sutton allowing him to set up a waterworks at Broken Wharf, also known as Poore's Wharf, west of London Bridge. There he set up horse-driven pumps to raise river water to a cistern, and pipes distributed it to nearby parts of the City. It was never more than a small supply, and by 1604 it was in the hands of one Thomas Parradine who was granted a new lease by the City. This allowed him to lay pipes into private houses and to negotiate payment with the occupants. It committed him to pumping at least 80 tons of water each day, of which 20 tons had to be supplied free at a conduit to be erected by the City. Broken Wharf could never have supplied more than a tiny part of London's needs, and eventually, in 1703, the London Bridge works took it over.

Parradine's 1604 lease contains much information about the practicalities of London's water supply. Among other very detailed provisions it includes a specific right for anyone authorised by the City to cut the pipes 'in time of peril and casualty of fire ... and freely to use the water ... for quenching of fire as often as need shall be.'

The general shortage of water that existed at this time can be seen from correspondence in the City records, which shows that even the rich and powerful could not expect a private supply. In April 1592, Lord Cobham, who had a house at Blackfriars, wrote to the Lord Mayor asking if he could take a 'quill' of water – a small pipe – from the conduit at Ludgate to his house. The Mayor replied that he had put the request before the Court of Aldermen who had the power to approve it. It is apparent from his reply that the necessary permission might not be forthcoming. He mentioned that the City was having discussions with an Italian, Frederick Jenibella, elsewhere called Genebelli, 'skilled in water works' who had proposed building a windmill at the fountain-head to improve the supply. If that was successful, he said, the City would be more likely to grant Lord Cobham's request. Genebelli's plans seem to have come to nothing, and more than two years later Lord Burghley wrote to the Lord Mayor on Cobham's behalf, renewing the request for a supply, which had not been granted.

More evidence of inadequate supplies can be seen in 1608, when the Lord Mayor wrote to the Lord Chamberlain to say that the quill of water formerly allowed to Essex House near the Strand must be stopped. The conduit water was very low and the poor were 'becoming very clamorous in this time of dearth,' so that it had become necessary to cut off several quills. Moreover, complaints had been made of the extraordinary waste of water at Essex House, where it was used not only for 'dressing meat' (i.e. preparing food) but also for the laundry, the stable and other offices that he suggested could be 'done otherwise,' though he did not say how.

Similarly in 1613, the Lord Mayor wrote to Lord Fenton. He too wanted a private quill 'out of the City's great pipe' to his house near Charing Cross. It was refused, on account of the frequent failure of the conduits to supply the City, 'provoking frequent complaints and clamours, especially from the poor.'

Sometimes people whose houses adjoined the conduits were tempted to connect a private supply without permission. As long ago as November 1478 William Campion of Fleet Street was found guilty of illegally abstracting water by tapping the conduit where it passed his house and running the water into his well. As punishment he was placed on horseback with a conical cistern on his head from which small pipes showered him. This was constantly replenished as he was taken round the City from one conduit head to the next, stopping at each for his crime to be proclaimed as his drenching continued.[3]

Colthurst's plan for a New River

The answer to the water problem came in about 1600, from Edmund Colthurst, one of those men of parts who thrived in Queen Elizabeth's reign. Originally from Bath in Somerset, he had earned his sovereign's gratitude during military service defending a castle in County Waterford in Ireland, and is often referred to as 'Captayne' Colthurst.[4] He was a benefactor of Bath, having ensured the survival of Bath Abbey, which he had inherited, by donating it to the city. By 1602 he was turning his mind to London's need for water, and all the evidence suggests that he and not Hugh Myddelton was the true originator of the New River. This question is discussed at the end of chapter three.

Precisely what Colthurst had in mind when he first prepared his plan is nowhere spelt out and has to be pieced together from a number of surviving documents. On 23 July 1602, he wrote to Sir Robert Cecil who owned the estate of Theobalds Park, north of Enfield, through which the New River still flows. The letter refers to his 'endeavour to bring a river through your park', and this may be the earliest surviving use of the word river for his proposed supply. He was writing because it had been suggested that before granting him permission to go ahead Queen Elizabeth would have to appoint a commission *ad quod damnum* – a kind of public enquiry to see who might be adversely affected by his plans. The letter continues:

> 'The water I mean to bring is spring, and no part of the River Lee, which in my simple opinion the Queen may pass without a commission of *ad quod damnum*, for I find the county most willing ..'[5]

What he meant by this was that spring water was subject to the ordinary rights of the landowner on whose property the spring rose. He was entitled to do with it what he wished, including channelling it through his neighbours' land if the neighbours were agreeable. By contrast, a river such as the Lea was subject to claims from a variety of sources – towns through which it passed, millers whose watermills it powered, farmers who watered their livestock at its banks and boat-owners whose barges depended on its continued navigability.

His letter shows that his intended springs were somewhere north of Theobalds, and at such a height that their route to London would pass through the park. This is consistent with the springs at Chadwell and Amwell that were eventually to become the twin sources of the New River, and no alternative springs have been identified that would have used this route.

Despite Colthurst's doubt whether it was necessary, the Queen did make enquiries with the City Corporation to discover its attitude. She also ordered the sheriffs of Hertfordshire and Middlesex, her representatives in the two counties affected, to find out whether any of their inhabitants would suffer loss or injury if the scheme went ahead, whether any navigable river would be adversely affected, and how large a channel should be permitted for the new watercourse. The answer to all this was that there should be no problems as long as there was compensation for landowners where the channel was cut, sufficient bridges to cross it, and a width of no more than six feet.

Colthurst's charter

All this had taken time, and on 24 March 1603 Queen Elizabeth died, without having given Colthurst the charter he needed to authorise such a major interference with the rights of the Queen's subjects. Undaunted, he renewed his application to her successor, King James I, and on 18 April 1604 James granted a charter to 'our lovinge subject Edmund Colthurst of Bath' by Letters Patent under the Great Seal of England. It is a lengthy document, and casts some light on prior events. First it sets out Colthurst's intentions, which it says were to provide a supply of water firstly for 'clensinge, scowringe and keepinge sweete divers fowle and unsavoury ditches in and about our said Citties of

London and Westminster, Which at this present are a very great annoyaunce .. and a cause often tymes of Sicknes ...' Colthurst, it continues, had invented and devised a means to bring a 'River, stream or watercourse' from certain springs in the county of Hertford, which would 'purge, scoure and keepe cleane and sweete' the ditches.

This shows some sophistication in Colthurst's approach. By offering free water to cleanse the stinking public drains, he was offering to provide a much needed service that would benefit every inhabitant. The claim that such foul ditches caused sickness was a topical one. Just the previous year, 1603, some 30,000 Londoners – about one in eight of the inhabitants – had died during one of the recurrent outbreaks of plague that afflicted the City. Colthurst was to claim, in a petition the following year, that his waters would not only cleanse the ditches but 'forever keep sweet, so that they shall be able to bear fish, if he may have the managing thereof.'[6] Only after setting out the public benefit does the charter turn to what must have been Colthurst's main purpose. Part of the water, it seemed, would be 'conveyed through pipes and other passages to particuler howses and places ... for the necessary uses .. of persons Who Wante Water.'

The document then records how James's 'late deere sister Elizabeth ... a little before her decease' had wanted the plan to be carried out, providing it brought no inconvenience to the citizens and inhabitants. Thus she had asked the Lord Treasurer, who had ensured that the Lord Mayor and aldermen approved of the work. Likewise the commissions *ad quod damnum* had led to enquiries in Hertford and Middlesex with the results already mentioned.

The charter then grants to Colthurst, his heirs and assigns the right to 'make digge and cutte one ditch or trench not exceeding in breadthe the measure of six foote' to bring water from springs in Hertfordshire and or Middlesex to the cities of London and Westminster and their suburbs. It also provides that because of the 'greate laboure, travaile, costs and expences' that would be incurred by Colthurst or his 'heirs, assigns .. or Deputies', they should have the whole 'benefitt, profitt and commoditie' for ever, giving no more than 'one thirde parte of the said river or streame' for 'private use', and reserving two thirds for cleansing the 'unsavory motes and ditches.' This extension of the charter, not only to Colthurst's heirs when he died, but also to his deputies is an important detail. It meant that the right was not personal to Colthurst – he could transfer it to others if he chose.

The charter goes on to provide that Colthurst would be liable to make a payment of £20 a year to the exchequer, starting once the works produced a profit. It also commands the population at large not to 'presume to lett, disturbe, interrupte or hinder' the work of Colthurst or his deputies, workmen or surveyors in doing the work or subsequently amending it or keeping it in repair. Nor must they meddle with any of the streams or watercourses, or the River Lea, in such a way as to 'hinder or diminishe' Colthurst's work. Further, nobody must then or in the future 'withdraw, derive or conveye away' the water 'by damminge, stoppinge up or cuttinge of the said Chennell' without Colthurst's prior consent.

Of course, the charter placed some obligations on Colthurst. Before cutting any land, whether it belonged to the King or anyone else he must reach agreement to 'satisfye and content' the landowners and occupiers for the 'losses, hurte and dammage' occasioned by the work. Further, where the new river anywhere along its course cut any crossing route, 'good and sufficient bridges' must be provided and thereafter maintained for ever 'for our lovinge Subjects to passe and goe over from place to place.' Furthermore, where the work involved digging trenches in the streets of London, Westminster or their suburbs, 'for layeing of pipes or for amendinge the same' the surface must be paved again and left 'in as good case .. as he or they found the same.'

In a nice touch, the charter also gives the occupiers of land cut for the river something in addition to mere compensation. It states that they could 'take and enjoy the whole benefitt of fishinge and fowlinge or any other pleasure of the same river stream ... not hurting the same water or alteringe the height or diminishinge the streame.' It also provides that the work should be carried to completion within seven years. Presciently, this time limit would not apply if the delay was caused by anyone who 'disturbed, molested, interrupted or hindred .. the worke', but only if Colthurst failed to complete through his own default, flowing from Colthurst's 'negligence and slacknesse' or his inability to finish the work. If that were the case, then the details of the charter were 'utterly voide, frustrate and of none effect, as if they had never byn.'

Finally the charter provided that if in future times 'it shall playnly appeare' that Colthurst's work has adversely affected the current of the river Lea or the Thames or any other navigable river, making them 'lesse navigable or passable with botes or barges or any other vessells', then Colthurst or his successors must make good the damage at their own expense within a year of the problem arising. Failure to do so would oblige them to restore 'the said springs and streames of water to their ancient courses' – again at their own expense – and the charter would then be void.[7]

Having obtained this patent, Colthurst set to work and began applying to landowners for their agreement. In a letter to Viscount Cranborne, a major landowner, Cranborne's agent has noted details of Colthurst's proposed route. It passed through Broxbourne, Wormley, 'Chestenhunt', 'Edlemonton' and Theobalds Park. This resembles the route eventually followed by the New River so closely that Colthurst has a better claim than Myddelton to be its originator, although it was of course Myddelton who carried the project to completion.

The role of the City

By early 1605 Colthurst claimed to have completed three miles of the work and tried to persuade the City of London to contribute towards the costs. The details of his three mile stretch will be discussed later. Three miles of waterway is such a substantial piece of work that digging the New River arguably began sometime in 1604, rather than in 1609 when Myddelton resumed the work with Colthurst's help.[8] It was around this time that the Common Council of the City of London began to take a closer interest in what was happening. First they appointed a committee to report on the proposals of 'Captayne Colthurst', and one of its 13 members was Sir Thomas Myddelton, one of Hugh's brothers.[9]

Alternative schemes were suggested, and before the end of 1605 the City applied for an Act of Parliament that would authorise it to bring water to London from the River Lea or the 'River of Uxbridge' – the Colne. A committee of MPs was set up to consider it, and among them was the member for Denbigh – Hugh Myddelton. If this new plan had gone ahead, Colthurst would have had nothing to show for all the efforts he had made, and he applied himself to making objections to that effect. He then appeared before the parliamentary committee, citing the merits of his own plan and the work he claimed to have undertaken. He seems to have satisfied the committee that his grant from the King would be prejudiced by the Act, and it was only passed into law in 1606 after an undertaking on behalf of the City that Colthurst would be compensated for any loss he suffered thereby.[10] By the time the Act was passed, its details had changed very significantly, perhaps because of Colthurst's intervention. Originally, the Bill had referred to river water from the Lea and the Colne. The Act that was passed made no mention of river water, but authorised the Mayor and citizens to bring water from 'the Springs of Chadwell and Amwell, and other springs in the countie of Hartford not farre distant.'[11]

Despite this similarity with Colthurst's charter from the King, the new Act gave the City greater powers. For one thing, the Act authorised a channel ten feet wide, rather than six. More important, like every other Act of Parliament it carried with it the authority of Parliament as well as that of the King, and as such, in the event of any dispute, it would inevitably be seen as a greater power than the King's letters patent granted to Colthurst. One legal oddity was included. The City was empowered to make terms with landowners for digging a trench ten feet wide through their land for use as a watercourse, but the Act specifically provided that the ownership of the land would not pass to the City – merely the right to dig the trench, gain access to it for maintenance as necessary, and run water through it in perpetuity. As the Act put it, 'leaving the inheritance of the New Cut in the owners thereof.' In practice this may not have made much difference, and it meant that if the scheme failed at some future time and the river ceased to run, the landowners would not be left with an inconvenient strip of land belonging to somebody else dividing their property.

Even after this Act the scheme remained under discussion, and in 1606 the City obtained a second Act of Parliament, entitled 'An Act for explanation of the .. Act for the bringing of a fresh Streame of running Water to the North parts of the City of London.' This stated that since the earlier Act was passed, 'upon view of the grounds through which the Waters are to passe by men of skill' it was thought better to bring the water in 'a Trunke or vault of Bricke or stone inclosed, and in some cases where need is, raysed upon arches' instead of an open channel. The Act therefore authorised the Mayor and citizens not only to dig the ground as the former Act provided for, but also 'where they shall think most meete' to make a trunk or vault up to ten feet wide, which could be buried or raised on arches as they saw fit.[12] This second Act has sometimes been taken to refer to a wholly different scheme, whereby the water would be enclosed for the whole distance from the springs to London. Its wording suggests that it is no more than clarification of what was needed to put the original scheme into effect. The first Act had only authorised the digging of a channel, the second one added that where necessary the watercourse might be tunnelled underground or raised on an aqueduct.

In 1606 things were happening behind the scenes. The Court of Aldermen reported that they 'well liked' and would recommend an offer made by one William Inglebert. He had proposed, on behalf of certain persons 'whose names are yet for some respects concealed', that they would bring water to the City from the 'springs of Amwell and Chaldwell' at their own expense. Little is known about 'Inglebert', who was probably William Englebert of Sherborne, who died in 1634,[13] but three months earlier the City had agreed to pay him £3 3s. 8d. 'for his payne in procuring the late Act of Parliament for bringing of water too this citye'. From subsequent events it seems likely that his unnamed backers included Hugh Myddelton.[14]

As that summer passed there is more evidence of the City's growing interest, and in September a payment of £5 6s.0d. to one Richard Staper was approved for his expenses in viewing the springs and making a survey of how they might be brought to London.[15] By December there was a map in existence called 'the Mappe of the new Cutt to bring the water from Amwell to Tibbolls'. ('Tibbolls' is Theobalds, on the route of the New River then as now). Whether or not this is Staper's survey is unknown. The map does not seem to have survived, and its existence is only known because two butchers from London were sentenced to hang for stealing it, together with some clothing, in the course of a robbery.

By this time, others were becoming interested in supplying water to the City, and in October 1606 two plans were under discussion in addition to Colthurst's. One was a proposal by one Ruddell who wanted to raise water from the Thames, but this seems to have gone no further. The other was by Inglebert and the others whose names were still being kept secret, and who now proposed to bring the water from Amwell and Chadwell – 'a body of running water a yard square' – most of the way in a trunk of brick 'for the sweet keeping thereof'.[16] Later that year another committee was appointed to look into the relative merits of Inglebert's and Colthurst's offers.[17]

Once the City had obtained its Acts of Parliament, Colthurst seems to have become worried that they might use their new powers to frustrate his scheme if he went ahead. He appealed to the City, and was given a promise that he might go ahead to complete the work and take all the profits, so long as he expected no financial help from the City and finished the work within two years of the next quarter day.[18] Matters dragged on and the men who were offering to back Colthurst must have decided that it would be more satisfactory to go ahead under the powers of the two Acts of Parliament than under his letters patent from the King, although in some ways the Acts were narrower. For example, they only authorised the bringing of water to the 'North parts of the City of London', whereas Colthurst had been empowered not only to supply London, but also the City of Westminster and all the suburbs of both cities.

Two things however may have made the Acts seem preferable. The first was that they allowed for a ten-foot channel to be dug, and this gave a better prospect of profit than the six feet allowed to Colthurst. The second was that they provided a means for settling disputes. Whereas Colthurst's patent simply required him to 'compounde, deale and agree with' occupiers and owners of land before cutting their ground, the 1605 Act set up a procedure for settling any problems. The Lord Chancellor would appoint sixteen landowners as Commissioners, four each from London, Middlesex, Essex and Hertfordshire. Any nine of them – always including at least two from London – would hear and settle the amount of compensation due in default of agreement. This provision must have seemed to offer more chance of carrying the scheme through to a successful conclusion.

At some stage Colthurst and his backers realised that since both Acts referred to the work being done by 'deputies and workemen' as well as the mayor and citizens, the City might be persuaded to transfer its powers to them as deputies to carry out the work. Accordingly in March 1609 Colthurst informed the City that as the costs were far beyond his means he had 'taken unto him persons of good sufficiencye of this Cittye that doe offer to undertake the worke.' He asked that the City should transfer to him its powers under the Acts. He suggested that the City might like to contribute £2,400 towards the cost, and if they did then two thirds of the water would be provided free for public purposes. Otherwise, he and his backers would expect the profit from all the water. At the same time he named Islington as the place the water would be brought to. This seems to be the first mention of Islington as the destination – the letters patent had not specified a place, and the Acts of Parliament spoke of bringing it to 'the north parts of the City of London', whereas Islington was well outside the City walls.

It has been suggested that the figure of £2,400 in return for which Colthurst was prepared to give two thirds of the supply may be an indication that he believed that £2,400 to be two thirds of the total cost of the scheme. If so the total scheme would only have cost £3,600, whereas it is known to be very much more than that – quite how much more will be discussed later. It seems more likely that Colthurst felt that £2,400 was the kind of sum the City might be prepared to pay for a flow of water to clean its stagnant ditches, perhaps at night when the water might otherwise be running to waste.

Colthurst's request for payment in return for two thirds of the water was one he was entitled to make under the terms of his charter, but the City does not seem to have been prepared to put money towards the scheme, even for a share of the water. They were however prepared to give him the benefit of the Acts – or so their committee recommended on 14 March 1609.[19]

The matter was to be formally decided at a meeting of the City's Common Council just two weeks later, and during that period Hugh Myddelton somehow took Colthurst's place. The most likely reason is that he was one of the anonymous backers, and now felt that the transfer of powers was more likely to go ahead if he, as a citizen of London and a prosperous merchant, was seen to be the promoter. Accordingly, on 28 March 1609 it was announced that the City had accepted Myddelton's offer to carry out the work. He was to begin within two months and to endeavour to finish within four years. In return, he and his heirs and assigns would be made the City's 'lawfull deputies, attorneys and agents.'[20]

By this time Inglebert had dropped out of the picture. According to a friend of John Aubrey he was later to be seen sitting in an old rug-gown like a beggar, next to an apple-woman at Parliament Stairs.[21]

Hugh Myddelton of Denbigh

Who, then, was Hugh Myddelton? He was born in about 1560, the sixth of nine sons of the governor of Denbigh Castle in the borderlands of Wales. They seem to have been a talented family. Of the brothers, William became an Elizabethan sea captain and also wrote poetry, Thomas (not to be confused with his unrelated namesake the dramatist) became Lord Mayor of London and was knighted, Robert became an MP, another became High Sheriff of Denbigh and another followed their father to be governor of Denbigh Castle. As for Hugh, he too achieved much. He is usually described as a goldsmith, but this word should not be read in its narrow modern sense. The Goldsmiths, who had existed since 1180, was one of London's twelve 'great companies' and its members could practice any trade they chose. Some members made and dealt in gold articles but others had much wider trading interests, such as financing trading voyages to the Indies and America. Some were starting to lay the foundations of a modern banking system by holding and advancing money. Myddelton had certainly dealt in gold and jewellery – he had supplied pearls to Queen Elizabeth and in January 1604 he was to be paid £250 for a diamond pendant given by James I to his Queen.[22] He was later to develop interests as varied as mining silver and lead in Wales and land reclamation at Brading Haven on the Isle of Wight. He was the Member of Parliament for Denbigh, and was among the members who in 1605 sat on the committee considering the City's first bill for a new water supply. It may have been this that first gave him an interest in Colthurst's scheme.

4 Sir Hugh Myddelton, an engraving of 1805 based on an earlier original.

Raising the money

As we have seen, by the end of March 1609 agreement had been reached as to the terms on which the New River could be constructed, namely the City of London's powers under the Acts of 1605 and 1606 deputed to Hugh Myddelton and others. At that stage the others involved were not publicly named, but there is no reason to doubt that they were among those named as shareholders – or rather, holders of Adventurers' shares as they were called – when the New River Company was eventually incorporated in 1619.

Joint ventures were well established as an ordinary part of commercial life by that time. Moneymaking ventures were often risky, and merchants spread the risk by taking shares in each other's schemes. Thus a trading voyage to the east required a suitable vessel to be obtained, fitted out and provisioned, and its captain would need money or goods to exchange for a valuable return cargo. The voyage might be profitable, or the vessel might sail and never be seen again. It was prudent to share the costs. So it was with the New River. The costs could only be estimated, success could not be guaranteed and its eventual profitability could only be a matter of conjecture. Not surprisingly Myddelton spread some of the risk, and he seems to have made an early decision that there should be thirty-six shares.

He may also have concluded that the venture was not so very risky, as he kept a sizeable holding for himself.

When he first began to sell shares in the enterprise is not recorded. The charter that brought the New River Company into being in 1619 sets out some of his reasons for so doing, in particular that he had found the cost to be 'greater and heavier than at first was expected, the success thereof doubtful and the opposicon made against it very strong.' What he did was to offer the shares on the basis that each one would initially cost £100. Its owner would be entitled to a share of the profits, if and when they appeared, but in the meantime he would also be liable to pay a proportionate share of any costs in excess of £3,200. In other words the £100 was the down-payment and not the final cost of the share. It was the admission price that gave the shareholder the right to any eventual profits – so long as he shared any further costs meanwhile – and at the same time it gave Myddelton some of the capital he needed to start work.

It does not follow that Myddelton started with £3,600 in his money chest, for two reasons. The first is that four of the shares were reserved for Colthurst. This may have been in furtherance of the agreement that he had obtained from the City at the time the 1605 Act was passed – that they would recompense him for what he had lost by not being able to carry out the venture himself. It may equally have been a private bargain between the two men as the price of his cooperation and help. The document by which Myddelton assigned shares to paying shareholders said that Colthurst's shares were given 'in consideracon of greate labour and endeavour by him bestowed about the said worke'. In any event, Colthurst was given outright ownership of two of the shares – providing he survived until the work was completed – and a life interest in two others, without any down payment and without any liability to contribute further when the costs exceeded the £3,200 raised by the other 32 shares. The agreement provided that when Colthurst died two of his shares would revert to Hugh Myddelton for his 'great industrie, travell and paines'.

The effect of Colthurst's four free shares was that the holders of the remaining thirty-two shares would have to fund the entire cost. In other words, each paid-up share would incur 1/32 (3.125%) of the costs, but would only receive 1/36 (2.78%) of any profits.

All these details are apparent from a surviving agreement that Hugh Myddelton made with one of the earliest shareholders or Adventurers, Sir Henry Neville. The document is almost certainly in the same form as those agreed with the other shareholders, and is not without interest. It is lengthy, witnessed at the end and bears Myddelton's seal. It records that Neville has paid £200 to purchase two shares, each being one thirty-sixth part of the enterprise, but they are not shares in a company, for there was no company at that time. It is a personal bargain between Neville and Myddelton. What Myddelton promises with each share is a part of the 'waterworks, river and new cutt, made and to be made, and of the profitt, benefitt, gaigne comoditie and advantage' made at any time in the future.

Myddelton also promises to use the money raised to carry out and perfect the necessary work 'as speedilie as may be'. He undertakes to provide annual accounts of money spent and earned and to pay Neville or his heirs the proper sums when due. He sets out the terms of the agreement by which Edmund Colthurst holds four shares. Neville agrees in return to make any further payments due from him if the costs exceed £3,200.

Precisely how much money Myddelton raised by selling these shares is impossible to say. Twenty-nine named individuals held the 32 shares at the time the company was incorporated, but this was not until 1619. Furthermore, some of those individuals only held their shares as trustees for Myddelton himself, as can be seen from his will which reveals that he owned thirteen of the Adventurers' shares at the time of his death. The reality may be that Myddelton wished to keep as large a share as possible in what he saw as a valuable enterprise, and only sold as many shares as he needed to.

CHAPTER TWO

The first ten miles 1604 to 1609

The weekly record – How the work was organised – Hugh Myddelton's role – The managers – Surveys and Surveyors – Labourers and Pieceworkers – Carpenters and other tradesmen – Contractors – Drums and Trumpets – Tools and Materials – Horses – The Ingen – Making the channel – Obstructions – Bridges – Frames – Compensation

The weekly record

Digging the New River was an enormous project. It would be a trench ten feet wide and several feet deep that snaked across the countryside for about forty-two miles. It had to be built to a very precise level, never gaining so much as an inch in height but always very gently sloping down, at the rate of no more than five inches a mile. That is a fall of just one inch for every 12,500 inches, an almost unimaginably gentle slope. The depth of water would be over four feet, but undulations in the land meant a cutting that could be much deeper.

Before about 1948 very little was known about the details of the construction. Most of the company's early records had been destroyed in a fire at their Bridewell office at Christmas 1769, so this lack of detail was not surprising. But there was in existence a careful record that set out all the costs of the work from 1609, not just until the London reservoir at New River Head was built in 1613, but right up to 1630. It came into being because King James I had agreed in 1612 to underwrite half the costs, including the past costs, in return for half the eventual profits as explained in the next chapter. The agreement he made with Hugh Myddelton provided that accounts must be kept and produced at regular intervals, and only then would the King's half be paid over.

It was not unusual for such records to be kept. In Elizabethan times, merchants who combined to share the risk of ventures or trading voyages expected an accurate record to be held, and Myddelton was certainly experienced in such matters. So the records would have existed even without the King's involvement. The very precise records that cover the start of the work, long before the King's involvement, confirm this. They show, for example, not only the names of every one of the labourers, but also how many days work each had done in any particular week. However, without the King's involvement these records would probably have been kept with the rest of the New River records and destroyed in the fire of 1769. Instead, they were in the possession of one office of state after another, and eventually surfaced in the Public Record Office in London.[1]

The accounts consist of vellum-bound books of paper leaves, containing hundreds of pages. The expenses of the project are listed week by week and carefully totalled. This was done first by Myddelton himself, later by his clerk Edward Hughes, and finally by William Lewyn who succeeded Hughes as clerk in September

1611 and remained with the company until his death in 1638.[2] Every page has been checked and signed by Myddelton and by the King's representative, who had to do so before the King's half contribution was authorised. They provide not only dates and amounts but also a wealth of detail as to what the money was needed for and to whom it was paid.

It is from these accounts that the figure usually given as the cost of the New River – £18,524 19s. 0d. – is derived. For reasons to be discussed more fully in chapter 6, the answer is not so simple. This chapter will deal with some of the practical day-to-day aspects of the project, including some of the costs of individual items, and the question of the total cost will be left until later.

How the work was organised

The first thing that is obvious from the accounts is the sanctity of the English Sunday. The standard week was six days long and Saturday was payday. Though men were often paid for less than six days work, they were never paid for more. Sometimes great floods or other emergencies were recorded, but seven-day weeks were not.

Payments were made to several categories of people. There were those we might call managers, including the Clerk, who were paid a weekly wage. Labourers and their overseers, carpenters and bricklayers were all paid by the day. There were also pieceworkers who were paid a fixed sum for doing a particular task or digging a particular distance of trench. Other sums were paid to those who provided horses, carts and drivers, or who undertook to build bridges for a fixed cost. Most of the timber needed for reinforcing the banks at weak points, making plank footbridges and constructing troughs to carry the New River over existing streams or vice versa was provided in bulk by one supplier.

Myddelton or his men also had to reach agreement with the occupiers and owners of the land that would be cut, and compensation had to be paid to them when agreed. Inevitably many of them were farmers with their own teams of horses, and very often they were also paid for providing men, carts and animals. Sometimes they chose to take on the job of building cart-bridges on their own land, and in such cases they were paid at the same rate as outside contractors.

The amounts paid need to be multiplied by about one thousand to give an approximation of present day values. Thus, a labourer who then earned ten pence a day, equal to five shillings (£0.25p) for a six-day week might now earn £250 a week.

Hugh Myddelton's role

At the beginning, there are very few records of payments to Hugh Myddelton. Then, in August 1611 he enters £162 16s. 11d. as the cost of his charges, time, labour and travel during the previous three years – equal to just over £1 a week. August 1611 was the month in which Myddelton made his preliminary agreement to secure the King's contribution, and that presumably caused the change in accounting. In the months that follow there are occasional entries to show his costs when he stayed at Hoddesdon, along the route of the river.

Then in January 1612 a weekly entry for £2 6s. 8d. appears, stated to be the cost of Myddelton, his man and the two geldings they rode. This becomes a regular payment every week until the completion of the work. 'His man' is never identified by name, and was presumably a personal servant. What exactly Myddelton did during these months is not usually stated, though occasional entries show that he was staying at Hoddesdon or meeting with the commissioners who settled compensation disputes. Much of the time he may have been meeting and negotiating with landowners. As for Myddelton's accommodation, a letter survives in the British Library to show that Miles Whitacres, who countersigned the New River accounts books for the King, wrote to a friend on Myddelton's behalf in April 1612. The letter is addressed 'To my right worshipfull freinde Sr Mychell Hicks knight give these.' Hicks's address is not given, but Whitacres writes 'from his majesties howse att Theobalds where I would be glad to see you,' and continues,

'Worthy Sr,

Mr Hughe Middelton of London my very good freinde, who hath undertaken the bringinge the new ryver to London; by reason of the nearnes of place to his workes; hath been desirous to lye att your lodge duringe the time the workes are neare that place. I have moved Hew Tilston thereunto, who dare nott, nor will nott give consent, without your leave which heareby I earnestly desire in his behalfe.

I am joined with him for the Kinge, and every day wee are to meete about that Bussiness and no howse can be soe convenyent as yours, he is a gentleman his majestie doth now favoure; ...: Thus desiring your answere wth the remembrance of my service to your good lady and your self, I take my leave and will Ever Remaine,

most willinge to doe you service,
Myles Whitacres.'[3]

The letter leaves open whether Myddelton may also have stayed as the King's guest at Theobalds Park during some of the work as the course of the river moved southward.

There is nothing in the accounts to explain how the workforce was accommodated. Many may have been local men who walked or rode from home. Certainly some of the labourers have the same names, or at least surnames, as occupiers of land who received compensation, and it seems likely that local people were employed. Later in the course of the works there does seem to be an increase in Welsh names among the workforce as though Myddelton had sent home for help, but where they lived as the work progressed is not explained. Presumably they lodged locally at their own expense, perhaps sleeping in barns.

The managers

One vital worker was the Clerk, who kept track of all the expenses of building the river in addition to his other duties. The first was Edward Hughes, who stayed from 1609 until 1611. William Lewyn then replaced him, and an entry on the first page of his account book suggests that Hughes had fallen sick and perhaps died. It records Hugh Myddelton's expenses during three days spent at Hoddesdon 'when Mr Hughes the Clarke was sicke, beinge with hym to take his accompte.'

Lewyn was to remain in that post for twenty-seven years, and his status was confirmed in 1619 when the King gave the New River Company its charter. That provides for 'our welbeloved subject William Lewyn, gentleman' to become the first Clerk of the new company in consideration of his 'long travell and attendance in and about the said Water Worke', and to hold that office for life during his good behaviour, either personally or by appointing a deputy. Like Hughes, he paid himself 12s. a week as clerk, and also charged his expenses for hiring horses if he had to travel to London. Where he was based is not known. To compile the accounts he had to have accurate lists of the names of all the workers employed each day, which cannot have been easy when there were sometimes hundreds at work. In later years the New River collectors, who collected money from customers, normally made themselves available in particular taverns or coffee houses at prearranged times, and it may be that Hughes and Lewyn similarly based themselves in inns and alehouses along the route as the work advanced.

As well as the clerk, Edmund Colthurst appeared on the payroll from the beginning, and his earnings were set at 14s. 0d. a week from the beginning of August 1609, slightly more than the clerk and almost three times as much as the labourers. He was later described as the overseer of the work, and it may well be that he was a clerk of the works who kept track of progress and which men were working at any time. Although he had made the original survey of the route years earlier, he was not the surveyor when the river was being dug.

Surveys and surveyors

There seem to have been many surveys of the route before the work began. This is hardly surprising in view of the very low elevation of the spring at Chadwell and the very careful level to which the channel had to be built. The first known survey, not of course included in the account books, is the one Colthurst had made before submitting his plan. We do not know when that was carried out, but it had been done by 1605, when Colthurst wrote to Viscount Cranborne asking for permission to cut the 'river' through his land. An attached note by Sir Walter Cope records that he had advised Colthurst to 'join with him some artist (i.e. surveyor) and try the levels' before troubling people 'but he refuses and says he will have the honour hereof himself. If it prevail not, he will bear the loss and shame.'

It seems to follow from this that Colthurst had carried out some kind of survey, and as mentioned in the previous chapter, a note by Cranborne's agent sets out the route. Another note says the water is to come from 'springs towards Hertford', all of which match the eventual route of the New River.[4]

The next survey was commissioned by the Corporation of London from Richard Staper, who was paid £5 6s. 0d. for it in September 1606. Its details are unknown, but it may have been the same 'Mappe of the new Cutt to bring the water from Amwell to Tibbolls' already mentioned, for the robbery of which two men were sentenced to be hanged.[5]

Then the account books show that Myddelton sought the assistance of a noted Cambridge mathematician, Edward Wright. In May 1609 he was paid £20 3s. 0d. for three surveys he made 'from Amwell to Islington and back again,' presumably to determine and then check the best route. Some or all of this survey work lasted for twenty days, as shown by wages paid to the labourers who accompanied him. He is said to have used a 'perspective glass' that may have been an early levelling instrument.[6] A week later Wright received £40 as an advance payment of salary to be what Myddelton called 'my arts man', and from September of that year he was paid £2 a week. This was a good salary – three times as much as Colthurst, eight times as much as the labourers and twelve times as much as the mole catcher. Myddelton went with Wright on the survey, and charged '£5 7s. 10d. that I spent in the first survey with Mr Wrighte'. Apart from his earnings, Wright did not cost much – 1s. 0d. for a line, and 1s. 2d. 'for a bord to make gages'.

There may have been a problem with Wright. On 28 September 1611 he was paid £1 for 'when he came to trye the Leavell in Chesthunte parke'. After that his earnings stop. One final laconic entry may also refer to him. This appears on 12 September 1612, and shows that £4 5s. 10d. was paid 'for sueing Mr Wrighte's bond toe Judgment & execution.' This suggests some financial irregularity. It is a feature of the story of the New River that those entrusted with money, such as collectors, had to provide sureties and these were often called upon if the employee was unable to balance his books. May it be that Wright, with his land surveying skills, was agreeing compensation with landowners and somehow muddled the accounts? The fact that the bond was sued 'to execution', i.e. enforcement of the judgment, shows that the action was successful.

Some problem is certainly referred to in a note at Gonville & Caius, Wright's college at Cambridge. It records that he died in 1615 and continues

> 'He was the first undertaker of that difficult but useful work, by which a little river is brought from the town of Ware in a new canal to supply the city of London with water, but by the tricks of others he was hindered from completing the work he had begun.'[7]

Whatever the reason, by the time the work resumed in November 1611 after a long disruption, Myddelton had a new surveyor in the person of Edward Pond, assisted on occasion by one Blagrave, who was probably the mathematician John Blagrave. Blagrave's home was at Swallowfield near Reading, where Samuel Backhouse also lived. Backhouse owned the land at Islington that was to be the site of New River Head and he was also one of Myddelton's original Adventurers. This may explain how Blagrave and Pond came to be employed. Pond is first mentioned in a note of 'Mr Midletons charges at Hodesdonne when he came downe wth Mr Ponde and Mr Blagrave toe take the plot betweene Cheshunt & Theoballs.' Later entries show payments to Pond, starting at a daily rate of 6s. 8d. and then settling at a regular weekly payment of £2 6s. 8d. which he received until October 1613, by which time the New River was running all the way to the reservoir at New River Head. Whereas such men as the labourers were paid 'wages', Pond's fee is described as being 'for his enterteynement', a courtesy that was also extended to Colthurst's more modest earnings.

Labourers and Pieceworkers

Labourers did most of the initial work of construction, and they were normally paid at the rate of 10d. a day, making 5s. 0d. for a six-day week. If they had to work in water, as sometimes happened, this increased to 1s. 0d. a day. Very often they were paid for much less than a full week. A typical week might have some men paid for six days, some for five or five and a half, or four, and so on all the way down to those who were only paid for a single day. In some cases it may be that workers had their own farm work to deal with and were only occasionally free, or in others it may be that all the work had to be delayed until one particular obstacle had been dealt with by a part of the workforce. Men were paid for working, not just for being there. Thus occasional entries show that if bad weather stopped the work, the men's wages were docked accordingly.

After a time a piecework system came to be used, especially for excavating soil. At first this was done by men working in gangs, with a single payment made to one of them, often for the distance dug in units of 1 pole (5½ yards). Thus, 'To John Gilderson and his companie for worke done by the pole, £3 10s. 0d.' and 'to Richard Akers and his companie for 44 pole done at the double gage £4 19s. 2d.' Similarly, on 30 December 1609 'Henry Stanly and his companie for 11 pole ¾ by them fully done at double gage £1 5s. 10d; more to them for 13 pole single gaged 15s. 2d.' The gage seems to refer to the depth of the cut. This of course varied as the New River sliced its precisely surveyed course through the undulations of the land.

The accounts show that men such as John Gilderson and Henry Stanly sometimes worked as daily labourers, and paying a single sum to a gang must have simplified the clerk's work if all the workers were happy to share the money between themselves. This system may have caused friction, or it may be that men preferred to be paid for their own individual output rather than taking a share of what the gang had done. Whatever the reason, the bulk payments soon disappeared for excavation work, and each individual labourer came to be paid for the precise amount of work he had done. How the work was allocated and how it was measured when finished is not described. Perhaps someone like Colthurst kept track and issued tallies to the men, a system that was used for centuries. Length was normally measured by the pole, but the amount depended on whether the work was single gauge, double gauge or treble gauge. Occasionally the depth was measured in feet. On one occasion 'A staffe of 16 foote longe to make a gage' cost 1s. 0d, but the size of a 'gage' may have varied from task to task.

As will be seen below, the description of the opening ceremony includes reference to 'the Measurer' as one of the workforce, possibly Howell Jones, and he may have been the one who kept tally.

Carpenters and other tradesmen

Carpenters were often employed, and typically earned 1s. 4d. a day. Thus at the beginning of the work on 5 May 1609 what seems to be an advance payment was made to 'Thomas Bilton the Carpenter before hande £3 8s. 0d.' Later, on 3 July he was paid 18s. 8d. for fourteen days' work, and his name appears at other times, including payment for repair work he did to the 'Ingen'.

One specialised trade used was that of shipwright. A number of these were employed for making and waterproofing the troughs that were built at Bush Hill and, in 1618, at Highbury. They were well paid, at 2s. 0d. a day.

Contractors

Contractors did some of the work. For example, many of the bridges over the New River throughout its length were built at a fixed price. One man, William Parnell, supplied most of the timber needed for works along the river. He also acted as a contractor for some works. Thus in May 1613 he was paid £100 'in full payment of the greate fframe at Endfeilde & for new makeinge the Dames at Ware.' Parnell was often paid in bulk, such as another £100 in November 1612 for 'provision of Tymber for use of the Ryver.' This contrasts with much more precise entries, such as in December 1614 when £2 9s. 4d. was paid to 'Wyddoew Tyllstone' for 'a Tymber Logge, toe sawe oute into planckes, toe kepe in store, to mende the frame as neede requirethe.'

Drums and trumpets

As the workforce built up, there may have been problems communicating with workmen strung out along the excavations. In March 1612 a drum was bought for 14s. 0d. 'to call the workmen,' with an extra 2s. 4d. for 'hoopeing the drume, braces & poyntes'. By October of that year 'mendeinge the Drume' cost 3s. 0d.[8] There is also evidence that a trumpet was bought and used for a similar purpose.

Tools and materials

It is very likely that some of the labourers who helped to build the New River came equipped with their own tools. There are certainly some entries in the account books for buying tools, but they are not sufficient for all the work that was done. The purchase of '2 dsen of spads and shovells – 17s. 0d.' in August 1609 is one of the few bulk purchases. In June 1612 'an iron spade to cutt the banckes' cost 3s. 0d. A 'shodd scavell', perhaps an iron-shod wooden shovel, cost 1s. 4d. In the past, wooden spades were sometimes preferred for working with clay, which does not cling to wood as it does to iron.

Handbarrows were as little as 1s. 0d. each. One wheelbarrow cost 3s. 4d in December 1611, but it may have been a large or special one, as the same amount paid for 'a new whele Barrowe & a hand barrowe and a hurdle' the following month. Soon after, 'a newe wheele Barrowe & Tymber toe make gages cost 1s. 5d., while just 2s. 0d. paid for 'a newe hand barrowe & mendeing 2 whele barrowes.' In June 1612, 2 new wheelbarrows cost 6s. 8d. A month later 'a newe whele Barroew pynned with Iron' cost 4s.

Baskets were used 'toe carrie earthe upon the Bancke' – 18 of them cost 5s. 6d. 'Hoddes' were also used, for carrying earth 'where the Wheele barrowes cannot goe', and 12 of those cost 18s. 0d. Rakes were bought in quantities of up to four. The price varied greatly from 6d. for 'a rake' to 2s. 0d. for an iron rake. In 1609, '4 iron rakes & staves' cost 4s. 4d. Two long rammers cost 6d. An 'iron crowe', presumably a crow-bar, was 4s. 0d. 'A dragge, a sawe and a hatchet' cost 4s. 0d. Waterweed was a problem from the start, and there are entries such as 'an old sith and a knife to cutt the weedes, 2s. 8d.' Black-smiths were often paid for repair work, such as 2d. for 'mendinge an Essex axe broken in the work'.

Nails were bought when needed, and were described as e.g. 6d. or 10d. (sixpenny or tenpenny) nails. This describes their weight, not their price. If 40 nails weighed one pound they were called sixpenny nails for the slightly illogical reason that 40 sixpences made £1. Likewise tenpenny nails, which were bigger, weighed in at 24 to the pound. A typical entry in November 1609 records that 200 sixpenny nails cost 1s. 0d., and in January 1612 double tenpenny nails cost 1s. 8d. per hundred.

By the time the workers were extending the network of pipes through London, the tools began to change. Thus in December 1616 'a greate Iron Twyvell, & a shovell shodd wth Iron .. to open faultes in the streetes' cost 4s. 0d., and 'three greate scoopes toe throughe oute water oute of the Trenche' cost 2s. 6d.

Horses

Horses were usually hired but in December 1609 'a nagg to drawe the Carte' was bought at a cost of £4. Its saddle and collar cost 4s. and 'his meate that week' 4s. 6d. During the long delay, in June 1611, 'a monethes grasse for the nag' cost 8s. 0d. When he needed shoeing, 1s.10d. to the smith paid for '5 shoes and 2 removes for the nagg' and 10d. for '2 shoes and 2 removes for the nagg' the following week.

Later, 4 horseshoes cost 1s. 4d. The farrier seems to have acted as a vet when needed, and there were occasional payments for 'a drincke and bloud lettinge of the horse.'

The Ingen

From August 1609 until the work was held up in early 1610 there are frequent references to 'The Ingen', which seems to have needed regular care and attention. A plough is also mentioned, and seems to be linked to the Ingen. This is consistent with a piece of machinery that the diarist John Evelyn wrote had been invented for the New River:

'A Country Fellow seeing them digging the Channel for the new River said that he would save them £2000, that is he would turn up the Earth with a Plough; and had strong Ploughs and Harness made purposely, which was drawn by 17 Horses and sav'd a vast deal of Expence.'[9]

In August 1609 'a plough, share, coulter, hooke, locke, pynnes & nailes' cost £1 5s. 8d. Later one Bateman was paid £1 'in parte for the Ingen', as well as 4d. for the whipletree and 1s. 10d. for mending the sullier. Later, 'Downes of stansteed' was paid 7s. 4d. for 'a legg, plates & pynnes, mendinge the sullier & for holing the coulter.' In September 1609 a 'wheler' and a smith were paid the large sum of £9 11s. 8d. for working on 'the Ingen'. By October new rudder posts, the yoke and some more timber for the Ingen cost 4s. 4d. It also needed tallow and nails, and a new shaft, costing 5s. 8d. In September a carpenter worked on it for a day, and '3 traces for the ingen' cost 2s. 6d. In October it had to be repaired with 2s. 8d. worth of 'cloutes & nailes'.

Working the engine, and moving it from place to place, continued through the autumn. In August £2 was paid to Mr Hellam, and 6d. more for bringing the plough from Ware. In September he had £2 10s. 0d. for five days use of his plough horses. In October John Adams was paid 2s. 6d. 'for carriage of the tumbrel & plough to Hodesdon,' and Hellam was paid £2 3s. 4d. for his men and 13 horses 'to draw the Ingen', the same payment being repeated later that month. In November Mr Greigose had 6s. 8d. for his horses to draw the Ingen, and a further 6d. to his men 'for their paines'. Later that month, Lupton had 8s. 0d. 'for his cattel to draw the Ingen' with an extra 6d. to his men for their pains, and John Sides also had 8s. 0d. with 6d. for his men's pains. Mr Bailie's man Giles was paid 2s. 0d. 'for his paines about the Ingen goinge'.

The Ingen had weights ('for carriage of the weighte 4s. 2d.'), and they needed watching – Harvey and Saringe were paid 8d. for 'watching the waights in the Ingen,' while Richard Williams and Thomas Levesey had 8d. for 'watching the Tumbrell'.

From these entries, the Ingen seems to have been drawn by a team of horses or cattle and connected with ploughing or breaking the soil. On one occasion when numbers are mentioned, no less than 13 horses were used.

Digging a cutting across meadowland would certainly be easier if the turf was first cut and the ground broken by a large plough. Perhaps the engine turned out to be more trouble than it was worth, as it does not seem to have been in use after 1609, other than a single entry in March 1610 which records a payment for carrying it 'home to mr throogoods.'

Making the channel

The accounts show that where the banks of the river needed to be built up, the ground also needed to be consolidated. This was done by the hooves of horses. Thus, there are entries such as 'one nagg xx tie (i.e. 20) daies to tread the earthe, £1', and 'to Goodman larke for his 2 horses, 11 days to tread the bancks and his boy, £1 5s. 0d.' Similarly John Saringe and Widow Shambroke were each paid 8s. 0d. for '4 horses to tread the bancks two daies'. The banks were also covered with turf in places. Thus John Rogers was paid 4s. 0d. 'for turfeinge of bankes in the chase,' while Richard Greene and Edwarde Hynde were paid £6 13s. 4d. for 'rayseing & turfeinge 80 roddes of bankes in Theoballs p'ke.'

Occasionally the route of the river passed very close to buildings which had to be strengthened. Thus in July 1612 a bricklayer and his labourer were paid for 6 days at 2s. 4d. per day 'to under Pynne Hollandes Barne, the trenche being Cutt under neathe it.'

Not surprisingly, boats were sometimes useful as the work proceeded. In October 1612 one shilling was paid for 'carrieage of the little boate to Chadwell', and two months later 10s. was paid to Thomas Roberts for the hire of 'a greate Barge, 3 weekes, tooe make the Damme at Chadwell.' Sometimes the first course taken was unsuccessful and had to be filled in again, and some of the compensation receipts record this.

Obstructions

Trees often blocked the passage of the channel and needed to be removed. No doubt the labourers took most such obstacles in their stride, but outside help was sometimes needed. So it was in December 1609 that the sexton at Broxbourne lent some ropes – perhaps the bell-ropes – to help pull down a tree and was rewarded with 3d. The same month Sir Henry Cox's carter had '2d. for his paines' in helping to pull a tree from the cut, and the same squire's 'bailie' had 6d. a week later for the use of his oxen for the same purpose. In May 1612 'fellinge 2 greate oakes' cost 2s. 0d. and another '3 greate trees' the same amount. Later 'a greate oake and 2 hornebeams' cost 5s. 0d., while a 'hathroene' came down for just 6d.

Bridges

The 1605 Act for constructing the New River imposed a duty on those who did the work to provide and maintain 'convenient Bridges and wayes for the passage of the King's Subjects, and their Cattell and carriages over or through the sayd New Cutte or River, in places meete and convenient.' This meant a plethora of footbridges and cart bridges. Some of these were provided at fixed rates by contractors, such as Messrs Nottingham and Springfield, who received several bulk payments for the construction of cart bridges, usually of brick. The standard rate was £2 per bridge.

Landowners whose fields were cut by the river often seem to have preferred to build any necessary bridges themselves, perhaps because they had their own men, animals and materials to hand. When this happened they were paid about the same as any other contractor. For example, in February 1613 Thomas Martyn was paid £4 11s. 0d., as compensation for allowing the New River to be dug through his land, and a further £11 12s. 0d. 'more toe hym for settinge up sixe Carte Bridges in his severall groundes & for gravellinge them,' as well as £1 2s. 0d. more 'for fillinge in 33 Roddes in his owne groundes.'

Footbridges were usually made of planks that were fixed to wooden 'sleepers' at each end. Typically, one with an 18 foot plank, two sleepers and a stay cost 5s. 0d. The company was liable to maintain all the bridges, and subsequently got rid of them where possible. In 1782 it was noted that they had been reduced to 196, down from 226 at the previous count.[10]

Frames

Normally the New River followed the contours of the land up the valleys of the little tributaries that flowed into the Lea, resulting in many loops to the west and back again. When it came to Salmon's Brook, at Bush Hill near Edmonton a different strategy was used. The valley here was quite narrow, and a great wooden trough was built to cross it, supported on 'arches of wood fixed in the ground' some of which were twenty-four feet high.[11] The trough was 660 feet long, five feet wide and five feet deep. It was caulked by shipwrights, in the hope of making it watertight, but eventually had to be lined with lead sheet. It survived in that form until 1788, when Robert Mylne replaced it with a new clay-lined earth embankment that still exists. The *Gentleman's Magazine* noted that the lead removed from the old trough and sold for scrap weighed almost fifty tons.[12] (*ill.5*)

Compensation

The 1605 Act provided that compensation would have to be agreed with owners and occupiers of land crossed by the New River, and also set out a procedure whereby Commissioners would be appointed to settle the amount where agreement was not reached. This was a vitally important power, for without it a single obstructive landowner could

5 *The former timber aqueduct at Bush Hill, replaced by the present embankment in the mid-1780s*

have made it impossible for the work to proceed – over 200 years later lack of such a power was to bedevil the construction of the Regent's Canal.

In many cases agreement was easily obtained, and sometimes no payment was expected. The vicar of Amwell, Thomas Hassall, allowed the river to be cut for over 200 yards through his land without charge, noting on the consent form that it was 'for the meere love I beare' to the city of London 'being borne therein.'[13] Hugh Myddelton had his own way of responding to this kind of gesture. In 1611 the new King James Bible in English was first published, and by 1612 an entry shows that Myddelton had bought 'a greate Churche Bible, geven to the parish of Amwell in good speede of the Water to the Cittie of London.' Later he also left £5 to the poor of Amwell parish by his will.

Where there were disputes the Commissioners were called in. Thus in September 1611, £2 3s. 9d. was paid to buy their 'dynner at Edmonton when they troade the grounde from Theoballs Pke to London.' A week later they had a sitting at the Exchequer chamber at Westminster, and their dinner there cost £7 17s. 0d.[14] Sometimes further compensation was needed after the cut had been made. In 1615 Edmond Nicholson of Bush Hill claimed that he had lost ground that had fallen into the river, widening the cut from 10ft to 16½ feet for 40 poles. He asked for £2 10s. 0d. for that, with a further £1 6s. 8d. for half an acre spoilt for corn. Myddelton agreed to pay these sums, but not a further claim for '53 or 54 geese, ducks & pullen at 8d. ye piece' which, according to Nicholson, had been lost 'by reason of the ryver & Ryver men'.

CHAPTER THREE

Completing the New River 1610 to 1613

The great disruption – Claim and Counterclaim – Progress of the Bill of Repeal – The Royal partner – Back to work – Work at New River Head – Completion: the three Myddeltons – Changing the course – Myddelton's River or Colthurst's Cut?

The Great Disruption

By the end of 1609 the work was going well. Ten miles of channel had been cut, and the New River was nearing the outskirts of Cheshunt, about one quarter of the way to Islington. Then the account books show that something went badly wrong. The weekly payments dried to a trickle as the average workforce dwindled from almost one hundred in December, to ten or fewer by March. Wright the surveyor was not paid after February, and even Colthurst's wages stopped by June. Soon the whole work seemed to be at a standstill. The clerk recorded it all, and his wages were the only invariable expense. (see chart, p.236)

Oddly enough, one new type of earthworker soon appears. In May there is a payment to John Nasing for '17 moules' at 2d. apiece. The next week one Smith is paid for '14 moules', and by the last week of May regular weekly wages of 3s. 4d. are shown, for 'William Smith, mould taker,' or 'William Smythe for ketcheinge of molles'. Sometimes he is paid extra for working six days, and one week he is paid an extra shilling 'for stuff to kill the mouls at Luks.' Plainly with no workmen to disturb them, moles were exploring the attractions of the soft new banks of earth, and undermining them in the process.

It was to be for almost two years that the work was disrupted, and Myddelton must have been near to despair at times. What had happened was that a group of landowners had turned against the New River and were determined to stop it. Their leader was one Purvey, often described as Auditor Purvey because he was one of the auditors of the income the King received from the Duchy of Lancaster. He owned land at Wormley, in an area where the presence of two tributaries of the River Lea would cause a great meandering loop of the New River, and this may have been part of his problem. Work on his land had already begun but he was now set on stopping the whole scheme, by having the 1605 Act repealed by Parliament. According to a contemporary document Mr Auditor Purvey and two others were the problem. They would not reach any agreement. They 'seemed to be well satisfied for a while, and afterwards .. began all this mischeifes out of mallice and spleene.'[1] The problem was coming to a head by December 1609, when the clerk booked an entry 'for my horsmeate at London comynge to you about mr Purvy, 8d.'

During 1610 events moved swiftly. In April Myddelton obtained a letter from the Lord Mayor of London to the Privy Council seeking the King's help to stop the hindrances to the New River. By May the opponents had mustered much support among the landowners of the House of Commons, so that one member wrote to a friend in Brussels that there was 'much ado' about the New River 'cutting ... through the Grounds of many Men, who for their particular interests do strongly oppose themselves to it, and are like (as 'tis said) to overthrow it.'[2] The account books show not only the lack of new work, but also some evidence of efforts to defeat the objectors. In April 1611 Hugh Myddelton was reimbursed a total of £14 5s. 9d. for various expenses including £1 each to two barristers for appearances, and dinners and suppers for 'the Hartfordshire men at severall times' – presumably witnesses. Over the months that followed the controversy continued, and some surviving documents set out the arguments of both sides.

Claim and counterclaim

Those who supported the Bill to repeal the earlier Acts of Parliament claimed that the New River would prejudice many of the King's subjects in Essex, Hertfordshire and Middlesex. It would damage the navigation of the River Lea by 'vessels of great burthen.' The water mills on the Lea would decay, and so would the water meadows. Cutting men's land would be a perpetual cause of quarrels 'being barred from their old waies and soe inforced to trespasse one another. – *No cause of quarrels – there would be convenient bridges where needed.*

Land would be spoilt – meadows becoming bogs and quagmires, arable turning into squallie ground. – *It is evident the soil is better next to the river, not worse.* Their ground in common fields would be mangled into 'quilletts and small peeces wherby the peeces cutt off being mingled among other mens are made unfit for that use. – *If any man's land is cut or divided the law allows him recompenses.* Sudden floods were already being caused. They would damage the meadows and arable land and would ruin many poor men. – *Not so – there are passages to let land water through.*

The right of access with horses and carts to maintain the banks will spoil the corn, and the Act gives no remedy. – *The law provides recompense, by agreement or using the Commissioners,*

The churches' tythes will be damaged. – *'Doctor Atkins will quarrel at a trifle ... for the cutt ... in his parish .. the tythe whereof is not worth above 2s 6d a yere.'*

The banks are thrown up ten feet on either side of the ten foot cut, and the Act gives no remedy.- *'The statute giveth recompence for all' in any case the land is made better not worse 'as by experience it is found'.*

The cut is 'a verie deepe ditch and Dangerous pit for Drowning of men and cattell as hath alreadie been proved.' – *'In one or two places the cutt is deepe, the necessitie of the place so requiring, but it is not Dangerous as it is pretended, neither was anie man or beast Drowned in it.'*

'the highwaies betweene London and ware wilbe annoyed and like to be made unpassable'. *The river does no harm to the road. 'Alsoe the river crosseth the highway but in two places where noe such inconvenience appeareth.'*

A document putting forward Myddelton's version began by pointing out that the work went back to Colthurst's petition to Elizabeth I. Her enquiries had led to juries for Hertfordshire and Middlesex swearing 'that it could not be hurtfull to any to bring the saide springes to London.' Furthermore, it claimed, Colthurst had laid out £1,000 and brought the stream about two miles. Then, Parliament had considered the whole position when the 1605 Act was passed and arranged for the City to compensate Colthurst. The 1606 Act was then obtained, and Myddelton had begun the work. He had now brought the river about ten miles at a cost of about £3,000 and had reached agreement with everyone whose land it crossed, 'except Mr Purvey and two more who will not be compounded with.' It claimed that 1700 men had worked on the scheme (although the records show that up to that time there were never more than about a hundred men paid in any week, some of them for just a day or two), and the work was 'likelie to prove profittable unto thowsands but hurtfull to none.' If the Acts were repealed, 'then were Colthurst undone, who att his great charge hath procured the saide pattent, and of whom both houses had great care in passinge the lawes.' Myddelton too would sustain great loss. Moreover, the City of London would be 'deprived of such a commoditie as the like was never nor cann be offred.'

Not only, it continued, had Myddelton caused his plans to be published in local churches, but to find out if there was any 'opposicons or dislike' he spent two months raising the spring head. Nobody had complained then or for many months after, whereas many had expressed their support for the work – including 'Mr Thomas Hassall, Mynister' until 'it came to Mr Auditour Purvey, being tenn miles from the heade, who seemed to be well satisfied for a while, and afterwards for reasons beknown to himselfe begann all this mischeifes out of mallice and spleene, since which time divers meetings and practices have bine used to the great hindraunce and hurt of the worke.'

There then followed a list of the 'Benefitte that by this ryver growe to the cittie of London and generally to all England.'

First, that in the daytime water would be served 25 feet high 'in any house in London or within the liberties or suburbes.' The present lack was 'lamentable to beholde' and poor people were forced to use 'foule and unwholsome water which breedeth great infections.' Then at night the water would run into the town ditches, the Tower ditch, the Fleet ditch and the common sewers. In hot weather the water could be run to cool the streets and cleanse the gutters 'wherby to avoide all ill aires and infeccons.' It would be ready and useful in case of fire.

Once south of Cheshunt, the river would be welcome to all, for at present 'if a dry summer happen' they have to 'dryve their cattell twoe or three miles to water. Above all, water would never hurt the land, but would 'mend both errable meadowe and pasture.'

The document then sets out the 'objections or malediccons againste the Newe Ryver, with answers thereto'.

It was said the River Lea would be weakened and made less navigable, but the people of Cheshunt and Enfield had for twenty years opposed barges going further upstream. Anyway, the commissions have established that the navigation will not be spoilt.

Had there been floods? Well, perhaps there had been: 'there was never workman or craftsman soe artificiall but gave first a rough shape or hewing, and after corrected as occation offred, wheras yett no great offence but easilie amended.'

Would land be crossed and cut off? – That could not be helped. 'Levell must be observed.' Was it of 'extraordinarie depthes'? Not any more. There are only three such places, and they 'shalbe mendid if we proceed in the worke'.

Were banks thrown up too high on both sides? They could be spread out, for the benefit of the land and would grow better corn.

Were there problems of 'entercourse and passages in the comon feilde?' Not so. Everywhere has been made passable either by bridge or ford, at 'great charge'.

What about floodwaters? Passages will be made over or under the stream for all watercourses and all land water that comes down furrows. The river was made so that when it 'riseth to a certeine height it passeth awaie without offence to any'.

Was there damage to church lands? If so it was only a 'small hindraunce, for we use but one Aker in a mile.'

What about the effect on mills? There was no water taken from them. In any case they were on the River Lea, 'where they have too much water'.

Did it damage the highways? Not at all. It was 'commodious for horse washinge and cattell drinckinge, firme and pleasant to passengers of all kindes.'[3]

Progress of the Bill of Repeal

In the House of Commons, things moved quickly. The repeal Bill had its first reading on 18 May 1610. On 25 May a deputation of dignitaries came from the City of London to try and persuade MPs to oppose it, saying that the water would be a great benefit to London and that Myddelton had already spent £3,000 bringing the work ten miles. The Bill still managed to continue its progress, with its second reading in June. By this time there was sufficient doubt in the matter for a committee to be appointed to go and see the works for themselves. Before they could do this the session would be over, so when Parliament rose for the summer break the Bill had gone no further.

Parliament resumed on 16 October 1610, but

MPs seem to have had other preoccupations and no decision was made about the Bill. Then, in February 1611 the King lost his patience with Parliament for a variety of reasons, and dissolved it as he had the power to do. It was not until 1614 that Parliament met again, and by that time Myddelton had resumed work and taken the New River to completion.

It was by no means the case that Myddelton could resume work as soon as Parliament was dissolved. Work had already been at a standstill for a year, and he could not know when Parliament might be recalled and the repeal Bill resume its progress. There were other difficulties. Although the amount he had spent on the New River by that time was probably less than half the £3,000 his supporters had claimed, he may have been short of funds. It may also have been very difficult to find new Adventurers once the work met difficulties. There was even talk of rival schemes being set up – one to bring water from Hackney marshes, and another from an Edward Hayes to tap another source.[4] If either of these had gone ahead they could only have endangered the profitability of the New River.

As 1611 continued, the opposition did not melt away. By August, the fact that Myddelton intended his New River to terminate in a pond at Islington became known. This was not quite what the 1605 Act authorised as it had envisaged that the supply would be taken to 'the north parts of the city of London'. It was said he had promised to take the supply to Moorfields from where it could be used to flush out the City ditches. Now, it was alleged, he planned to

'bring this water to a pond in a field between Islington and Clerkenwell .. where he may vent it most to his profit ... whereas by the statute the whole stream is to be brought to the north parts of London, which the city engaged to do by bringing it to Moorfields to keep the city sweet.'[5]

Myddelton was in difficulty by now, and the whole future of his scheme must have seemed very uncertain. He applied to the City of London for an extension of the time-scale under which the work had to be finished. This was granted and the date for completion was put back by five years, to April 1618.

This removed some of the pressure and, fortunately for Myddelton, more help – of a kind – was not far away.

The Royal Partner

By 1611 King James I was 45 years old and had shown himself to have a general interest in the well-being of his subjects. He had been the author of the 'Counterblaste to Tobbaccoe', a furious condemnation of what he saw as the evils of the new fashion of tobacco smoking, thereby showing a grasp of a danger that was not to be generally recognised for more than three centuries. He had caused a new translation of the bible into good English to be made. What became known as the King James Bible remained the standard version until the late twentieth century and its English is still admired. As far as water supply was concerned, he had been ready enough to take on Queen Elizabeth's support of Colthurst's scheme. Perhaps he might be ready to help the New River again.

There was another reason for James to take an interest. His finances were largely dependent on Parliament and were not on a very secure footing. If he used his power to ease the New River's completion, might he not take some share in its profits? Thoughts such as these plainly occurred to the King and his advisers at around this time. It is even a possibility that the opposition to the project had been orchestrated by those close to him, with a view to gaining him some advantage from it. There is no hard evidence of this, but it an odd fact that the two principal opponents had royal connections. Auditor Purvey was employed as auditor to the royal revenues of the Duchy of Lancaster, while Dr Atkins of Cheshunt was one of the doctors to King James I and after him to King Charles I.

As the summer of 1611 progressed, Myddelton was in negotiations with Lord Salisbury, the King's Lord Treasurer, and by November there was a written agreement between them. This was then followed by a final agreement in May 1612, and this was made directly between the King and Hugh Myddelton. Exactly how and why this happened remains a matter of conjecture. It may be that as the work dragged on and met setbacks, Myddelton found it difficult to raise more funds. He had kept thirteen shares, and when the work came to a temporary standstill he may have been left with insufficient resources of his own and a parcel of remaining shares that nobody wanted to buy. It may be that the King's intervention was an altruistic one to help a project that he believed to be of great public benefit. Whatever the reasons, the upshot was that the King agreed to take a financial interest. In effect, he would provide half the cost of digging the New River in return for a half share in any future profits. Because of this the financial interest in the New River was thereafter divided into two halves or 'moieties' – the King's moiety and the Adventurers' moiety, and this continued until the twentieth century.

The progress and scope of negotiations may be judged from an entry in the account books in September 1611 suggesting that much was already agreed in principle and a draft agreement being drawn up by then. It shows £1 paid to a George Crooke for drawing articles to pass between the Lord Treasurer & Myddelton for his Majesty to have 'halfe the proffitt, payinge halfe the charges' when the water is brought to London. One Mr Walter was paid £3 for his counsel thereon, his clerk 5s. 0d. for engrossing it, and the Attorney General £10 as his fee.

In its final form as sealed by the King, the document is an odd mixture of promises and hard financial terms. It spreads wordily over several large sheets of parchment, but its main provisions are easy to set out.

First, there were promises of royal patronage and support. The King bound himself and his heirs to do all he could to help the completion and future viability of the New River, 'and will also .. withstand and remove all such unjuste and unlawfull impediment which shall or may give lett, disturbance and hinderance to the bringing of the said waters.' There was also a small practical gesture – he would allow it the right of free passage through royal lands, which in practice referred to Theobalds Park.

Then it turned to the kind of problem that had already blighted the project. If anyone tried using any 'tumultuous or other rude or unlawfull' methods to hinder the course of the river, his Majesty would, on hearing of it, cause it to be 'suppressed and reformed.' He commanded his subjects not to:

> 'moleste, inquiett, trouble or hinder the said Hughe Middleton ...bringing the saide springes ... to the cittie of London ... upon paine of his majesties highe displeasure and upon such other paines and penalties as by anie laws or statutes of this realm are or may be inflicted upon them.'

This injunction was taken seriously. When a 'seditious fellow' persuaded the water bearers of London to raise a petition against the New River, a warrant was taken out to bring him before the Recorder of London, who was a judge and also, whether or not the seditious fellow knew it, one of Myddelton's fellow-Adventurers.

The King also promised to support any future applications for Acts of Parliament for the benefit of the New River, if any were needed 'to redresse or supplie anie defecte' in the earlier Acts. The agreement continued with appointment by the King of one Myles Whitacres to verify what costs Myddelton incurred. Such costs were to be entered in account books signed by both men.

Now came the most important part of the agreement. The account books, duly signed, were to be produced to the Lord Treasurer who must within twenty days thereafter pay one half of all such sums to Myddelton 'out of the treasure of his Highnes, his heires and successors remayning in the Exchequer.'. The Lord Treasurer was also to appoint a suitable person to check future payments and disbursements once the water had been brought within a mile of the city of London, and was beginning to be distributed to individual houses 'in or near the said Citty'. It envisaged that the King would continue to pay the costs of the distribution of water and the maintenance of the New River.

The agreement also approved of one charitable wish that Myddelton had asked for. As an exception to the general rule that New River water was to be sold for profit, Myddelton might at his own cost provide one pipe out of the main:

> 'to serve the poor people gratis about Saint Johns Streate and Aldergate Streate which are not able nor fitt to paie for their water, to be enjoied by the said poore perpetuallie.'

Myddelton for his part, in return for all this Royal bounty, promised to pay over 'one halfe of the benefitt, profitt and comoditie of the said water,' for ever.

This agreement must have transformed public attitudes to the New River. It would still have been open to its opponents to pursue the Bill for repeal of the earlier Acts, but any chances of success had been greatly reduced because defeating the New River would inevitably also damage the King.

Now everything was in a place for the completion of the work.

Back to work

Construction work resumed as soon as the King's financial help was promised. Between March 1610 and October 1611, the average number of labourers and pieceworkers employed was just over two. In November 1611, when the initial agreement was signed on the King's behalf it rose to 16, by March 1612 to 200. At the end of May 1612, by which time the King had sealed the final agreement, it was about 250 and in July of that year it reached its peak of just over 300.

New Year 1612 must have seemed a moment for optimism, and Myddelton distributed more gratuities than ever before or after – £15 7s. 0d. This was described as gratuities given 'as a token of the newe yeare, tooe such as have geven greate furtherance tooe the workes & have taken greate paynes & have done many kyndenes therein.'

Work went quickly from then on. Theobalds Park was reached in August 1612, and by March 1613 workers including 'William Mollitrapp' were digging the cutting '6 fote depe ... in the Bowleing alleye in Hornseye.' Can there really have been such a name as Mollitrapp, or had William Smith the erstwhile molecatcher earned himself a nickname? The same month saw excavations at 'Strowde grene.' Many entries at this time suggest work being finalised and

6 The New River by Myddleton Road, N22. Watercolour by C. Yardley, c.1870

C.YARDLEY

tidied, with many men involved in 'botominge' the channel.

As the New River entered Islington parish an enormous loop was needed to the west before the channel could cross Hackney Brook, a little tributary of the River Lea. This loop was to have the distinction of being one of the shortest-lived major stretches of the New River, being replaced by a much shorter embankment and wooden frame less than five years later.

On Easter Eve that year some largesse was distributed – £2 'geven amongste the Anciente workemen, wch hath Contynewed wth us from the begnnge.' At last the end was in sight. In May 1613 Richard Bennet was paid £21 6s. 8d. for '160 payres of postes and rayles, from Horneseye to the Duccinge Ponde at Islingtonne & for setting them up.' A week later Robert Handes was paid £1 10s. 0d. for 'making upp all the ffences ffrom Stroude Greene toe Islingtonne'.

As the river reached Islington it had to cross the highway, now called Essex Road, just north of the junction with present day Cross Street. Here Steven Boone built 'a greate Brick Bridge att Islingtonne towne end, being 18 foot wyde,' and was paid £7 3s. 6d. for it on 15 May 1613. By that stage, the workmen were almost within shouting distance of New River Head.

Meanwhile, up river, the work continued, such as 'cleeringe and botominge all the Trenche from Theoballs pke to the Troughe in Gyrton pke', and wydeninge 80 poles, 3 foote wider & a foote deper in Rye feilde.'[6]

Work at New River Head

Near the top of Islington Hill, on a southern slope overlooking the whole of London and Westminster, Myddelton had chosen the highest spot to which he could lead the New River. Here it would reach the last stage of its journey as an open stream, and flow into a great circular reservoir, from where it would have only two possible exits. It would either pass through a cistern into one or other of the wooden main pipes, or it would run to waste. Running to waste was something that could not be entirely avoided once the flow of the New River had begun, and surplus water was run into a ditch from where it found its way to a lower pond, and any overflow down to the River Fleet.

What Myddelton built at an old duck-flighting pond that had long been there was a large round reservoir to provide a head of water-pressure, where water could be stored to even out fluctuations between supply and demand. It had a house at the water's edge, where one of his men would live to keep charge. The basement of the house had a cistern into which water from the reservoir flowed, and from there it could be directed into one or other of the main supply pipes. The house also had a counting-house, where money would be checked and stored as it was collected from customers. A circular brick wall enclosed both house and reservoir.

To generations of Londoners, the house was known as the Water House, while the whole site, then as now, was New River Head. Work started by the summer of 1613, when £100 was paid for a stock of bricks 'for the Conndyt heade at Islingtonne.' By August a carpenter was making 'the frame for the Sestern howse' and by October the wages of carpenters and sawyers came to about £90.

The structure was well protected. In November Ferdinando Jefford was paid £27 'for Iron Barres and Casementes for the wyndowes of the Sesterne howse, for Lockes and keyes, hookes & hinges, for spikes, broade nales & other Iron worke, for the howse. Later he was paid 3s. 4d. 'for three greate Iron Crosse garnetts for the newe wyndowe into the Sestorne howse,' while 'a lock & Keye, staple & nayles for the Counting howse doore att the sestern howse, and a payre of hinges' cost 7s. 0d.

Steven Boone, had built various brick structures along the course of the New River, and he was entrusted with 'the Brick worke & Chymneyes for the howse att the Ponde heade' at a cost of £102 17s. 0d. He also built the brick wall, which cost £138 and was finished in August 1613. Tiling the roof, and plastering the counting house, cost £14 14s. 0d; timber for doors, windows and floors cost about £40, while planing and laying a deal floor in the 'Mydele rooms' cost £12 10s. 0d. There were tool-rooms, garrets and stairs. There was a surprising amount of glass in the windows – 220 feet, which cost £4 14s. 0d. Inside the cistern, a gallery was made 'toe stand upon toe turne the stopp Cockes'. On 21 March 1618 'a greate Gate, made att Islington toe goe to the Sestorne howse,' together with its ironwork and nails, cost 11s.10d. There were 'wyer grates that geve ayre into the sestorne howse' and on 5 April 1617, 'oyelinge' them cost 3s. 4d.

Completion: the three Myddeltons

The moment when the New River was finished has been recorded in histories of London ever since, because Hugh Myddelton chose to have a theatrical opening ceremony. It took place on the afternoon of 29 September 1613.

At least three Myddeltons were there, and one of them left a piece of verse written for the occasion. Hugh was there, as was his elder brother Thomas, who was a prominent public figure who had that day been elected the next Lord Mayor of London. Finally, his namesake Thomas Middleton was there. He was unrelated, but was established as a writer of verse and a playwright. He chose to write a long verse describing the occasion, and later published it, perhaps in the hope of favour from his wealthier namesakes. They rode out from the City with the previous Lord Mayor, the Recorder of London, who was one of the Adventurers, and many of the aldermen.

A description by Anthony Munday, a contemporary, describes the opening ceremony. It began with a procession of sixty of the workmen, in their best clothes and wearing flat, round Monmouth caps in green, led by a drummer and a trumpeter. They circled the dry excavation that was about to become the Round Pond carrying the spades shovels and pickaxes with which the work had been done. Then, they formed up in front of their visitors, and one of them began to recite a long verse.

It praised their efforts, and included a kind of rhyming roll call:

> First heer's the Over-seer, this tried man,
> An ancient Souldier and an Artizan.
> The Clarke, next him Mathematician,
> The Master of the Timber-worke takes place
> Next after these: the Measurer in like case,
> Bricke-layer, and Engineer; and after those,
> The Borer and the Pavier. Then it shows
> The Labourers next; Keeper of Amwell-Head,
> The Walkers last: so all their Names are read.
> Yet these but parcells of six hundred more
> That (at one time) have been imploy'd before:
> Yet these in sight, and all the rest will say,
> That all the weeke they had their Royal pay.'

Many of these can be named from the accounts. Edmund Colthurst, certainly an old soldier and artisan, was probably the overseer. William Lewyn was the clerk, Edward Pond the mathematician, William Parnell the master of the timber. The Measurer may have been Howell Jones, who was later given the tenancy of the Water House and a legacy of £20 in Hugh Myddelton's will. The bricklayer was Stephen

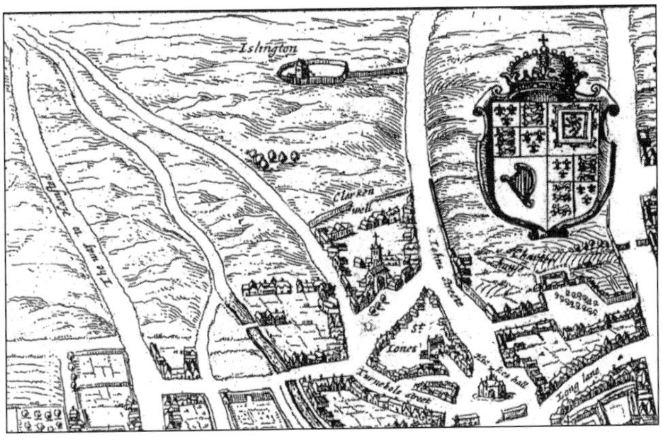

7 The earliest known depiction of the Round Pond and the Water House (top centre), from a map of London c.1620. It fails to show the course of the New River running north-east after it crosses St John Street.

Boone. The Engineer's identity is unknown, and this is unfortunate as this is one of the earliest examples of the word engineer being used in a non-military context. Perhaps it was Evelyn's 'country fellow', the man who designed the 'Ingen' described in chapter two.

Once the verse was over, 'the flood gates flew open, the stream ran gallantly into the Cistern, drums and trumpets sounding in triumphal manner; and a brave peal of chambers – small mortars used for firing salutes- gave a full issue to the intended entertainment.'

Oddly enough the account books do not record the cost of all these jollities. The only unusual entry that week is for 3s. 0d. 'given to the workmen in breade & bere for labouring in the nightes.' Perhaps Hugh's way of thanking those who had helped was to pay for the entertainment out of his own pocket.

Changing the course

Even before the river was complete there were changes. Many receipts show that landowners were paid for a cut on their land that was then filled in again, while others refer to a new cut being made.

The first major change was at Highbury in 1617 to 1618. As we have seen above, the original course made a long detour of well over a mile to the west and back again the same distance, in order to cross Hackney Brook (*p.217*). This was as far west as Ring Cross at Holloway Road, now identifiable at Ringcroft Road. Work was still being done there 'bottoming' the river as late as July 1615. It was soon obvious that a stretch of embankment on a more direct course might serve better, and Highbury Bank was built. The method used was to construct an earth embankment – for which over three thousand loads of earth were carted – and then build a wooden frame or trough along it to contain the water. The frame was built by shipwrights and because of its visible wooden sides became known as the Boarded River. It has often been described as 462 feet long, but when John Lowthorp FRS measured it in June 1704 to calculate the flow of the New River (8½ million gallons a day), he found it to be 420 feet long, 42¾ inches wide internally and containing water 30½ inches deep.[6a] Where it crossed Hackney Brook there was a brick arch that used twenty thousand bricks. The new bank had a watchman whose wages are recorded, and in November 1618, £11 1s. 0d. was spent on 'tymber, boordes, nayles & workmanship toe make a little wachhowse for hym to bee in when itt Raynes that lookes to the Newe Bancke.' The technology that kept water out of ships does not seem to have been right for keeping water inside a long trough, and it and similar structures on the New River leaked continually. The boarded river survived until 1776, when Robert Mylne built a higher and stronger embankment that included a channel for the water. This in its turn survived until 1865, when the water in that section was diverted into underground pipes.

Major works continued to be needed even after the river was open. There had been a large trough for the river at Hawe Mores since 1612, reinforced with oak piles twenty feet long. The work did not last and in January 1615 a 'new troughe att Hawe mores' cost the large sum of £26. It took six loads of timber, 200 wharfing boards, 34 days work by the carpenter to frame the trough, as well as carrying ten 'loades of stuff' and buying 50 pounds of iron spikes and nails. To make it waterproof, there were 27 pounds of oakum, 12 quarts of tar, 64 pounds of pitch and rosin, 6 pounds of tallow and 2 'cawkeing Cheecills'. Sixty-four loads of clay were needed for the foundations, and a hundred and twenty loads of gravel. Finally, Edward Curtesse had to be paid £2, for carting 'three score loades of Rubbyshe toe fyll upp the pitt where the Cleye was digged in my ladie Cock's ground for Haw mores.'

Another new trough was needed in March 1615, at 'Gyddinges' at Hoddesdon. There is now a Geddings Road there by Woollens Brook, and this may be the place. There it took 30 days of the carpenter's work 'toe frame the troughe', as well as thirteen days for a bricklayer and his labourer. The carpenter and bricklayer were each paid 1s. 6d. a day, the labourer 1s. like other labourers. The materials included the usual timber, 2500 bricks for the foundation, which together with some sand and lime cost £3 14s. 9d. Oakum, pitch, tar and rosin were used to waterproof the structure, with the help of 'a caske and a mopp'. The whole job cost about £20.

Sometimes the banks burst. In March 1615 it cost £5 to fill the 'holes in waterie Lane .. being galled and worne awaye with a breache of the newe Ryver by occasion of the laste greate fludes.' Another new flash was needed in Newmans Grove in August 1615. That took 34 days of carpenter's work and '1000 elme boordes and 1400 double ten penny nails.'

Another early change to the river happened in 1649-50, and involved the building of what become known as the Dark Arch in Islington. When first dug, the water ran in an open channel for about 400 yards by the side of Lower Road, now Essex Road, between present-day Cross Street and the end of Colebrooke Row.. This seems to have caused problems, and in November 1649 a committee was formed 'to advise and order the making ... an arch of brick through the upper parte of Islington and to put the same in execucon when and how they think fitt.' The channel that was then built lasted for over two centuries. In 1851 a new deep sewer was to be laid along Essex Road, to which each house would be connected. W. C. Mylne, the Company's engineer, advised the Board that the house drains would all cut through the Dark Arch. He proposed laying a 36-inch cast iron pipe along the route as an 'adjunct' to the Dark Arch, whose capacity, he reminded them, had become inadequate. The work was approved and completed in October 1851. It seems from this that the Dark Arch remained in use, but probably became redundant in 1856 when there were major changes in the flow to New River Head. Perhaps it still remains under Essex Road.

Myddelton's River or Colthurst's Cut?

It has long been accepted that without Hugh Myddelton there would have been no New River. By contrast, Edmund Colthurst has been seen as a minor player. It may be useful to examine his role at this point, to see whether he deserved better.

First, there can be little doubt that Colthurst designed the route the New River eventually followed. This we know from a combination of sources. The charter he was given by James I simply refers to springs in Hertfordshire. More of Colthurst's intended route appears from letters he wrote to Lord Cranborne asking for permission to dig through certain land. These show that the water was to come from 'springs towards Hertford,' which fits Chadwell and Amwell. The route he described to Cranborne's agent passed through Broxbourne, Wormley, Cheshunt, Theobalds Park and Edmonton, just as the New River does. Because the scheme could only work if the water followed a steady and almost level route, Colthurst's intended source can be located by following the contour, and this leads upstream to Chadwell Spring. It seems to follow that he alone deserves the credit for planning the route.[7]

When Colthurst planned it is unknown, but it was certainly no later than 1602. On 23 July 1602, he wrote to Sir Robert Cecil who owned the estate of Theobalds Park, north of Enfield, through which the New River still flows, about his 'endeavour to bring a river through your park'.[8]

Colthurst's charter confirms that Queen Elizabeth had considered his plan before her death, and she died on 24 March 1603. By contrast, Myddelton's first known link with the scheme was not until 1605, and then only as one of the Members of Parliament who sat on the committee for the 1605 Act. Indeed, he could hardly have sat on the committee had he been one of the scheme's promoters.

When the work of digging the river was interrupted by the machinations of Auditor Purvey in 1610, Colthurst's interest was recorded in a document that set out Myddelton's case. It began by pointing out that the work went back to Colthurst's petition to Elizabeth I. Furthermore, it claimed, Colthurst had laid out £1,000 and brought the stream about two miles. If the Acts were repealed, 'then were Colthurst undone, who att his great charge hath procured the saide pattent, and of whom both houses had great care in passinge the lawes.'[9]

Next, we know from the accounts that Colthurst was paid every week throughout the whole period of active construction. We also know that Myddelton gave him four of the original thirty-six Adventurers' shares. This was done before the King had bought a 50% stake, and it means that Colthurst was originally given a shareholding worth more than 10% of the total. Myddelton's deed of agreement with one of the other Adventurers shows that Colthurst had not paid for the four shares and, unlike the other Adventurers, was not liable to make any further payments for extra costs.

Nobody except Colthurst received free shares in this way, and it supports the view that Myddelton had agreed to take over Colthurst's scheme and to pay him compensation in shares as well as wages for his work.

Finally, there is evidence that Colthurst had made substantial progress in digging the river before Myddelton was involved. This comes from two sources. The first was in 1605 when the City of London began to obtain its own Act of Parliament for bringing water to London. Colthurst protested that he had already begun work and 'brought the river three miles towards London'. This would have been an absurd claim to make unless it was substantially true, though a later document, not by Colthurst, suggested it was nearer two miles than three.

The second is that Colthurst's claim to have begun the work is supported by an entry made in Myddelton's accounts in May 1613. By that time the river had been dug almost as far as Islington, and various last minute tasks up and down the river were being finished off. The entry shows that men were paid £15 0s. 0d. for 'Cuttinge the trenche from Chadwell too Amwell, foure foote wyder in the topp & a foote and half wyder in the bottome.'[10]

This entry points unmistakeably to widening a piece of Colthurst's original work. Colthurst's charter from the King only authorised a cut six feet wide. When Myddelton began work he did so under the 1605 Act of Parliament, and that authorised a cut ten feet wide. It follows that any part of the river previously dug by Colthurst would need to be widened by four feet. This did not need doing immediately – the trench he had dug would provide a level from which the work could proceed downstream. It was only as the work neared completion that Myddelton would have wanted to standardise the width of the river from Chadwell all the way to Islington to achieve the best flow. The trench of course had sloping sides to prevent the banks falling in. That is presumably the reason it only needed to be widened one and a half feet at the bottom, compared to four feet at the top. It seems that Myddelton had decided to use a slope that was less steep than Colthurst's, perhaps because of the recurrent problem of banks caving in.

Colthurst would of course have started digging at the source, as there is no other way that he could have been certain he was digging at the right level. This entry then provides another piece of evidence that Chadwell and Amwell were his intended springs although their names are not spelt out in the 1604 charter.

Similar work may also have been needed south of Amwell, but it would not necessarily stand out in the account books, as not all the entries are as detailed as the one described. There is certainly one that shows the cut being widened three feet in Rye Field at Hoddesdon, which is just about three miles from Chadwell Spring. That was done even later, at the end of August 1613, barely a month before the grand opening ceremony at the Round Pond.[11]

From all this it seems that Colthurst both planned the route and dug the first two or three miles south from Chadwell Spring. This work seems to have been done sometime in 1604. Colthurst then stopped work while Parliament was considering the 1605 Act. We know that he subsequently applied to the City at various times for their support in allowing him to complete the work. When work resumed in 1609 under Myddelton's direction, Colthurst worked on the scheme, and he continued to do so until his death in 1616.

There is no reason to suppose that the New River would ever have been built unless Colthurst had planned it, and it now seems plain that he dug the first part long before Myddelton was involved. He deserves to be known as the originator and at least the joint engineer of the New River with Myddelton. Perhaps the stretch from Chadwell Spring to Rye field, its route little altered for four centuries, should become known as Colthurst's Cut.

CHAPTER FOUR

Source, storage and supply

The source of the New River – Reservoirs – Wooden pipelines – Making wooden pipes – Intermittent supply – Water in the City – Water for the West End – The cost of water – Trade supplies

The source of the New River

The source of New River water might seem too obvious to need discussion. The King's letters patent to Colthurst referred to springs in Hertfordshire. The 1605 Act spoke of 'the Springs of Chadwell and Amwell', and this phrase was repeated in the City's transfer of its powers to Myddelton in 1611, and the deed whereby King James took a half share in 1612. When in 1619 the King granted the charter that incorporated the whole enterprise, the corporate name was 'the New River brought from Chadwell and Amwell to London.' It is true that some of these documents also spoke of 'and other springs .. not farre distant from the same' but they certainly did not authorise taking water from the River Lea. Had not Colthurst written to Sir Robert Cecil as early as 1602 'The water I mean to bring is spring, and no part of the River Lee'?[1]

Despite all this, the records show that soon after the completion of the New River, water from the Lea was being diverted into it. As can be seen today, the Lea wanders in winding channels and backwaters in the flat-bottomed valley between Hertford and Ware. It was here that Myddelton chose to divert some of its waters into his own, by cutting a channel that linked the two. The dispute this started was to roll on in lawsuits for over a century. The Lea was only navigable by barges of shallow draught, but it was important to the town of Ware. Barges constantly took cargoes such as corn and malt downstream to supply the London market, and the bargemen did not take kindly to interference.

Exactly when the abstraction from the Lea started is not known, but the timber contractor Parnell received a payment in May 1613 which included the re-making of dams at Ware. 'Toe Mr Parnell in full payment of the greate fframe at Endfeilde & for new makeinge the Dames at Ware £100.'[2] The New River account books include many of the expenses, both of the work and the associated legal costs. In October 1618 Commissioners went 'into the Countreye' and spent three days in the execution of the commission 'for takeing in p(ar)te of the river of Lie, viz for their supper & break faste att Ware the first nighte being 30 No'mber with them and theire followers £5 10s.0d.' The next three days they spent at Hoddesdon at a cost of £8 5s. 0d, and the next at Waltham Abbey where their dinner cost £2 5s. 0d. Then there was £2 14s. 0d for three days hire of a 'Coache' for some of the Commissioners, and their 'horsemeate' was also paid for by the company at a cost of £5 15s. 0d.[3] During this period Commissioners appointed by the King travelled around and heard the views of interested parties. Their findings seem to have favoured the New River, and by November 1618 a cost of 10s. 0d. is shown for scouring and cleansing the ditches to let in the backwater.[4] Then in September 1619, there was a flurry of payments as the matter was concluded, evidently

8 Chadwell Spring, one of the principal sources of the New River, much as it appears today.

to the Company's satisfaction. A payment of £2 4s. 0d. went to the Attorney General's clerk 'for draweinge and engrosseing the Commission and Articles for the King toe signe, for the takeing in of water out of the Ryver of Lee & other things enquireable by the said Commission for the good and benefit of ye Newe Ryver', with a further six shillings 'To Mr Attorney's man that keepes his studdie doore.'

William Lewyn, the New River clerk, had to ride to Oakingham to get the King to sign the Commission, and his expenses were £1 6s. 8d., while another ten shillings went 'To Mr Secretarie Nanton's Clarke'. Lewyn also went riding round the countryside to deliver the good news, and charged £1 10s. 0d. 'ffor horse hire for three dayes, & for horsemeate & mans meate, too Carrie ye Commisioners warrantes, to the Shereiffe of Essexe toe Chencford, & to ye Shereiffe of Hartford & for labouring ye Commission's toe meete att Ware & Waltham Abbey'.[5]

The main works followed in June 1620, with carpenter's work, and the purchase of twenty piles and a hundred wharfing boards for the building of 'a damme in the Meyne River, too tourne in the streame to our Ryver'.[6]

Despite these efforts there was trouble at Ware within months. On 2 December the King's representative Mompesson and Hugh Myddelton went there to speak to the justices and the bargemen about the 'Ryver of Lee,' and stayed for dinner and breakfast. Despite that, on 16 December a messenger had to be sent 'toe Ware toe ffetche upp some of the Bargemen, that broke down the Damme.'

What is obvious is that even though Myddelton started off without any right to abstract water from the Lea, he acquired it by 1619. From then on the Lea was a major component of the New River's supply, and the broken dam was rebuilt as often as necessary.

Taking water from the Lea continued to cause much resentment. In 1670 Charles II appointed commissioners, including Sir Christopher Wren, to report on the conflicting interests. Wren was already much involved in the rebuilding of London after the Great Fire of 1666. As such, his sympathies may have been more with London's biggest water supplier than with the interests of country millers and bargemen, though other members may have balanced this.

The report concluded, in any event, that the amount of water taken from the Lea could have no discernible effect on its navigability.

Despite this, it seems that the New River Company was forced to reduce the amount it took from the Lea about that time. This can be gleaned from one of the incomplete minutes that survived the 1769 fire. In 1670 John Grene, shareholder by marriage and salaried Clerk, was seeking to renew his maintenance contract for the New River. In doing so he claimed to have increased the flow to London despite the fact that the intakes from the Lea had been reduced from one 17 inch and one 12 inch to one 8 inch and one 6 inch pipe. This means a reduction to just 23% of the previous supply.[7]

It was not until 1739 that Parliament gave the New River Company the statutory right to take water from the Lea. The Company had to pay the river Trustees £350 a year in perpetuity, and in return was empowered to build a gauge six feet wide and two feet deep, with a floating beam that allowed a constant supply from the Lea into the New River, irrespective of variations in the water-level of the Lea. This was built in 1741 with the occasional supervision of Henry Mill, as described in chapter 13. In 1770, when Robert Mylne was joint engineer with Mill, it was replaced by the 'marble gauge' a disused structure that still exists, formerly marked with a stone bearing the date 1770 and the names 'Mill and Mylne, Engineers.' The present intake from the Lea passes through a substantial brick structure, the New Gauge House, built by William Chadwell Mylne in 1856. It has an arrangement of floats and plates that limit the intake to 22½ million gallons a day.

Reservoirs

Reservoirs were needed for at least three purposes. First, they provided a head of water to fill the mains during hours of supply. Second, by providing a large area of relatively still water, they allowed any impurities that had been carried along by the force of the current to settle to the bottom. Much had already settled along the course of the New River, and any that was left by the time the water reached New River Head formed a thick muddy deposit that was very occasionally cleaned out. Third, they smoothed out fluctuations in supply and demand.

The first of the company's reservoirs was the Round Pond at New River Head. The fact that it was immediately surrounded with a brick wall suggests that it was expected to be the only reservoir at that location. If so, it must quickly have become inadequate as it was soon supplemented by adjacent outer ponds. These were referred to as 'store ponds withoute the sestorne walls', and were rented from John Adkinson of Islington by 1617.[8] These ponds seem to have become larger as time went by. In 1664 Edward Fawcett, who was also 'Innkeeper at the Angell at Islington', tenanted the surrounding farmland. He petitioned the company for compensation for 'his ground in the fields next above the Waste ponds', alleging that he had lost more than an acre of ground by enlargement of the ponds and the banks caving in because of the flow of water.[9] A lower pond, also referred to as the 'wast(e) pond and groundes' was being used by 1614, rented from Abraham Mussgrove, apparently John Backhouse's tenant, for £32 10s. 0d. a year.[10]

The water from New River Head passed into pipes, some in the cellar of the Water House and some in a small cistern house on the edge of the outer pond, before being turned into one or other of the mains. Originally these cistern houses contained only wooden pipes, but in 1732 they were converted to lead, which was said to be much more convenient.[11] (ill. 9)

The next major reservoir was the Upper Pond, built in 1708 at what is now Claremont Square to supply the higher parts of the West End, as described in chapter 12.

Another reservoir, the West Pond, was built in the Hanging Field west of New River Head in 1781. It was supplied by waste water from a new waterwheel, and from it pipes were laid to serve about seven hundred customers in Clerkenwell and the Battle Bridge area near King's Cross, previously supplied direct from the Head.[12]

The St John Street reservoir was built in 1805 on vacant land between the New River and St John Street, and was oval in shape. Its purpose was to give a better supply to the east parts of the City, with an iron main along City Road

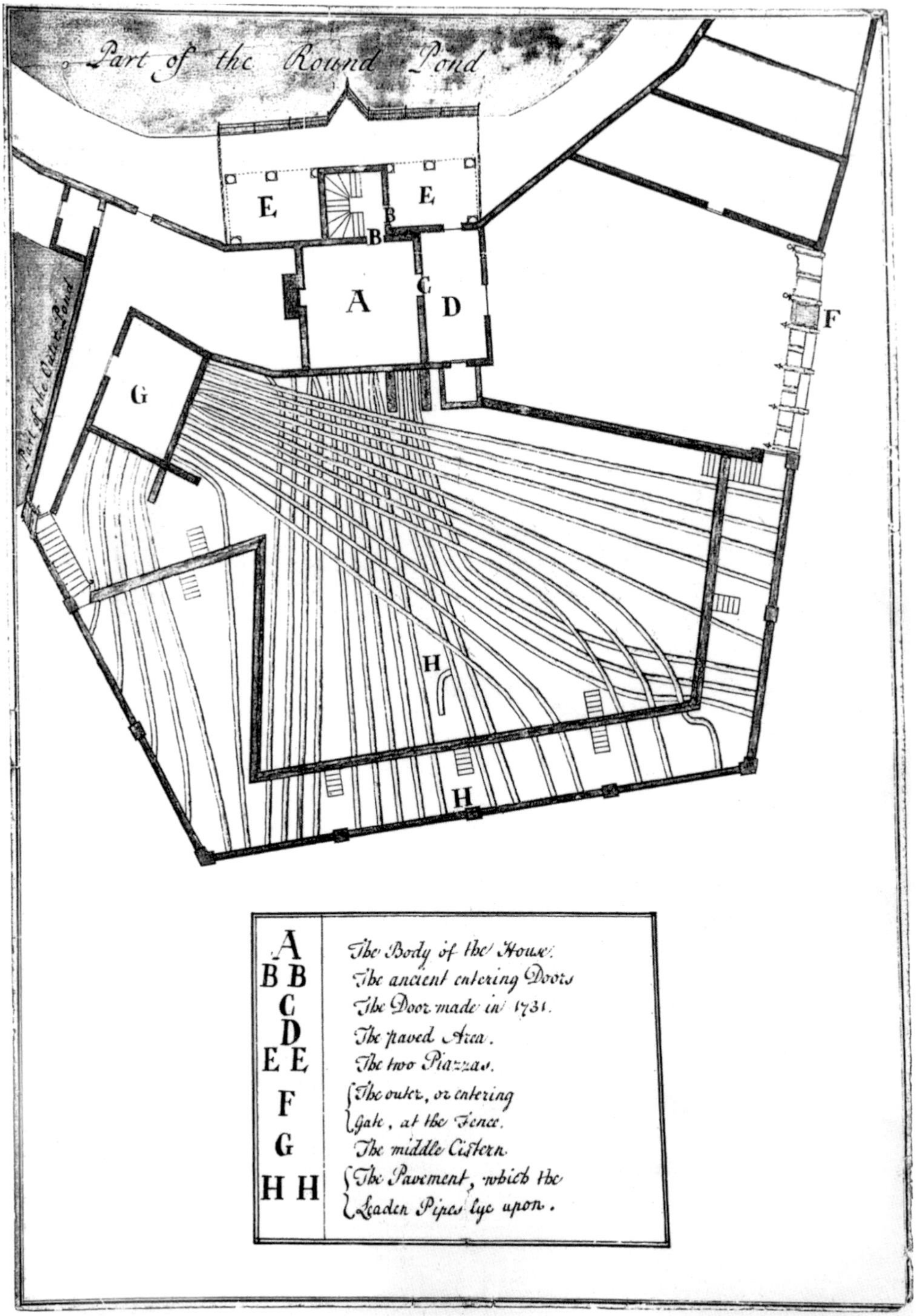

9 Plan, after 1731, showing how lead pipes from the two cisterns under A and G had been laid on a pavement in the yard behind the Water House at New River Head. These replaced earlier wooden pipes that were much bulkier. They still remained connected to a distribution network that was entirely composed of wooden mains until after 1800. The work was probably carried out by Henry Mill.

10 Wooden water mains of the New River crossing the Fleet river. The distant tile kilns were in what is now King's Cross Road, near Bagnigge Wells.

as far as the Hoxton turnpike. The cost of building it was about £600. By 1857 it had become redundant because most of the New River water was now served from Stoke Newington, and on Mylne's advice it was filled in and let as building land.[13]

Wooden pipelines

Even before the New River had been dug as far as the Round Pond at Islington preparations were under way to begin distributing the water around the City of London. This required the laying of miles of wooden water mains in trenches dug through all the principal streets, beginning with those closest at hand. The preferred wood for pipes was elm. It had the advantage of being durable underground even when wet, though all pipes eventually rotted. As early as 1616 a plumber was paid to place the ferrules where 'the wooden pipes were Deceyed and new ones placed'.

Elm also has the merit of being a wood with an irregular and twisted grain that does not split easily – this was useful in pipes, just as it was the reason that elm became the standard wood for the broad, thin seats of Windsor chairs whose other parts were made of beech. It has been said that elm lasted underground for anything from four years to twenty-five. According to William Chadwell Mylne the range was even greater. He gave evidence to a committee in 1821 that 'in two miles of wood you may find a hundred places where it would decay in two years, while the rest is sound.'[14]

As early as 1612 men were being sent into the counties around London to locate and order suitable elm timber. In January 1615 Richard Percevall was paid 15s. 0d. 'for his paynes and travell into Kente and Essexe toe look uppon Elmes for pipes.' Similarly Richard Parkes spent '3 days goeing into Barkshire toe marke oute Elmes for pipes, 3 days into Essex to choose Tymber ditto and 4 days toe Dartford toe marke Tymber, and 4 dayes for hymselfe and his horse to Sir John Garrett's in kent toe choose Tymber.' There are many similar entries, such as 'for Avereys Chardges and horse hire to

11 The joint between two lengths of elm water pipe

Meyden heade tow marke oute Elme timber for pipes – 7s. 6d.'

Because of the poor quality of roads at that time, timber for the New River Company was almost invariably carried by water, and unloaded at the Bridge house on the south bank just downstream from London Bridge, which belonged to the City of London, and where there was a wharf known as 'Pipe Borers Wharf.' Pipes were also wharfed at 'beare keye'. In December 1615 Thomas Mathewes, wharfinger was paid £6 for the 'wharfage and carriadge of 180 loades of Elme att 8d. per Loade,' and on 30 December 1615 George Hubberd was paid £5 8s. 4d. for the 'carriadge of fiftie loades of elmes from beare keye to the Greene yarde.' Similarly in March 1616 the labourers at Tower wharf were paid £1 2s. 0d. for loading and removing 44 loads of pipes. On 6 March 1613, Sir Henry Neville – who was one of the Adventurers – was paid £67 'toe make provision of Elmes for ye use of the workes.' The same day £30 went to Mr Pawlinge for '26 loads, six ffote of Elmes, att 23s. the Loade, for ye use of the workes', together with 17s. 0d. 'for the Landeing thereof att the Bridg house'.

Many different suppliers were paid for elm timber, mostly at about the same price, such as George Hurte who was paid £50 for 50 loads in March 1613, and Thomas Heathe the same amount in April 1613. In May 1613 Thomas Cock was paid £105 for '100 loads elmes to be delivered att the Bridge house.' In September of that year Robert White had £157 10s. 0d. for '150 loades of Elmes for pipes'. Over a century later, a letter of 1731 explained the current cost. The New River Company were said to pay £2 3s. 0d. a ton for elm timber and expected 50 feet of pipe to the ton. This works out at 10d. per foot for the raw timber, which still had to be bored out.

It was the continuing demand for elms that led to the long rows that were planted along field boundaries until the nineteenth century, many of which survived until attacked by Dutch elm disease in the 1970s.

Making wooden pipes

The elm trunks were cut into lengths, usually about 8 feet long. One log at a time was then chained tight to a horizontal frame with the help of windlasses. Wedges were driven to stop it from rolling. The frame had wheels and could be drawn backwards or forwards by ropes, along a fixed track between wooden guide rails, so as to push the log against the drilling augers that cut out its centre.

The drilling was a slow process, done with spoon-like augers, beginning with a small one and progressively using larger ones. The drills were turned by simple machinery, usually horse-driven but sometimes water or hand-powered. The largest pipes had an internal diameter of 7 inches, but 3, 4 and 6 inches were more usual sizes. There was a pit underneath in which the chips accumulated.

In 1731 Sir James Lowther wrote to a friend about a visit he had paid to the New River offices 'where they have a wharf and a yard by the Thames, and saw them boring small pipes by men, and larger by horse engines with great ease.'[15] In 1779 a testing machine for pipes was purchased. Its details are unknown, but a Dr Grant was paid £10 10s. 0d for 'the engine for trying the strength of wooden pipes in the Yard.' Dr Grant had been named some years earlier as a supplier of fir timber, which was sometimes used as an alternative to elm, as shown by minutes in 1693, 1770, 1814 and other years.[16]

As well as having their centres drilled out, the pipes were shaped at their ends. One end would be pointed like a pencil, the other would have a tapering round socket cut to the same angle. The outside would have had any branches roughly trimmed off with an axe, but was otherwise left unfinished. The bark was usually left on, as this was believed to prolong the wood's life underground. When the pipes were laid, in trenches through the streets, each was driven into the end of the next. An iron hoop was sometimes forced over the socketed end first to reduce the risk of splitting, and the account books show these being bought in bulk, for 5d. and 7d. each.

Pipeboring was usually paid for as piecework. In April 1613 Richard Parkes was paid £6 in part payment for 'boreing of pyepes'. In June 1615 Richard Parke had £20 as a part payment for boreing pipes, and John Bartlemewe £10.

A forked trunk was sometimes carefully bored to make a 'piece of three holes', to split a water main into two branches. Some of the elms bought proved useless for pipes and were sold on – between 1613 and 1630, £166 2s. 0d. was gained from the 'sale of crooked and other timber.' In December 1752, the works committee concluded that 'only one Horse Ingine for boreing pipes is absolutely necessary ... 3 men are sufficient to supply ... any emergency .'A Board minute from March 1767 records that 'Mr Wilson pipeborer attended & agreed to deliver 400 yds of 7" at 5s. 6d. p. yd and 4d. for each gage joint. Mr Gregory agreed to deliver 300 yds, Mr Legg to deliver 400 yds. Mr White to deliver 300 yds on the same terms.' These simple methods of making wooden pipes continued even after 1800, as the Company minutes show.

In July 1801, William Murdock wrote from the Boulton & Watt works at Soho, Birmingham. Boulton and Watt had already supplied the company with steam engines for pumping water, and Murdock wrote about a new machine. This could bore out logs to make water pipes by removing the whole core in one usable piece, instead of making a vast pile of useless chips. The New River surveyor, Robert Mylne, was ordered to find out more. Whatever his enquiries showed, nothing further happened at that time. Five years later, in April 1806, the Clerk of the yard reported that the boring engines were very much out of repair and required new cogs for nearly all the wheels. Mr Mylne was again told to investigate, and in September he was authorised to carry out a trial on Murdock's boring machine, using fir timber. This seems to have been satisfactory and in November 1806 the board authorised £50 to be paid for Murdock's 'machine for boring pipes vertically and extracting the core.'

It seems the new machine was still powered in the traditional way. In April 1807 a board meeting decided 'that a new horse be bought for the boring engine, and the favour was requested of Mr Tedder to look out for a strong blind one.'

Intermittent supply

It is an odd feature of the New River system that its water mains were empty most of the time. Because of the rudimentary joints every eight feet or so, the system was intrinsically leaky. If the mains had been kept permanently filled, the usage of water would have exceeded anything the New River could supply and low points in the streets would have become permanent quagmires. Normally the pipes were buried throughout their length, as they are today. This protected them from frost, from accidental damage, and from children, who quickly discovered that a hole bored in a main would produce a delightful fountain on water days.

In some places, the routeing of pipes caused difficulties. Pipes from New River Head to the West End had to cross low ground after crossing the Fleet River and the resulting dip reduced their flow. To improve this they were raised on trestles in places. A diary from 1773 says that to the north of Capper's Farm, at the back of the British Museum, 'the pipes of the New River Company were propped up in several parts to the height of 7 and 8 feet, so that persons walked under them to gather water cresses, which grew in great abundance and perfection.'[17]

The system was controlled by a network of stopcocks, turned with 'greate iron keyes' weighing as much as 30 lb. Householders generally had a single tap at the end of the lead quill, which ran into a cistern or water butt in the kitchen or cellar. Many of them left it permanently turned on. Two or three times a week one of the New River turncocks would pass through the district turning on the supply to particular streets for an hour or two. During this time the mains ran full, the cisterns filled to overflowing and the water was then turned off until the next 'water day', as it was known. This supply varied from district to district. In Soho the flow was never very good because of its distance from New River Head and the low intervening ground. In 1767 it was allowed seven hours three times a week, while the Grosvenor Square district, even further away, had a total of twenty-four hours a week.

It is a surprising fact that even when iron pipes replaced wooden ones all over the New River district between 1810 and 1820, the supply continued to be only intermittent. It was not until 1904 that the New River Company could finally say that all its customers had a constant supply.

Water in the City

The City of London was the first priority for laying water mains. It was London that had obtained the Acts of Parliament from which Myddelton derived his authority, and London had the first claim when the water arrived, though at first care was taken by the Company not to impinge on areas in the southern parts of the City already supplied by the London Bridge waterworks.

The first water main was laid from the Water House across open fields to St John Street, where in October 1613 400 yards was being paved after the pipes had been laid. From there the main went down to Smithfield and Newgate, where it branched to the east and west. In January 1614 over 1000 yards was laid from 'Pye corner to Ludgate, & Newgate to the cross in Cheap.' The same year extensions went west to Temple Bar and to Holborn Bars. Side-shoots sprouted from these first mains as time passed. The accounts show that in March 1615 a branch was going to the west through 'pysheing Alleye' later called Pissing Alley and now sanitised as Passing Alley, which still runs west from St John Street.

By 1615 there was a supply in Fleet Street, Fetter Lane and Shoe Lane, and stopcocks were being installed from Temple Bar in the west to Coleman Street in the east. In 1616 a pipe went from the 'Sestorne howse to Greyes Inne'. The network of pipes spread quickly. Any householder who wanted a supply would arrange for a small lead pipe to go from his house to the mains, and a brass ferrule was driven into the wooden pipe to which the lead quill could be soldered by New River workmen.

The normal supply was through a pipe with a half-inch diameter and this piece of standardisation would lead to a fundamental and intractable problem. Sir Christopher Wren considered the matter almost a hundred years later, and concluded that different sizes should have been used at different levels. If customers were all to have an equal supply, those on higher ground where the pressure from the reservoir was lower would need larger taps, and those on lower ground smaller ones. This exercise was never attempted. (*Appendix 3*)

Because the city streets were narrow and thronged all day with traffic from pedestrians to lumbering horse-carts, much of the pipe laying had to be done at night. This led to regular expenditure on 'candells', as well as links, pitch soaked torches which could be set alight, as in '4 dozen and a half of lynckes toe worke in the nightes'. They cost 2s. 0d. a dozen. There were also more durable sources of light, such as '3 greate lanthorns to work the night in the streets', which cost 4s. 4d. in November 1613. Not only was work done at night but men were also paid to 'watch nights in the streetes when the trenches ley open.'

Pipes were moved through the streets on a pair of big wheels. The first set was worn out by April 1615, when 'a newe payre of Coache wheeles and an extree (perhaps an axle-tree) to drawe the sixe ynche pipes, the old one being broken' cost 13s. The same week also showed the purchase of '4 greate Ashen Leavers toe lyfte the greate pipes att 8d. a pece.' By December 1615 a 'newe payre of Coache wheles and extreye to drawe the pipes ' cost 10s. An 'iron cheyne' was also used to haul the pipes, and '4 lynckes' to repair it cost 10d. Pipes soon needed repair and 16 yards of canvas for 'seareclothes to mend the pipes' was bought together with 20 pounds of hard tallow, pitch and rosin, and 'small cordes to bynde the seare clothe to the pipes' for 19s. 4d.[18]

The buried wooden mains displaced a lot of earth, and contractors were paid 8d. a load for removing it. Between February and June 1616 one Richard Pressegrove was paid £61 10s. 8d. for carting a total of 1846 loads, from Whitecross Street and Chiswell Street to Moorgate, from Chick Lane 'along the wall to Byshopsgate', from Bevis Marks, from St Paul's Churchyard to 'the 4 spoutes at Leaden Hawle Corner', from Mark Lane, Mincing Lane and 'gratious streete', and from 'Byshopsgate streete withoute the gate to the Barns at Shorditche.'

The position in 1629-30 is shown by a book in the Public Record Office, a slim neat ledger of rents received in those years. There were almost 1500 houses supplied by then, and the mains extended down St John Street and Goswell Road all over the City as far as St Paul's in the south, Aldgate and Houndsditch in the east, and Temple Bar, Chancery Lane and Gray's Inn Lane to the west. All the tenants are listed and it can be seen that no favouritism was allowed. In Bassishaw Street, Sir Hugh Myddelton paid his £1 each half year, while William Lewyn the Clerk paid 10s. 0d. for the supply to his house by St Bartholomew's Hospital.[19] After that time the proliferation of water mains never really stopped. At a board meeting in 1656 it was noted that the existing six mains running 'from the Waterhouse to Towne will not serve the present tenants with water,' and it was ordered that another main should be laid, down St John Street and through Smithfield and Old Bailey to Ludgate.

Water for the West End

Westminster and its suburbs certainly had a need for water, especially when the first streets and houses began to be built around St Martin-in-the-Fields and elsewhere. By 1638 the inhabitants of Covent Garden were asking for New River water. A board meeting considered it and decided not to supply there yet, partly because of the uncertain political climate – the English Civil War was looming – and partly because they still did not have a constant surplus of water at New River Head. Supplying water became increasingly difficult as the distance from New River Head increased, and this may have explained a reluctance to serve Whitehall.

By 1705 the West End was divided into two 'grounds' by the New River Company, each with its own Collector. Mr Maximilian Apprice had the half closest to New River Head. It was roughly square, with its eastern boundary formed by Lamb's Conduit Street, Red Lion Street and Lincoln's Inn Fields. It reached south as far as the Strand, and west as far as St Martin's Lane. To the north it went as far as the new building had then reached, along Great Russell Street and Great Ormond Street. At that time the area to the north of Oxford Street still consisted of open fields.

The second collector, Thomas St Hill had his ground to the west of Apprice's, beginning at St Martin's Lane. His southern boundary was 'Pell Mell', as far as St James's Palace, and then up St James's Street, across Piccadilly and west as far as Stratton Street, then east to Golden Square, north to 'Tyburn Road', now Oxford Street, and east to meet Apprice's ground near present day Centre Point.

A report made to the Treasury in 1724 shows that New River water ran in a main at Charing Cross, and a supply had been 'for many years used in all parts of Whitehall'. The company had recently cut off the supply because they were not being paid for it, saying that they had only agreed to supply a fountain in the Privy Garden, and that the other branches had been joined without their knowledge. The authors of the report, including Sir John Vanbrugh from the Whitehall Office of Works, had been searching for a copy of the company's charter in 'all the Offices of Record' in the hope of disproving this, but had 'not been able to meet with any footsteps of it by which we might see whether any reservation of water was made.'[20]

Whitehall had also been served from a spring in Hyde Park and by a small waterworks in Orange Street, behind the present National

12 Elm pipes of the New River Company dug up near St Anne's Soho. A photograph of the 1880s, when excavations to construct Shaftesbury Avenue dug up these old pipes

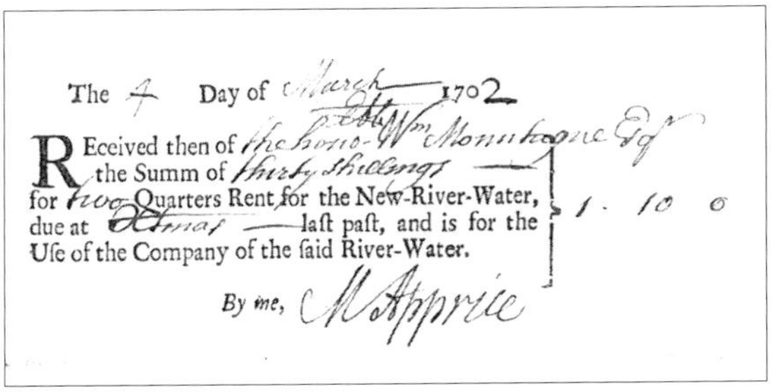
The 4 Day of March 1702
Received then of the hono. Wm Monntague Esq
the Summ of thirty shillings
for two Quarters Rent for the New-River-Water, 1. 10. 0
due at Xmas last past, and is for the
Use of the Company of the said River-Water.
By me, M Apprice

13 *A receipt for the supply of two quarters of water to 'Wm Monntague Esq', in March 1702. It is signed by Maximilian Apprice, collector of the Holborn and Soho areas since 1677 (see Chapter 11).*

Gallery. In 1725 during a drought Vanbrugh reported that he had 'endeavoured to recover some of the springs about the mews and St Martin's Lane which have either been diverted or choked up many years ago; and has so far succeeded in this search that he believes the additional quantity of water which will now be gathered from them will be sufficient to supply both the Cockpit & Whitehall without any further aid.'[21] It seems from this that New River supplies did not go far to the west or south of Charing Cross.

The cost of water

From the beginning, New River customers had to pay a connection charge, known as a fine, followed by quarterly payments – the method still used for supplies such as electricity. The quarterly payments were fixed and did not depend on usage, as there were no meters used before about 1830. The amount of payment depended on the size of the premises, and whether the water was to be used for trade purposes. The connection charge was usually £1, though some paid odd sums like £1 4s. 0d. and larger users were charged £4, £5, £10 and in one case £25. These were presumably intended to include a contribution towards laying the mains. The total of these fines for the first five years to November 1618 was £2183, and this is consistent with other records that show there were over 1500 premises supplied by that time.[22]

By 1700 competition, particularly from the London Bridge works, meant that the company was connecting new tenants without the traditional fine.

From the outset there were standardised formal agreements for the supply of New River water. To lawyers a water supply was not like an ordinary bargain for the sale and purchase of a quantity of goods. It was a transaction that would continue, presumably for many years and there would have to be provisions for enforcing the continued collection of charges down the years. It would have to include certain guarantees as to what was being provided. Equally, there would have to be some way of preventing customers from reselling part of their water to their neighbours and thus depriving the New River of customers. What if an ordinary householder obtained a connection at a modest charge and then set up a brewery or public wash-house that ran the mains dry?

The law's answer was that this kind of transaction was equivalent to a lease of property for a term of years. The same kind of provisions that protected landlords from bad tenants and vice versa would be the basis of the relationship between the water supplier and the consumer. Thus the potential customer signed a lease, and was always thereafter referred to as a 'tenant' of the New River water. This meant a lengthy document, of course, that needed careful drafting. Hugh Myddelton's first leases were probably modelled on those already used by the Broken Wharf waterworks. The first leases were all made between the householder and Hugh Myddelton. Once the company had been formed, the agreements were made with 'the Governor and Company of the New River brought from Chadwell and Amwell to London.' At one of the first meetings, on 30 November 1619, it was resolved that the existing draft of the lease should be 'enrowled in the Ligier Booke verbatym' to act as a precedent for all future leases. They were thereafter preprinted in the standard form, with gaps left for details such as names, addresses and amounts. To make them look like handwritten leases a typeface known as Civilité was used that resembled script.

What the customer leased was 'one Watercourse conveniently furnished with Water running in and through one small Branch or Pipe of Lead containing half an inch of Water or thereabouts.' Water leases contained provisions to cover most eventualities. The place where the rent was to be paid was always set out. In 1616, before the company was incorporated, this was at Hugh Myddelton's house, which was at that time in Westcheap. In 1661, shortly before the Great Fire of London, it was at the telling house on the west side of the Royal Exchange. By 1689 rent was to be paid at the Water House, and this continued until at least 1785. In practice, householders could arrange to pay their rent to the local collector who gave attendance at coffee houses and inns at pre-arranged times for that purpose. From the earliest leases there was a penalty of 2s. 6d. for each failure to pay the rent when demanded, and for each time water was allowed to run to waste, 'except in time of Frost,' when the tenant could leave the tap one quarter on to prevent freezing up. There was also provision for cutting off the supply if the householder breached the terms of his lease, by failing to pay the rent or otherwise breaking the terms of the agreement. To enforce this, the company kept the right to enter the premises 'as often as shall be convenient to view the said Cock and Pipe ... and to see that the said Water shall not be given, sold, taken away, or run to waste.' In return the company promised that the water would be turned on by the turncock 'three days in every week at least'. If they failed to do so without good cause and repairs were not carried out within fourteen days of the company being notified, the householder might withhold his rent until the fault was mended.

Cutting off a tenant's water for non-payment was a sanction included in all water-leases. In November 1725, the New River Company's clerk wrote to 'Mr Edward Stephenson, over ag(ain)st Old Man's Coffee House, Charing Cross' to explain why his tap was now dry:

'Sir, Yours I opend at the Board, and tis a General order to the Collectors not to suffer the Tenants to be in Arrears but to keep them strictly to half yearly payments. The Collector, being called in, informed the Gentlemen that he had directed your pipe to be left out of the tree, he having called on you for the rent abundantly often to no purpose.

Yr Humble Serv't

Jasper Bull.'

Trade supplies

It was always recognised that trades using water paid special rates. As early as 1615, when most householders paid £1 to be connected, one unnamed tenant, possibly a brewer or dyer, paid £25.[23] In 1770 Messrs Fawcett and Curry, distillers in Chiswell Street paid six guineas to be connected and the same amount as rent. The following year George Crump who ran a Dye House at Spitalfields was charged £40 a year for his supply. In 1630, St Bartholomew's Hospital had paid just £2 a year, the same as Sir Hugh Myddelton paid for his own house.[24] By 1810 St Bart's – somewhat larger by then – was paying £33 a year, and Christ's Hospital, including the masters' houses, £50.

By the 1850s meters were available, and trades using them were charged £1 14s. 0d. per thousand hogsheads – one hogshead being 54 gallons. Brewers were charged for the quantity of beer they brewed, at the rate of £2 2s. 0d. per thousand barrels. Distillers were charged just half this rate, but based on the quantity of water supplied to them, not their output of gin. Public houses, eating houses, bakers, pastrycooks and butchers all paid 20% more than private houses of the same size. Printers paid 25% extra, chemists from 50 – 100%. Steam engines were charged at the rate of £10 a year for each horse-power. Workhouses paid a rate based on a shilling a year for each pauper.

CHAPTER FIVE

More help from the King 1616 to 1631

Signing up the citizens – An Adventurer's deed – Founding the New River Company – The first Adventurers – King James rebuffed – Myddelton's baronetcy – A whiff of competition – King Charles sells out – Proclamations and warrants

By 1616 there was a problem with the New River. The costs continued to mount, while the citizens of London showed a considerable reluctance to sign up to the supply. This must have vexed Myddelton and his fellow Adventurers, whose investments were turning sour. Above all, it affected King James, for he had not only encouraged the scheme, but his fifty per cent investment meant that his potential loss was as much as Myddelton and all the others put together. Not surprisingly, he was persuaded that the great public benefaction deserved some more royal help.

There were two ways in which the King could help. The first was for him to use his influence on reluctant customers. The second was for him to turn Myddelton's unstructured venture into an incorporated company.

Signing up the citizens

It would have been beneath the King's dignity to write a direct plea to the Lord Mayor and Aldermen of London asking for help, so two days before Christmas in 1616 the Privy Council did so on his behalf. The letter reminded the mayor of the City's role in the history of the venture and of the expense and efforts of those who had funded it. The work, after all, was for the public good. It provided sweet wholesome water and prevented fires. It was not to be supposed that two Acts of Parliament and one Act of Common Council had been passed for no other purpose than to prejudice those who had undertaken such deserving works. The King therefore commanded, and the Council required, the Court of Aldermen to provide that all such houses in the City and Liberties as either of necessity or convenience might use the water should be required to do so.[1]

This put the City in a difficult position. The King had no right to force anyone to sign up for New River water, yet there was obviously some force in what he said. Less than a month later came a test of the City's resolve. The City had a small water supply at Dowgate near Thames Street, and pumped water from there to a public conduit head. Some local brewers petitioned to be allowed to take over this supply and offered to continue to pump water to the conduit, thereby saving the City £20 a year. In return they would take water for their brewhouse for making beer. They must have heard of the pressure to take New River water, as they offered to 'take in Myddelton's water,' but only for domestic purposes.[2] It seems likely that the petition came at this time because the brewers knew there were moves afoot to enforce the uptake of New River water, and were trying to win a concession before they were obliged to make terms, at business rather than domestic rates, with Myddelton.

14 King James I. Oil painting by Paul van Somer.

The King evidently heard of this petition, and in February 1617 the Privy Council wrote once more to the Lord Mayor to say that it was deemed expedient to refuse the application, the more so as the brewers could so plentifully be served from Islington. The New River accounts record the cost of that piece of assistance – £1 2s. 0d. to Sir Clement Edmonds and five shillings to his clerk 'for the Lordes l(ett)res to the Lord Maior & Alldermen for steye of the Brewers Licence to sett an Ingynne to serve them with water.'[3]

It seems that the City bowed to this pressure and the word was put out that subscribers were needed. One of the earliest documents to survive from the records of the New River Company is a damaged and incomplete minute from a board meeting in July 1620:

> 'Ordered there shall bee delivered from Sir Giles Momp'sons to William Lewyn clerk .. of all the Certificates signed by the alldermen & their deputies of all such (as have not) retorned their answeres, that they are willing (to take) in the water, & that the Clarke wth the assistance (of Mr) Rowland Bachowse & Mr Roberte Bateman, goe (into the) severall Wardes and demaund of them, whie they doe (not take) in the water, & yf they refuse, to complayne of (them to) the Alldermen of the Ward or the Lord Maior.'

Sir Giles Mompesson was one of the King's trustees for his share of New River profits, and received £200 a year for the sinecure of being the King's surveyor of the profits. A year later he was impeached for abuse of certain monopolies, and left the realm with some haste.

Few records remain of the steps taken to enforce the taking of New River water, but one entry survived in the Parish Books of St Michael Bassishaw. Apparently there were 18 in the parish who took New River water, but another 29 were 'able but unwilling'. One of the unwilling was Jo. Bancks, and his refusal is recorded – he was evidently quite happy with things as they were. He said that his family was small, and he had a pump holding a large store of water and a large cistern for rainwater; further he maintained a 'poore aged man' by paying him to bring conduit water, at the rate of four tankards for a penny, and likewise his house was unfit to receive New River water, in consequence of vaults and pavements that would need expensive Mason's work to connect it. Even if he could have it free, without fine or rent, he would be unwilling to take it.[4]

Nevertheless many must have been persuaded, and gradually the number of subscribers crept up. It is interesting that Mr Bancks thought it worthwhile to point out that by his existing system he was maintaining 'a poore aged man,' who fetched his water. It has been observed that this kind of social interdependence flourished under the old conduit system.[5] Dealing with a water company turncock, who might need to be bribed to provide an adequate supply, was a very different kind of relationship.

An Adventurer's deed

One of the earliest agreements that Hugh Myddelton made with one of the Adventurers who backed him somehow survived among the New River records. It was made with Sir Henry Neville. The deed is dated 8 May 1612, just six days after King James I had agreed, in effect, to pay half of the costs in return for half of any future profits.

It is a lengthy and carefully drafted document setting out the agreement between Myddelton and this particular Adventurer, and is probably almost identical to those made with the others. Myddelton had divided the whole enterprise into thirty-six shares, and the document confirms Neville as the purchaser of two of them. It begins by setting out the names of the parties, and the details of the 1605 and 1606 Acts which empowered the City of London to build the New River. Then come the details of the agreement by which Myddelton received his power to carry out the works in place of the City, followed by the agreement in which the King agreed to take a 50% share. It then records the fact that Neville has on an earlier date paid £200 to Myddelton 'towards the effectinge and performinge of the said waterworks by him.'

Myddelton then confirms the grant to Neville, in return for his £200, of two full 1/36 shares in the 'moiety' or 50% of the enterprise which does not belong to the King, entitling him to 2/36 'of the said waterworks, river and new cutt, made and to be made, and of the profitt, benefitt, gaigne, commoditie and advantage which ... at anytime hereafter shalbe made'. Myddelton further agrees not to relinquish the enterprise, and if 'by or through anie impossibilitie' the work cannot be completed 'before the first daie of Aprill which shalbe in the yeare of our Lord God according to the computacon of the Church of England 1613', then he Myddelton will repay Neville's due share – one sixteenth – of any surplus funds. Myddelton also promises to provide a 'true and just accompt' of the 'cost, charges, and of the gayne, benefit and advantage' each year, and to pay Neville his due share.

The agreement then records that 'Edmond Colthurst of the Cittie of Bath, Gent' has four shares 'in consideration of greate labour and endeavour by him bestowed about the said worke'. Neville for his part agrees that if the total cost of the work exceeds £3,200 and if a 'full and perfecte accompte' is provided, he will pay his 1/16 share of the extra costs. Whereas Neville's share of any profits is 2/36, his contribution to any costs beyond £3,200 is 2/32 – a slightly larger proportion. This is of course because Colthurst has been given 4 'free' shares, on which he will receive all the profits but on which, unlike the other shareholders, he is not liable to pay any further calls for expenditure. Accordingly, the other shareholders between them have to pay what would have been due on his four shares.

Edmund Colthurst, it has to be said, received less than he may have expected from Myddelton's generous gift of four shares for his lifetime. He certainly worked on the construction of the New River both before and after the completion of the Round Pond, for records show that his wages of fourteen shillings a week were paid until August 1616. But then they stop, and it seems that he died years before the shares began to pay any dividends.

Founding the New River Company

By 1619 the New River was a going concern. It was short of customers, there were still many distribution pipes to be laid, and there were no profits yet; but it was plainly here to stay. But what exactly was it? It amounted to two springs, more than forty miles of open waterway, a reservoir, a house and a network of wooden distribution mains, and it all belonged to Hugh Myddelton. He had privately reached individual agreements with a number of other people – including the King – as to how any profits should be divided, but there was no unified structure.

There was only one solution, and the King agreed to provide it. By letters patent under the Great Seal, he granted a charter that incorporated the whole New River enterprise – and thereby made it a distinct legal entity that existed independently of Myddelton and the others who ran it. The corporation would have a name, perhaps a little wordy by modern standards – 'The Governor and Company of the New River brought from Chadwell and Amwell to London' – and it would have its own seal with which to bind itself to agreements, and the power to sue and be sued in its own name. The charter that achieved that purpose is a massive and self-important document, florid, repetitive and neatly lettered, running to ten thousand words or more and spreading over a sheaf of eleven great vellum skins. Its contents are interesting, partly because they show how such an early company was set up and partly because of certain provisions designed to maximise the company's profitability. It should be remembered that although the King might grant a charter to any such enterprise, this was one in which he himself held a 50% share. Ostensibly, he was acting to safeguard the continued existence and good management of a public utility, but he was also protecting his own investment. Would he do so impartially, or would the royal thumb nudge one of the scale-pans to give – his – new company an advantage it had never hoped for?

The charter recounted the history of the enterprise and Myddelton's role in it. But it noted that although the work was long since completed it had not 'yeilded such profitt' as hoped for. This was said to be partly because of the continuing costs, and partly because of the unregulated nature of the enterprise. The charter then proclaims that in order to settle and establish the work, half to the use of the King and his heirs, half to the use of Myddelton and the Adventurers in due proportion, the persons named and their successors shall for ever be a corporate body. The persons named, including Myddelton and seven other members of his family, amounted to twenty-nine in total, and between them they held the 36 Adventurers' shares. Most had just one share but seven, including Hugh Myddelton, had two each. The King was not a member of what became known as the New River Company, and he had no powers to intervene in its management.

As to the running of the company, one of the 'most sufficient and discrete' members was to be elected from time to time as Governor. He was to call meetings as necessary. There was also to be a deputy Governor and a Treasurer to receive the profits and make necessary payments. The charter appointed Hugh Myddelton to be the first such Governor, Robert Bateman to be his deputy Governor and Rowland Backhouse the Treasurer until replaced by election. It was provided that any five or more members, including either the Governor or his deputy, should meet as necessary from time to time with power to grant leases of the water and to decide 'all manner of business matters' to preserve and maintain the supply of the water and the collection of the proceeds. The meetings were also empowered to appoint employees, such 'Stewards, Clarkes ... Officers and Ministers' as necessary. Once a year, within ten days after the first Tuesday after the feast of All Saints there was to be a meeting held in the City of London or its suburbs, attended by at least seven members including the Governor or his deputy, to elect a Governor, deputy Governor and Treasurer. They would hold office for a year, but twelve or more members might replace them within that period 'for reasonable cause' or if they died or went away.

The legal basis on which the company held the course of the New River was then defined, but in words unintelligible except to land lawyers.[5a] There was also a power to buy a suitable building to use as a 'hall or meeting place'.

Just before the final provisions of the charter is one of the most surprising parts of the whole document. It begins as a kind of royal instruction to the public at large as to how they must treat the New River. Few who began to read it may have bothered to continue to the end, yet they would have been wise to. Most of it is predictable enough. They must not throw earth, rubbish, soil, gravel, 'dogges, cattes,' or cattle, carrion or unwholesome or unclean things in it. They must not use the river for washing nor break down its banks, pipes, ponds, bridges or houses. They must do nothing to hinder or annoy its current, nor run any sink, sewer, tannery or ditch into it. Neither must they presume to lay pipes or other devices to take its water, whether from the New River itself or from any supply pipe or quill, except where authorised in advance and in writing by the company. They were not even to make any new ponds, ditches, pits or trenches near the New River that might take its water, nor plant sallows, willows or elms within five yards of its banks, or to cause any other nuisance or annoyance.

Then, buried towards the end of that long list appears something quite new. Without so much as a full stop and straight after the references to tree planting and other nuisances comes the grant of nothing less than a monopoly to the new company. No one, it says, must attempt to bring any other river or 'pipe for conveyinge or bringinge of water' from any place whatsoever to the Cities of London or Westminster or to the borough of Southwark without the permission of the New River Company, on pain of incurring the King's high displeasure.

The original Acts of Parliament had never suggested that the right to bring water from Chadwell and Amwell should be a monopoly, and it seems doubtful that Parliament would ever have agreed to such a far-reaching provision. It amounted to a massive interference with the rights of the citizens of London to arrange their own affairs with regard to one of life's necessities. Here was England's capital, in need of good water supplies, apparently being fettered as to where that water should come from. It made no difference apparently that the New River might run dry, turn muddy or taste bad; no-one might seek to supplant it.

It has to be remembered that the charter to incorporate the company was not issued by Parliament. It was the King, using some of the vestigial powers contained within what is called the Royal Prerogative, who issued it. What makes the provision even more astonishing is that by this monopoly provision he was not merely enriching a group of his subjects – the Adventurers – but at the same time benefiting himself as much as the rest of them put together.

Why was that monopoly provision slipped into the charter? There can be little doubt that it was deliberately tucked away into one of the more uninteresting parts of the document. Other actions by the King at around that time may suggest the answer – that he was increasingly concerned that the company might fail even at this late stage.

In later years the New River Company tried to have its royal charter confirmed by Parliament, but failed to gain sufficient support on three occasions, in 1621, 1624 and 1642. The main difficulty may have been the monopoly as monopolies were a contentious issue at the time.

Obtaining the charter was not without cost, as the account books show on various dates from December 1617 onwards. The first legal fees, for a 'paper Booke for the Corporation' were 3 guineas. Then the Attorney General charged £22 for passing it, and his doorkeeper 10 shillings. Mr Beale had £14 12s. 0d. for drawing it up, and his clerks a further £12 for engrossing three copies for the King, Privy Seal and Signet. Fees at the Signet 'being three skinnes' were £6 6s. 8d., at the Privy Seal were £4 6s. 8d., where the two Clerks had £4, the chamber keepers 6s. 8d. One 'Clarke that followed itt and broughte itt home' was paid ten shillings. The fee for 'passing itt under the Greate Seal' was £24. 4s. 0d. After all that effort, the final 4s. 8d. 'ffor a Boxe for itt' seems very reasonable.

The first Adventurers

The 1619 charter sets out the names and descriptions of the Adventurers as they were on 21 June 1619. Although they held thirty-six shares, there were just twenty-nine Adventurers, and thereafter that was the maximum number of Board members allowed to attend and vote at weekly meetings and general courts. (The order of their names has been rearranged so that relatives appear together. Those who held two shares at the time of the 1619 charter are indicated).

Hugh Midleton, Cittizen and Gouldsmith of London.(2)
Hugh Midleton, sonne and heire of Hugh Midleton, Gouldsmith.
William Midleton of London, Draper.
Richard Midleton of London, Grocer.
William Midleton of London, Gouldsmith.
Sir Thomas Midleton, Knight, Cittizen and Alderman of London.
Henry Midleton, sonne and heire of David Midleton, late of London Gent. deceased.
Timothy Midleton of London, Esquier.
Sir Henry Mountague, Knight, Lord Chief Justice of the Court of Kings Bench.
Sir Robert Killigrewe, Knight.
Sir William Burlacie the elder, Knight
Sir William Burlacie the younger, Knight
Sir Lawrence Hide, Knight.(2)
Nicholas Hide of the Middle Temple, London, Esquier(2)
Sir Henry Nevill, Knight.(2)
John Packer, Esquier.
Samuel Backhowse, Esquier. (2)
John Backhowse his sonne and heire, Esquier.(2)
Rowland Backhouse of London, Mercer.
Robert Bateman of London, Skynner
William Bateman of London, Grocer.
John ffaror of London, Skinner.
Edward Pritchard of London, Skinner
Humfrey Hall of London, Girdler.
Peter Vanlore, Merchant stranger.(2).
Marmaduke Rawden of London, Clothworker.
Henry Vincent of London, Letherseller.
James Bearblocke of London, Gent.
Gabriell Newman of London, Gouldsmith.

Some of these descriptions, such as grocer or mercer sound modest enough, and may suggest small tradesmen, but they were of course members of the powerful City Livery Companies: the Adventurers were wealthy men.

Peter Vanlore may sound the most modest of all – just a merchant, and a 'stranger' or foreigner at that – yet it is no accident that he owned two shares rather than one, for he could possibly have financed the whole venture on his own. Born in Utrecht he was a jeweller, merchant, banker and moneylender. He had sold jewels at Queen Elizabeth's court and continued to do so when James followed her to the throne. One record reveals that in February 1604 the King authorised the payment to him of £11,477, being the remainder of the price of a 'jewel', and in June of the same year £7,631 16s. 1¼d. as part payment of another debt. Vanlore's reputation in his lifetime was such that his alabaster monument in Tilehurst church, Berkshire, where he became lord of the manor in 1604, and died as Sir Peter Vanlore in 1627, carries the confident inscription:

> When thou hast read the name "Here Lies Vanlore",
> Thou neesdst no story to inform thee more.'

Some of those named were merely trustees who held shares on behalf of Hugh Myddelton, perhaps to gain him extra votes at company meetings. The last two named, Bearblocke and Newman, were certainly in this category as their trusts are disclosed in a company minute from the 1630s, and there were probably others among the seven other Myddeltons named.

King James rebuffed

If the King had hoped that forming the New River Company would solve all the problems, he was to be disappointed. New customers were connected, but in a trickle rather than a flood. In March 1618, a year before incorporation, the King considered taking over the whole project to himself. To that end he had started enquiries to find out at what rate of yearly pension each of the Adventurers might be prepared to deliver his shares up to the King. In June of that year the Privy Council directed that since the New River had not done as well as expected and might be improved to the king's advantage either by taking it 'wholly into his Majestie's hands, or otherwise by letting it wholly to such undertakers as have the other moytie'. The Chancellor of the Exchequer, Master of the Rolls and two others were deputed to meet with Myddelton, and afterwards report back with their opinion as to what should be done.

Nothing seems to have come of that, and the following year the Privy Council again started enquiries to see whether the Adventurers might either sell out to the King, or buy out his share. Again, nothing transpired.[6]

In 1622 the Lord Treasurer renewed enquiries on the King's behalf. Perhaps the Adventurers would be prepared to sell their shares to the King at a reasonable price? The Adventurers were not interested. Without refusing outright, they delayed and played for time, suggesting that the King might somehow be able to help the company further, perhaps with the collection of bad debts. Back to the King went a report that it was doubtful anything could be done 'without more pressure than the tymes will well beare.'

The report finally spelt out the stark truth. By buying a half share in the enterprise the King had committed himself to be most affected by its future profitability or otherwise. The report continued:

> 'they have gotten this advantage, that his Majesties moitie being undivided from theirs cannot be improved without improving theirs. And they being manie, the losse of their moitie devided in manie parts is the easier to beare than his Majesties which fals all upon himself. How to drive them from this hold we yet see noe means.'

Eventually the New River Company produced a small profit, and for the year ending Michaelmas 1622, £433 2s. 7d. was available as the King's share. This cannot have seemed very much of a return for the money and effort invested by the King.

Myddelton's baronetcy

Despite these disappointments, the King chose the year 1622 to bestow an honour on Hugh Myddelton. Earlier in James's reign, he had created a new form of hereditary title – that of baronet. Like a knight, a baronet gained the prefix of 'Sir', but whereas a knighthood died with its owner, a baronetcy passed on through the male line. The baronetcy was invented as a way of raising revenue, because it was available for purchase to any knight or esquire of good repute with lands worth £1,000 a year. It cost £1,080 to become a baronet but as with modern domestic appliances, the payments could be spread over three years.

The King chose to forgo this charge in Myddelton's case, and on 19 October 1622 he became Sir Hugh Myddelton of Ruthin in the county of Denbigh. The grant listed the three achievements that had brought him this honour. One was his land reclamation work at Brading Haven on the Isle of Wight, and one was his development of silver mines in Cardiganshire. Heading the list was:

> 'For bringing to the city of London with excessive Charge and greater Difficulty, a new Cutt or River of fresh Water, to the great benefitt and inestimable preservation thereof.'[7]

King James was never to see the benefit of all his efforts on behalf of the New River. On 27 March 1626 he died, and was succeeded by his son, who became King Charles I.

A whiff of competition

By now, things were even less promising for the new company. London had been badly affected by an outbreak of bubonic plague in 1625. According to one contemporary account, it claimed 35,000 lives, so that many houses were left empty and the company's income slumped.[8] This is confirmed by early company records showing that whereas there were 1549 premises supplied in 1618, this dropped to 1372 by 1630.[9]

During that difficult period came the first of a series of competitive pressures that would affect the way in which the New River Company developed over the ensuing centuries. By 1630 a new water scheme was being planned by a Sir Charles Herbert, Sir Walter Roberts and others. They proposed to supply London with water from Hoddesdon in Hertfordshire in an enclosed conduit, the method previously favoured by Inglebert. Roberts, in support of his scheme, was scathing about the New River:

> 'Middelton's water by reason of the foulnesse and muddinesse of it (coming in an open trench)

> being found by experience not to be fit for many uses, and to faile, many times for a whole weeke or fortnight altogether.'[10]

He also pointed out that the constant growth of London was causing problems of supply, with 'houses in Covent Garden, St Martin's, St James's, St Giles', Drewry Lane, Lincolne's Inn and Holborne being short of good water, especially in the new buildings there.'

King Charles became interested in this scheme at an early stage, because its promoters were offering to pay the Crown no less than £4,000 a year, simply in return for the King granting his approval to the necessary patents and authorities. There was a plan to raise the necessary funds with a lottery, and the whole enterprise has a faint air of financial raffishness, but it seems to have appealed to the King.

King Charles sells out

The King renewed the enquiries his father had begun to obtain a better deal from the New River. By 1630 the Crown had received only about £4,470 in return for the investment made by King James. The prospect of competition from the Hoddesdon scheme can only have made the New River's financial outlook seem bleaker, particularly when it was promising to pay the King almost as much each year as the New River had paid in almost twenty years. Perhaps for that reason King Charles eventually decided to accept a compromise that had been suggested, after negotiation between his advisers and Myddelton. At least it had the merits of simplicity. The Crown would give up all its rights to any share in the future profits, in return for a single down payment of £500, followed by a guaranteed annual payment of £500 for ever. The necessary paperwork was completed on 18 November 1631. By it, the King transferred his interest not to the company but to Sir Hugh Myddelton.

Myddelton dealt with this change of circumstances very simply. Just as the Adventurers' moiety had been divided into 36 shares, he split the King's moiety into 36 shares. These shares would in future be known as King's shares, and they would always be worth less than the others because they came encumbered with the 'Crown Clog'. In effect, £500 a year would be deducted from the dividends payable on those 36 shares in order to pay the Crown, so each would receive about £13 a year less than an Adventurer's share. Unlike Adventurers' shares, they came with no right for their holders to vote or take part in the management of the New River Company, and so would always be worth less.

As time went by, of course, dividends tended to increase, and gradually the value of the two classes of shares came to be almost identical.

From Myddelton's point of view, the agreement must have seemed something of a coup. He already owned thirteen of the thirty-six Adventurers' shares, either directly or through nominees, in effect 18% of the entire business. Now his holding had increased to 68%. Sadly he was not to enjoy it for long, as he died on 7 December 1631 less than three weeks after buying out the King.

King Charles had not struck a very good bargain. The Hoddesdon scheme came to nothing and was eventually forgotten, whereas the New River still flows. The Crown – or its nominees – continued to receive a flat £500 a year, whereas by 1897 the dividends due on the King's moiety exceeded £100,000 a year. Even in Charles's short lifetime the dividend would have exceeded £500 within four years of his selling out, £1000 by 1639 and almost £1400 by 1648, the last full year before he walked out to be beheaded on a scaffold in Whitehall.

Proclamations and Warrants

One of the ways in which the New River Company was helped by its royal partner was that the original declaration by James I in 1612 included a commitment to suppress any 'tumultuous or other rude or unlawfull course, by force, sleight, clamors or otherwise . at any time or times hereafter ... to the hinderance, lett or opposition of bringing of the said springs and water.' This led to a flow of royal proclamations which continued to issue and which, after polite reminders from the company, were issued afresh by new sovereigns. This continued even though the royal interest had been reduced to a fixed annual sum of £500, payable whether or not the company made any profit at all.

The proclamations were generalised requests 'for the careful custody and well ordering of the New River', but more specific help was also to be had, from the Privy Council if not direct from the sovereign, when the occasion demanded. The earliest example dates from 1615:

> 'Whereas Hugh Midleton hath brought a river of water unto Islington and from thence convayed the same by pipes into divers partes of the citty of London to the great benefit and commodity of the inhabitants of the said citty; forasmuch as complaint is made unto us of many abuses and misdemeanors daylie committed and donn in and upon the said river, by lewde and ill-disposed people, in cuttinge the bankes and letting out the said water, to the inconvenience and prejudice of the tennantes, casting in dogges and filth, and letting in sewers and other fowle and unclean water, to the annoyance of the said water; breakeinge and carreinge away the bridges, vaultes and rayles standinge in and upon the river; taking and carryinge water out of the said river in licquer cartes, tubs or barrels, and stealing branches and cockes from the pipes without any composicion, together with many suchlike abuses and annoyances: these shalbe therefore to will and require yow that, upon informacion given unto yow by the said Hugh Midleton yow cause the offenders to be ymediatly brought before us, to answere in their misdemeanours in that behalfe, whereof they may be assured his Majestie wilbe very sensible, beinge to the prejudice of soe worthie a worke, wherein his Highness is soe deeply impressed.'

In 1689, under William and Mary, there was a new proclamation to protect the New River. It prohibited the taking of water from it, fishing, and watering cattle, and even forbade keeping domestic geese or ducks on it. It also gave the Company the power to enter premises to search – in daylight hours – for any branch pipes laid without their knowledge.

This royal willingness to assist the profitability of a privately owned company is perhaps explained by the company's special nature. True enough the Governor who asked the King for support might be motivated by nothing more than a wish for greater profit, yet the underlying enterprise, as the chief provider of water to England's capital city, had an undeniable public benefit. Thus, there was always a certain duality about the nature of the New River Company and this sometimes stood it in good stead.

CHAPTER SIX

Cost and Concealment

The surviving records – What did it cost to dig? – How many men did it take? – How fast could they dig? – How did labour costs compare to the total cost? – What was the cost of maintaining it? – A culture of secrecy – Mr Wilkinson's gratuity – A puzzling reticence – Corporate amnesia – £6,000,000 compensation

This chapter will seek to answer some questions about the original cost of the New River before turning to a separate and much later matter. That is the way in which officers of the New River Company claimed to be unaware of the original cost, despite being asked many times, from about 1812 right up to the time when it was taken over, and paid compensation, by the Metropolitan Water Board in 1904.

The surviving records

Hugh Myddelton had ensured that careful records were kept of the costs he incurred building the river, and the original books of account still exist in the Public Record Office. The tall slim books are covered in a single thickness of flexible goatskin vellum that was once cream but has darkened with age, soot and handling. Inside its protection the pages, almost three times as high as they are wide, are made from a thick hand-made paper that is still fresh and clean after four centuries. The writing was done with a broad nib in a dark, rusty brown ink that has never faded. It is careful, almost meticulous, but the words are hard to read because nearly every letter is somehow different from any modern script. As for the figures, they are easy except where the Royal auditors have added their own totals in a clumsy version of roman numerals.[1]

It is an odd fact that the books lay neglected for centuries. The first published source to quote much detail from them was not until 1948. Of their authenticity, there can be no doubt. Not only did Hugh Myddelton sign every page, he made other entries. As J. W. Gough pointed out, the first page begins with the entry in his distinctive handwriting 'Mo(nie)s paid and Dysbursed for the bringinge of watter from the springs of Chadwell and Amwell to the City of london...'[2] It is also clear that Myddelton himself totalled the books as they went from week to week, a wise precaution as he would have to swear to the correctness of the sums he thereafter demanded from the Treasury. One entry in September 1629 describes the purchase of a similar book. 'For a Greate Booke of Dutche Paper fayrely bound in Vellum and clasped and ruled in spaces to make a Rental booke, and for paper, £2.'

So the writing, though difficult, is legible and the figures present no real difficulty at all. From this it might seem that finding out the cost of the New River would be simple, and efforts have been made in the past to transcribe and analyse the records. One figure that has been quoted as the total cost in a number of publications since 1948 is £18,524 19s. 0d., and it has the merit that it can be reached, almost precisely, by two quite separate routes.

First, from the account books, the accumulated costs as at November 1614 were £18,525 Second, Treasury records still exist of the amount paid to Myddelton to honour the King's agreement to pay 'as well the one halfe of the monie already disbursed, as the one halfe of the mony to be disbursed'. By 1617, when the November 1614 bill was finally paid, Myddelton had received £9,262 9s. 6d. from the Treasury – almost exactly half of the total just given.

It is tempting, then, to accept that the New River cost about £18,500 to build. Unfortunately, there are a number of problems with that figure. It is easy to assume that because Treasury payments to Myddelton ended with the November 1614 accounts, then that must mark the end of the river's constructional phase. This is simply not so. Construction continued in many ways. The reason the Treasury payments stopped may simply have been that the business was beginning to generate some income as the first customers were signed up, and therefore the King's half of the costs could be met from half of that income, even if there was not yet any surplus to pay dividends. It seems to follow that we cannot blindly accept November 1614 as the moment of completion, and that it would be wrong simply to include the costs to that date.

The next problem is to decide what it is we are trying to cost. Is it just the New River itself – the channel from Chadwell spring to Islington – or does it include the distribution network of pipes to all parts of London? Whichever of those options we choose, that still leaves open the question of what cut-off date to choose.

This is not a frivolous point. As far as the New River is concerned, no sooner had it been dug than further money had to be spent on it. This was not just the ordinary expenditure of maintaining an open waterway – cutting waterweeds, and restoring the banks. The channel was being altered almost from the moment of its completion. Mostly this took the form of reducing its length by building embankments or cuttings to reduce the number of meandering loops that made up the original route. This process started within weeks of the water first flowing and continued long into the twentieth century until the original route had almost been halved. What date should we choose for completion?

Next, should the infrastructure of pipes to the City also be included in the cost and, if so, at what date should that be measured? It seems illogical to exclude this part of the system, for without it the New River has no purpose. Yet it is difficult to include because, just as the channel of the New River was being constantly shortened, so the pipe network would inevitably be lengthened, the first main pipe quickly followed by others as the network spread underground like the roots of a tree and as London grew in size down the years. Should the cost of the network be measured at the moment when the first customer received the first connection? If not, when?

Perhaps the answer to the growing list of conundrums is that there is no one simple answer. Better to ask a series of questions if any of the answers are to be useful. What follows is an attempt to show from the accounts such things as the size of the workforce, how much of the total was incurred in paying the labourers who dug the channel, how much it cost to build the many bridges that crossed it, and how much went in compensation to landowners.

What did it cost to dig?

The total expenditure by the time of the grand opening September 1613 was £11,053. About £1000 of this related to elm timber bought to make wooden mains, and the first pipeboring costs, which all relates to the distribution network. In round figures, then, it cost £10,000 to dig what we might call New River Mark I. Many thousands more were spent in later years to improve that original channel, a process that has continued ever since.

The original channel was about 42 miles long. If we deduct 2 miles to allow for the work Colthurst had done in 1604-5, that leaves 40 miles, or 70,400 yards. The cost of £10,000 divided by 70,400 works out to about 2s. 10d. a yard for a trench ten feet wide and with an average depth of five feet, inclusive of timber where needed, bridges, all wages and some compensation to landowners. Although the depth of water was only about four feet, undulating ground meant that the cutting was often much deeper in order to keep the bottom almost level, and five feet seems a likely average.

The banks sloped inwards, and if the ten-foot width was thereby reduced to two feet at the bottom, the cross-section was 30 square feet, or 3⅓ square yards. Dividing this into the cost per yard, each cubic yard of excavation cost about tenpence. This figure includes all bridges and timber and some compensation to landowners.

If this figure seems very low, it can be usefully compared with costs given by the canal builder Robert Whitworth. Preparing an estimate for a proposed canal in London a hundred and sixty years later, in 1773, he noted the 'Expence of the common Cutting' at 'fivepence per Yard'. His accompanying measurements show that 'Yard' means cubic yard. His estimate shows that this is merely the cost of the excavation, as he lists the cost of building embankments, locks, bridges fences and compensation to landowners separately.

How many men did it take?

The construction workers are all listed week by week, and seem to have been exclusively male. Some are paid at lower rates of 6d. or 9d. a day and might be boys, but these are few in number, well below 10% of the total. Where women's names occur it is either as landowners hiring out horse teams or, very occasionally, in entries such as 'Goodwife Essex, for bere' or the occasional payments to Alice Crew who supplied nails.

Taking the digging of the channel first, perhaps the most interesting question to a modern reader is not so much the cost in money terms, because values have changed so much, but the cost in human terms – how many days work for people using spades, shovels and wheelbarrows. This is a question that can be answered with some accuracy, as long as the limitations are understood.

Labourers are easy to count as long as they worked at daily rates, for they were meticulously counted by the number of days they worked in any week. The complications come when they were paid at piecework rates, as they often were. When on piecework, the payments were much less regular. Sometimes a pieceworker received two or more separate payments in a week, sometimes none, and the amounts paid vary greatly. It seems they were probably allocated a particular section of measured work to do, and when it was finished they were entitled to payment. Someone, perhaps Colthurst, was the overseer of this system, and he may have kept written notes which were not retained once the details had been entered in the accounts books.

It is therefore not possible to say precisely how many days work any of the labourers had done when they were on piecework rates. The accounts show that labourers and pieceworkers were drawn from the same group, as many of their names appear in both categories on different occasions.

From this it seems likely that their daily earning as pieceworkers will have been broadly similar to their ordinary daily rates. If the piecework system was used to provide an incentive for them to put their backs into the job, it may well be that they were able to earn a little more under that system.

From this assumption, it becomes possible to estimate the size of the workforce. As labourers normally earned 10d. per day, or a premium rate of 1s. 0d. when standing in water, it should not be too far out to assume that pieceworkers averaged 1s. 0d. per day. From this we can convert the amount paid to pieceworkers each week into the number of man/days.

The chart on p. 236 uses these calculations to show the approximate work-force month by month during the construction period, based on a full six day week. In other words, if 400 men were paid for 3 days one particular week, that would be shown as a workforce of 200 for the full six day week.

The chart also shows the proportion of the workforce being paid daily rates, and the proportion on piecework. The fluctuations reflect changes in the type of work. The basic excavation, which could easily be measured, was usually piecework.

The total cost of labourers, pieceworkers and tradesmen for the period from the beginning of August 1609 to the end of September 1613 is about £4,700. That is a period of fifty months, but for twenty of those months work was at a standstill, so the real constructional phase lasted for 30 months.

Averaging out the labour costs over the 30

months gives a cost of £157 per month, and using the assumptions already discussed this is equivalent to 128 men regularly working a six day week. In other words, the New River was dug in 30 months by an average workforce of 128 men working a six day week.

In fact the work force fluctuated from day to day. The maximum number at work on any single day was just over 300.

How fast could they dig?

The total length of the New River when it was built was about forty-two miles. To calculate the work done by Myddelton's men this has to be reduced to forty miles, to make allowance for the preliminary work Colthurst had done.

Forty miles is 70,400 yards. Ignoring the twenty-month standstill, the actual construction was done in thirty months. This period contained 130 weeks, and at six working days each week, 780 possible working days. Dividing 70,400 yards by 780 days gives the answer that the work progressed at an average of 90 yards each working day. Another way of looking at this figure is to say that each full-time worker can be credited with 1/128 of the total length, or 550 yards, over thirty months.

Of course not all the workforce was engaged in digging, and much effort went into such activities as raising and consolidating the banks. Once the channel was made there were frequent collapses of the sides – referred to as 'calving in,' which we might call caving in, and much time was spent removing the resulting debris, described as 'casting out calves.'

How did the labour costs compare to the total cost?

By 29 September 1613, the New River was complete and running all the way from Chadwell to the Round Pond at New River Head. Up to that date, the total money expended was about £11,053. This can be broken down as follows:

Managers	£1092
Daily labour (including carpenters)	£2030
Pieceworkers	£2713
'Quarterage'	£138
Moletrapping	£14
Horsework	£427
'The Ingen'	£29
Timber	£1404
Bridges	£664
Legal	£189
Compensation	£848
Costs at New River Head	£268
Elm & pipeboring	£1033
Bricks, lime, tools, etc	£204

In these figures 'Managers' means Hugh Myddelton, the various surveyors, Edmund Colthurst, Clerks and those employees who received a regular weekly wage. Quarterage covers quarterly payments to the first walksmen, who were appointed to care for the river. 'Timber' consists mostly of payments to one contractor William Parnell, who supplied all kinds of timber for 'wharfing' or strengthening the banks, for some of the bridges, and for frames and flashes where the channel crossed, or was crossed by, other streams. The costs for elm and pipeboring all relate to preparing main pipes for distributing water through London streets.

The figure for compensation only includes amounts paid by 26 September 1613, and further sums were paid later. Some of the largest amounts of compensation were paid in Islington, such as to Sir William Compton who was paid £56 15s. 2d. 'by reason of the Cutt & banckes ... for a trenche cutt throughe...196 poles of mead(ow)e grounde, 94 poles of pasture groundes & 61 poles of wood grounde..'. The total length cut through his land was 351 poles, or 1.1 miles.

What was the cost of maintaining it?

Soon after the New River Company was incorporated, Hugh Myddelton offered to be responsible for the maintenance of the river for the fixed annual sum of £800. These payments began in 1620 but were inadequate and increased to £1,000 a year in 1622. This covered ordinary maintenance only and not changes in the stream.

By April 1665 Gregory Hardwick the Clerk,

and John Grene who would succeed him, were offering to maintain the river for a fixed fee of £1000 a year. Then as now new management may have been expected to cause job losses, but they made a point of saying that they would not remove any of the existing servants 'soe long as they do their duety.' This offer was eventually embodied into a written agreement whereby Grene contracted 'for maintaining the Contry work .. with all troughs bridges & flashes' for a period of five years ending on 25 March 1670

When 1670 came, Grene offered to continue for three more years at £1000 a year. The maverick Simon Myddelton offered to undercut him, by doing it for £800. Grene claimed it had formerly cost the company nearly £1700 a year, and said he had supplied the city with 'a greater plenty of water' notwithstanding 'the helpes out of Lee River was reduced'. After discussion, Grene's contract was renewed.

A culture of secrecy

That, then, is a summary of some of the costs disclosed in Myddelton's account books. The remainder of this chapter deals with what appears to be the discovery, and immediate suppression, of these books in 1845, by those who might have been expected to trumpet their existence – the directors of the New River Company.

By way of introduction, an odd claim appears in *The Waterworks of London* by Zerah Colburn, published in 1867. He said that no accurate description of the New River had ever been published, the officers of the company having always refused particulars of their works for publication. He continued

> 'At any rate they have repeatedly declined to contribute a paper upon them to the Institution of Civil Engineers, and beyond a few details scattered in various tracts and reports, the library of that body has absolutely no account of this, the principal undertaking for the supply of water to London.'

Colburn explains that he had been given little co-operation by the New River Company, and contrasts it with the help given by the engineers of other water companies. If his claim stood alone it would hardly merit a mention, but it does not because of an astonishing fact contained in the Company's own records.

Mr Wilkinson's gratuity

The minutes of a General Court of the New River Company in January 1845 include the following:

> 'Mr Wilkinson the collector desiring to present to the company a book of prints with written and other descriptive matter principally relating to the New River and the parishes through which it passed to London, and it appearing that Mr Wilkinson had another book relating to the original formation of the Company etc., obtained from various sources, the subject was referred to a committee (Mr Miles and Mr Berens) and on their report & recommendation the Board ordered that upon Mr Wilkinson giving up the latter Book also, and the papers in his possession from which it was compiled, and not proceeding any further in such enquiries the sum of £50 should be given to him.'[3]

Alexander Wilkinson had been employed as a collector since 1841, and was to remain with the company until he retired in 1877. At that time, £50 was a large amount. By way of comparison, the company's labourers were paid less than £40 a year. Why should the company have been prepared to pay such a large sum to suppress a piece of historical research? What could the books have contained?

Part of the answer may lie among the company's own records, in a vellum-covered foolscap book of ruled paper containing a handwritten 'History of the New River.' The only clue to its authorship is on the flyleaf, where it has the initials AW and the date 1844.[4]

What the book contains is a meticulous investigation of the subject by reference, among other early records, to documents then at the office of Land Revenue and now at the Public Record Office. It has to be stressed that the book is not written in vague terms. It begins with quotations from early published sources, but then goes on to set out in minute and accurate detail the costs and income of the New

River up to 1632. It gives chapter and verse for its sources, and they include the account books kept by Hugh Myddelton's clerks, and signed by him on every page. They were books whose existence seems to have been overlooked by historians of water supply – apart from A.W. – for more than three centuries, as the fascinating detail they contain was nowhere referred to until 1948.

There seems little doubt that A.W. is Wilkinson. It is obvious from the minute quoted above that Wilkinson had been 'proceeding in enquiries' that led to 'another book relating to the original formation of the Company etc., obtained from various sources,' before January 1845. The Clerk's working agendas for several other meetings between September 1844 and January 1845 include the heading 'Wilkinson's New River Book', but if the matter was discussed at those meetings no minutes of the discussions were made – in itself a significant omission, as the minutes were normally full and meticulous. A.W.'s book fits the description closely, and the date 1844 is spot on. The likelihood of some other A.W. having been engaged on an identical project in the same year, and his notebook turning up in the Company archive, seems impossibly small. It follows that the Company paid a large sum to suppress an accurate historical account of its own origins.

A puzzling reticence

Why should the New River Company, normally proud of its ancient foundation, have felt shy about such a work? The answer may be that by this time London's water companies had been for some years under the scrutiny of a hostile public who saw them as purveyors of water that was overpriced and barely fit for use. An example is Charles Dickens' complaint in 1855 that he was 'usually left on a Monday morning as dry as if there was no New River Company in existence – which I sometimes devoutly wish were the case ..'[5] It has to be said that New River water was of a better quality than that supplied by some of its competitors from the Thames, but its quality was not beyond reproach, and its flow was often inadequate.

Because the true cost of building the New River had somehow been forgotten, the company had sometimes been asked what it was, and appeared not to know. The loss of company papers in the 1769 fire was the usual reason given for this ignorance. An example of the Company's stance on this point can be seen from a leaflet sent out under the Governor's name in 1812, during a period when the Company's charges were under attack. In this, he said that the belief that the shares had originally cost only £100 each was 'absurd', and that 'the formation of their works at the time of Sir Hugh Myddelton cost, according to the best authorities, £500,000.'[6]

The matter became important in 1821, when Parliament had appointed a Select Committee on the Supply of Water to the Metropolis. They wanted to know what capital the water companies had invested in their businesses, in order to assess the reasonableness of their dividends, and the charges they made for water. Most of the London water companies were relatively new, and had this information to hand. The New River Company apparently did not know what the river had cost. Accordingly William Chadwell Mylne, who had succeed his father Robert Mylne as the Company's Engineer in 1810, had valued it at present day prices in 1815 when the subject was first raised.

Appendix 4 to a Parliamentary report in 1828 explains the position:

> 'The capital of the New River Company is invested first, in the aqueduct called the New River, and the accessory works .. for bringing the water to London; second in lands & houses all originally purchased with a view to some purpose of the waterworks... third, in steam engines, water wheels, pipes and other machinery for the distribution of the water. The company are not able to state the amount of the first two portions of this capital otherwise than by valuation, *all documents relating to far the greater part of them having been lost by lapse of time or destroyed by a fire in the year 1769.* (Italics added.) The first and second portions of this capital are valued by the Company at £600,000. The third .. as nearly as can be ascertained from the Company's books, at £438,725.'[7]

It has to be said that Mylne's 1815 estimate may well have been accurate at current values. It is also the case that if the early records really had been lost and the figure was unknown, making an estimate at current values might have been the only way to proceed. But if it had been known that 'bringing the water to London' cost little more than £18,000, the £600,000 estimate may not have found such ready acceptance.

Corporate amnesia

Thirty years later the subject was raised again, and in 1851 W.C.Mylne found himself giving evidence to another select committee. During cross-examination about the capital of the New River Company, he confirmed that the return showing a figure of £1,421,717 was made by the Secretary.

> *Q. Of that sum, is £500,000 the sum subscribed by the shareholders, and £921,717 the sum which you have laid by from revenue?* – I do not understand the return exactly; I never knew what the subscription was.
> *Q What has been paid by the shareholders?* – I do not know; after the fire which took place, I do not believe there was a single document to show.
> *Q If any return has been made, is it unsatisfactory?* – We know that the capital which has been spoken of here was arrived at by an estimate in 1821; when the first question about water supply arose. I was called on to make an estimate of what the works would have cost at that day; I did that in company with Mr Murdoch, of Soho, who is since dead; that estimate is in the returns given to Parliament in 1821; from that period the outlay has been regularly kept and added to it, which additional outlay in improved works makes that capital of £1,421,000.
> *Q – Did you make the return in 1821?* – Yes … I made the estimate.
> *Q At present you are not able to tell us the total amount of the capital of the New River Company?* – Only from this paper.
> *Q Only by the returns at the date of 1821?* – Exactly; there was no document whatever saved from that fire.
> *Q When was the fire?* – My father was engineer to the company 40 years before myself. I think it took place before his appointment.
> *Q. That fire burnt all your books?* – Yes, our books were by the Thames side, close to the foot of Blackfriars Bridge; the whole of the papers were destroyed.
> *Q. In what year was that?* – About 1769.[8]

The revealing thing about this passage is that, however little he may have known in 1821, Mylne still appeared not to know in 1851 what the New River had cost to build. Yet he had been the Engineer of the New River Company for forty years by then, and it was only six years earlier, in 1845, that the board had agreed to pay £50 for Mr Wilkinson's books 'and the papers in his possession from which it was compiled', on his agreeing not to proceed any further in his enquiries.

Did the Board members not know that their engineer would be giving evidence to a select committee in 1851? Had they forgotten to spread the glad news that at last they knew the cost of the New River? Had he been told and forgotten it?

In passing, it is surprising that Mylne thought the fire had taken place before his father's appointment as surveyor to the New River Company. Not only was his father's appointment more than two years before the fire, but Robert Mylne was the architect of the attractive building that had replaced the burnt offices. That was completed only ten years before William Chadwell Mylne was born and was still used as the Company's only office until 1819, by which time Mylne had had been working for the Company for fifteen years.

Another year went by. Mr Mylne found himself giving evidence again, to a committee on the New River Company's Bill of 1852. This was promoted by the Company to obtain an Act of Parliament, which among other things would declare what their capital should be deemed to be.

> '*Q. Were those items of land purchased taken at the old prices?* – The land was valued at the prices of that day; all the documents have been burned; *we have no record whatever to guide us.*' (Italics added).[9]

To Mylne's 1815 valuations were added other items of expenditure. The Act was passed, and

Parliament thereby declared that 'the capital expended by the Company in carrying out and completing their works now in existence amounts to the sum of £1,519,958 and upwards.'

Down the years the same questions were occasionally asked, the same answers given. By 1898 a Royal Commission, chaired by Viscount Llandaff, was sitting to consider whether the water companies should be taken over by a public authority. If there was to be such a takeover, compensation would have to be paid to the companies, and somebody would have to decide how much it should be.

At one of its hearings, on 23 January 1899 the Governor of the New River Company was giving evidence. He was not able to say how much of the company's capital represented real estate and how much waterworks – 'I think it has always been kept all together, so that I do not think I could give you any idea what the different lands cost.'

Q- Can you tell us how that figure of £1,500,000 .. was arrived at?
A- They went into it all at the time of the Act of Parliament; they had the figure before them at the time.
Q – I want to know what was gone into, and what was the result?
A – It was the evidence of 1852; I really cannot carry it in my mind exactly how they made up the amount.
Q Very well, you cannot tell us. Your secretary (i.e. the company secretary), perhaps, would be able to tell us something about that?
A – I do not think that he would be able to give you any further information.
The next day the questioning turned to when water had first been taken from the River Lea, something easily discovered from Myddelton's accounts, and Mr Pope, counsel for the company, was asked by Lord Robert Cecil,
Q. All we want is the date when the Lea began to be used.
Mr Pope – I am afraid we none of us know.
Q – I do not suggest you can carry your memory back Mr Pope, but you must surely have some record of when you first made your works, which enabled you to take water from the Lea?
- They were all burnt. We have not those records, because whatever they were, they were destroyed by the fire.
Q – I am quite satisfied with whatever statement Mr Pope makes. If he tells me the information is not in the possession of the company, I will take that.
Mr Pope – I do not undertake to say that. But if it is not, it is because we have not got it, not because we are withholding it.[10]

£6,000,000 compensation

In due course Parliament decided that the water companies should be taken into public ownership. Under the Act compensation had to be paid, and this was based on the amount of the company's capital. A Court of Arbitration was set up to decide the issue of compensation, and heard evidence from all parties. It consisted of a retired Lord Justice of Appeal, a retired Permanent Secretary and an eminent engineer. They had to decide the value of each of the private water companies that was to be taken over. Before the matter was decided in the case of the New River Company there had been appeals to the Court of Appeal and the House of Lords. Never during those proceedings was the true cost of the construction of the New River disclosed.

The final outcome for the New River Company was that it reduced its claim from £13,260,144 to £8,214,163 and was finally awarded £6,000,534. At the request of the New River Company this was to be apportioned by the Court among the holders of King's, Adventurers' and New shares. The result was that a holder of one of the King's or Adventurers' shares received water stock worth £67,800 as well as 1365 £1 shares in the new property company. A separate arbitration decided the amount of compensation for loss of office by those shareholders who sat on the board. They claimed £396,255 but were awarded £76,917 17s. 10d.

Many still felt the compensation awarded to the companies was over-generous. When the Chairman of the Southwark and Vauxhall, on hearing the result, proclaimed that he would 'go and take poison,' his QC is said to have commented 'The only poison he'll take is a bottle of champagne.'

CHAPTER SEVEN

New River People

Shareholders and meetings – Loyalty oaths – Storing valuables – Governors and deputies – Beating the clock – Treasurers and auditors – Clerks and Secretaries – General Surveys – Surveyor/Engineers – The Beadle – Collectors – Walksmen – Turncocks and Paviours – Engine workers – Hungry labourers.

From its incorporation in 1619 until it was taken over by the Metropolitan Water Board in 1904, the New River Company was run according to rules laid down by its charter. How this worked in practice, and how it affected the lives of the people who owned or worked for the Company, is the subject of this chapter.

Shareholders and meetings

The Company's charter of 1619 required the holding of regular meetings. These seem to have settled into a routine of weekly meetings originally on Tuesdays but later on Thursdays at 11 am. There were also more formal meetings, known as General Courts. These dealt with such things as electing officers, administering oaths of loyalty, granting leases and other important matters.

Early records are incomplete because of the 1769 fire. The first meeting of the Company was on 2 November 1619 at the chambers of Sir Henry Montague, one of the Adventurers. He had previously been the Recorder of London, and was now the Lord Chief Justice. Later meetings were held at private houses, often Hugh Myddelton's, which was at first in Little Wood Street and by 1627 in Bassishaw Street, and sometimes at taverns or coffee houses.

In 1633 and 1635, after Hugh's death, meetings took place at Thomas Myddelton's home, in Lothbury, and by 1640 in Threadneedle Street after he had moved there. In 1649 a meeting was held at Simon Myddelton's house in St Paul's churchyard, when he was appointed Treasurer. In 1663 it was resolved that dinner would be provided at future meetings. In 1664 there were meetings at the treasurer's house in St Paul's Chain, a road that led from the Cathedral to the river.[1]

Many of the shareholders must have lost their homes in the Great Fire of 2 to 6 September 1666. The incomplete records from that time suggest that it was after the fire that meetings began to be held at taverns. Thus on 25 September 1666 a General Court was held at Mr Clifton's tavern in Covent Garden, and in December 1666 at the 'Devill & St Dunstan' Tavern near Temple Bar, and later at the Kings Head Tavern in Chancery Lane.[2] In 1687, a meeting is described as being at 'the New River Office', and this may be a reference to the premises at Puddle Dock described in the next chapter.

There is a complete lack of minutes for the period from 1691 to 1741. After 1742 meetings of the 'works committee' were sometimes at Bridewell Precinct or at the Water House, presumably if there were inspections to make there. They also met at the Thatched House tavern in what is now Essex Road, Islington before going on an inspection of the river. Even as late as 1761 a book about London noted 'The

Governor & Directors keep their office at a coffee house in Ludgate Street where every Thursday they hold a board for appointing officers, granting leases and redressing grievances'[3]

An unplanned meeting was held on Christmas Day 1769 'at Peel's coffee house in Fleet street, on the late accident of the New River office being burnt down on Sunday morning last, being Christmas Eve', as the minutes recorded.

Loyalty oaths

The founding charter provided for the Governor and officers to take an oath of loyalty to the Company. The Clerk's oath, for example, included promises to attend when required, to use no fraud or falsehood, to keep the secrets of the Company so long as they were not 'hurtful to the Common Weal,' and not to hand over any Company documents without the approval of the Governor, Deputy or Treasurer. This procedure was extended to other employees, and it became the practice that once a year at a General Court the whole staff would pass in front of the Directors to be reviewed.

Of course such oaths could not prevent all misbehaviour. A surviving letter to a Deputy Governor shows that after Richard Holford's term as Secretary ended in about 1780 there were enquiries about his dealings with timber suppliers while in that post:

To: Rev Mr Berners, Woolverstone Park, Ipswich, from Jo. Searle, North Town near Maidenhead.

> 'Rev'd Sir,
>
> You ask whether Mr R. Holford ever receivd any present of myself & the other persons who serve the New River Company with Elm Timber while he was Secretary to the Company? I answer that he receivd of each of us regularly two Guineas on the day we made our Contract, except the year he quitted the office of Secretary when he told us we should make him a present of a piece of plate – as we did not know what piece of plate he would like best we desird him to buy it himself an we would pay him again – He did so – and Old Mr Morris paid him the Mony, which was to the best of my remembrance between 7 & 8 £ – we had no communication with Mr Rd Holford at any other time as stated above.'[4]

Holford was also accused that after the 1769 fire, 'all the books and papers which the fire had not consumed were sold to a Cheese Monger,' by him, that he had not accounted for the sale proceeds, and that he had not been authorised to sell 'those invaluable records and papers.'

Even as late as the 1850s the charter was observed to the extent that the employees, including collectors, turncocks, paviours, and plumbers were required on being appointed to appear before the Governor and members to swear an oath that combined allegiance to the sovereign and faithful service to the New River Company, abjuring fraud, falsehood and deceit in favour of honest diligence, true accounting and obedience to lawful orders.

Storing valuables

There was a 'counting-house' at the Water House where some cash was presumably stored, but the Collectors were supposed to pay their takings to the Treasurer, and this may have been at his place of business. In 1633 a chest with three locks was purchased for the Company's charters to be kept in. It was stored at the Governors house, and he, his Deputy and the Treasurer each had a key to just one of the locks. How long this method of storage continued is unknown, but it seems to have been effective. Despite the destruction by fire of the area including the Governor's house in 1666, and of the Bridewell offices in 1769, the early deeds have virtually all survived to the present day although many other company records were lost.

Governors and deputies

Hugh Myddelton was appointed to be the Company's first Governor by the founding charter. This was not a life appointment, unlike the Clerkship to which the King appointed

William Lewyn for life. There was an annual election each November, but Myddelton continued to hold the post. When he died on 7 December 1631 his brother Sir Thomas, the former Lord Mayor, was elected in his place and served for less than a year. At the next General Court for electing officers in November 1632, Sir Hugh's eldest son William, who had become Sir William on succeeding to the baronetcy, was elected in his place. He held the office until about 1652, and was the last Myddelton to be Governor of the Company. Later Governors included Henry, Second Earl of Clarendon, and his younger brother Lawrence Hyde, Earl of Rochester.

Beating the clock

In 1785, Robert Mylne wrote to James Watt's partner Matthew Boulton in Birmingham to ask him to attend a Board meeting in London to discuss an engine for New River Head. He stressed that the Board met 'exactly at eleven o'clock.' This punctiliousness is confirmed by the later practice known as attendance money, whereby members were paid to attend the weekly meetings punctually. Whether this was to save them from being out-of-pocket or to encourage a larger attendance is not explained. It probably started after 1827, when the average attendance was 8 and before 1874 by when the average attendance had climbed to 20, out of twenty-nine members.

James Searle, the clerk, was asked to research the whole subject of attendance money in 1894, and prepared some notes. They show a weekly fee of £2 per member from 1837, with £1 extra for those there by 11 am from 1848. In 1850 this became a fixed sum of £300 a year 'for division among those in the boardroom at 11 o'clock'. By 1878 what he called 'the present arrangement' was in place, at a cost that he put at £148 a week.

Mr F.W. Drake who worked at New River Head from the 1880s recalled years later the way in which it had operated at that time. He thought it did not apply to the Governor, Deputy Governor, Treasurer or Auditor, as each of them received a salary, though Searle had noted that £2 extra was available for the Governor, or his deputy in his absence. That left twenty-five members entitled to attend. Fees of £5 per member per meeting were allowed, making the total the relatively large sum of £125, (£148 according to Searle,) which was split among those who turned up. Members who failed to attend the meeting received nothing, their £5s remaining for division among those who did attend. Meetings started promptly at 11.00 a.m., and any member who arrived late received only £2, the remaining £3 of his payment being left for division among the punctual. Under this system, those who arrived promptly on days when factors such as bad weather kept others at home might receive £10 or so, the equivalent of hundreds of pounds today.

To prevent arguments in those days before time-signals, a local watchmaker attended just after 10 every Thursday morning with a chronometer to check the accuracy of the boardroom clock – Clerkenwell was, as it happened, a watchmaking district. As 11 o'clock approached the auditor stood, pen in hand, and as the clock struck he drew a line under the names of those who had arrived.

Some members attended from as far away as Bristol, Norfolk and North Wales, and wealthy men could sometimes be seen running across the yard from the Directors' Gate as the minute hand neared the hour. It must sometimes have meant a cheerful start to the meeting.

Treasurers and auditors

Rowland Backhouse, one of the Adventurers, was appointed Treasurer by the charter, to hold office until elections were held.

It was a salaried post, and there was sometimes competition to fill it. In 1656 Simon Myddelton was Treasurer.[5] In 1661 he failed to be re-elected and appealed to the meeting to be told who had voted against him, but this was refused.

It has to be said that Simon Myddelton was an unusual man. He was Sir Hugh's seventh, and youngest, son and was born in about 1612. He was admitted to the Goldsmiths' Company in 1641, by right of patrimony based on his late father's membership. By 1651 he was in business as a linen-draper on the south side of St Paul's Churchyard. Seven years later, he acquired the King's moiety of New River shares from his nephew, and subsequently became the Company's Treasurer. According to the nephew, he never paid for the shares, and a lawsuit ensued. Precisely what he did wrong as Treasurer is not recorded, but he seems to have been dismissed. Some years later, in about 1664, he applied to become the Company's secretary – a more menial post than Treasurer – and supported his application with a letter of recommendation from King Charles II.

In it, the King called him 'a person every way fitt, and whose interest in the said River being equall to all yours will be a sure pledge for his integrity in that Trust.'[6] This praise, with its reminder of Simon's enormous shareholding, might have been expected to help, but instead it brought the derisive reply that 'such letters were to be had for five shillings.' The New River members refused to accept him, saying that he had once been mad, had spoken traitorous things and when Treasurer had failed to hand over certain dividends. They said he was unfit to be their clerk, and replied to the King that he was 'a person unfitt to execute the office of Clerke, and humbly begg his majesties excuses that they do not comply.'[7]

Simon Myddelton then claimed he had been unwell from a violent fever when he had spoken the 'traitorous words', but was still refused the job. Nevertheless, he remained a man of substance, and one of his daughters Sarah married Robert Harley. It was because of this marriage that Harley, who was to play a significant part in the Company's affairs around 1700, acquired his shareholding.

By 1681 Thomas Darwin was Treasurer, but he became bankrupt in 1696 when his business as a woollen-draper in St Paul's Churchyard failed. Large sums of the Company's money had been in his hands and were lost, £7,000 according to one version, 'not less than £20,000' on another.[8] Banking was in its infancy, carried out by merchants such as Goldsmiths, and it was not unusual for them to fail. Because of this risk, the practice developed of requiring those who handled the Company's money to provide guarantees. Thus, when Aime Garnault was elected treasurer in 1782, he transferred £15,000 worth of 4% bank annuities to the Company, and William Berners – who happened to be Deputy Governor – stood surety for a further £10,000 for him.[9]

The charter mentions the keeping of books 'true Accompts of all matters and things'. To confirm this was so, shareholders were appointed to act as auditors. In 1620 four were appointed – Rowland Backhouse (who was also Treasurer that year), Peter Vanlore, Robert Hyde and Henrie Vincente. In 1622 they were ordered to 'devyde & apporsion' what was due to the King and what to the Company. By 1670 there were just two auditors. In 1782 the two directors acting as auditors were ordered to be paid £5 each twice a year, and this was increased to £25 in 1794. In 1840 the first full time auditor was appointed. By 1904, just before the Metropolitan Water Board took over, the auditor's salary was £250 a year. This was the same as the Deputy Governor and Treasurer, but much less than the Governor, who received £600 by that time.[10]

Clerks and Secretaries

Ranked above the remaining staff was the Clerk, who was often a shareholder. The first Clerk, William Lewyn, had been appointed for life, subject to good behaviour, by King James I in the charter that formed the Company. His salary was set to be £100 per year 'when the companie shall first receive any profitts of the said workes.' He remained in office until his death in 1638, when Josias Berners, who held four Adventurers' shares bought from the Backhouse family, succeeded him. His successors were also usually shareholders. Like a modern company secretary, he acted as a channel of communication between board members and staff and attended all weekly meetings and General Courts. He made the rough minutes, later carefully transcribed into a big ledger by a junior clerk.[11]

One way in which King Charles II sought to

use his grandfather's goodwill with the New River Company was by supporting applicants for vacant posts. Thus in September 1667 he recommended John Grene for the post of Clerk, vacant on the death of Gregory Hardwick. He pointed out that Grene had married Hugh Myddelton's grand-daughter Elizabeth – another of Simon's daughters – and said that he had been 'serviceable in several works.'

John Grene got the job and held it until his death on 29 March 1705. He had acquired great wealth by his marriage to Elizabeth, for she owned four shares in the New River. She had died on 9 December 1675 and was buried in the parish church at Enfield, next to which the New River flowed.[12]. Grene later married their servant Joanna who bore him more children. As clerk of the Company, he earned £100 a year,[13] and more by undertaking the maintenance of the river for the fixed annual sum of £1000.

A fragmentary minute from 1742 shows that Jasper Bull, described as the Clerk was 'to be Secretary', but the distinction, if any, between these posts is not explained. A newspaper report of the 1769 fire notes that his house was also burnt and calls him 'one of the clerks.'

General surveys

From as early as 1622 what became known as general surveys were an annual event. That year it was ordered that Hugh Myddelton, Rowland Backhouse the Treasurer, John Backhouse and three other Adventurers should go to survey the river from Islington to Ware, to see the state of the work and to make a report to the next court. As many others of the Company as were willing were 'entreated to take the payne to goe with them.'

Surveyor/Engineers

Trying to establish when the company first employed a surveyor to supervise all the works is complicated by different uses of the word surveyor. When James I appointed a man to check the accounts on his behalf, that person was known as the King's Surveyor of the New River, whereas he was really an auditor. In 1634 one William Grace, described as 'general surveighor' was ordered to be dismissed until he accounted for certain disbursements, but nothing is known of his work.[15] Later, the men who supervised the walksmen were known as river surveyors and this has caused confusion. For example John White was commemorated by a tombstone at Enfield parish church that proclaimed 'I served the New River Company as surveyor from Ladyday 1691 to Midsummer 1723.' So he did, but Company documents show that he was simply the 'river surveyor' for Enfield and parts to the north.

White's tomb also bore a verse:

'Here lies John White who day by day,
On river work did use much clay,
Is now himself turning that way,
If not to clay, to dust will come,
Which to preserve takes little room,
Although enclosed in this great tomb.'

Copy letters in the letter book of Jasper Bull for August and September 1723 address White as 'country surveyor,' and by 23 September he appears to have resigned suddenly on some point of principle. Bull's letter to him on that day expresses the 'very great surprise' his letter had caused members. It asked him if he would not 'take care of their affairs till they have had the opportunity of providing otherwise, and in the meantime they shall be ready to hear what you have to alledge, and to do you all imaginable justice.' He did not die until 1741, by which time he was 83 years old, but he seems to have rejected this offer.[16]

A list of salaries of the Company's officers from about 1700 confirms there were then three 'surveyours'. Ephraim Green was 'citty surveyour' with a £50 salary and the duties of overseeing employees at the Water House and in the City. John Winch was the surveyor from Islington to Bush Hill and earned £30, while John White was surveyor from Bush Hill to Ware and also earned £30. None of these was the equivalent of later surveyors who had overall responsibility for all practical aspects of the water supply system.[17]

The post of 'Engineer and Surveyor of the

works' as it was called in 1725 in the earliest document known to use that description, was held by just three men between 1718 and 1860. They were Henry Mill, from 1718 or earlier until 1767, Robert Mylne from then until 1810 and his son William Chadwell Mylne from 1810 until 1861. The minute books show that they reported directly to the board and their advice was generally taken. Above all, it was recognised that they were professional men who could not be expected to devote the whole of their working life to the New River Company.

We know little enough about Henry Mill, but he certainly designed other waterworks as well as being engineer to the New River, such as those at Northampton and for Sir Robert Walpole at Houghton Hall in Norfolk. Thereafter, according to the funeral inscription placed by his sister at Breamore church near Salisbury, 'Declining to engage in many other Employments that would have been attended with greater advantages, Contenting himself with the Satisfaction of having been able to make such good use of his Talents for the Service of the Publick.'

Robert Mylne in his turn was surveyor to St Paul's Cathedral and Greenwich Hospital as well as the New River Company. In addition he travelled all over England and Scotland by coach, designing bridges, canals, drainage schemes and houses. He was punctilious in seeking leave from the New River Board before any long journey, but his diary shows that he was frequently away for weeks at a time.

William Chadwell Mylne became his father's assistant in 1804 and succeeded him in November 1810, a few months before Robert's death on 5 May 1811. He too had his own professional practice, and as well as waterworks in Birmingham, Colchester and Lichfield made a number of journeys to France to advise on new waterworks in Paris, beginning in 1816 within months of Napoleon's defeat at Waterloo. At the same period he was busily arranging the changeover from wooden to iron mains for the New River Company, and when this was complete in 1819 he was awarded a gratuity of £1,000 in addition to his usual salary for the extra work. Similarly, between 1852 and 1856 the major improvements required by the New River in common with all the London waterworks interfered with his private practice, (which by that time included waterworks at Hamburg in 1845) so that the Company paid him another gratuity. Soon after, in 1861, he retired. His first son, Robert William Mylne (1817-90) assisted him for many years, and became a recognised authority on water supply. His second son worked for the New River Company without achieving his father's status, and retired in 1875 having been River Surveyor.

The Beadle

The post of beadle existed for a time in the early days of the Company. The accounts show that Adolphus Iremonger held the post from 1619 until at least 1630. It seems that his status was far below the Clerk, to judge from his salary of £12 a year compared with the Clerk who averaged £75 during that period.

Collectors

Collectors had some status within the Company, and were well paid. In about 1635 it was ordered that there should in future be 'six Collectors of the Rents and arrerages due ... to have onely twelve pence out of every pound they shall collect and pay unto the Treasurer ... without any other standing fee or wages.'

A summary of the Company's accounts in 1670 shows that there were at that time seven collectors. They were allowed to keep a shilling in each pound – i.e. 5% – on all the water rents and arrears they collected, as well as on the 'fines' – the connection charges paid by new customers. By 1684 there were eight collectors, still earning 5%. Some had more profitable walks than others, and their earnings that year varied from £72 to £31.[18] In 1756 there were said to be fourteen collectors, still earning 5%. By 1904 the percentage varied between 2½% and 5%, and some collectors earned over £1,000 a year.

As early as 1635, a collector had to find two

people who would each stand surety of £400 to guarantee his rendering a true account, before he could be appointed. There are records of these sureties being called in, as in the case of Thomas St Hill who was one of the two West End collectors for about twenty years. In 1725 he defaulted and the Clerk Jasper Bull wrote to each of his two sureties:

> 'Sir, I take this first opportunity of informing you that Mr St Hill is deficient in his account ... and it will behove you to make provision for clearing the same.'

On the same day, he had written to St Hill calling him to come in to account, and reminding him that he had failed in his promise to do so. He ended 'I do assure you that your person will be safe', presumably meaning that he would not be taken into custody. In an almost fatherly way he ended one letter to St Hill 'Irritate not, but be advised by, yr friend etc, J.B.'[19]

No fewer than four other collectors defaulted in their accounts between 1724 and 1728. Copies of letters from Jasper Bull refer to William Wyat, Mr Mellichamp, James Collinson and Rice Morgan. In particular he had a long correspondence with Mellichamp's father between 1724 and 1728, who seems to have made numerous promises of payment that were never fulfilled. This spate of difficulties almost certainly stemmed from what became known as the South Sea Bubble, when a period of frenzied investment was followed by a ruinous collapse in stock prices. Collectors, who held cash for a time before they had to account for it, may have been tempted to gamble in the meantime. To make such temporary use of the Company's money was regarded as more acceptable then than it would be today.

Collectors were responsible for signing up new customers, arranging for connections and disconnections to be done and monitoring the state of the pipes in their districts or 'walks'. They also had to collect the quarterly 'rents' from customers, which they did by waiting at certain taverns or coffee-houses on pre-arranged days.

Thus in 1811 one collector had the printed note at the bottom of his receipt: 'Attendance at the Crown and Magpye Tavern, Aldgate High Street, on Tuesdays and Fridays from Twelve to One o'Clock.'

Similarly in 1815 Islington tenants were served by a collector who 'attends every Wednesday at the Angel Inn.'[20]

Collectors were also required to live in their 'walks'. In 1785 they were reminded that their silver plates or tickets of office were to be worn, or at least carried. Perhaps because the collectors habitually sat in the gloom of taverns and coffee houses on pre-arranged days, waiting for their tenants to come in and pay their water-rent, they were given an allowance of the price of 12 lbs of candles twice a year. This was known as candle money, and continued until 1831, by which time gas lighting was ousting the use of candles in London. In that year the board decided to stop the allowance and substitute 'a pair of dark mixture trousers at the time they receive the rest of their uniform. Mr Berdoe has agreed to make such of the best second cloth, lined with stout cotton, at 23s a pair.'

Walksmen

From the earliest days of the New River walksmen were appointed, each of whom was responsible for a section of the river. Each had a labourer as his assistant, and it was their task to patrol their section, keeping the banks in good order and cutting waterweed. Originally each man looked after about one mile of bank. By 1859 this was increased to an average of one and a quarter miles each, and their daily hours were increased so that they worked from 7am to 6pm 'during daylight'.[21] It was an old tradition in the Company that the walksman looked after the right or upper bank, facing downstream, and his labourer the left bank. The route of the river meant that the left bank was often an embankment built on lower ground and it generally needed more attention.

Walksmen sometimes provoked complaints, as in 1783 from Mr Breton of Forty Hall, Enfield. A loop of the New River ran for almost

3½ miles through his park, and he claimed that it had been damaged and widened to twenty-one feet in places. His osier beds were damaged, and he said the walksmen were very insolent. They mowed down his grass on the banks and took it away for hay in their boats. He said they also generally brought dogs with them and disturbed his game.

Turncocks and paviours

In 1700 there were eight turncocks, each earning £20 a year. It was their job to go through the streets turning on and off the valves that provided each district with its two or three hours of water on alternate days.[22] Paviours were also employed, to attend to the constant work of unearthing, repairing and making good when the wooden mains leaked.

By 1756 there were said to be twelve paviours and sixteen turncocks. In 1814 there were twenty-eight, of whom nine earned 21s. and the rest 18s. Turncocks had circular brass plates with the Company's insignia, and were reminded in 1785 that they must wear them.[23] The Company also employed supervisors, later known as foremen, who reported to the Collectors. In 1814, they were paid £1 7s. 0d. a week.

There were persistent rumours that bribing the turncock was the only way to be sure of a good supply. Sometimes paviours also succumbed to the temptations their work offered, like John Barker of Islington Walk who was dismissed in 1803. He had gone into another man's walk and made five unofficial connections to houses in Nelson Terrace, in return for a five shilling bribe.[24]

Engine workers

The word engine, sometimes abbreviated to gin, was used in a much more general sense in the past. It included any 'ingenious' apparatus. Thus, pumps worked by horses turning a geared shaft were called horse engines or horse gins, and a spring-operated rat trap was called a gin-trap. Similarly, the machines used for boring pipes were engines, whether they were operated by the power of men or horses.

In 1756 there were twenty men employed boring pipes, as well as horse engines for the same purpose.[25] Their status is not easy to judge, as they were paid piecework rates. It seems that the Company paid for the machinery they used, perhaps because its highly specialised nature and considerable cost put it in a different league from a craftsman's tools that he bought for himself.

The records of New River board meetings after 1769 are sufficiently complete to shed some light on the way they treated their employees, and the engine workers provide a good example. When John Smeaton's Newcomen-type atmospheric engine – a precursor of the steam engine – was finished and ready to set to work for pumping water at New River Head in 1769, he recommended a worker to 'undertake its care'. Previously a man known as 'Hardy the Horsekeeper' had tended the horse-engine. Now he was followed by one Forrester, who was known as the 'fire-engine' worker. It was not until 1802 that the engine at New River Head was referred to as a steam engine rather than a fire engine, even though the Company had been buying steam engines from Boulton and Watt since 1785.

In 1773 the job had gone to one Marley, and he agreed to 'work the fire engine himself without any assistance' and thereby had his wages increased from 15s to 18s a week. The engine worker's status increased over the years. In 1802, one Edward Hughes, by then referred to as the 'Steam Engine worker' was awarded a gratuity of 10 guineas in addition to his wages, for extra work he had done. By 1804 his earnings had reached £89 a year and were then increased to £100. In 1813 his salary rose again, to £110 and in 1820 to £125.[26]

His duties were not always performed as well as they might have been, as the board minutes show, and yet the way he was treated shows a considerable amount of tolerance for human frailty. In 1792 the Company secretary had to warn him of his 'peril if he dared to disobey the orders I had delivered.' In July 1801 he was reprimanded 'for improper behaviour to Mr Mylne and the Labourers at the

Water House, and was told if a similar Complaint is made he will be discharged.' In 1813 he was admonished for carelessness after inadvertently cutting off one of the mains.[27]

Worse was to come. In 1815 a public official from the coal meters office had inspected a coal delivery being made at New River Head, and found that many bags had been accepted by Hughes which contained short measure. When he spoke to Hughes about it, he seems to have been told to mind his own business and keep out of the yard, and the inspector thus reported the whole matter to the Board. Three weeks later Hughes was called before the board to explain. As the minutes record, his explanations were not accepted and he was found to have been 'at the least guilty of great inattention and neglect, and deserved to be dismissed.' In view of his length of service he was severely reprimanded and told he would 'probably be reduced to some subordinate situation.'[28]

Despite this reproach, the board ordered Hughes a £10 gratuity in 1819 for apprenticing his son, and if he had ever lost his status as engine worker, he had regained it by 1820, when his salary was increased from £110 to £125. Some backsliding followed, and in 1824 he was 'severely reprimanded' and fined £2 'to be put in the poor's box' for obstructing householders in Myddelton Square and dispersing some gravel they had laid.[29] Sometime in the 1830s he retired, and in 1837 Mylne reported the death of 'Edward Hughes, formerly steam engine worker...having been 52 years in the Company's Service. The Board, out of Respect ordered £24 ... towards his funeral.'

At least two other deaths were linked to the steam engines. In May 1816 the Clerk reported an additional charge of £5 19s. 2d. in the wages bill for burying R. Walsh 'it appearing that his death was occasioned by an accident he met with in fixing the New Steam Engine, the same was ordered to be allowed.'[30]

This contrasts with an occasion in 1823. Joseph Hind, a stoker, had been found dead in the engine house and was thought to have fallen from the top of the boiler. 'Mr Mylne having been directed to enquire into the state of his circumstances and if necessary give £5 towards burying him, this day reported that he was a single man and had sufficient property to pay the expenses of the funeral.' The following week a payment of 1 guinea was approved to 'Mr Everard, the surgeon who attended him.'[31]

In 1848, Roderick the engine stoker suffered a 'heavy affliction in his family ... two children having died within four months, one being burnt to death on Christmas Day last, and his wife who had been many months ill now lying dead.' It was ordered that he should receive £2 from the poor box.[32]

Hungry labourers

The labourers based at New River Head had a much lower status than engine workers. By 1800, the long-running wars against Napoleon had forced up the price of basic foods, and the New River workers began to ask for higher wages. In December 1800, the Board resolved that

> 'Taking into Consideration the Application of the Turncocks for some relief during the present high price of Provisions it is Ordered that they be allowed the addition of two Shillings per week to their Wages during the Pleasure of the Board.' A few weeks later they ordered that all the Walksmen and their Labourers on the River should have 'the Addition of sixpence per week for Bread over and above the present allowance of one shilling per week.'

The following July they agreed that the labourers in the streets should have an extra shilling per week.[33]

Around this time, the labourers at New River Head petitioned the Board, in the following terms:

> Gentlemen,
> We humbly intreat you to take into consideration the present Extravagant price of every necessary of life and the almost Impossibility for us at our present wages to procure them ... It is unnecessary for us to Inform you that our present wages will scarcely supply our familys with the single article of Bread ..[34]

This seems to have achieved a small increase,

and in June 1802 as prices continued to rise they tried again:

> 'Little reflection will convince anyone that the small sum of 12 shillings per week is very inadequate to obtain the Necessarys of life unless in a very limited degree as the Price of Provisions of all kinds is at so enormous a pitch.
>
> Your Petitioners humbly hope you will take it into consideration and grant them that satisfaction the urgencies of the time has compelled them to ask.'

In June 1804 this petition was finally granted, and their wages were raised from twelve to fifteen shillings a week, and later to seventeen shillings. Another pressure on wages came from the activities of the press gangs, who scoured all towns for able-bodied men to be pressed into service in the Royal Navy. A Board meeting in 1803 heard from the Street Inspector 'that on account of the Press for Seamen there is difficulty in finding labourers', upon which they increased street labourers' wages from fourteen to fifteen shillings a week. A year later the Street Inspector wrote to the Board again:

> 'Gentlemen, The Labourers in the streets gave me notice that they would leave the Works – I wished them to remain in the Works till you met again which they have done – their complaint is that they are as much entitled to 17s. per week as the labourers in the yard, this difference they have long complained of. I thought it my duty to inform you of the same, as strangers will not do for the Works.'

The Board reluctantly gave him the discretion to regulate their wages according to their length of service, but in no circumstances to pay a common labourer more than seventeen shillings. At around the same time their foremen's wages, and also the paviours', were increased from £1 to £1 2s. 0d., and it was noted that they often had to work from six o'clock in the morning to eight or nine in the evening.[35]

By 1814 labourers were being paid 18s. 0d. a week, an increase of 50% since 1800. Over the same period, Hughes the engine worker had only seen his wages increase by about 25%, but he earned almost three times as much as a labourer and was better insulated against increases in the price of basic foodstuffs. This rate of wage inflation later went into reverse, and a labourer's contract more than fifty years later, in 1867, agreed to pay Alfred Heath just fifteen shillings a week. The standard printed form he signed provided that if he were dismissed for misbehaviour he would not even receive such wages as he had earned in the week of his dismissal. William Chadwell Mylne, who countersigned for the Company, had struck out this harsh clause.[36]

CHAPTER EIGHT

Premises and Problems

PREMISES – The Water House at New River Head – The Oak Room – Puddle Dock – Bridewell Precinct – Dorset Garden – Later buildings at New River Head
PROBLEMS – Water theft – Bathers and swimmers – Fishermen – Polluters

The New River Company needed offices and pipe-yards from its earliest days, and later needed engine-houses of various kinds for pumping. This chapter deals with those buildings, but not with the practicalities of water supply, or of changes to the various engines and machines used, which will all be found in other parts of the book. It also looks at some of the recurrent problems that faced the owners of a long open stream full of fresh running water that passed temptingly close to places where people lived.

PREMISES

The Water House at New River Head

The building always known simply as the Water House stood by the Round Pond at New River Head, and both were built in 1613. Its design has been attributed to Inigo Jones but there seems to be no support for this except that it is in a style he might have favoured. There are tiny thumbnail sketches of it on some early maps, and it can also be seen in two early pictures. The first is a 1637 portrait of Sir John Backhouse, who owned the land the Round Pond was built on, and was one of the original Adventurers. He is shown in a three-quarter length portrait, standing by a table, and his right hand rests possessively on the frame of a small painting that shows the Round Pond, the Water House beyond it, and the skyline of London, dominated bythe spire of Old St Paul's Cathedral in the background. Because the house is merely one detail in a small painting within a painting, it is tiny and is unlikely to be meticulously accurate. The house it shows has a tall chimney stack at its western end, a pitched roof with the gable end facing north, and a small wing under a slightly lower pitched roof extending to the east. It is not symmetrical, and there is no sign of a colonnade facing the water.

The second picture is among six small drawings made by Wenceslaus Hollar for the Company in 1665. Some of them also show the poignant view of Old St Paul's Cathedral in the background, destined to be destroyed in the Great Fire of London a year later. It shows the building with a colonnade facing the water, and many later drawings include this feature.

The first occupant of the Water House was Howell Jones. He had worked for Myddelton as an overseer during the digging of the New River, and then became the supervisor at New River Head. Myddelton liked him, and in 1620 he was awarded 100 marks (a mark was 13s. 4d.) 'in consideration of his greate paynes & sevice in the water workes.' He was also left a legacy in Myddelton's will. It may be that he or his wife set up a small business inside the brick wall at New River Head. After his death a board meeting resolved to choose who should succeed him 'looking to the walke and water house &c at Islington'. They also noted that the building was presently occupied by his widow Joane, resolved that she should be evicted and

15 The New River Head from the north in the earlier part of the 18th century. The figures are in front of the outer pond. Beyond it the brick wall, round pond and water house were all built in 1613.

ordered 'that none shalbe there suffered hereafter to sell drinck or kakes, or to use victualling in any sorte whatsoever.'

In the 1630s the Company had a lengthy lawsuit with Sir John Backhouse, who had succeeded his father as the owner of the land around the Water House. He claimed that they only had a licence to use it, whereas the Company claimed to have to have bought the freehold. In 1639 they resolved 'out of theire love and respect to Sir John Backhouse' to allow him a 21 year lease 'of a chamber in the waterhouse neer Islington'. This never seems to have been completed, and may have been a negotiating ploy of some kind.

The original Water House was gradually extended over two centuries, then almost entirely demolished when new offices were built in 1819. John Grene, a wealthy shareholder and Clerk to the Company from 1667 until his death in 1705, made the first major alteration. The changes he made included the magnificent Oak Room, which still survives and is described below.

Robert Mylne made the next major changes in 1782. He was a distinguished architect and served as the Company's Engineer from 1767 until 1810. He extended the building to provide more accommodation for himself and his family, and strengthened parts of the old structure with new brickwork. Two inscribed stones he inserted are preserved above the windows of the Oak Room on the outside of the west end of the present building at New River Head, and record that the building was erected in 1613 and restored in 1782.

Mylne's work seems to have added considerably to the appearance of the building. In 1815, by which time the sprawl of London was lapping all round it, it was described as follows:

> 'At the New River Head is a house, ornamented with vases and quoins, surrounded with a variety of flourishing trees, and fronted by this noble sheet of water, which altogether gives it the appearance of a nobleman's villa.'[1]

The original building, with its modifications, survived until 1819. The Company then decided to sell its valuable offices in Blackfriars and move to a new building at New River Head. William Chadwell Mylne had by then succeeded his father as Engineer, and he reported to the board on the state of the existing building. His report raises the interesting possibility that the old Water House may have

16 View of the area around New River Head by Wenceslaus Hollar, 1665. Old St Paul's is in the distance.

been re-erected elsewhere instead of being simply demolished.

> 'Having carefully looked over the Old Buildings now standing I find there are a great portion of tolerably good materials which will be extremely serviceable in the erection of a new house on the same plan, so much so that I consider the expence of pulling down the same, and erecting it on your ground adjoining Lloyd's Row, St John St, will not cost more than about £200, and I should therefore recommend that it be done by your own Carpenter.'[2]

The Oak Room

John Grene, Clerk from 1667 to 1705, and wealthy from marrying into the Myddelton family, lived at the Water House and added rooms including The Oak Room in about 1693. Also referred to as the Court Room, this room was the finest in the house but does not seem to have been normally used for Board meetings. It has fine oak carving, some of it attributed to Grinling Gibbons, and an elaborate painted plaster ceiling, with a portrait of William III in armour. According to Vertue, the ceiling was painted by 'Mr H. Cooke.'[3] In 1782 Robert Mylne the surveyor reported to a General Court that 'The Court Room at the Water House, Islington, has been cased with 9 inches of new brickwork, for the better preservation thereof and of the House Cistern underneath the same.'[4]

In 1819 new offices were built at New River Head, but the Oak Room with its fittings was retained inside the new structure. There it remained for almost another hundred years. When the Metropolitan Water Board took over the New River Company in 1904 the Oak Room was excluded from the transfer, but the new Board agreed to purchase it and its fittings, and did so in February 1904 for £2,000. In 1913 the Metropolitan Water Board decided to build itself a headquarters at New River Head. The old building was demolished, but the components of the Oak Room were retained and built into the first floor of the new structure (*ill.74, p.218*). In the process it was moved through ninety degrees, so that its main windows faced west. When first built it had windows on three sides, and must have had good views over the surrounding countryside.

The carving has a watery theme, and has been described as follows:

17 The ceiling in the Oak Room at the New River Head. In the centre is a portrait of William III. According to Vertue, it was painted by 'Mr H Cooke'.

'There are fishing lines and a frog, water weed, willow leaves and flowers, the overthrow centring on a duck and other birds, including partridge and a pewit; some of the smaller birds bowing down stems of wheat'.

'There are further panels of oak carving over the windows and doors. The quality of these six smaller panels is said to be less good, but two are enchanting and, in workmanship and design, as worthy of Gibbons as is the overmantel itself. Both are for overdoors, the first having singing amorini, peaches, flowers and chains of shamrock slung over wooden nails, the other interlacing wreaths of forget-me-not and primrose flanked by ribbons which trail over flower-decked wings. The amorini are sensible rather than pretty, the designs delicately balanced and delightful. To see them is to pronounce them the essence of Gibbons, directly inspired by him even if, as seems unlikely, they were carved by another's chisel.'

'The other small panels have bulrushes with fringed drapes, palms and laurels, trumpets with oak and laurel wreaths, but their quality is not quite up to the two described.'[5]

The ceiling needed maintenance from time to time. In 1868 it was taken down, 'and the timbers above, being much decayed, were replaced with new and stouter beams; the ceiling was then replaced being very strongly screwed up with specially made screws and cups.'[6] The main ceiling painting was restored by Mr D. A. Holder in 1922. By 1935, some renovations and replacements were needed, and an independent steel structure was built to support the floor of the room above it.

During the Second World War, it was decided to remove the oak carving and the ceiling to a place of safety. The work was entrusted to Maple & Company, the furnishers. They were able to remove the carvings, but on inspecting the ceiling they found it to be in one piece and beyond their ability to remove. Because of this, only the oval painting was removed. All was replaced in 1945, when it was found that the painting had suffered by its removal and reinstallation. It was therefore restored once more, by W. Freeman & Son.[7]

Puddle Dock

By 1669 the Company had an office at Puddle Dock, close by the Thames just east of Blackfriars. Nothing is known about the premises, not even their precise location. The charter that incorporated the New River Company authorised the acquisition of 'one convenient Messuage, Tenement or Howse within the City of London or its suburbs,' but there seem to be no surviving records of such a purchase. All the early meetings of shareholders took place at private houses, or later in taverns and coffee houses. The Company's early water leases specified where payment was to be made and where notices could be left. Originally this was at Myddelton's home, later at the 'telling house' on the west side of the Royal Exchange. Whatever the 'telling house' was, it was in an area destroyed in the Great Fire of 1666. Three years later, in December 1669, a new water lease to a saddler near Fleet Street provides that complaints of non-service should be made 'to the Governour, or to the members that meet weekly at the Clerk's Office near Puddle-Dock.' This may be the earliest mention of meetings there. By 1687 the incomplete records from that time show that a board meeting was held 'at the New River Office' on 1 December 1687, and this presumably meant the building at Puddle Dock.

One possible reason for having premises at Puddle Dock is that elm timber for water pipes could be landed nearby. In 1613 and thereafter timber had been landed at Bridge house wharf in Southwark, but a surviving note from between 1656 and 1661 records that the Corporation of London was asking £40 a year rent for what had previously been used free of charge, and this may have prompted a move to other waterfront premises.

The Company remained at Puddle Dock until 1717, when a notice appeared in newspapers on 8 August to say the office had moved 'from Puddle-Dock into Bridewel Precinct near Fleet-Ditch.' A list of 'persons the company pays rent to' dating from sometime after 1742 includes an annual rent of £8 to a Mrs Katharine Morgan 'for a piece of ground lying in St Andrew's

Wardrobe.' This is the name of the small City ward that includes Puddle dock, and it may hold a clue to the location of that first office. There seems no other reason for the Company to have had land there.[8]

Bridewell Precinct

When the Company moved its offices and yard to Bridewell Precinct in 1717, they took possession of first one and later a second substantial building. The second included land and a wharf, of which they took a long lease from Humphry Ambler for £800 on 22 July 1742.[9] There was a substantial house occupying a prominent position overlooking the river, and a wharf in front of it where boats could unload the elm logs, which were turned into water pipes on the premises. The main house is seen in two contemporary views of buildings fronting the Thames.

The first is the Buck's Long View – a panorama of the Thames from Millbank to Whitehall, published in 1749. Here the house is shown as a small sketch, broadly accurate but lacking any useful detail. Much better is an oil painting from about 1750, perhaps by Samuel Scott, and now on display in the Guildhall Art Gallery. It looks across the Thames to the mouth of the Fleet Ditch, which had been greatly improved after the Great Fire of 1666 when it was widened to admit shipping as far as Holborn. It is shown with a high arched bridge in the Venetian style. To the left of its entrance are first of all an unknown building, and then the New River Office standing at the back of its log-piled yard. It appears to be a handsome red brick building with a tiled roof. It has three full storeys, and attic windows flanking a central stone sun-dial. A woman is looking out of a first floor window, while two smartly dressed men stand in discussion by a pile of large elm trunks on the wharf in front (*ill.18*).

Here the Company remained for over fifty years. Then, on Christmas Eve 1769, came the disaster that destroyed most of the Company's early records and much else besides. A newspaper described it:

> 'Yesterday morning between 2 and 3 o'clock a fire broke out in one of the offices of the New River Company in Bridewell Precinct, which consumed that and all the other offices, together with the house of Mr Bull, one of the clerks, and all the furniture, books of account &c.'

On 27 March 1770 the Company decided to surrender their leases of the site of the burnt offices back to Bridewell Hospital, and the assignment was completed on 21 February 1771. On giving up their lease the Company agreed to leave behind 'the crane, the office lately fitted up out of that part of the house left unburnt, the fences, walls, gates and charter room, and the paving of the yard.' They were to take away 'all shops, stables, sheds, mills and engines.' Bridewell Hospital paid the Company £900 for the early surrender of what must have been two valuable leases.[10]

Dorset Garden

In July 1750, almost twenty years before the disastrous fire at the Bridewell offices, the Company had providentially taken a long lease, at an annual rent of £140, of some adjacent land known as Dorset Garden, belonging to the Duke of Dorset. It had a river frontage of 62 feet, formerly known as Bagge's Wharf, and had on it 'the shed or low building ... lately used by a company or copartnership of carpenters as a compting house.'[11]

It had once been the site of the Duke's or Dorset Theatre, built by Wren after 1666 and demolished in about 1720. The New River Company had for some reason decided to take the lease when it became available in 1750, and immediately sublet it to Messrs Boddicoate & Pitcher, a firm of timber merchants.[12]

In 1759, Robert Mylne had won an open competition to design the first bridge over the Thames at Blackfriars, and had also been appointed to supervise its construction, which was not completed until 1769. The works included covering over the Fleet River and building embankments at Blackfriars. This had the effect of increasing the size of the New River Company's wharf at Bridewell precinct as well as the adjacent land they owned. This

18 Detail from a painting of the outfall of the river Fleet into the Thames at Blackfriars c.1750, of the school of Samuel Scott. An elegant foot bridge spans the Fleet across what is now New Bridge Street. As can be seen here, the Fleet was a substantial inlet used by boats, which in those days could reach the present location of Holborn Viaduct. Blackfriars Bridge was built in the 1760s by Robert Mylne and the Fleet was then paved over. The offices of the New River Company, burnt down in 1769, fronted the riverside. They are to the left of this picture, just to the right of the spire of St Bride's church. On the riverside was a wharf for the reception of elm trunks from which to make water pipes.

is probably how Mylne developed the connection with the New River Company that led to his appointment first as joint surveyor with the elderly Henry Mill in 1767 and then as sole surveyor in Mill's place in 1771.

Following the fire at Bridewell Precinct, the adjacent site at Dorset Yard, which had a river frontage of 140 feet 6 inches, must have seemed an ideal location for new offices. On 3 May 1770, the Company resolved 'that a new House containing a Court Room, Offices and Apartments for the Clerk of this Company should be erected at Dorset Yard.' The building was to be erected 'as soon as may be, together with Stables Work Shop and Mill and Sheds proper and necessary for the Works of the Company.' Mylne set to work and produced a neat classical plan for new buildings consisting of a central block flanked by single storey wings containing sheds and workshops. (see ill.19)

Oddly enough, the Company had already started to recover possession of the site six months before the fire. The new minute book recorded some earlier decisions, including one of 29 June 1769 when it was ordered 'that the surveyor be empowered to treat with Mr Bodicoate concerning his quitting Dorsett Yard and making void all Agreement now subsisting between him & the Company.'

The first stone of the new headquarters was laid on 28 June 1770; the builder was one Sylvanus Hall, and the work was finished in 1771. The cost was £1,952 and the Company ordered that it should be insured for £2,000 at the Hand-in-Hand Office. The work had been outside Robert Mylne's ordinary duties, and he was given a gratuity of £200 'in consideration of all his extraordinary services'. It was built 'in a very uniform neat style' according to the historian Noorthouck in 1773. Its address was sometimes given as 'Dorset Garden, Salisbury Court', as in a 1775 water lease, and sometimes as 'New River Office, Salisbury Square', as in a notice dated July 1812.[13]

In 1819, the Company moved to a new building at New River Head. Wooden pipes had just

19 The new headquarters of the New River Company at right angles to the Thames on the site of Dorset Garden, opened in 1771. They were designed by Robert Mylne after the old offices, just to the east (ill. 18) were destroyed by fire in 1769

gone out of use, and so there was no longer any need for a timber wharf on the Thames. The site was valuable because of its river frontage – there were no railways yet – and all bulky goods came by water. The land was thus sublet to a newly developing industry, in the form of the City Gas Light Company. Their gasworks needed wharves to land the coal that was its raw material, and they took a 71-year lease of the site from Lady Day 1819 at a rent of £2,000 per year. In due course, the gasworks moved to Barking, and in 1883 the City of London School moved to a new building on the site. The school building is still there, now converted to offices, while the school has moved to a site near Puddle Dock.

Later buildings at New River Head

The original Water House of 1613, somewhat extended, was in use until 1819. In that year James Donaldson of Bloomsbury Square, tendered to build 'A New Court House with Secretary's Apartments and the necessary offices' for the Company for £3,500, and thereafter built it. The new structure incorporated the central parts of the old building, including the Oak Room. The plan to have apartments there for the Secretary was not fulfilled. William Chadwell Mylne continued to occupy the upper parts as his father had done from 1767, and a nearby house was rented for Mr Rowe the Secretary.[14]

The new building was completed in 1820 after some delays. Mylne, who continued to live there, offered the Board the use of the Oak Room for meetings if the new part was not completed on time. It seems to follow that he, and his father before him, must have enjoyed the use of the Oak Room as their best room. The first Board meeting was held in the new offices on 30 March 1820. According to a writer in the 1820s, the new Board-room was 'a fine lofty apartment, much larger than (the Oak Room)'. Water supply became more complex in the decades that followed, the new building proved too small, and extensions were built at various dates. In 1862, the apartments occupied by the Mylne family for almost a hundred years were taken over and converted to offices. Around that time the Oak Room began to be used as the Directors' Luncheon Room. Later, drawing offices and other extensions were attached to the premises. The result was a building that looked, in the words of an old member of staff, as though it had been brought out in monthly parts.[15]

When the Metropolitan Water Board took over London's water supply in 1904, its first offices were at Savoy Court in the Strand. There were sixty-six Board members, and for lack of space at Savoy Court they met first at the offices of the Metropolitan Asylums Board on the Victoria Embankment and later, during the First World War, at Armfield's Hotel in South Place, Finsbury. In 1913 the Board decided to have a new headquarters building with a boardroom at New River Head. There was a com-

20 *Looking from the north across the Outer Pond and the round Pond to the Water House in 1824. the new offices built in 1819 are the three bays with semi-circular panels at the top.*

petition, and a design by H. Austen Hall was chosen. The foundation stone was laid in July 1915, but labour troubles and the First World War delayed the work. A photograph from 1914 shows the rambling old building still in use, with recruiting posters pasted to the adjacent wall; not the famous pointing finger of 'Your Country Needs You', but a uniformed bugler sounding his instrument under the slogan 'Fall In'. In June 1916 the Ministry of Munitions issued an order suspending work, and it did not resume until January 1919. The offices finally opened in May 1920, and the new Board-room saw its first meeting on 2 July. The total cost was £324,205.

The building was of three storeys, but had been designed to accept the weight of a further floor if needed. That floor was then built in 1934-6, giving the building its present form. A long curving laboratory for water testing was then built as a separate structure to the north-west of the site, and opened in 1938. It had a staff of seventy, with sections covering biological, bacteriological, chemical and chlorination aspects of water quality. Its design was intended to provide the maximum possible amount of north light to the laboratories, and it was set back from Rosebery Avenue to protect instruments from the vibrations of passing trams.

After the privatisation of Thames Water in 1989 and its centralisation in Reading, the office building and the laboratories became redundant. Both buildings were listed as Grade II buildings, with the Oak Room having a starred listing. This precluded demolition, and they were then converted to luxury apartments, which were sold on long leases. The Oak Room remains inside, carefully protected and available for hire to residents and others.[16]

PROBLEMS

Water theft

From the earliest days of the New River there were those, in both town and country, who preferred to take their water rather than to buy it. This was sometimes by dipping into the open stream, sometimes by making an unauthorised arrangement with a neighbour who paid for his supply and sometimes by making a private connection to the main, either secretly or with the collusion of employees.

In June 1614 the accounts record the payment of five shillings for two warrants from Mr Recorder to 'bringe the bruers before him that fetche water from the Ryver', and also the payment of four shillings to Richard Greene for 'watcheing 4 nightes toe take the Bruers that fetched water.' Even this did not end the practice, and two weeks later three men were being paid eight pence a night each watching in Goswell street for 'the Brewers' liquor cartes.'[17]

A 1632 minute directs that any 'Beadle or other person informing of stolne or concealed branches' was to be rewarded at the Governor's discretion.[18] When offenders were detected the Company usually made some financial 'composition,' in effect fining the offender. Thus a note in the accounts records the receipt of £1 from 'severall who cutt the water out in the Countrey.' If a customer was caught giving water away there was a similar composition. A Mr Batten paid £2 in such circumstances.[19]

Diversion of water from the river was sometimes blatant. In 1669 the Privy Council issued a warrant to justices of the peace at the Company's request authorising the arrest of Thomas Izard of St Margaret's, John Cooke of Stanstead a carpenter, Robert Boram of Hodgdon a 'collermaker' and Robert Martindale of Hogdon, husbandman. It was said they had diverted the New River 'by making Damms cross the Current, to rune it into their own Grounds, whereby the River Streame is much Abated and in Danger to become uselesses, these are therefore to will and require you to Repaire to the severall Dwelling Places, or wherever else you shall find them, and them and everyone of them to apprehend, and in your Company to bring to this Board.'[20]

A similar warrant four weeks later, signed by Privy Councillors including the Archbishop of Canterbury, the Bishop of London, the Duke of Ormonde and the Lord Chamberlain, named Joseph Prickman of Theobalds, Josiah Gallard, Nicholas Mutton and Robert Welch, all brewers, for causing the banks to be cut 'whereby .. the City of London will be put to great Exigencys for want of Water.'[21]

One of the letter books in which the secretary Jasper Bull kept copies of letters he wrote at the board's direction contains a number on this subject. In May 1723 he wrote 'To Mr Noland in Denmark court, Exeter street.

> Sir, The compa. having information that you have clandestinely enjoyd their water these 20 years , for two houses and have paid for one only they have comanded me to inform you that if you appear not tomorrow before them at their office in Bridewell Precinct by 4 afternoon they'l forthwith direct process to be comencd against you, Yr servt JB"

Despite being delivered by hand this brought no reply, and two days later it was followed by another threatening to cut off his supply.

In June 1723 it was the turn of one of those whose land adjoined the New River: 'to Mr Tho Nash Gardner near Newmans flash Edmonton.

> Sir
> The New River Company being very certainly informd that you have frequently both by night and by day taken great quantityes of water out of their River for the supply of your Physick garden near Newmans flash Edmonton they direct that you desist from doing so, or they will forthwith give direccon for process against you with the utmost rigour this is what I have in command
> yr servt JB'

In 1724, members out on a general survey noted with regard to a buried portion of the river in Islington, 'These underground Conveyances are often bored & great quantity of Water stolen at the time of the Year when it is most wanted by the Company's tenants, the discovery is impossible & if a Walksman is off his watch or sleeps or is bribed, all of which is likely to happen, the Company is greatly prejudiced.'[22] In 1740 the Company had to take legal advice on this topic. Mr Richard Holland had an agreement with the Company to have a one inch pipe drawing water direct from the New River at Hornsey Sluice, for the use of his dwelling there. He had now supplemented it with a three-inch pipe that took the water to a brew-house, and had even closed Hornsey Sluice while he installed it despite being told to desist. The Company was advised that its remedy was an action for damages for diverting water and for obstructing the river by shutting the sluice.

Bathers and swimmers

The New River was always an attraction for bathers. As early as June 1614 two labourers were paid three days each for having 'looked to Kepe out Swymers in Whitsonne holidays.' In March 1616 'Sympson the Messenger had 2s. 6d. for his 'ettendance att the pond to kepe oute Dogges and Swymmers.'[23]

In July 1728 Jasper Bull wrote to 'the Reverend Mr Davies, Schoolmaster at Enfield:

> Sir, The Company being this day informed by their Surveyor that your Boarders do frequently wash themselves in the River, and you seem resolute in Justifying 'em therein they direct me to inform you that they have by printed papers publiquely forbid the same on account of the great damage accruing to the banks and bed of the River thereby, and that sundry persons have been lately committed to New prison for the same, and that they hope you'l desist from Giving incouragemt thereto, and prevent farther inconvoeniences,
> these I have in comand who am,
> yr very humble serv't, JB.'

The lure of refreshing water was not to be denied so easily, and in the summer of 1770 the Company had to advertise:

> 'New River Office Bridewell Precinct
> August 16, 1770
> Whereas a great Number of idle and disorderly persons have assembled together in the Fields between Islington and Newington & parts adjacent and have by bathing and washing themselves in the New River broke down the Banks and done other damage to the said River and have also in a most atrocious, indecent and illegal Manner committed many other offences highly injurious to the property of the Company and to the Public in General. This is therefore to give Notice that the said Company are determined to prosecute with the utmost Severity of the Law, all such persons who for the future shall be found so offending.'[24]

Occasionally a bather was caught and prosecuted. One such was Liscombe Price Junior of Islington, and in November 1770 he was able to escape the consequences of his crime by signing a solemn promise 'never to be guilty of the like offence' and agreeing to pay the Company's costs. The following year the Company advertised a forty-shilling reward for the prosecution of anyone bathing between Islington and Newington.[25]

The problem was still troubling the Company ten years later in June 1781, when a General Court decided that an advertisement 'to prevent persons washing in the river' be inserted three times on the front page of the *Daily Advertiser*. This offered a reward of £2 for information leading to a successful prosecution. Notice boards were also to be painted and 'affixed to posts on different parts of the river about Islington as formerly, to prevent persons trespassing by Bathing or otherwise.'

In 1781 a West Pond had been made not far from New River Head. This supplied houses in Clerkenwell and at Battle Bridge near King's Cross. In 1783 forty-two of the householders signed a petition, complaining that their water was 'so thick and unclean' from 'the number of people continually bathing therein' that they could not use it without prejudice to their health and constitutions. The Board ordered that a brick wall with a locked door must be built around the West Pond.[26]

In August 1801 the Company received an anonymous letter. It asked that the public 'may not be permitted to bathe in the new river between Duncan Terrace and Colebrooke Row

– which they now are in the habit of doing all day long to the great annoyance of this Town and more especially the female part'.[27] The Board considered this, and ordered the Collector 'to call on some of the respectable inhabitants in that part and inform them that the board will contribute a part of the expence in prosecuting any person whom the parish officers may think proper to indite for the nuisance.'

On 17 August 1801 a second letter came:

> 'Sir,
> It is with very great shame that the inhabitants of Colebrooke Row should be annoyed by such a set of Worthless Rascalls who are always, especially on Sunday, Washing their nasty rotten Hides in the New River Water near the City Road, a place of great passage, and a great and abominable Shame for a rich Company to suffer such indecency. It is expected by the Neighbourhood that your Company will immediately put a Stop to such Shamefull Practice or strictures must be put upon them in the papers.'[28]

This was signed 'Rob't Yelton', but the Clerk noted that it was believed to be from some anonymous source, and described it in the minutes as being 'couched in very indecent terms.' Apparently an Islington cow-keeper called Rhodes had also visited Robert Mylne to complain of the same nuisance.

Sometimes such bathing led on to other things. In 1809, John Tyre of Islington appeared before the Middlesex Sessions, a court held at Hicks's Hall in St John Street. He had gone bathing in the New River and afterwards ran naked in the field in front of the houses in Highbury Place. The court declared his behaviour subversive of public decency and sent him to Newgate Prison for two months.[29]

In July 1830, a committee went out on one of the periodic river surveys, and described the problem in their report. 'The river between Newington and Islington is the great resort of bathers and when their number is stated at from 800 to 1000 in the course of every 12 hours in the summer season the Board will not be surprized to learn that the banks are destroyed, the wharfing carried away and the bed of the river in a constant state of disturbance, in one particular spot their nuisance has widened the river to not less than 60 or 70 feet giving it the appearance of a large dirty pond. The committee are at a loss to suggest a remedy for this growing evil, but they deem it necessary to call the attention of the board to the subject.' Two years later, the survey measured 'those portions of the River side which would be best secured against nuisance, near London.'[30] The Company later provided water free to public baths, and the existence of these combined with stretches of the river being piped underground and the fencing of other parts seems to have eventually cured the problem.

Fishermen

Colthurst's charter from the King had given all fishing rights to the occupiers of the land through which the New River passed. The 1605 Act, which Myddelton had used instead of the charter made no such generous provision, and the New River Company seems to have decided it owned the rights. Nevertheless, most old illustrations of the New River include the depiction of anglers, even as far into London as the last stretch that passed in front of Sadler's Wells.

A fragment of a burnt minute records that in April 1769 the Board ordered that 'no person whatsoever be permitted to fish in the Pond at Islington or that part of the river between the Ponds and Sadler's Wells except (members) of the Company' and other authorised persons.[31] They took particular exception to the use of 'drag nets' and in 1785 sued a Mr Hart of Bluechurch, Enfield, who had been seen by New River staff emptying roach, dace, chubb and perch from his net.

Fish were not only confined to the open reaches. In October 1812, *The Star* reported that a New River turncock 'opening a plug opposite the eastern lodge of the Ordnance office in Pall Mall, caught about a dozen fine eels, nearly two feet in length, which came out of the pipe

21 Fishing in the New River. The illustration, published in 1819, shows the river running between Duncan Terrace and Colebrooke Row in Islington. Today gardens and grass verges cover its former passage. The Regent's Canal, which emerges from its tunnel at Colebrooke Row, was constructed beneath the New River.

in about as many minutes – some of them nearly as thick as a man's wrist. The singularity of the occurrence attracted a great number of spectators.' Shellfish also thrived in the New River. In 1868, the Chief Engineer Mr Muir reported to the Board that 'an extraordinary accumulation of mussels' had been found in the large pipe between the reservoir and filterbeds at Stoke Newington, amounting to 300 barrow loads.

The lure of fishing extended to staff. In 1813 Tingey the walksman was discharged when the board learnt that he 'neglected his business very much & was continually fishing the river' despite being frequently spoken to.[32]

Polluters

The New River must often have received effluvia that those along its course wanted to dispose of, and the Company was hardly likely to advertise such components of its household supply. One notorious case was that of the eccentric Portuguese Baron Ephraim d'Aguilar. He had a riverside house with stables at what is now Lamb's Mews, Colebrooke Row, Islington, and kept a variety of farm animals in a neglected and filthy state, whose dung and occasional corpses went straight into the New River. In 1800 his neighbours complained to the Company, and the nuisance was eventually stopped.

CHAPTER NINE

A Lost Fort in London 1642

The English Civil Wars – A map of the forts – London prepares for war – The Venetian ambassador – 'A Schotch Man and a Lyar?' – The lie of the land – 'Animadversions of Warre' – The Fort Royal – A sermon at the fort – Slighting the fort – Hollar's drawings

The English Civil Wars

The English Civil Wars did not affect the New River Company as much as might be expected. One small benefit that they perhaps brought was the end of the proposed rival water supply by Sir Walter Roberts and others, already mentioned in chapter five. There was a slight hiccup in the level of dividends, in that they fell by about 10% in 1643 and 1644, after a period of steady increases. By 1645 they reverted to the former level, and continued to rise thereafter.

At least four of the shareholders supported the Royalist side. By October 1643 Sir John Backhouse was a prisoner at Windsor Castle, and his Alderman brother confined in the Tower of London, while Richard Nevill and Lawrence Hyde were still fighting for the Royalists. This is set out in a warrant directed to the New River Company ordering that dividends due to them should be paid to one Captain Bushell of the Parliamentary army, who was owed certain arrears.[1]

Two of Sir Hugh Myddelton's sons, by contrast, fought for Parliament. William, the second baronet, served as a colonel, while the fifth son, Henry, commanded a troop of horse.

A map of the forts

The last thing one might expect to learn about Islington Hill was that it had been the site of a fort during the English Civil War. Yet there is a map, admittedly not drawn until a century later, of London 'as fortified by order of Parliament in the years 1642 and 1643' which plainly shows a substantial fort on Islington Hill. Those were the years when London seemed to be at its greatest risk of being attacked by the Royalist armies. From 1641 onwards, relations between King Charles I and his Parliament had steadily worsened. Sending his family to the Low Countries, the King had retreated first to Windsor, and later to York where he had more support. His eventual strategy would be to try and launch a three-pronged attack on London, from the west, the south and the north.

The map shows the cities of London and Westminster, and the borough of Southwark across the river, ringed with a continuous line of defensive earthworks, the so-called lines of communication, along which occasional forts are marked. Just one stands out from the rest. As the wall passes through Clerkenwell a single line goes up and away from it, ending some

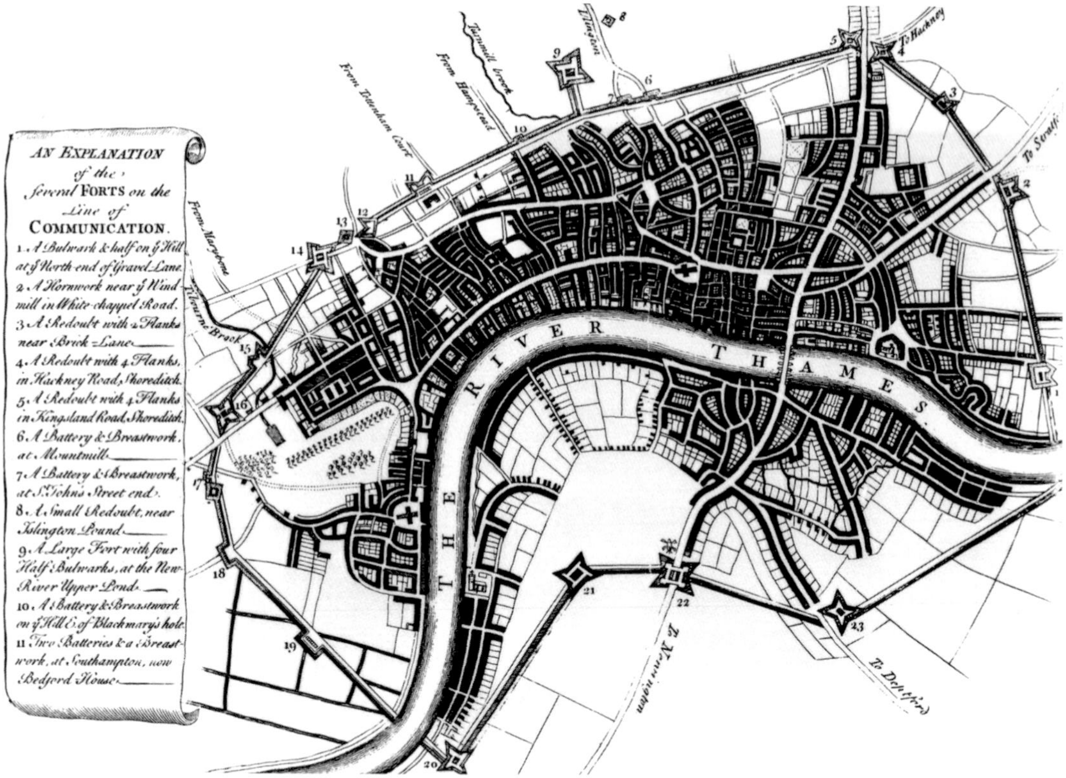

22 Map of the fortifications during the Civil War of the 1640s. The Fort Royal, roughly on the site of the western part of today's Claremont Square reservoir, is prominently displayed.

distance north of New River Head at a star-shaped fortification. The caption describes each of the forts, and this one it calls 'a large redoubt with four half bulwarks at the New River Upper Pond.'

This description raises an obvious question. The Upper Pond was a well-known landmark *by the time the map was drawn,* but it had not been dug until 1708, more than sixty years after the fortifications had apparently been built. If the fort had been on the site of the Upper Pond, digging the pond would have destroyed it. How did the mapmaker know precisely where the fort had been? Something else was intriguing. It was easy to see the point of building a strongpoint, for example, where the line of fortification crossed a major road, but there was no road up there. The main road, which passes east-west along the north side of the Upper Pond reservoir, now called Pentonville Road, was not built until 1756. In the 1640s the nearest main road had been three hundred yards to the east, passing on the far side of the Angel Inn. Surely if the fort was anywhere it would have been over there?

London prepares for war

It was easy to confirm that fortifications had been authorised. On 7 March 1642 Parliament had given the Lord Mayor and citizens of London the power to 'trench and stop' all highways and byways leading into the City, and also the power to 'fortifie and intrench the places aforesaid with such out-workes and in such places as they shall think meet.' Just five points of entry to the city were to be allowed, at Charing Cross, St Giles in the Fields, St John

Street, Shoreditch and Whitechapel, and these were to be guarded.[2]

Many histories of London dealt with the story of the fortifications, and it seemed that there were two main contemporary sources on which they all relied. The first was the Venetian ambassador and the second a Scotsman called William Lithgow.

The Venetian ambassador

In those days, long before the unification of Italy, the 'serene republic' of Venice was still a major figure in world trade. As such, she sent her ambassadors to the main capitals, both to promote her interests and to send back reliable reports about current affairs. These reports were addressed to the Doge and his senate, but normally they went first to six 'sages' appointed by the senate, who read all such reports in a room that can still be seen in the Ducal palace at Venice. Once they had been dealt with the reports found their way to the Ducal archive, and there they remained in the centuries that followed, somehow surviving the periodic floods and invasions that afflicted the city.

Those reports provided a rich vein of historical information about the countries they described, and British scholars began to read and translate them in Victorian times. Eventually they were published by the Stationery Office, as part of the vast series known as the Calendar of State Papers, and are easily accessible. They are oddly reminiscent of the weekly letters written home by family members away at school or overseas, in the days when letters were still the usual way to pass on news. They are full of detail, much of it unimportant but all part of the need to communicate. It is as if a certain number of words must be written for the letter to be complete, regardless of whether the week has been full of drama or tediously ordinary. Because of this, they are full of information.

Venice's man in London in 1642 was Giovanni Giustinian, and he wrote as dutifully as the schoolboy who knows that his letter will be checked for grammar, length and content. Thus what he has to say about the fortifications is buried among a mass of other information about people, events, politics and motives. As might be expected, he seems to have been generally well informed – at one point he reported back that he had 'seen the letters of many lords of the Court' as well as speaking to people who had been present at major events. On 17 October 1642 he wrote of how soldiers were posted at all the approaches to London, and how the main highways were blockaded with timber and thick chains of iron. A week later, he noted that the 'trained bands' of city soldiers had been ordered to 'stand ready to their arms at the first touch of drum'.[3]

On the same day Parliament made a further order, for the speedy fortification of London and the building of outworks.[4] Two weeks later, Giustinian wrote describing what that meant in practice, adding the little details that are so revealing:

> 'There is no street however little frequented that is not barricaded with heavy chains, and every post is guarded by numerous squadrons. At the approaches to London they are putting up trenches and small forts of earthwork, at which a great number of people are at work, including the women and little children.'[5]

Two weeks later, on November 21, he wrote again. The city was in a great stir. All the guards had been doubled and there were cannon in the main streets

> 'constantly attended by artillerymen with their fuses burning to be ready for all emergencies. At the trenches outside .. they are working incessantly with a great number of pioneers … they are making every preparation which is likely to prove effective for offering a stout and valorous resistance for an open city which is so populous.'

In the same letter he gave some detail of how the costs of the defences were being raised, writing of course as the representative of a Catholic state whose sympathies must have been with Charles and his Catholic wife Henrietta Maria, and not the Puritans who opposed him.

> 'To meet the expenses of these levies and of so many other requirements which multiply

> hourly, they are making application to everyone, without distinction, for contributions. Those who do not promptly consent have their plate taken by force, with the best of the goods which are found in their houses, and are subsequently sent to prison, without remorse, as enemies of the state and adherents of the contrary party. Seventy of the most substantial merchants of the mart are now in prison for this cause being determined to perish rather than give any encouragement by the profusion of their fortunes to those arms which are directed against their legitimate sovereign.'[6]

The City of London has records that give some details of the fortifications the City had ordered, including 'a battery and breastwork on the hill near Clerkenwell towards Hampstead way'. Although imprecise this does fit the location of the Upper Pond, which overlooked the road to its west that followed the valley of the Fleet, leaving Holborn near Gray's Inn and leading towards Hampstead.

Giustinian left London in December 1642, and his secretary Gerolamo Agostini, who considered the English 'an inhuman and barbarous people', took over writing the weekly letters. In March 1643, Agostini wrote that Parliament, 'dreading the approach of the Royal forces and .. not able to trust their safety to the devotion of their citizens' had decided the whole circuit of London must be fortified, and had sent to Holland for engineers for that purpose. They had already begun the work with great energy, but he predicted that it would take a very long time and be very difficult to defend. A week later he wrote that the work was proceeding with incredible cost and effort,

> '.. they do not even cease work on Sunday, which is so strictly observed by the Puritans.'[7]

He also wrote of the continuing efforts to raise money needed for the defences, with the help of 'paid troops, who sack the houses and shops of everything without any reference to the amount due, so that everyone is trying to escape, and already a large number of the houses are empty, some of the shops closed and the rest contain little or no merchandise.'

By 15 May 1643, he was able to report that the forts around the city were

> 'complete and admirably designed. They are now beginning the connecting lines. As they wish to complete these speedily and the circuit is most vast they have gone through the city with drums beating and flags flying, to enlist men and women volunteers for the work. Although they only give them bare food, without any pay, there has been an enormous rush of people, even of some rank, who believe they are serving God by assisting in this pious work, as they deem it.'[8]

A week later he claimed there were no less than 20,000 people working voluntarily and without pay on the fortifications, which would be completed in a few weeks. They were already beginning to place guns on the principal positions. Another week later, on 29 May, he had to report on a sadder aspect of Puritan England:

> 'The people here are still very busy with the work of the fortifications, and equally so over the destruction of crosses and figures. This very day there was a great concourse to pull to pieces the royal monuments in the church of Westminster, which was one of the finest ornaments of the city, admired by all foreigners for its antiquity and the perfection of the beautiful marble carvings.'[9]

Agostini's vivid picture is certainly consistent with the fact that a massive line of defences was built. Whether he dared to visit any of the forts to examine them closely seems doubtful – London was in the hands of Parliamentarians opposed to the Catholic King Charles, and a representative of a Catholic state like Venice must have needed to use some discretion. Sir Kenelm Digby, a royalist, was taken into custody for showing too much interest in the fortifications at Whitechapel. The King, at Oxford, did receive 'particulars of the fortifications' from John Webb, who was deputy to Inigo Jones the King's surveyor, but these have not survived.[10]

'A Schotch Man and a Lyar?'

For a detailed description of the fortifications we have to turn to William Lithgow, who published a small book on the subject in London in that same year, 1643, entitled *The Present Surveigh of London and England's State*. One surviving copy, in the British Library, has the words 'a Schotch Man and a Lyar' angrily scrawled next to Lithgow's name on the title page. Does this mean the work is not to be trusted? It seems that Lithgow had travelled to distant lands in his youth and then published an account of his travels, which from time to time was plainly adrift from the facts. This did little for his credibility. On the other hand his 1643 book, published in the very city whose current state of fortification he set out to describe, has not been shown to be inaccurate, and is generally accepted by military historians as being correct.[11]

Lithgow confirms Agostini's description of the vast numbers who had gone out to work on the fortifications, and claimed to have spent some two months witnessing the toil of groups drawn from every trade in the City. He then describes his lengthy walks around the whole circuit of the earthworks – walls defended with ditches and occasional forts that he describes in great detail. At last he describes arriving at:

> 'Islington Hill where there is erected a most rare and admirable fortification, called Strawe's Fort, but now Fort Royall. It hath eight angles, and a specious interlarding distance between each of the cornerd bulwarks. This fort is marvellous perspicuous and prospective, both for city and countrey, commanding all other inferiour fortifications near and about that part of the enclining grounds. The north east corner bulwark is doubly altified above the rest of the worke, carrying, on the two sides thereof, six cannones royall; and the two south and west corners are mutually charged, on each of them, with two half-culverins of brasse; and the east promontoriat corner adorned with three whole cannon. The altified bulwark is twice pallosaded; and, at the root of the work, answerable to the top of the inmost ditch, it is strongly barrocaded: the middle place, between the two ditches, is enravelled all about with low wooden stakes, and long pikes of throwne pointed iron: and without all which works there is a breastwork cast up, and made defensive, either for the first assault, or for the second invasion.'[12]

The lie of the land

This description could hardly be clearer. The fort was indeed upon Islington hill, and Lithgow's words show why that place had been chosen. Of all the forts that can be seen on the map, it is the only one on high ground. As he reports, it was 'marvellously perspicuous and prospective, both for city and for countrey, commanding all the other inferior fortifications near and about.' In other words, it had an excellent view in all directions. What an advantage that was in an age when messages could travel no faster than the speed of a galloping horse, unless there was a line of sight to enable communications with flags or other visible signals. Further, a commander on such a vantage point could see for himself a vast sweep of country on the northern and western approaches to London.

One other thing Lithgow mentions points to the authenticity of his description. Anyone visiting the site today can see how steeply the ground falls away to the south and the west, but less to the east and least of all to the north. Lithgow describes the fort as having its north-east corner 'doubly altified above the rest of the worke' – made much higher than the others. So it would need to be in any fort built on that particular spot if an all-round view was wanted.

'Animadversions of Warre'

A search for books about fortification dating from that period reveals that one in particular had been published in London just three years before the works began, in 1639. It was called *Animadversions of Warre* and its author was described as *Robert Ward, Gentleman and Commander*. He had dedicated it to the King and to the Earl of Warwick, a Royalist, so he would have had little sympathy with London's

23 *A treatise on fortification and other military matters published in 1639, three years before London's Civil War fortifications, including the Fort Royal on Islington Hill, were built.*

puritan fort-builders. But it was in London that it was published and printed, and it would be surprising if such a recent work did not come to the attention of those designing the fortifications. It deals, among other aspects of warfare with 'diverse new inventions, both of Fortifications and Stratagems' and it has engravings showing how earthworks had been thrown up to make forts in recent European conflicts, and precisely how they were proportioned, equipped, defended and attacked.

What Lithgow described in such meticulous technical detail is one of the typical structures of the civil war, of a kind that was being thrown up with ferocious energy in threatened or strategic towns all over England. No stone masonry was used in the construction, though the earth was in places reinforced with timbers. The approaches were 'pallosaded' or protected by palisades, lines of strong wooden stakes with sharpened tops, driven deep into the ground in close rows to make an obstacle for men and horses. He also refers to sharp iron pikes or stakes driven into the ground for the same purpose, all to delay attackers in the open where they could be picked off by defenders shielded by the ramparts of the fort. The complicated outline, not a square but with what Lithgow calls eight angles, is designed so that those on the ramparts above have a clear line of fire down to every part of the base of the structure, making the walls much riskier to attack.

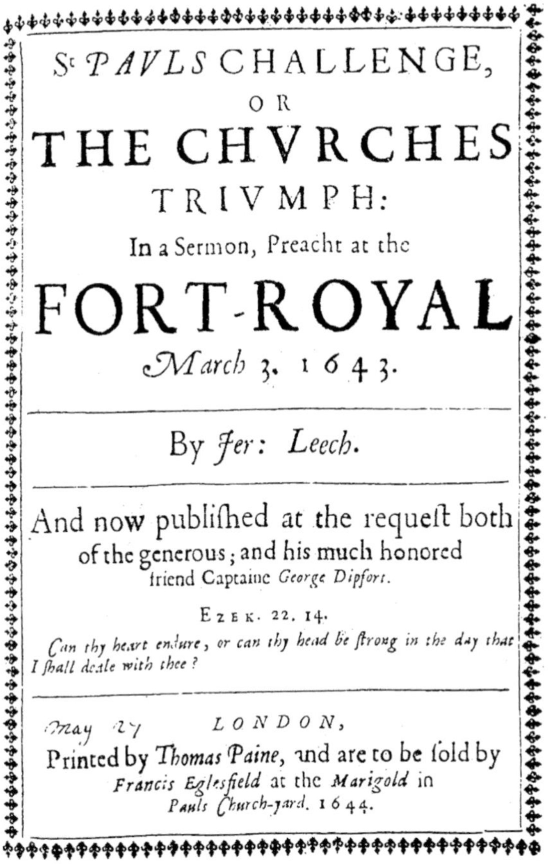
St PAVLS CHALLENGE,
OR
THE CHVRCHES TRIVMPH:
In a Sermon, Preacht at the
FORT-ROYAL
March 3. 1643.

By Jer: Leech.

And now publiſhed at the requeſt both of the generous; and his much honored friend Captaine George Dipfort.

Ezek. 22. 14.
Can thy heart endure, or can thy head be ſtrong in the day that I ſhall deale with thee?

May 27 LONDON,
Printed by Thomas Paine, and are to be ſold by Francis Eglesfield at the Marigold in Pauls Church-yard. 1644.

24 The title page of Leech's sermon 'Preacht at the Fort-Royal'. The site of the fort became the New River Upper Pond and is now the Claremont Square reservoir.

The Fort Royal

One of the most useful parts of Lithgow's description is that he gives the names by which the fort on Islington Hill was known – 'Strawe's Fort, but now Fort Royall.' At first sight 'Royall' seems an unlikely name for a fort built by Puritans whose enemies were the Royalists. But it seems that 'Fort Royal' was a term of art referring to a major fort of its type. In the same way the 'Cannons Royal' that Lithgow says were on the north-east bulwark were one of the largest sizes of cannon then in use, firing an eight-inch iron cannonball weighing 63 lb. and with a range of 1500 paces. The other guns he describes, half-culverins, only fired a 9 lb. ball but had a range of up to a mile.

A sermon at the fort

The name Fort Royal helped to locate another document that cast some light on the structure and its use. It is, by modern standards, a rather dull and long sermon, on the text 'If God be for us, who can be against us?' According to the title page it was 'preacht at the Fort-Royal, 3 March 1643' by one Jeremiah Leech. It survives because the preacher's 'much honoured friend Captaine George Dipfort' was generous enough to pay for it to be published. Of Captain 'Dipfort', all that seems to be recorded is that there was a Captain George Dipford, listed as one of the officers of the Blue Regiment of the London Trained Bands.[13]

What the sermon perhaps does is to provide a reminder that this was a war being pursued by people who took their religion seriously. Why was it preached on that particular day, 3 March 1643 old style, i.e. 3 March 1644? The day was a Sunday but there does not seem to have been any particular news that week, and the war was entering one of its most bitter stages, with each side tasting its share of victory and defeat. Perhaps Captain Dipfort thought his men needed a pep talk.

The sermon runs to nineteen pages, and anyone hoping to learn about the Fort Royal will read it with growing despondency. One might optimistically hope that it would at some point turn to earthly matters and give a description of the surroundings, or the occasion, or the congregation to whom it was preached – but Leech was made of sterner stuff than that. Page after page he thunders on, reminding the garrison how God had broken the chariot wheels of the Egyptians when they tried to pursue the fleeing Israelites across the Red Sea, how likewise the Angel of Death had slain a hundred and five thousand Assyrians in a single night for presuming to fight Hezekiah, how in short God looks after his own. The only reference to his hearers is when he tells them never to forget that God is with them 'when you go forth into the field, and while you lye here in your fort.' It was probably very inspiring on its day, but an Agostini might have made it more informative for the present day reader.

Agostini had made one telling observation about the forts in a letter he wrote on 27 March – and it was one of the few passages in his letters that he sent in code. Having referred to the state of the fortifications he went on:

> 'The shape they take betrays that they are not only for defence against the royal armies, but also against tumult of the citizens, and to ensure a prompt obedience on all occasions. In consequence of this, to furnish the most important positions, the city itself has decided to raise 6000 foot and 2000 horse, whom they have already begun to enlist."[14]

This is an interesting claim. It seems to be the case from Lithgow's descriptions of the other forts that they were protected on all sides, and not just facing outwards. Was this simply to increase their impregnability, or did those in authority really feel the populace might turn on them? It is worth remembering that, as Agostini himself had noted, the vast efforts made to complete the fortifications were by volunteers working without payment. Furthermore, the Parliamentary forces defending London were volunteers – the so-called trained bands who were drawn from all the trades of London. Would all this have been possible unless the London populace had largely supported Parliament against the King?

Slighting the fort

One reason that the fortifications of those years are less well known than might be expected is that Parliament, once triumphant, ordered their destruction. There was no longer any need for London to be a fortified city, and on 2 September 1647 came the order 'the lines of communication ... and all the forts upon and about the same be forthwith slighted and demolished.'

Despite the demolition work, traces of the fort could still be seen as late as 1756, when the historian Maitland described them. He takes as his starting point the garden of Merlin's Cave – a public house just to the west of New River Head. Its position is marked on many old maps, and a pub called the New Merlin's Cave remained nearby until the 1990s. Maitland continued:

> 'From there a covered way (the course of which is still to be seen) ran to a large bulwark at the Upper Pond belonging to the New River Company, the greatest part of which is still to be seen, adjoining the said Pond on the west, and the Eastern part thereof is occupied by the western part of the said Pond.'[15]

The 'covered way' he describes was a path protected by earth banks to allow troops and supplies to get to and from the fort, which was detached from the main circuit of the lines of communication, without exposing themselves to fire. It seems to have followed the line of present-day Amwell Street and can be faintly seen in some old engravings.

In 1746 Dr Cromwell Mortimer, secretary of the Royal Society, traced the remains and noted those which could still be seen. He shows the plan of the fort in a way that fits Lithgow's description of it. A drawing of about 1730, after the Upper Pond had been built, shows some signs of raised earth along the route of the covered way.[16]

Hollar's drawings

Although there seems to be no drawing of the Fort Royal, some traces of the earthworks may be visible in some drawings made by Wenceslaus Hollar for the New River Company in 1665. Only suggestions of ditches and mounds can be seen, incidental to the scenes he was drawing and conveying very little sense of the extent of what must still have been there (*ill.16, p.88*). Hollar probably had no wish to glorify such remains as he saw. He was originally from Prague, had come to England as an artist under the patronage of the Earl of Arundel in 1637, and served on the Royalist side when the Civil War came. He had been captured and had then escaped to join Arundel in Antwerp, not returning to England until about 1652. There, according to a later biographer, he suffered from 'the smallness of prices' paid by print sellers who took advantage of a poor man.[17]

The drawings Hollar made around the Water House at New River Head are not his only connection with the New River. One of the fragments of documents that survived the 1769 office fire refers to an order in 1663 to 'agree with some skilful Artist to draw a map of ... several wooden pipes and their severall Boars with .. particular streets and places in which they are layd.' Four years later a fragment from 1667 records 'At this court it is order'd that Mr Treasurer doe (pay?)... Holler £20 for drawing up the Mapp which he had promised.'

It is hardly surprising that in the aftermath of murderous civil wars, that had set brother against brother and son against father, there was a desire to put the past behind and begin afresh. The forts seem to have been forgotten. A brief flurry of interest was caused in the 1820s with the appearance of a sketchbook containing what purported to be detailed drawings of the fortifications, supposedly made by 'John Eyre, sometime Captain of General Cromwell's regiment.' Sadly it soon became obvious that they were entirely spurious, cobbled together from descriptions such as Lithgow's. They depict the forts as being built of stone, which was simply not the case, and there are other errors impossible in a genuine work.

For the time that it was there, the Fort Royal must have been a major part of the lives of those who built, garrisoned and supplied it. At the time of writing, there is not even a plaque to show where it stood.

In 1708 the eastern part of the fort becaome the site for the New River Company's Upper Pond. In 1856 that pond was changed into a high brick-walled reservoir, strengthened by sloping earth banks. Now the whole structure is covered by grass and shrubby trees.

Thus, by pure chance, the site of the Fort Royal is marked by a structure that has more than a passing resemblance to the fortification Londoners built for protection against the King's army.

CHAPTER TEN

The water plot 1701

The water plot – After the fire – Lord Clarendon's complaint – Declining dividends – The higher grounds – Competition from Hampstead – Change at London Bridge – The Marylebone conduits – The opposed leases – The bankrupt goldsmith – A blueprint for blackmail – Winners and losers.

It was the fate of the New River Company that each new century brought a clutch of major problems. In 1700, it was a combination of competitive pressures and inadequate supply. In 1800, it was renewed competition and antiquated pipework. In 1900 it was the legislation that would end the company's independent existence by 1904. This chapter deals with the problems around 1700.

The water plot

One of the strangest events in the history of the New River took place around 1700, and can now be pieced together from documents dispersed between several archives. It seems that a small group of wealthy men hatched a plan to take over two of the three main components of water supply to the City of London – the London Bridge Works and the Marylebone conduits. They did so with the help of nominees and subterfuge. By so doing, they would be well placed to force the New River Company to split with them such water rents as the citizens would pay. Before the scheme was fully in place, the Common Council of the City realised what was happening and tried unsuccessfully to back out from what they had agreed. In order to understand the background, the position of the New River Company just before 1700 needs to be explained.

After the fire

London's best-known disaster, the Great Fire of 1666, did not affect the New River Company as much as might be expected. Although there was a loss of income from customers until rebuilding was under way, the works at New River Head were out of reach of the fire, whereas the London Bridge waterworks was completely destroyed. Rebuilding those works was seen as such a priority after the fire that they were given a special exemption from the Rebuilding of London Act of 1666. This provided that all new building must be of brick or stone, except for the London Bridge waterworks which might be rebuilt in wood. Despite this concession, there was a delay caused by disputes within the Morris family, and it was not until 1668 that the work was finished.

During this period, the New River Company was not idle. As well as repairing its former supply network, it extended new mains into southern parts of the City previously supplied from London Bridge. Despite claiming in 1667 that it would not do 'soe unworthy a thing,' it had within months begun laying its new mains and offering to supply former customers of the bridge works. This led to a complaint from Mary Morris that

> '.. Cittizens may bee in a short time compelled to (be) served from them at unreasonable rates, when they shall have beaten down all other waterworks & specially this, which is more ancient & furnished much better water than the new River.'[1]

Perhaps because of this expansion, the New River Company continued to thrive and its dividends grew, at least for a time.

Lord Clarendon's Complaint

In October 1699 Lord Clarendon, who with fourteen shares was the Company's biggest shareholder, wrote to Robert Harley, another shareholder. Later to be made Earl of Oxford, Harley was a prominent Member of Parliament and would soon become the Speaker of the Commons, Secretary of State to Queen Anne and one of the most powerful figures in the land. He had been a shareholder since 1694 as a result of marrying Simon Myddelton's daughter Sarah, who owned New River shares. Clarendon was urging Harley to attend a forthcoming meeting of the New River Company:

> 'If you are here I believe things may be putt in some order, otherwise .. I shall despair of it ... the best improved works will go to ruin.'[2]

When Clarendon wrote of the improved works, he was speaking of a topic that was to preoccupy those concerned with the company for years to come – how to modify Myddelton's works to supply houses on higher ground than it had ever been designed for.

As the year 1700 dawned, the New River Company was in trouble. Its treasurer Thomas Darwin, 'woollen draper of St Paul's Churchyard'[3] had become bankrupt in 1696 and departed his house leaving large debts. Most of the company's ready cash, which had been in his hands in those days before bank accounts, was lost. The bankrupt Darwin seems to have been for some reason under a cloud for at least ten years before his final ruin. In September 1686 he wrote a cringing letter to 'His Excellency the Lord Lieutenant of Ireland at ye Castell in Dublin' – that being the Earl of Clarendon's job at the time. It seems from the letter that there were already divisions in the company.

> 'I presumed .. to trouble you with a letter and give you an accompt as you desired of the proceedings in the New River; butt nott having had yr honr and favor of a line from you in answer ... causeth me feare your by some false representation angry with me ... I have ... faithfully and freely served yr Exell's to the utmost of my power, and am very much troubled I have now reason to feare I am in displeasure; I am as ready and as willing to serve you as eaver, and it may be faithfullyer than them that pretend more.
>
> You were pleased to say in the letter to the Company that ... you would name some to bee removed to make things goe smoothlyer, and now I am certainly tould I am one of those. I have not obstructed any yr commands, nor opposed any of the company's business; soe am bold by this humbly to begg yr Exell favor and good opinion and .. favor of a line from you that I am in good opinion and shall continue in the place I am notwithstanding the malys of ill men.'[4]

Whatever the reasons, the company was in trouble, and a drop in dividends from 1696 until 1712 confirms this.

Declining dividends

Partly because of its expansion after the Great Fire, New River dividends had dipped only briefly at that time, and recovered their previous levels by 1670. In 1685 Lord Clarendon was able to write to his brother Lord Rochester about New River shares, extolling their value:

> '.. it is visible that revenue does daily more increase than land can do; and by some new rules which we have lately made, a very considerable improvement will appear within a year.'[5]

From 1670 they climbed steadily upwards until 1696, but then they began to drop. Apart from the money lost in Darwin's bankruptcy, the major problem was the difficulty of supplying newly built districts, such as Soho, which were on higher ground than the City. This meant that competitors were starting up who could offer a better supply to those parts and might in due course threaten the New River all over London. Meanwhile, down in the City renewed competition from the London Bridge waterworks was forcing the New River Company to cut its prices. Even worse, there were moves afoot to increase the quantity of water the London Bridge works could supply, and that could only intensify this competition. The New River Company had spent money in various attempts to hold its position and this meant less was available to pay dividends to shareholders, which fell by almost a quarter from 1696 onwards. This provoked great anxiety among the small number of wealthy people who held New River shares and who had come to depend on the twice-yearly payouts. Unlike a modern public company where shareholders leave management in the hands of the directors, most of the holders of Adventurers' shares were on the board that met to discuss and vote on all important decisions. Inevitably their anxieties led to factions and cabals forming within their ranks.

The higher grounds

When the New River was first built, the West End barely extended north of the Strand. As new houses were built further north and west during the later parts of the seventeenth century, it became increasingly difficult to supply them from New River Head. The first problem was one of height – the new buildings were not as high as New River Head but they were significantly higher than the City of London, and this lowered the water pressure. The second problem was distance. Water running through pipes is subject not only to leakage, but to friction, and this progressively reduces the flow of water as the distance increases, so West End customers received little more than a trickle of New River water as long as it was supplied from New River Head.

Competition from Hampstead

Among a collection of Robert Harley's papers now at Nottingham University is a letter from one Evan Jones, dated 1 October 1701. It is mostly concerned with promoting pumping machinery designed by Jones but it also gives a summary of the extent of competition from the Hampstead Waterworks in the West End. He said the Hampstead works were able to provide water at higher pressure than the New River, and this seems likely as the water came from higher ground. He also listed a range of smart streets north of Piccadilly, from Swallow Street to Berkeley Street, whose occupants already had New River water but were

> 'so uneasie at the ill servitude that they are inviting the Hampstead Waterworks to lay in pipes in those Streets, which if not speedily prevented will be some hundreds pounds per annum out of the Company's present Income in those parts only.'

He also claimed that the sluggish flow of New River water meant that their mains froze up first in the winter, so that some of their tenants defected to the Hampstead waterworks, 'but if the New River water be raised 15 or 20 foot or above, its Currant will be as swift and strong as the Hampstead Which will prevent the Inconveniencies of ffrost that now affects it..'[6]

The Hampstead Company had an office in Denmark Street, near today's Centre Point, and was said to have two seven inch mains supplying that neighbourhood. Their supply seems never to have been large enough for them to be a real threat to the New River, yet they took some of its customers.[7]

Change at London Bridge

The company's main competitor in the City was the London Bridge Waterworks. For over a century since Morice had founded it in 1582 it had continued to provide a supply of river water. Although it had to pump every gallon it supplied, waterwheels provided the motive power so the only pumping costs were those of building and maintaining the machinery. Its other great advantage was the fact that its source was within yards of its customers' houses. Although the New River could supply the City by gravity without any pumps, its costs included the constant maintenance of a stream over forty miles long, with crumbling banks and constantly growing waterweed.

The London Bridge works could only change the balance substantially in its favour if it upgraded its works to pump more water more cheaply, and extended its area of supply. This was something the Morris family did not choose to do. Then, in about 1700, came someone who did, or so the histories say. A typical account of what happened is that a goldsmith called Richard Soame or Soames bought out the Morrises, constructed better waterwheels and then sold shares in the works at a great profit.

The actual sequence of events pieced together from several sources was much more complex than this. Richard Soame was the ostensible purchaser from the Morris family, but he was acting for three other men called Higginson, Lake and Stafford. They in turn were only trustees, acting for seven men who were actually providing the finance.

The true purchase price was £43,000. Of this, £38,000 was destined for the Morris family and £5,000 for Richard Soame. Three City magnates provided £10,000 each. Heading the list was Sir Stephen Evance, who was a goldsmith and entrepreneur who speculated on trading voyages. His nature glistens out in a letter he wrote on an unconnected matter to the East India Company's Governor at Madras:

> '... but I am in with both sides, so they can do nothing but I presently heare of itt.'

The other main backers were Charles Hopton and John Abington. Four others put in smaller sums – Laurence Parker, Charles Shales, John Deacle and Robert West. Each of the purchasers acquired a share of future profits, and so did Richard Soame who became entitled to 18% of the business, worth about £6,800.[8]

The first move came in June 1701, when Thomas Morris asked the City to be allowed to lease another arch of London Bridge in addition to the two his waterworks already used. His reason was that the existing engines 'cannot draw sufficient Quantities of Water at lowe Tides' to serve his customers properly. This seemed a good enough reason, and a subcommittee was asked to seek out the views of the Bridge-masters and the 'Rulers' or leaders of the Watermen, Lightermen and Wharfingers. Those were the trades that might be affected by any interference with the navigation of the bridge. Then, on 18 June 1701, when their views had been obtained, a note shows that the committee was going to ascertain the views of the clerk of works and 'Mr Sorocold, engineer to Mr Morris'.

Now it can be seen, from documents in a lawsuit seven years later, that Sorocold, of whom we will hear more, was not on any view Morris's engineer. He had signed a six-year contract to be Soame's engineer almost a fortnight earlier, on 6 June 1701, and the contract included a provision that he would not work on any water supply in London except for Soame. Other documents, unknown to the Common Council, show that Soame had already signed an agreement to purchase the London Bridge works from the Morris family, but it was 'at his request kept private and not published.'[9]

The application was plainly made in Morris's name to hide Soame's involvement. For the same reason Sorocold was put forward as Morris's engineer when he was Soame's. For a time the deception was successful and meanwhile the plan was advancing. Surprisingly, the various users of the river made no objection to an arch being blocked. It was said that it would be a positive boon to the lightermen, whose wherries – small passenger craft – found the fourth arch dangerous as they could be swept through it by the current and 'dashed in pieces' against moored vessels. The wharfingers also approved, it seemed, because erecting an engine in the fourth arch would increase the area of calm water downstream of the bridge where vessels could be moored while they were unloaded. All that was required was a protective framework of piles to prevent vessels being drawn into the waterworks.

Then in July, the committee approved the application and its members signed a report to that effect. This was presented before the Common Council on 10 July, and they remitted the matter to the committee, having empowered them to negotiate terms with Mr Morris. Soame's name was still nowhere mentioned in any of the documents.

On 22 July the committee reported again. They had viewed the arch and perused the report. They had discussed the matter with the Bridgemasters, the rulers of the watermen and lightermen, the bridge house artificers and Mr Sorocold the engineer. They reported that the engine would not prejudice the navigation or obstruct the river. They proposed the grant of a lease for as long as the City had power, subject to certain conditions. It should be subject to Mr Morris making good any damage caused by his default to the arch, pier, stonework or houses of the bridge, and to his providing at his own expense as many fire cocks – hydrants – in the City streets as the committee should direct.

Thus in little more than six weeks an application to permanently block one of the arches of London Bridge had been considered and was being recommended for approval. A contract was then drafted which gave Morris the right to the fourth arch for three hundred and eighty-one and a quarter years. This odd length of time was so that the lease should last for as long as the two earlier leases, which ran for 500 years from the date of the first in 1582.

In return, Morris was to make a down payment of £300, and thereafter pay a rent of just ten shillings a year. He must also supply private houses – except those using extraordinary quantities of water, or used for trade – for no more than £1 a year, instead of £1 4s. 0d., and charge no 'fine' – connection charge – as from Midsummer 1702. On the face of it, this seems a remarkably favourable lease to Morris. The annual rent of ten shillings was nominal. Morris was being offered the right to sell Thames water from this arch for almost four hundred years in return for a single payment of £300. Why the generosity?

The answer is to be found in the final proposed condition:

> 'That neither the two former nor this licence shall not be assigned to the Governors of the New River Water nor to any other person than is specified in the said former licences...'

This condition shows that the City was by this time very much alive to the risks of a water monopoly and the wording suggests that there was nothing in the existing two leases to prevent the Morrises selling them on to the New River Company, and thereby giving it a virtual monopoly, which would enable it to push up its prices at the expense of the citizens. Thus the City was trying to cure this defect, not realising that Morris had already sold out to Soame. Soame had been right in thinking that his name should be kept out of it, for he had family links to the New River Company, as the committee might easily have found out.

The proposed contract or licence was then read before the committee on 31 July, agreed, and ordered to be entered in the Book of Grants for Mr Morris to sign. He did so, the City's Controller countersigned it, and Morris paid over the £300. On 21 August 1701 the details were read out to the Common Council. At that stage, there must have been some small opposition and a vote was called for. The opposition lost and the proposed licence was agreed by 93 votes to 23. That might have been expected to end the matter, but it could not be finalised until the Lord Mayor affixed the seal of the corporation to the licence – normally something that would be a mere formality.

At about that time, light must have started to dawn on some members of the City Corporation. Perhaps Soame or those about him became indiscreet once they thought the matter was settled. Whatever the reason, the Lord Mayor refused to seal the deed. There then followed two years of struggle between the two sides. The City tried to find reasons for going against the advice and decisions of its committee and Common Council, while Morris – or those who acted in his name – produced counter-arguments and meanwhile went on to exercise their new rights. They did this by starting to build the new waterwheel and pumps, and also began laying new water mains in the City to cater for the improved supply. This may have been done on legal advice to show that Morris was exercising his rights under the agreement and thus make it harder for the City to back out.

Meanwhile, there had been several developments in what had become a battle between 'Morris' – or Soame's backers – and the City fathers, who were by this stage even divided among themselves. Historically the City's legal adviser was known as the Recorder of London, and Salathiel Lovell the current incumbent of that post had been asked to apply his mind to the problem. His answer was that the Lord Mayor should not seal the lease to Morris. He reached this view as follows.

First, the committee that recommended it did not know that the River Thames was a Royal Port, of which the navigation and free passage belonged to the Queen and all her subjects. It would be a common and public nuisance to obstruct it with waterworks. The Lord Mayor had a franchise to keep the river clear and might forfeit his franchise if he sealed the lease to Morris and thereby appeared to allow the obstruction.

Perhaps the Recorder knew that this argument had its weaknesses, particularly as the Morris family had blithely been obstructing two other arches of the bridge for over a hundred years, with the City's blessing and without any complaint. He continued on a different tack.

> 'Next I am of the opinion that if this grant might be lawfully made, yet this lease ought not to be sealed.'

His principal reasons were first that Morris, he said, had misled the committee as to certain unspecified aspects of his existing leases, then secondly

> 'The lease now drawn doth in no sort answer the good intention and design of that committee; who to prevent the exaction of the New-River Water men, intended to hinder the Bridge-water to come into their Hands or Power; which is not prevented by this deed.'

This comment reveals how matters had changed between 1613 and 1702. Myddelton's great benefaction of the New River was now seen as a source of exorbitant charges, and the New River Company as one that would abuse its power if given the chance. The Recorder also claimed there had been an element of deceit:

> 'I am of Opinion that the City is not bound in Honour neither to execute such Intentions, when they find the Matter is not legal, and such Consent gained by Surprize, Misinformations, and untrue Suggestions: Nay, even a common Person, who may make a Contract by Word or Writing, is not bound by it, if it was fraudulently or deceitfully obtained.' [10]

Nowhere does he spell out precisely what deceit he is referring to. He then pointed out some further weaknesses in the drafting, and ended up by saying that even if those were rectified he would still advise against the lease, for various reasons including the fact that its provisions, he said, were unenforceable in law.

Unfortunately, from the City's point of view, his advice had not been obtained before the City committed itself. The licence had been offered to Morris, and he had signed it and thus agreed in law to be bound by it. Further, he had paid his £300. He (or his backers) had gone ahead with the building works, and with laying new pipes in the City streets. He even claimed they were reducing water rates as the lease provided and losing money thereby. Was it not too late for the City to back out?

Advice on this point had also been sought, from three of the most senior lawyers in the kingdom, Sir John Hawles, Sir Edward Northey and Sir Simon Harcourt. Each one of them was either a current or past solicitor general or attorney general, Harcourt was a future Lord Chancellor. They advised in October 1702, and each of them separately concluded that the Lord Mayor was bound by the order of the Common Council to affix his seal.[11] All three opinions were apparently read out at a meeting on 8 October 1702, yet still the Lord Mayor refused to affix his seal. He must have had very powerful reasons for taking that course; yet they were never spelt out and must remain a matter of conjecture.

It is by no means clear who was behind the various machinations on either side. Robert Harley was certainly taking a close interest in the proceedings, presumably to protect his financial interest in the New River Company. One letter in his archive is in effect a confidential warning shot to the New River Company. The writer says he was at a meeting of the Court of Aldermen in November 1702 when two people attended claiming to represent the New River and publicly opposed the sealing of the new lease to Morris. They claimed that Morris had offered to do some deal with the New River, thereby putting in doubt his promise to reduce water rates. The writer had obviously been asked to help the New River interest in some way, and now complained

> 'This disabled me from doing anything more towards an accommodation and made the other party so shy, that I can't ask him a question tending that way. So far as I can find among the Common Council men, this opposition ... has done Mr Morris a service, and so far exasperated the Common Council against the New River Company that they will take upon them to seal the lease if the Court of Aldermen defers it beyond next week. Some of the Aldermen themselves, who violently opposed sealing the lease, grow cooler since those gentlemen appeared for the New River because their opposition now will be construed as an opposition to the interest of the City... If that company would desist from all further opposition, I believe I could yet be an instrument of serving them, which I would gladly do for the sake of my Lord Clarendon, and for that truly great man your friend, for whom I have all the honour due to so much merit...'[12]

This letter seems to confirm that the New River Company was not behind the 'Soame' purchases, but it also raises new questions as to what was going on. What does it all mean? Had the writer been asked to try and reach an 'accommodation' between the New River Company and Morris? Presumably he had, or why write in these terms? If so, can this mean anything other than a private agreement to avoid genuine competition between the two suppliers? At the same time, is he playing a double game by secretly working to try and prevent Morris from even getting his lease, in which case no accommodation would be needed? The writer of that letter was Robert West. Although his letter gives no hint of it, the trust deeds relating to the purchase of London Bridge Waterworks show that he was one of the investors. He had put in less than any of the others, just £2,000. His warning letter to the New River Company perhaps shows how obscure the whole transaction was. Why should one of the secret investors be helping the principal competitor of the waterworks he was investing in? Was he simply there as Harley's inside man?

The incident when New River representatives tried to influence the Court of Aldermen was not the only opposition from the Company. There was also an appeal from the New River Company to the Attorney General, urging on him that Morris's new waterworks constituted a public nuisance by obstructing one of the arches of the bridge. That was an extraordinary piece of hypocrisy, whose underlying motives must have been transparently obvious. The business of the New River Company was to distribute water from its own private channel, which was nowhere any closer to the River Thames than at its terminus at New River Head – well over a mile from the Thames. Its only legitimate interest in the Thames navigation was that it purchased quantities of logs for making water pipes, some of which doubtless arrived by river. Yet in this respect it was hardly different from any other company or citizen – most of London's goods arrived by water in those days.

This attempt by the New River Company to obstruct Morris seems to have outraged the City. We know that because it provoked a petition to the Queen from the Common Council of the City, signed on their behalf by Sir William Ashurst, a former Lord Mayor. What that sets out shows how much public attitudes towards the New River company had soured since the welcoming celebrations of 1613.

Having set out the citizens' need of water for ordinary uses and also in times of fire, the petition continues

> '... the Proprietors of the New River Waters taking advantage of these Necessities of your Majesty's subjects have extracted from them (and also for the Prisons and Hospitalls of this Citty) unreasonable Fines and Rents'.

The petition then set out how Morris's application for the fourth arch had been carefully considered before it was agreed to, and then

> 'the Proprietors of the New River finding such further supply of your Majesty's subjects with water would very much prevent their aforesaid exactions have applyed themselves to your Majesty's attorney Generall ... to make use of his Name in an information ... for a nuisance in obstructing the Passage through the said arch'.[13]

At the end of it all, the City lost the argument and the new proprietors of London Bridge Waterworks embarked on more than a century of renewed competition with the New River Company, that would only end when they were taken over by their larger competitor in 1822. George Sorocold had built them new pumping equipment, but although they held their existing territory, their efforts to advance it do not seem to have been successful.

The Marylebone conduits

Meanwhile another dispute related to the City's water supply was taking place, and once more members of the Soame family were involved. At that time, almost all of the City's water was provided either by the New River or the London Bridge works. The City still had rights to water from springs in Marylebone and elsewhere that had formerly been fed to conduits in the streets. Most of these had ceased to function when street improvements were made after the Great Fire of London, and the City was prepared to lease out the right to use the springs.

There was a joint application from several individuals including Bartholomew Soame, Richard's father. Some of the others named had also been named with Richard Soame in the trust deeds relating to the purchase of the London Bridge works, though the City would never have seen those private documents. The City saw no difficulty in agreeing to grant this request, although at the hefty annual rent of £700, which contrasts strikingly with Morris's ten shillings a year. This was apparently acceptable to the applicants, and three of them signed a bond that committed them to take the lease, subject to a penalty in the enormous sum of £10,000.[14]

Then, as the dispute over Morris's licence dragged on, the applicants suddenly seemed to be in no hurry to sign. On 20 January 1703, the Court of Aldermen noted that, despite their bond the applicants had not bothered either to reply to enquiries or to appear and explain their reasons. The court ordered that the draft lease should be sent to them to complete. Months went by, and the matter was frequently mentioned before the court, but nothing transpired, and still Soame and the others gave no reason. Then, in July 1703, came an explanation of sorts. The City had

> 'sent the draft lease to Mr Bartholomew Soame for him and the others to peruse ..or send their objections in writing... A servant of the said Mr Soame's son came .. and insisted that the said lease ought to be conditional, that if the waterworks in the fourth arch of London Bridge should be abated upon the proceedings of law, then that lease to be void.'

The 'proceedings of law' referred to was an application to the courts to have the waterwheel in the fourth arch removed on the basis that it was a public nuisance. What Soame junior's agent was saying was that unless Morris kept the right to have a waterwheel in the fourth arch, he was not signing for the Marylebone waters. This on the face of it was an extraordinary posture to adopt. Surely Soame and his partners must want to supply water from the Marylebone conduits they had agreed to lease? They could only benefit if a potential competitor like the London Bridge works was prevented from improving its works. How or if the servant of Soame's son explained this position is not recorded, but the explanation may have provoked incredulity.

Three more weeks passed and eventually Bartholomew Soame was prevailed upon to attend in person. His position was unchanged – he wanted a provision inserted that the Marylebone lease should be void

> '...if Morris should be evicted .. from enjoying the licence lately granted to him for placing an engine under the fourth arch of London Bridge.'

He was given two days to reflect upon the matter, and appeared again before the court on

29 July 1703, this time with his partners, when the record notes that '...they did peremptorily refuse to execute the lease..' and the order was made that another copy be prepared, and tendered to Soame and his partners to sign. The aldermen had evidently smelt a rat and intended to force Soame and the others to comply whether they wanted to or not, in accordance with their bond to do so.

The Opposed Leases

The extraordinary position had thus arisen that the City had agreed to grant two leases relating to water supply. One of them the City was now trying to wriggle out of, while Soame and his backers were trying to enforce it. The other one the City was determined should be signed, while Soame and his partners were trying to avoid it.

In the event, the Marylebone lease never was signed. The City then sued the guarantors of the bond that had been given, and was awarded nine years' rent – £6,300, plus legal costs all the way to the House of Lords.[15] It may be that Soame and the others never intended to use the Marylebone supply, and applied simply to prevent any third party from taking it and thereafter competing with the London Bridge Works. If so, those who guaranteed the offer had cause to regret doing so.

The bankrupt goldsmith

Who was Richard Soame? Histories of London credit him with having taken over the waterworks at London Bridge, improved them, and sold shares in the enterprise at a great profit. But who was this man who could put his hands on the colossal sum of £38,000 that he was said to have paid the Morris family to buy out their interest – the equivalent of millions at present day prices?

All the published references to him related to his dealings at London Bridge, often described in identical terms as though they had simply been copied from one book to the next. Sometimes he was described as a goldsmith, but nothing else about him or his background was ever mentioned. The Goldsmiths' Company confirmed he had been a member, introduced by his father Bartholomew in 1695. Was this the Bart Soame whose name appeared as a member of the New River Company? The apprenticeship books showed that Bartholomew Soame had become an apprentice in November 1648. More usefully, the entry gave his father's name and address – Sir William Soame of Little Thurlow in the County of Suffolk.

It turned out that there were some Soame family papers at the Suffolk county record office in Bury St Edmunds, deposited many years ago, and some went back to the years around 1700. What those papers, and others in the Public Record Office, show is that Richard Soame was an entrepreneur who lost more often than he won.

One old case suggests that he had become bankrupt,[16] but before about 1720 records of bankruptcies are rare. He had also been a party to two Chancery cases, and both recorded money problems. One was started by an Antwerp merchant who had supplied him on credit with 'parcells of good pictures done by good and able painters, and fitt for the adorning of stare cases and houses ... at the cheapest rates at which the same could be bought in Antwerp.' Now the merchant wanted payment. Three London merchants brought another case against him, claiming that he owed them over £11,000. In his answer, Soame acknowledged the debt and offered to pay it as soon as he was able. [17]

The final confirmation of his problems came from a scribbled note on a legal brief among the Soame family papers in Suffolk. On 30 November 1704 Richard Soame was made bankrupt, and on 24 April, presumably the following year, he 'Surrenders himself a Prisoner to Q's bench & fleet also.' The Queen's Bench Prison and Fleet Prison were both for debtors, and that day must have marked at least a temporary end to his financial adventures. Other papers showed that he had long since mortgaged his interest in the London Bridge Waterworks to a relative.[18]

What this shows is that in 1695 Richard Soame was finishing his apprenticeship. Within five years he was – apparently – contracting to buy London's second-largest waterworks. Four years later he was bankrupt and in prison.

The records also show that his father Bartholomew was bankrupt in all but name by this time. He had been born in 1630, and was his father's sixth son. In a society where it was normal for the eldest to inherit, he was doubtless expected to make his own way in the world. At the age of 18, he was apprenticed to a goldsmith, Simon Myddelton. This gave him a link to water supply, for Simon was one of Hugh Myddelton's sons and owned shares in the New River and was its Treasurer in the 1650s. His apprenticeship ended six years later, and he was admitted as a freeman of the Goldsmiths' Company. He does not seem to have been a working goldsmith, and Simon's business was as a draper.

In due course Bartholomew married a merchant's daughter, who bore him three girls and five boys of whom the youngest was Richard. Bartholomew went on to hold office within the Goldsmiths'. In 1690 he became one of its wardens, and in 1694 Prime Warden – the most senior officer. The Company was the most powerful of all the livery companies, so Bartholomew must have been a man of influence and in good standing at that time.

In that same year, Bartholomew also strengthened the Soame connection with the New River Company. Hugh Myddelton by his will had left one Adventurers' share to the Goldsmiths' Company, its income to be used for charitable purposes. The Goldsmiths accordingly appointed one of their number from time to time to hold this share in trust for them and, by virtue of holding it, to be their representative at New River company meetings. On 22 October 1694 Bartholomew was chosen for this role, and he held it until 23 December 1702, when he was replaced having asked 'to be relieved' of it.

His brother Edmund was Deputy Governor of the New River Company by that time, having acquired four shares in the same way as Robert Harley did, through marriage to one of Simon Myddelton's daughters.

In the light of later events, it may be significant that Bartholomew's appointment to the New River was not merely because he was Prime Warden at the time the vacancy became due. The Goldsmiths' records show that he was one of three members who had offered themselves for the task and he was chosen only after the matter was put to the vote. It seems he wanted for some reason to be present at New River meetings, although the post would have brought him no income or obvious benefits. Subsequent events raise the possibility that his asking to be relieved of this office in 1702 may have been less than entirely voluntary, like the letters of resignation of dismissed cabinet ministers at the present day.

Up to that time, Bartholomew was doing well. At some stage he gained the occupancy of the family seat at Little Thurlow in Suffolk, something he can hardly have expected as a sixth son. It came about because his nephew Sir William Soame, who had succeeded to the baronetcy in 1684, died at Malta on his way to take up an appointment as ambassador to the Ottoman court at Constantinople. He was childless and left the house and estate at Little Thurlow to his uncle Bartholomew for life. Bartholomew, then, might have seemed destined for a dignified and prosperous old age at his country seat. It was not to be. Soon after 1700 his affairs went rapidly downhill. A document preserved among the Soame papers records that in 1706 he transferred 'all the goods, household stuff and implements of household' set out in a – now missing – inventory to John Soame of London, in part settlement of an unpaid debt from 1700. It is possible that this was an artificial transaction to keep family possessions out of the reach of creditors, or it may have been a genuine transfer to settle part of his debt. The debt in question was for just over £2,000 plus interest, and Bartholomew had entered it jointly with his sons Richard and Edmund, all described as goldsmiths, together with one 'Henry Gray of London, Merchant'.

By 1712 he was in need, and in May one of the Goldsmiths' courts ordered 'that Mr Barth'w Soame, a poor member of this court, have 40 shillings paid him out of Mr Morrell's gift', one of the charitable funds they administered. Three months later they ordered that Edmund Soame should instead receive the 40 shillings 'that was formerly to be paid to his father'. The reason for this is unexplained, but it may be that if the money had been given direct to

Bartholomew his creditors would have been entitled to seize it. This Edmund was Bartholomew's son, also a member of the Goldsmiths' Company, not to be confused with Bartholomew's brother Edmund the deputy governor of the New River Company.

The small size of this charitable payment is revealing. Forty shillings might be a useful sum to a poor man, but it was hardly a large sum even in those days. It suggests that Bartholomew was virtually penniless. If it seems surprising that the Goldsmiths were not more generous to one of their own, that may be because they were weathering a severe financial crisis at the time.

Bartholomew's finances do not seem to have improved. All members of the Goldsmiths' Company were liable to pay quarterly dues, and in his case they had accumulated unpaid. At a meeting in August 1716 'it being moved on behalf of Mr Bartholomew Soame that he, having served all offices in this company and for many years past having laboured under great misfortune, might be discharged from the arrears of quarteridge: it was put to the question and ordered accordingly'. By then Bartholomew would have been 86 years old, and there seems no reason to doubt that he had been impoverished for many years past.

A blueprint for blackmail

One tantalising final document fits somewhere in the story of the takeover of the London Bridge works and the Marylebone conduit leases, and it may well point to the purpose of the whole elaborate exercise. It is tantalising because its author chose to date it with just two words – 'Thursday night'- and there is nothing else to pinpoint its date. It is written by one John Stafford and addressed to 'Mr Jenkins'. It is nothing more or less than a proposal for blackmail from someone at the London Bridge Waterworks and aimed at the New River Company.

John Stafford was one of the three trustees who were involved in the purchase of the Morrises' interest through Richard Soame, and he was also one of those who signed the guarantee to take the Marylebone conduit lease. Whose particular interest he was acting in is not explained – he speaks in the letter of acting for others, including some he refers to as 'some pretty stiff ones'.

As for the Mr Jenkins to whom the letter is addressed, his name does not appear elsewhere in connection with the New River Company, nor among the various parties involved in the Soame purchase. However, a guide to London published in 1708 says that the chief proprietors of the London Bridge Waterworks at that time were 'Mr Somes, Mr Jenkins, Mr Stafford, Mr Dunwell, Mr Gold, Mr Dearing &c'. Of those names only 'Somes', or Soame, and Stafford appear elsewhere. Perhaps this was the same Jenkins. None of those named, incidentally, is on the list of those including Sir Stephen Evance who actually put up the purchase price.

It may be then that Stafford, representing one group of shareholders was writing to another, possibly reluctant, shareholder to tell him what needed to be done. The letter runs to almost four pages, and contains some detailed calculations. The following extracts give the gist of it.

> 'Mr Jenkins, Sir, After I parted from you I was musing by myself which produced the following Scroll which I present you with to justify my demand of two fifths.
>
> I judge the rents of the N.R. to be about £11,000 p.a., the Bridge Water about £4800, Nett Rents £15,800. 2/5 amounts to £6320, deduct 4800 = £1520 Gained to ye Bridge Water.
>
> Now it may be objected, why should the N.R. give us £1520 p.a. but if what I have to offer does not prove they will be gainers by so doing, I shall think I have not given any reason for my demand; and if what I do offer should likewise demonstrate that ye N.R. cannot be gainers but on ye contrary considerable losers by their not allowing 2/5 then I hope it will be allowed as a good reason for their complying therewith.'

Stafford then sets out at length five reasons why the London Bridge works have the upper hand. Firstly, with the five engines London Bridge will soon have in use they can supply all the tenants (i.e. customers) they presently have. Second, within two or three months they could put up at least eleven more pumps in the various arches they hold, to supply eleven seven-inch mains, each of which would serve:

'500 tenants one day and 500 another day, which would be 1000 tenants for each main, at 20 shillings, though some would pay considerably more, it would then be £11,000 p.a.'

Third, any extra tenants they gain 'must be from the New River chiefly'. Fourth, certain 'streets and parishes' have already asked for the London Bridge supply to be extended to them. Fifth, whatever they gained would come straight out of the New River Company's profits because their expenses would stay the same.

He continues by explaining that if they only got 5000 extra tenants, the New River could only compete by lowering their rents, and continues rather menacingly:

'Now after all that I have said I must Conclude with this. That I esteem My L. Clarendon & Mr Secretary to be persons of so much worth and honour & of so sound judgment that were this an Affair of my own I could after their mature and impartial consideration of this Scroll lay the division of my own fortune at their Mercy with a full Assurance of their Justice, but You know there are so many persons concerned & some pretty Stiff ones, that I cannot depart from my demand. I am, Sir, Your very humble Servant, John Stafford.'[19]

Taking this letter as a whole it seems to be a demand, which Stafford is telling Jenkins must be put to the New River Company. The reference to 'Mr Secretary' in the same sentence as Lord Clarendon can only refer to Robert Harley, who was so called while he was Queen Anne's Secretary of State. Whether Stafford intended it or not, the letter certainly ended up in Harley's possession, and is among those in his archive now.

Reading the whole letter, Stafford's message to the New River Company is stark. It amounts to this: 'At present we, the London Bridge Works, receive less than a third of the total income of our two companies. We want more, and would settle for two fifths of the total in return for doing nothing, if you were prepared to pay us the difference. If not we are in a position to take it, and much more, by extending our supply, which we can do easily and cheaply. Any tenants we gain, you will lose, and your income will fall. Pay up or face the consequences.'

Despite the letter's flowery closing lines, this was nothing but blackmail. To add insult to injury, Clarendon and Harley as the largest shareholders in the New River would suffer the biggest loss from such an exaction. It must have taken a brave or foolish man to address such a demand to someone in Harley's position of power at that time.

Whether the demand was ever acceded to seems unlikely. Stafford's dabbling in waterworks was to cost him dear. For whatever reason, the rent due on the Marylebone conduits was never paid. The City therefore sued Stafford and the other two guarantors who had signed the bond, for £6,300 being nine years rent at £700 a year. The City won, so Stafford and his co-guarantors appealed to the House of Lords. They lost and were then liable to pay the £6,300 and all the costs of both sides. One of Stafford's co-guarantors was Bartholomew Soame, who was all but bankrupt, so the entire loss would have fallen on Stafford and the other guarantor John Adams.

Winners and losers

After all the years of scheming, who had gained? Richard Soame was bankrupt and, for a time at least, in prison. His aged father Bartholomew was a ruined man, not too proud to take a small handout from the livery company he had once led. The Morris family, who had once relied on the income from their grandfather's waterworks, sold it and helped Soame to conceal his identity from the City but still had to sue for the money he had promised them. George Sorocold, innocently involved, had the shame of seeing his family turned into the street when Soame stopped paying his salary and rent. Stafford and Adams, at the very least, found their involvement an expensive one. Even Sir Stephen Evance, one of Soame's three main backers in the London Bridge purchase, a goldsmith and banker who had been the King's Jeweller in 1697 was bankrupt by 1721.

The New River Company, by contrast, was over its temporary setback and its dividends were on the way up again by 1713.

CHAPTER ELEVEN

Wind, horse or water? 1702 to 1705

The Reverend Lowthorp – Wind, horse or water? – The Gentleman's Magazine – Mylne's commonplace book – 'Sr Christ. Wrenn ...' – Wren's report – '... and severall other persons...' – Lowthorp at Highbury – An experiment with pumps – Or a windmill? – Lowthorp tries again.

The Reverend Lowthorp

When the Earl of Clarendon, the largest shareholder in the New River Company, wrote to his fellow shareholder, Robert Harley, about Company affairs in 1699, his tone was pessimistic and he used words such as despair and ruin.[1] This turned out to be prophetic, if the Reverend Lowthorp is to be believed. John Lowthorp was an Oxford graduate, whose holy orders may have been little more than one aspect of a well-rounded education at that time. He had a considerable interest in science, which was then called natural philosophy, and was admitted as a fellow of the Royal Society in 1702.

The Royal Society of London for Improving Natural Knowledge had been founded with the encouragement of Charles II in 1660, and Sir Christopher Wren was one of its founding members. It may have been Lowthorp's connection with the Royal Society that brought him to the attention of the New River Company. The company asked for his advice on technical matters relating to the improvement of the water supply on at least seven occasions between 1704 and 1711. It does not follow that that was the full extent of his involvement, given the loss of company papers in the 1769 fire. His surviving letters and reports come not from the New River archives but from other sources, such as Robert Harley's vast correspondence. They are sufficient to show that Lowthorp was a regular and, presumably, a paid adviser.[2] The advice that he gave mostly has its place later in this chapter. He merits a mention at this stage because the last surviving document that he wrote to the company confirms the pessimism that Lord Clarendon had expressed some twelve years earlier. It was in 1711, and he described the Company's efforts at that time as follows:

> 'All their attempts to remove one defect have still served to discover another ... and till this difficulty be overcome all proposals of this kind will be imperfect, and the estimates of the charge and profit to be expected will be wild and at randome.'

This chapter will examine the succession of proposals and decisions that led him to that gloomy prediction.

Wind, horse or water?

One of Lowthorp's reports, written in 1704, helpfully sets out some basic principles regarding pumping machinery. It has a neat heading: *'An answer to the Demand of my Opinion concerning the use of Engines (in generall) in the Company's Service, Delivered in May 1704'.*

By way of introduction he reminds the reader that 'the necessity of making some sort of engines for the raising of the New River water at Islington to a convenient height having often employed the company's time and divided their opinions' and explains this as the reason for the summary that follows. Lowthorp then starts from the basic propositions that the company's tenants, and therefore revenues, would increase if the supply were improved, and that some kind of pumping was required at New River Head. He goes on to provide a succinct analysis of the technology available at that time:

'All the usual engines for raising water may be reduced to three sorts, namely, those powered by the wind, by horses or other animals, or by water.'

He continues:

'Wind engines are so very uncertain, from frequent calms and storms, that they seem altogether unfit for the Company's service, which is continual and equal.'

'Horse engines are very convenient for most purposes and I think the only objection that can be made to them, is the great and continual charge of the horses and servants that must attend them. The constant charge is always proportionate to the work required and cannot be determined till that be agreed; but that being once settled, 'tis easy to form an estimate of this from the following rules:' (which he then sets out)

'From these rules it readily appears, that in the particular case of sending water to Soho in one six inch main ... will require the constant work of 6 horses... so that it seems very reasonable to me that the company should enquire after and consider all other expedients before they have recourse to these engines that are so chargeable and ought for that reason to be their last refuge.

Water engines of all others are most desirable, and if the company have water enough to spare, there will be no great difficulty to erect and employ them. But if not .. they may next consider whether the same water that shall be found necessary to work the engines may not, after it hath performed that office, be restored to the cisterns and pipes ... as if it had flowed immediately from the pond.'[3]

It seemed to be Lowthorp's view, then, that for the New River Company a windmill was out of the question, a horsemill was too expensive and should be a 'last refuge', while a 'water engine' – a waterwheel – would probably be the right solution if carefully designed for the site. In view of subsequent events, it is worth bearing in mind his simple analysis of the problem and its solution.

The Gentleman's Magazine

This is a convenient stage also to look at the views of another expert. One early printed source raised the surprising possibility that Sir Christopher Wren had been consulted at this time and had written an opinion as to how the New River supply to the West End could be improved. None of the standard histories mentions any involvement by this best known of British architects. Could it be right? The source was *The Gentleman's Magazine*, a monthly periodical that first appeared in 1731 and did not finally cease publication until 1914. It was the first such publication to call itself a 'magazine' – the word was formerly confined to storehouses for arms and explosives – and Dr Samuel Johnson was a frequent contributor. It contained a wide range of articles on literary, historical and topical subjects. One issue, in 1753, includes two pages of text with no preface or introduction beyond the single sentence *'Thoughts of Sir Christopher Wren concerning the distribution of the New River Water; not published in his Works or elsewhere'*.[4]

The text that follows begins:

'Being desired by some persons of honour concerned in the New River water, to give them my thoughts about the most profitable distribution of the water; and particularly how the high parts around Soho Square might be supplied; I have, as well as my age and the continual avocations of publick business would permit, applied myself to make the best inquiries I could ...'

The paper then goes on to analyse the weaknesses of the distribution pipework, to consider various remedies that had evidently been proposed and to suggest his own preferred solution – of which more in due course.

Was this a genuine piece, and if so how had it been overlooked? The only modern work that mentioned it attributed it to Wren's son, also named Christopher, perhaps making that assumption because the publication was dated thirty years after Wren's death. But this seemed wrong. For one thing, Wren's knighthood was not hereditary and his son was plain Christopher, whereas the magazine refers to Sir Christopher. Then again, the reference to Soho Square plainly relates to the difficulties the company was experiencing around 1700, and that would fit in with Sir Christopher speaking of his age and the 'continual avocations of his public business'. Wren was 68 years old in 1700, had been Surveyor of the King's Works since 1669 and was involved in the construction of St Paul's Cathedral until after 1710.

Mylne's commonplace book

A document then came to light that helped to answer the question. Among the papers of the New River archive is a commonplace book of Robert Mylne, the New River Company's surveyor and engineer from 1767 until 1810. It is a foolscap sized leather bound notebook of blank pages, with Robert Mylne's signature on the flyleaf. Inside are various entries, some handwritten and some pasted in, all oddments relating to the New River. One of them is the text of the Wren report, carefully written out in full, and even identifying its source as the *Gentleman's Magazine*.

On closer examination it seemed that Mylne had also come across the article, and had asked somebody, perhaps a clerk, to copy it out in full. At the end is a short paragraph in what appears, from signed letters elsewhere, to be Mylne's own handwriting. What he wrote at the end of the Wren article was:

> 'There is no date to this paper. It may be supposed to have been wrote before the High Pond Service was established. He died in 1723. Tho' he is wrong on some particulars: Yet the hand of the Master is visible in this Sbozo.'[5]

Here, by a remarkable chance, was Mylne's private opinion on the very question of the authenticity of this piece, and it was an opinion deserving some respect. For not only was Mylne the 'surveyor' – in effect chief engineer – to the New River Company from 1767, but from October 1766 he was the surveyor of St Paul's Cathedral, both posts that he held for over forty years. In carrying out his duties at St Paul's he must often have needed to refer to Wren's notes and drawings. It was even Mylne, as it happened, who was responsible for the erection of the famous memorial tablet to Wren inside the cathedral, which tells the – classically educated – reader simply to look all around if they seek his monument: *lector, si monumentum requiris, circumspice.* Thus, by the pure chance of his two main occupations, Mylne was uniquely qualified to judge whether a document attributed to Wren and concerning the New River was genuine. What else can he mean when he speaks of 'the hand of the master' being visible in what he calls 'this Sbozo'?

Sbozo is a word that calls for an explanation. It is not in English dictionaries, nor bearing in mind Mylne's origins, in Scottish ones. He had underlined the word, perhaps indicating a foreign origin. A modern Italian dictionary provides the answer. Sbozo is not there, but Sbozzo is – a word used by painters meaning a rough outline or sketch, which fits well enough. Mylne had studied architecture in Rome for some years while on the Grand Tour, so the use of such a specialised word perhaps supports the view that the handwriting, and therefore the opinion, is indeed his. Mylne's note that the paper was 'before the High Pond service was established' would put its date before 1708.

'Sr Christ. Wrenn ...'

It seemed that Wren had indeed been consulted and that his views as printed deserved some scrutiny. Yet was there not still a possibility that the opinion was somebody else's, to which Wren's name had been attributed to make it seem worth publishing, and that Mylne had been taken in by the deception? Fortunately, confirmation of Wren's involvement then turned up among the letters in Robert Harley's correspondence now at Nottingham.[6] In June 1702 Edward Allen, Treasurer of the New River Company, wrote to tell Harley of a meeting to be held at the Water House at ten o'clock the following Friday, 12 June,

> '..to consider and settle (if itt may bee) how the water may be raysed and improved ... it were hoped to have Sr Christ. Wrenn and severall other persons who have proposed Engines ... to discourse largely about all matters relating thereunto and come to some resolucon thereon.'

That chance survival of a letter that many would have consigned to the wastepaper basket seems to put Wren's involvement beyond dispute. Taken together with Mylne's opinion it authenticates the *Gentleman's Magazine* article. It also usefully provides a date that was proving elusive. Other archives had already yielded copies of various proposals by those who had proposed solutions to the same problem, but they were undated. Here at last was a date to hang them on.

Wren's report

Wren's report makes a good starting point because in it he goes into much detail about what he regarded as the underlying faults of the distribution system for New River water once it left the Round Pond. Because it is not easily available elsewhere, the report is set out in full in Appendix 3. For present purposes a selective summary will be sufficient.

Wren began by setting out that he had been asked to give his 'thoughts about the most profitable distribution of the water, and particularly how the high parts about Soho Square might be supplied.' He went on to say that on looking into the present state of the matter he found fundamental mistakes had been made from the outset 'and every day since new errors have been added.' What should have been done at the outset was to draw an exact street map. The height of the reservoir above the Thames should then have been measured, and also the height of any hills and high ground. The height from reservoir to Thames should then be divided into four parts – so if it was 60 feet, then 15, 30, 45 and 60 feet regions. It could easily be shown by experiment that water would flow more strongly the further any given tap was below the level of the reservoir. Accordingly to ensure an equal supply to people in the higher parts as in the lower, there should be four different sizes of orifice for the four regions, the sizes calculated with some exactitude. The lowest ground would have the smallest, the higher ground the biggest. Furthermore, long mains should be avoided, as they slowed the velocity of the water. It would be better to have an intermediate cistern at some distance from the main reservoir, which could be filled directly by the main and could then in its turn supply local branch pipes. Such pipes should always, if possible, run level.

He summed up the problems:

> '1. There seem to have been more mains laid at first than are necessary; for the old undertakers having expended much money in bringing the river to the pond, were in haste to be reimbursed by taking in tenants ... as they offered; and as the city increased, they increased the branches, and lengthened the mains, carrying them down, and up, and down again, until the mains failed of carrying the quantity desired, being obstructed by air, or filth, or too long a run.
>
> 2. There was little care taken of levels, and so the lower parts of the town have too much by a great proportion, and great wastes are there made, and accidental breaches and leakages soon exhaust a whole main, whereas the upper parts and the most remote were too scantily supplied...
>
> 3. The ferrils which are put into the pipes, seem all of a size; which should be regulated according to the levels; every region having its peculiar size, to bring the force of the water to an equality.'

Wren then turned to the particular problem of the Soho neighbourhood. He observed that the New River officers were in favour of one proposal which involved a pump engine powered by three horses which it was said could raise sixty 'tuns' of water an hour to the height of thirty feet, whence it would go down again

25 Sir Christopher Wren, from a painting by Godfrey Kneller

into the mains. The supposed cost was said by the 'undertaker', or engineer as we might say, to be under £300 and the horses would cost £150 a year. Wren doubted this. The pump engine would cost 'very much more' than £300. He did not believe three horses could do that much work, and even if they could there would still need to be nine horses rather than three, to allow for changes. Two men would be needed to tend the horses. As for the costs of keeping the pumps in order 'the engine itself will spend, in brass, iron, leather, and oil, more than the feeding of another horse.' If it went wrong it would cost money to repair, and meanwhile the tenants would be left without water. There would also be the cost of the tower, up which the water was to rise thirty feet, and stables would have to be built for the horses.

Sir Christopher was not in favour of the horse pump. 'I think an engine is not adviseable, if the place can be supplied without one, as I think it may.' His solution was very simple. He had gone with some of the company's men to Soho Square to see how much water the six inch main could deliver. Thirty tuns an hour, he concluded. There was a piece of higher ground at Soho Square, just nine feet below the level of the pond. A cistern should be built there, supplied direct by a seven inch main. This would provide the necessary water. He ended with a summary of this finding, and a courteous flourish:

> 'So that I am confident a 7 inch main, running into a cistern, day and night, built properly at Soho and thereabouts, would be more useful than an engine; which is submitted to better judgment.'

Submitted it doubtless was, but it does not seem to have been followed. More mains may have been laid but nowhere is there a mention of a cistern at Soho Square. Other proposals were afoot, and if they came from less distinguished sources they may yet have been persuasively presented..

'... and severall other persons...'

There is nothing in the paper to identify the contractor whose three-horse engine and thirty-foot tower Wren refers to. The details resemble, but do not quite match, the others that survive, and doubtless other proposals have been lost. Only one of them had always been in the New River archive, the others have turned up more recently, from various private collections

One of them has the merit of bearing a date. Among Robert Harley's papers is an original letter three pages long from one Evan Jones, dated 1 October 1701.[7] It begins:

> 'Honoured Sir, According to your desire I have made the following Observations of the Advantages your Company of the New River Water will Reape by haveing the Water Raised at the River head 15 or 20 foot high, and the Disadvantages that will accrue if not Speedily done.'

There follows a carefully structured and persuasive argument. It deals with the newly built West End, where the New River had a competitor in the form of the small Hampstead Waterworks. Jones claimed there were several thousand families in what he called the 'Upgrounds of this district', most of whom would take New River water if it could be 'effectually served'. By contrast, he said that many existing customers around Swallow Street had such a bad supply that they were begging the Hampstead company to lay pipes in their streets. Jones suggested raising the New River water by fifteen or twenty feet to prevent these ills. He presumably had in mind some kind of water tower, but does not explain it.

> 'The advantages of my engine is in the Easinesse, Quicknesse and Strength of its Motion With the Improbability of its not being often out of Order. And since I have finished the engine I have now at work I find £40 per annum will keep all the engines in repaire as will be required to raise two seven inch mains of water 20 foot high besides some few horses to keep the motion agoing, and by laying pipes at Islington, would overpay that charge'.

He goes on to claim that the engine has parts in reserve so that if any fault develops they can be used until the others are refitted: 'By which Rule the worke need not stand still half an hour at any one time'. Finally Jones delivers a warning, and one that the New River Company might have done well to heed:

> 'Many may give in proposalls and demonstrate matters seemingly above plaine. But oftens when Notions are putt in practice they fall much short of Expectation. What I propose to perform is not to say what may be done but what is actually at work. All which I leave to your Honour's most serious consideration, That am, Yr Hon's, Most humble and obedient Serv't, Evan Jones.'

On close examination, this letter is surprisingly vague as to detail. The language is flowery and there is a good deal of repetition. He repeatedly returns to the theme of the thousands of families who would gladly take New River water if only they had the chance, putting it in a slightly different way each time. He does say what the annual running costs of the engines will be, but not what the purchase price is, nor even how many engines will be needed – just 'all the engines ... as will be required'. How many horses will be needed to do the work? His answer seems to be 'some few horses to keep the motion agoing'. He writes of an engine he has finished, but does not say where it can be seen working.

What he proposes is a horse engine to 'raise two seven inch maines of water 20 feet high'. The letter stands alone, and the name of Evan Jones does not appear in any of the other company documents of this time. Was he one of the 'severall other persons' who were asked to attend the same meeting as Wren eight months later, in June 1702? Was he even perhaps the 'undertaker' whose proposals were favoured by the officers of the company but so disparaged by Wren? There is insufficient detail in his letter to say either way. One difference is that Wren talks of a proposal to lift the water thirty feet high, whereas Jones, in this letter at any rate, does not venture beyond twenty.

The next document is also one among Robert Harley's papers, but this time among those that have found their way to the British Library.[8] It is undated, but the heading summarises it:

> *'A proposall for raising the New River water at Islington made by Charles Beckingham to the New River company.'*

Who Beckingham was is unknown. The proposal gives no indication of his occupation or address, though it does end with a request that he should be given the house at New River Head to live in, so as to keep his machines running and maintained. As for his proposal, like that of Jones it is rather vague. He speaks of raising the water at Islington to supply four main pipes 'to be continually supplied with as much water, and as full as now they are, or can draw off.' Each main would supply 'three times the number of tenants as it now doth' and 'the water shall rise ... 12 feet higher than now it rises.'

He offers to provide the materials for what he calls 'the experiment engine or engines' at his own expense, and that he will keep them 'in good repaire and continually working at his own charge and cost.' His charge for this is to be 'a sum of money not exceeding 50 pouns' for each of the four mains, payable within one month of satisfactory completion, and thereafter £200 a year for so long as the engines work. He goes on to offer that if the company wants to have the same rise in height on any of their other mains, he will provide it for £25 each main and £25 a year thereafter. Finally, before asking to live in the Water House, he stipulated that no one but he should be employed to work the engines.

Beckingham's proposal is at least precise as to cost. But what on earth is his 'experiment engine'? One clue may be the sentence:

> 'That in the making of this experiment engine or engines or in the working thereof the water shall not be thereby wasted or let out from the ponds or cisterns at Islington or afterwards (broaches in the main pipes only excepted).'

There is no obvious reason why a horse-engine should 'waste' water, save that which the horses drink, and the same could be said of a windmill. It sounds as though Beckingham was planning a waterwheel that would be turned by the water of the New River as the London Bridge wheels were turned by the current of the Thames. It would have required some fall of water to make it work, but the water that turned the wheel need not be wasted – it could be still be run into one of the mains which served the lower parts of the city. The fact that he regarded the engine as experimental, and wrote of providing all the necessary materials – rather than supplying the engine – at his own expense is consistent with a waterwheel. Such a wheel would be large and heavy, and would have to be assembled on site. The reference to 'broaches in the main pipes' not being his responsibility would apply to any pumping system, where the increased pressure might well cause broaches or bursts in the wooden pipes. On balance, it was probably a waterwheel he planned. If so, as things turned out the company might have been wise to have accepted his proposal.

Lowthorp at Highbury

The company, then, had some conflicting suggestions. For Wren it was no engine at all, just a cistern down in Soho Square. For Evan Jones it was a horse engine lifting water twenty feet into some kind of header tank. For Beckingham it was probably a waterwheel that would pump water twelve feet higher than it was.

No decision was made, and in May 1704 Lowthorp wrote the report already mentioned, favouring a waterwheel. At the end of that report he had suggested that the flow of the New River needed to be measured and also the levels of the various mains, before deciding which type of engine to use. That task he was asked to do, for in the same bundle of Harley papers is Lowthorp's *'Report of several experiments and observations concerning the quantity of water constantly conveyed to Islington by the New River'*. This is dated 9 June 1704, within a month of his earlier report, and describes the simple method he used. He went to Highbury Frame, the wooden aqueduct that carried the New River high over Hackney Brook in the north of Islington. This had very regular dimensions, more so than the ordinary winding course of the New River, and having calculated the quantity of water it held, he simply measured the time a floating object took to travel from one end to the other as it was carried along by the current. This enabled him to conclude that the stream conveyed 1680 tuns an hour, or more than 40,000 tuns a day – sufficient to supply 80,000 houses, which he said was more than the total number in London and Westminster. In the light of his earlier report, this seemed to pave the way for a waterwheel, his preferred method, even if the waste water from the wheel would need to be saved by being fed into a main and used to supply some district on lower ground.

An experiment with pumps

All this might have been expected to bring things to some swift conclusion, but it was not so. The next document to shed light on these events is among a batch that turned up at a Christie's auction in 1988, and is dated almost a year later, in April 1705.[9] It seems that a committee had been set up to consider the matter, and they required a report from the collector who served the district around Holborn, Soho and the higher parts, the exotically named Maximilian Apprice. He had been a collector since 1677, and if his name sounds remarkable for a humble collector from the waterworks, it should be borne in mind that collectors were allowed to keep 5% of the monies they collected. This could amount to a considerable sum – Apprice's area took in a hundred streets and served over two thousand customers – and the job may have had other perquisites. The Earl of Clarendon's diary from the 1680s has many references to one Thomas Apprice whom he sent around the country on various personal errands – perhaps Maximilian was related (*ill.13, p.57*).

Ephraim Green, another long-standing employee as the company's City Surveyor, who supervised work at New River Head for a salary of £50 a year, was asked to join with Apprice in preparing the report. This sets out the problem. The existing mains were insufficient to supply Apprice's customers or those of his colleague Thomas St Hill who had the area west from St Martin's lane to the Strand, 'Pell Mell', and St James's, thence up to Stratton Street and Golden Square. They said there had to be either two new mains laid or an engine at New River Head to raise the water twenty feet higher than it was and thereby force more water through the existing mains. A new main to Apprice's walk at Bloomsbury, 1600 yards from the head, would cost about £550 plus £100 or so for the land needed. That to St Hill's walk at Dean Street, about 3000 yards, would cost about £1000 plus something for the land. None of this expense was necessary, they reported, if an engine at the New River Head could add twenty feet of height and supply two mains in each walk on alternate days with one third more water than they currently received.

The committee considered the report, and after discussion it seems that Apprice favoured a thirty foot increase at the head. By way of practical suggestion Green then suggested an experiment – to obtain some pumps that could be worked at the head to raise the water just twenty feet higher, and see what effect this had on the supply to Golden Square, which was reckoned to be the highest ground the company served. The committee approved of this, so Green set up two double handled and two single handled pumps, and had them worked by a total of eight men:

> 'which upon the first & second Tryals, broke 2 pipes of the 6 inch maine, but that being repaired, and 6 pumps set at work againe on the 5th of September 1705. Wee whose names are hereunto subscribed did find the water rose out of the 3 inch pipe on the west side of Golden Square about 4 Canes (or 14 ft), which without the pumps would not rise there one cane.... In Soho Square also wee found the water whilst the pumps were working, to rise about 4 canes, but without the pumps would rise but 2.'

The three shareholders who signed this report were the oddly-named Mr Bempde, whose obituary in due course would say he was 'possessed of a vast estate', Mr Lane, and John Grene who was also the company secretary at a salary of £100 a year, and unrelated to the City surveyor Ephraim Green. Their report concluded from the pumping trials that great benefit would accrue from a pumping engine.

Or a windmill?

Then, for the first time in the surviving papers, a windmill was seriously proposed. The committee reported that the cost of an engine with a windmill would be £1000, with running costs of £80 a year. An engine without a windmill would cost just £550, but its annual running costs would come to £160 'according to an estimate delivered on Friday last to the weekly meeting'. Unfortunately, the estimate has not been found and so its authorship is unknown.

So more than a year after Lowthorp's report – which had warned the company that windmills seemed 'altogether unfit for the company's service' the committee was putting forward a windmill as their first option. The second engine they refer to, 'without a windmill' could hardly be less helpfully described. It was probably a horse mill, as its annual cost of £160 is twice that of the windmill and there is no obvious reason why a waterwheel should cost twice as much as a windmill to keep in repair.

Lowthorp tries again

More months passed, and Lowthorp reported again. Once more the document is among Harley's papers. It is undated but begins with a note from Lowthorp that he had intended to put it before the General Court in November 1705, but sickness prevented him.[10]

The tone of this report is rather different from his earlier one. Previously he had said that it was 'most certain' that proper engines would improve the service, and that it did not appear any other expedient would have equal success. Now he was less sure. He seemed to agree with Wren's earlier view – though he does not mention Wren – that perhaps the problem was not the lack of height but rather the 'unreasonable and unequall distribution of the water after it enters the town'.

> 'I have no intention by what I have said to obstruct the design of erecting an engine for raising the water at Islington, but I should not act faithfully with the company if I did not dissuade them from such suddain and immature resolution, as I easily foresee will prove much more chargeable to them than they yet apprehend'.

He goes on to propose that the supply should be reorganised with the aim of providing a good service in the City even up to first floor level. If any engine is found to be necessary, it should be powered by nothing but the company's own water. Before any such engine was erected, or any work done beyond laying new pipes where necessary 'all the circumstances of the charge and profitt shall be so clearly estimated that no room shall be left to fear a disappointment.' This can only mean that he still believed that if pumping was necessary a waterwheel was the only suitable method.

Obviously the necessary enquiries would involve a lot of work, and Lowthorp finally got to the point, asking to be made General Surveyor to the company 'with a reasonable salary' so that he could deal with 'this troublesome and difficult undertakeing'.

Perhaps the company would have been wise to accede to this request. They seem not to have done so, as a document exists to show that Lowthorp was still angling for that job six years later, in 1711. In the intervening years the new works had been delayed again and again. Finally, in 1708 the work had been done, but in a way that was quite against what Lowthorp had advised.

CHAPTER TWELVE

Sorocold's Solution 1707 to 1711

Sorocold's 'Proposalls' – An Upper Pond – The New Works – The landlord of The Angel – A mill with two motives? – Trouble with the mill – Yarnold and Preston – A mill with six sails – Reaping the whirlwind – 'A foot too narrow ...' – The square horse-works – The mystery of Sorocold – Early works – Sorocold in London

Sorocold's 'Proposalls'

In 1707 the members of the New River Company at last reached a decision on how the supply was to be improved. In doing so they ignored the advice they had received independently from two members of the Royal Society – Sir Christopher Wren and the Rev. John Lowthorp – and opted for a solution that was elaborate, expensive and experimental.

All the earlier proposals had involved pumping the water twenty or thirty feet up as Wren put it, 'to fall again into the main'. He pointed out that this would need some kind of tower, and went on to point out the disadvantage. The increased pressure could be maintained only for so long as the pumping continued. As soon as it stopped – for any reason – the pressure would instantly drop. To quote Wren again, 'If the engine breaks the repair is chargeable, and the while the tenants want water.'

Traditionally the design of the New Works has been attributed to George Sorocold, but without referring to any documentary source that confirms this. It is now possible to identify such a source and so put the matter beyond dispute. It is a document in the vast archive of New River papers inherited by the Metropolitan Water Board, passed on by them to Thames Water and now in the London Metropolitan Archive, where it is catalogued as a 'proposal for raising the New River water by George Sorocold.' It seems to have escaped notice in the past, perhaps because it does not bear a date, and perhaps because of the number of documents in the collection. It is a single folded sheet in a legible and decorative hand, presumably the work of a scribe or clerk, and very different from Sorocold's own rough scrawl, which exists elsewhere.[1] Like so many other documents of its type from that time, its heading provides a good summary of its contents:

> *'PROPOSALLS for raising water at Islington for the use of the governor and Company of the new river, to serve Mr Apprice's and Mr St Hill's walks abt. 20 foot higher than now they are served. by Geo: Sorocold.'*

This is a promising start. As already noted, Apprice and St Hill were the two collectors covering the West End at the relevant time.

After the heading the Sorocold proposal goes into detail:

> 'There being a piece of ground abt. 26 foot higher than the surface of the water in the present ponds at Islington and not above 300 yards distance, being the lands of the Rt. Honble. the Earl of Clarendon,

1st I propose to make a pond at that height and distance to hold about 6000 tuns of water for a sum not exceeding 150£.

2d I propose to erect a windmill at the head of the out pond which chall fill the upper pond: the sd. windmill and all it's materialls not to exceed the sum of 470£.

3d This windmill in time of wind shall serve two maines to each walk – every other day and in case of the slacknesse of wind then the upper pond to supply that defect.

4th That if the wind shall not be sufficient to carry the work and that the upper pond shall be drawne off. Then I propose to supply these defects with horse sufficient to do the work at my charge for ye sume of 80£ p. ann.

And as to ye yearly charge of servants to attend and work the said mill as also the continuall ware & tare thereof; I propose to undertake the whole for the sum of 40 £ p ann.

Being ord'ed to make a report abt the service of the tenants in the town of Islington, upon a strick enquiry I find – that the landlords of many houses, and other housekeepers are willing to lay in the water, when it shall be brought, – whereby I compute the whole of Islington may bring in above 200£ p. ann.'

The proposal goes on to set out calculations to show that the contents of the new pond will be sufficient to keep Apprice's and St Hill's walks supplied for ten days without the help of the windmill.

Company records show that new works consisting of an Upper Pond and a windmill were indeed built in 1707-8. The pond was dug on land belonging to the Earl of Clarendon and at just about the height and distance mentioned by Sorocold. It seems safe to take the document as evidence of Sorocold having been the engineer, just as tradition tells us. Once more Robert Mylne provides help with this attribution as there is a note in what looks his handwriting on the outside folds of the single sheet – *'New River water, Proposal by G. Sorocold to Raise water to the upper Pond – Very probably adopted'*.

An Upper Pond

Of all the proposals for improving the supply, Sorocold's is the only one to suggest that an Upper Pond should be dug on the hilltop. It proved to be the one feature of the New Works that stood the test of time. As recently as 2003, the reservoir that still stands on the same site was refurbished and brought back into use after having been unused for about ten years.

At one stroke, the Upper Pond provided both the extra height that was needed to supply the higher districts and a large reserve capacity to smooth out any fluctuations between supply and demand. Thus, although it went against the proposals of Wren and Lowthorp, it completely answered Wren's objections to the idea of a water tower, which had been that the supply would instantly fail if the pumps stopped working for any reason.

It is interesting to note that Sorocold was offering what we might now call a complete package. In summary, his proposals amounted to capital costs of £620 for digging the pond and building the windmill, and thereafter £120 a year to be paid to him. In return, he would supply and pay the necessary staff, keep the machinery in repair and supply horses as and when needed to supplement the windmill. And – if his appraisal was right – the annual payments to him would be more than offset by the extra £200 gained from new tenants in Islington, whose properties had previously been too high to be supplied.

Taken as a whole, it must have seemed a very attractive proposal. It would finally settle the complaints of poor supply to the West End while opening up a new range of customers in Islington. Islington then was no more than a village, but it was already starting to expand.

It might be said that there is still a certain lack of detail in Sorocold's proposals. He does not mention the costs of building the extra mains that will be needed to pump water to the new pond and thence to link it to Apprice's and St Hill's mains. Nor does he deal with the costs of supplying water to Islington. That would be a completely new supply – what would be the cost of buying or leasing the land to lay the pipes in, and what about the cost of

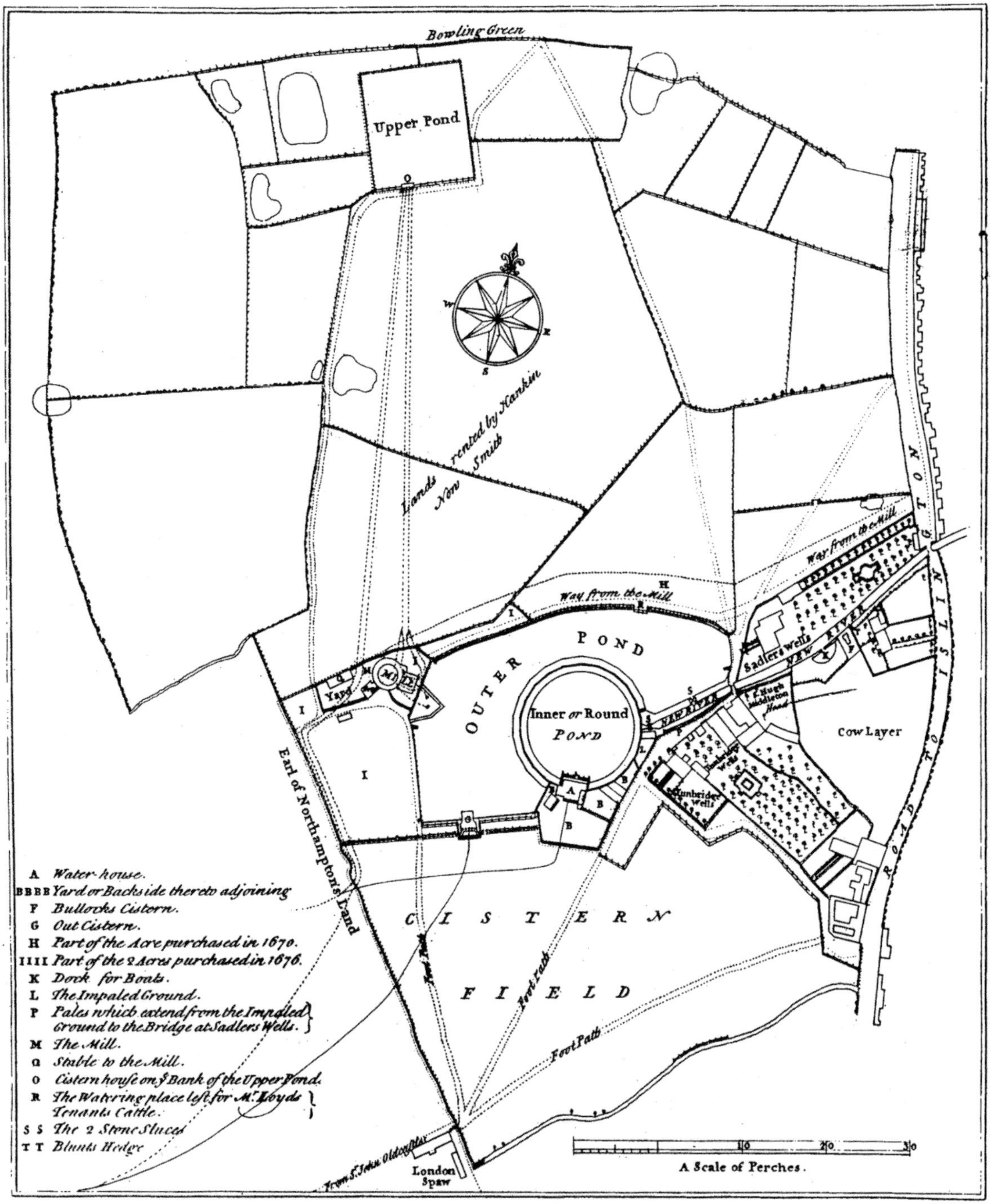

26 Plan, possibly the 'Plan of the New River Head' engraved by James Cole in 1741 at a cost of 2 guineas, for a lawsuit between the New River Company and the Lloyd family. The square adjacent to the right side of the windmill 'M' is the 'square horse-works', built in about 1720 to provide extra pumping and shown in many illustrations. The dotted lines are pipes through which water was pumped to the Upper Pond, and then flowed back down with greater pressure to join the mains flowing from the outer pond.

the pipes themselves? We are not told. Sorocold is keen to sell his plan and just mentions the supposed benefit in vague terms – '...Islington may bring in above 200£ p ann.'

Neither does he spell out any details of how the horses will pump the water when the windmill is not turning. No ordinary windmill could be worked by horses, yet the proposal does not mention an extra set of pumps for the horses to be harnessed to. There is reason to think that he intended to construct a dual-purpose building. This would have needed a windmill tower on top, with shafts geared down to the water pumps below, and room for the horses to tramp round somehow in the base, with a system of beams, shafts and cogs so that they could work, presumably, the same pumps. If this was his plan, did anyone ask him whether it had ever been done before, and with what success?

Above all, nowhere does Sorocold explain how many days a year he thinks a windmill will work on this relatively sheltered site, well below the summit of Islington Hill. The question is rather brushed aside by his offer to provide horses when necessary 'if the wind shall not be sufficient' for a flat fee of £80 a year.

The New Works

There is no record of the New River Company meeting that finally decided in favour of Sorocold's proposals. It may have been an acrimonious one. Was Robert Harley there, perhaps determined that this matter must be forced to a conclusion after the endless dithering of the past ten years? Others present may have been very doubtful. Was Lowthorp asked for his views? Did no one remember his written advice from 1704: '..Wind engines are so very uncertain, from frequent calms and storms, that they seem altogether unfit for the Company's service, which is Continuall and Equall'?

Whatever the doubts the plan went ahead. Because it involved the acquisition of rights over land, lawyers were involved and deeds were prepared, which have survived and give some detail. As to the land on which the Upper Pond was to be built, it did indeed belong to the Earl of Clarendon as Sorocold's proposal said, jointly with someone else. It was a small part of some fields used for pasturing animals. These had been leased to one Henry Hankin, and his lease still had another 17 years to run. The conditions of his lease did not allow for such things as ponds to be excavated. Fortunately, the Earl of Clarendon was a major shareholder in the New River.

Three documents accordingly came into being between March and May 1708.[2] By the first Clarendon released Hankin from any liability for breaching his lease if he allowed the New River company to dig a pond on one acre of the land. By the second Hankin undertook to the New River Company that as soon as he had the necessary licence he would sublet that acre to the company for £10 a year 'to dig the same as they shall have occasion for the convenience of their works.' The same document records 'whereas the licence ... is not yet obtained & the sd govr & compy have found it necessary for them forthwith to begin to dig the said acre of ground, and the said Henry Hankin hath agreed not to oppose the same.'

It seems from this that there was some real urgency at last to make a start on the work, perhaps because of the importance of finishing this enormous excavation – which would have to be dug by hand – before bad weather made the ground unworkable.

The landlord of *The Angel*

The third document is of some interest, and seems to have been a concession given to Hankin in return for his compliance in letting the digging begin ahead of time. Anyone who has played the English version of the property-dealing board game Monopoly will recall that one of the least valuable squares is called *The Angel, Islington*. This district took its name from a pre-Reformation inn, which stood at the southern tip of the village of Islington. Until its demolition in 1819, it was a substantial old place with a galleried courtyard in which plays had been performed in Elizabethan times. Hogarth and Rowlandson both drew scenes there. Long into the eighteenth century it was still used as a final stopping point for travellers heading towards London to stay a night. In

1819 it was rebuilt as a coaching inn, but that was in its turn replaced in 1899. The 1899 building, which still stands, began as a hotel, was then a Lyon's Corner House Restaurant from 1921 until 1959 and has been used as a bank since 1982.

Henry Hankin, it seemed, owned or leased the Angel Inn. By the third document the New River company agrees to provide a supply of water 'from the pond now making' into the yard of the Angel Inn before the 29 September 1708, 'in sufficient quantities for the use of the said Henry Hankin .. and the customers resorting thereto, their horses and cattle' in return for the yearly rent of 'a peppercorne at the feast of St Michael ye Archangel, if the same shall be lawfully demanded.'

It seems to follow that the pond was being built in the summer of 1708. The windmill was already built by this time – a deed of 6 November 1707 dealing with the right to lay pipes between the windmill and the pond refers to '...the windmill work lately erected ...'. It might have been expected that the problem was at last solved, after all those years of discussion and all the advice. Sadly, it was not so.

A mill with two motives?

There are several reasons for thinking that what Sorocold designed was no ordinary windmill. Quite apart from the fact that it was a tower mill and had six sails, both very unusual features in England at that time, it seems to have contained a horse mill in the base as an alternative motive power. If so, it may have been unique. There are four descriptions of the windmill which, when taken together, suggest that was so. First, Sorocold's own proposal says

> '4th That if the wind shall not be sufficient to carry the work and that the Upper Pond shall be drawne off. Then I propose to supply these defects with horse sufficient to do the work at my charge for ye sume of 80£ p. ann.'

He does not say that the horses would be working inside the structure, but neither does he exclude the possibility. Next is Defoe's description of 1726, which is set out in full on p.135:

> '...and this higher Basin they fill from the lower, by a great Engine worked formerly with six sails, now by many Horses constantly working;'

This is at best ambiguous. He may be referring to the windmill tower or he may mean that the horses were all in the Square Horse-works, which was built at the side of the windmill soon after 1720, or he may be referring to both.

Then, however, comes a description in *The Builder's Dictionary* of 1734, which is accurate in many other respects. Having described the new mill erected near the windmill (presumably, the square horse-works), it says '... both of which are drawn by horses.' On the face of it, this must mean that in addition to the square horse-works, the windmill tower was still being used for pumping, but with horses instead of sails. If so, it was indeed a dual-purpose structure.

The clinching piece of evidence comes among some undated notes under the heading 'New River Engine' in a notebook kept by Thomas Coke, a landowner for whom Sorocold designed garden fountains. After dealing with the cost of the 'Windmill Engine att Islington wch works 4 Engines that raise the water to a Pond 24 feet higher than where the Mill stands,' it continues:

> 'This Mill is a foot too narrow at the bottom in the circumference to work well with Horses when the wind fails, as it was intended it should.'

Leaving aside for the moment the fault he describes, this can only mean that the windmill was indeed a mill designed for two motive powers. It is unfortunate that no drawing of what must have been a very unusual mechanism is known to have survived.

The pumps in the windmill base may have survived until at least 1769, as a note added to some pumping calculations, possibly by Robert Mylne the engineer, records that 'both horse engines were at work'.

Trouble with the mill

The best evidence that the 1708 works were not an unqualified success comes from a report Lowthorp wrote for the company on 16 July

27 New River Head from the north east c.1753. Sadler's Wells is on the left. The building to the left of the windmill tower is the 'square horse-works', built c.1720.

1711.[3] This was some three years after the completion of the 'New Works' – the Upper Pond and the pumps that filled it – which had been hoped to rescue the company's fortunes. Unfortunately, Lowthorp does not spell out what problems there may have been with the new works – perhaps they were already too familiar to those who would read his report. Having criticised the lack of specialised technical knowledge on the part of the company's servants, including the secretary, Ephraim Green, Lowthorp continues,

> 'The want of this knowledge I conceive to have been the occasion of a great part of the expenses the company has been put to for some years past, which has sunk their revenue ... from £15,000 to £11,000. All their attempts to remove one defect have still served to discover another ... However, what is already past cannot be recalled. All that remains to be done is to make the best use of the New-Works they are capable of, and to remedy all other defects with the greatest certainty and at the least charge.'

This reference to making 'the best use of the New-Works they are capable of' hardly sounds like a ringing commendation for Sorocold's efforts, and suggests there may have been something radically wrong in the design.

Yarnold and Preston

Further information comes from a document in a small bundle relating to New River Company affairs between 1700 and 1713 that was auctioned by Christie's in 1988.[4] It seems to have come from the family papers of the wealthy Mr Bempde, who had New River shares and took a keen interest in the company. It is undated, but it refers to the windmill as existing, and defective, so must be after 1707. It also proposes to leave the question of payment for certain proposed works to be decided by the Earl of Rochester. As the Earl died on 2 May 1711 it follows that the faults must have been apparent by that time, barely three years after the work was first done.

The document is a proposal by two people whose names occur nowhere else in the New River papers – John Yarnold and John Preston. It proposes the construction of a large building, fifty feet by forty, to contain 'a Horse Work Ingin for fforceing Waters', consisting of an upright shaft, a cog wheel, two horizontal shafts and other equipment including twelve pumps to be worked by ten horses. This they say will pump water both to the Upper Pond and to a new cistern in Bloomsbury fifty feet by thirty, and six foot deep together with two new pipe mains. The proposal explains that all this work is necessary because the present system allows air to be drawn into the mains, forming 'an oppression of air that lyes in the pipes' – what we might call an airlock. It is said that when the work has been done 'you may be assured your tenants will be served to their satisfaction' – a claim that must have had a dreadfully familiar ring.

Wren, it seems, was perhaps right when he had observed that the mistakes in the pipe layout were fundamental.

The reference by Yarnold and his partner to the windmill being defective is this:

> 'Note. That after I have brought the horse work to perfection, I will alter the Windwork soe as to make it goe much easier than it does, and raise more water.'

Plainly there was some fundamental problem with the windmill, and it is a pity they do not set out what it was. Whether Yarnold and Preston did carry out any work for the company is not recorded. Probably not, at least in the full form they proposed, as there is no record of a new cistern being built at Bloomsbury at that time. There certainly was a large new building containing a horse engine on the site by the 1720s, immediately adjacent to the east side of the windmill. It became known as the 'square horse-works', perhaps to distinguish it from the windmill, and can be seen in many illustrations from then on including one by Canaletto. It continued in use until the 1760s, as John Smeaton described it being at work with four horses in 1766. Who built it tradition does not say. Perhaps it was Yarnold and Preston after all.

A mill with six sails

What exactly was wrong with the windmill? Contemporary publications do not provide much help, apart from two books. Daniel Defoe mentions it in his *Tour Through the Whole Island of Great Britain* published in 1726:

> 'The New River, which is brought by an Aqueduct or artificial stream from Ware, continues to supply the greater Part of the City with Water, only with this Addition by the way, that they have been obliged to dig a new Head or Basin at Islington on a higher ground than that which the natural Stream of the River supplies, and this higher Basin they fill from the lower, by a great Engine worked formerly with six sails, now by many Horses constantly working; so from that new Elevation of the Water, they supply the higher Part of Town with the same Advantage, and more Ease than the Thames Engines do it.'

If Sorocold's mill did have six sails, it was technically very advanced for England at that time, and this may have brought its own problems. All of the well-known illustrations of the windmill at New River Head show it without its sails and are no help on this point. There are just two documents that support Defoe's description. One is a map of London by Morden and Lee published around 1720. At New River Head it shows a conventional symbol to depict a windmill, which although tiny unquestionably has six arms (*p.136*).

The other is a topographical engraving of the buildings in Red Lion Square by Sutton Nicholls. Sketched in tiny rough outline along the northern skyline are clusters of buildings, one of which is marked 'Islington' and includes a windmill. It is such a minor detail of the picture that it is little more than a squiggle, but under a magnifying glass it can be seen to have six sails. There is no other record of a windmill on the hilltop at Islington which could have been visible from the direction of Red Lion Square, let alone one with six sails, and it seems to follow that Sorocold's mill had six sails.

Reaping the whirlwind

The other book with some detail about the windmill is *'The Builder's Dictionary, or Gentleman's and Architect's Companion'* which has some interesting information about the windmill. It dates from 1734 and, unlike Defoe's, contains information about storm damage not referred to in other publications. It is as follows:

> 'About 30 years ago, there was a Wind-mill erected near the New-River, between London and Islington, with six Wings, being the admirable Contrivance of that ingenious Architect Mr Surrocole, in order to convey Water from the lower Ponds, through Pipes under Ground, to a new one made on the Top of the Hill, consisting of an acre of ground, which serves successfully to supply the great Increase of new Buildings of London, especially the West-ward, but a sudden Gust of Wind, or rather a Whirle-wind, blew it down about 20 Years ago: however it was soon restored: it was also on the 20th of November 1720, blown down again, by a terrible high Wind that then happened; but the Proprietors have not thought fit to put up the Sails again, but erected another Mill near it; both of which are drawn by horses.'

As to the first damage referred to, no date is given but it is interesting that it is described as a 'sudden gust of wind' rather than a storm. One of the known hazards of windmills is that they are very susceptible to damage if the wind suddenly reverses its direction. This is very unusual, but can happen when there is an advancing thunderstorm in hot weather. The phenomenon is known as 'tail-winding'. At best it tears the cloth from the sails, at worst it can reverse the direction of the machinery and cause a fire by friction, or in the case of a tower-mill – as Sorocold's was – the cap and sails may be torn off completely. It is apparently something that a skilful miller is always on the alert for.

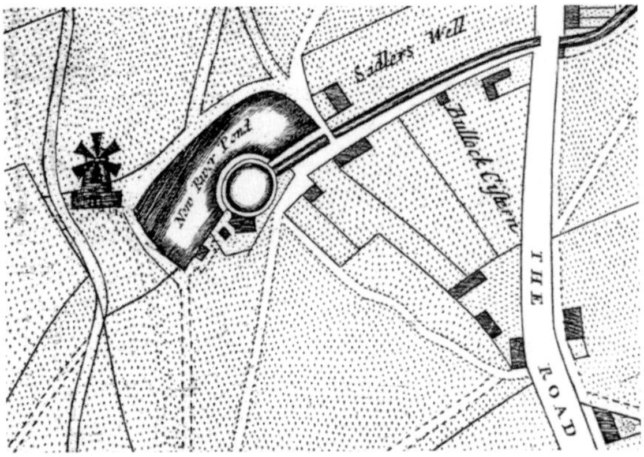

28 Early map by Morden and Lee c.1720, confirming that the windmill had six sails, as Defore and others describe it, instead of the more usual four.

The second occasion when damage was caused sounds like a more general storm. Weather records from that period confirm there was such a storm on 20 November 1720. A news-sheet from the time, the *Post-boy* which provided shipping information, records a 'violent storm' that day which dismasted a Lisbon-bound ship off Ramsgate, drove a frigate on to Sandwich Flats, caused great damage to about 20 coasters at Harwich, and damaged houses on the east coast as well as driving an enormous whale ashore at Padstow. The *Post-boy* does not mention a windmill anywhere, but perhaps it was only concerned with coastal damage. There was a move to restore the windmill sails in 1742, when the works committee so recommended, but nothing ever came of this.[5]

'A foot too narrow...'

Quite the most useful information about the windmill's faults came unexpectedly, in a dusty muniment room, the old dovecot of Melbourne Hall in Derbyshire. The purpose of going there was to see a few letters written by Sorocold, who designed fountains for the formal gardens there, and kept up correspondence with Thomas Coke the owner of the house, who was away in London. In an old worn notebook that had entries concerning the gardens and had no known link to Sorocold, the words 'New River Engine' at the top of a page suddenly stood out. Astonishingly Coke, who was interested in the technicalities of water pumping for his garden, had jotted down some notes of what must surely have been told him by Sorocold about the New River works – two pieces of information possibly not recorded anywhere else.

Underneath the heading 'New River Engine' he had written:

> 'The Charge of makeing the Windmill Engine att Islington which works 4 Engines that raise the water to a Pond 24 ft higher than where the Mill stands came to £1073 9s. 11d.'

There seems no reason to doubt the accuracy of this precise sum recorded in the private notebook of a man who had regular dealings with Sorocold in the early 1700s. Even if this cost covers all the expenses including digging the pond and laying the pipes, it is well above Sorocold's written estimate, which cannot have pleased the Company. Then, after some notes about the cost of pipe-boring at the New River yard, the entry continued:

> 'This Mill is a foot too narrow at the bottom in the circumference to work well with Horses when the wind fails, as it was intended it should.'

This confirms the dual nature of the mill as well as identifying its weakness. The fault is a serious one and almost impossible to remedy. Once a circular brick tower has been built, there is no practicable way of increasing its internal dimensions. A one-foot difference in the circumference would only have been a very small percentage of the total – little more than 1%. The writer probably meant diameter rather than circumference, which would have been nearer a 4% error. If so, it may have meant that the horses were walking in a circle that was too small for them to use their strength efficiently. As can be seen today, the internal diameter of the base is barely 22 feet 6 inches, and this does seem very small for horses working heavy machinery. Although records exist of single horse-mills as small as 18 feet, 24 to 26 feet is more usual, and 28 to 36 feet and larger not unknown. One early engineer, writing in 1734, explained it as follows:

> 'When a horse draws in a Mill, Waterwork or Gin (engine) of any Kind... great Care should be taken that the horse work be large enough in Diameter, otherwise the Horse cannot exert all his Force as he goes round .. The Horse Work should not be less that 40 feet in diameter wherever there is room for it ... In a Walk of 19 foot Diameter I have known a Horse lose two fifths of the force that he exerted in a 40 foot Walk.'[6]

How was such an error made? The likely reason is that Sorocold was trying out an untested theory – all his previous expertise seems to have related to waterwheels. One writer who examined the circular base that remains at New River Head wrote that by its date it is one of the first tower mills to have been built in England. He noted that there is much irregularity in the brickwork, and comments that millwrights accustomed to building wooden mills 'had not yet developed the skill with bricks which characterises 19th-century tower mills.'

So it seems that after all those years of indecision, the New River Company had plumped for a dual-purpose mill that was seriously faulty. Not only was the windmill unable to survive high winds to the extent that it was put out of action twice in the first twelve years of its life, but according to Yarnold and Preston it needed attention 'to make it goe much easier than it does' within three years of being built. As for the horsemill in the base, it had been built too small to work properly, and that could not be cured.

The slow decline of the windmill structure can be seen in many drawings from the eighteenth century. At first it is shown with its cap and finial but no sails or arms. Later the cap has gone, and there is castellated brickwork at the top. By about 1790 the upper parts were removed and it was reduced to its present stump, roofed, and used for storage.

The square horse-works

Soon after 1720 the building known as the Square horse-works was put up, abutting the east side of the mill tower. There are many illustrations showing the two buildings together (*ill.27, p.134*). It may have been a costly way of pumping water, but it did at least work for over forty years. It lasted until about 1770, by which time Smeaton's 'fire-engine' was working. In 1779 the minutes mention the place 'where the horseworks formerly stood, near the tower at Islington,' so it had gone by then.[7]

In the circumstances, it is not surprising that Sorocold does not seem to have continued as the company's engineer. In 1709-11, the company sought advice from Lowthorp again, from Yarnold and Preston as mentioned, and from one Robert Aldersey who had made a water pump at Blenheim Palace for the Duke of Marlborough. Sorocold's name is nowhere to be seen.

If all this is correct, how does it come about that the faults have been unpublished? Most accounts that give a reason for the failure of the windmill blame a lack of reliable winds. Even *The Builder's Dictionary*, which knew about the storm damage, called the windmill *'the admirable contrivance of that ingenious Architect Mr Surrocole'*. Perhaps it was simply that those at the New River Company who had laboured so long before making the wrong choice were in no hurry to publicise their mistake. Perhaps it is also because Sorocold's other innovation – the Upper Pond – was a lasting success once the pumping difficulties were overcome. By 1725 it was being written;

> 'As to the ... part of the Town about Hanover Square.. that part is now plentifully supply'd by the new River, who follow all the new buildings thereabouts with their Water faster than the builders can finish them and find that their Water will rise at least Eleven foot higher than the surface of any ground thereabouts.'[8]

There are still so many uncertainties about Sorocold's involvement in these events that it is time to look at what is known about him.

The mystery of Sorocold

George Sorocold has long been a puzzle to those interested in the early engineers who empowered England's industrial revolution. In the 1690s and early 1700s he seemed to be everywhere. All over England, town after town received the benefit of waterworks designed by him. Liverpool where he was concerned in the design of its first dock, made him a freeman of the city. At Derby he was credited with the design of machinery for a silk mill that was arguably England's first factory. In that age before canals were being built, he designed systems of locks and weirs to make rivers, including the Cam, navigable for cargo vessels. He was admired and praised by his contemporaries, usually with the word 'ingenious' somewhere in the description. He was a married man with a large family.

Then, after 1711, it is as if he suddenly disappeared, without trace and without comment. There are works attributed to him after that date, but unlike his earlier works there never seems to be any unequivocal proof that Sorocold was involved. Historians have searched likely records in vain, without finding even so much as the date or place of his death.

The only faint clue that something had gone amiss in Sorocold's life comes from a letter written in 1717. There were moves afoot at that time to revive a scheme for making the River Derwent navigable as far inland as Derby. Sorocold had surveyed and mapped the proposed works many years before, and had given evidence to the House of Lords about it in 1703, but the work had never gone ahead. Now, in 1717, the mayor of Derby was writing to a member of the House of Lords, Baron Parker. He enclosed a copy of what he called 'the map that was done by the ingenious, unfortunate mathematician, Mr Sorocold.' This is generally taken to suggest that something unpleasant had happened to him, but it need not necessarily have been fatal. The misfortune might be no more than the money difficulties he suffered in the aftermath of Soame's bankruptcy.

What can reliably be said about Sorocold's life and career? Various branches of the Sorocold family, with the surname spelt in a variety of ways, had long been established in Lancashire. The one who was probably George's father also had some property interests in Derbyshire. George's date of birth, probably in the late 1660s, has never been established and the first firm date for him is 15 May 1684. On that day *'George Sorocold, of Lancashire'* was admitted to Emmanuel College, Cambridge. He entered with the status of fellow-commoner, rather than as a sizar like most students. This meant that he was making full payment for his place there and suggests that he was from a prosperous family. The college still has a silver tankard that he presented, according to the custom of the time. It bears a Latin inscription recording it as his gift – *Ex dono Georgii Sorocold Coll: Eman: Commensalis 1684.* Around this inscription as well as the arms of the college and framed by decorative plumes, foliage and fruit can be seen the Sorocold family coat of arms, a profusion of *fleur de lys* and turrets. The tankard has a lid, its thumbpiece elaborately formed in the shape of crossed dolphins.

Unfortunately, George Sorocold's year of birth cannot be established from the date of his admission to Emmanuel. He might have been fifteen or eighteen, or some other age. From the quality of the tankard he was expected to make his mark in the world, but he seems not to have done so at Cambridge as there is no record of his ever having matriculated or graduated from there.

The next landmark date was to be less than seven months later. On 7 December 1684, at All Saints' Derby, George was married to Mary Francis, daughter of a respected burgess and later mayor of Derby. Nor does that ceremony gives us a safe indication of his year of birth, as youthful marriages were not unknown. Boys only needed parental approval to marry if they were between 7 and 13 years while for girls it was only from 7 to 11.

One thing that is recorded about the course of that marriage is surprising. It comes from the writings of Ralph Thoresby, in his enormous guide to Leeds, which was published in 1715 but must have been many years in the writing:

> 'Our ingenious hydrographer, Mr George Sorocold, has already had thirteen children (of whom eight were living at the same time) all single births, and all nursed by his wife, before he was twenty-eight years of age.'[9]

If accurate, this suggests at the very least a high level of fertility in both spouses. Perhaps the marriage less than seven months after he had gone up to Cambridge was one of urgent necessity. Thoresby was a contemporary of Sorocold's and a highly regarded antiquarian and local historian. In his publications are a number of references to Sorocold's work, and where these can be checked they seem to be wholly accurate. Thoresby also collected a personal museum of antiquarian curiosities, and two of these, a hat-band made of snake vertebrae and some samples of lead water-pipe, one a foot in diameter, he records as given him by Sorocold. Thoresby's use of the present tense ('has already had thirteen children') suggests that Sorocold was still alive, but is not conclusive, given the vast size of the book, as this particular passage may have been written years before the publication date of 1715. It may also be significant that although Thoresby gives a list of waterworks built by Sorocold, what he calls 'Islington new-works' is the last in time, and they were completed in 1708.

Early works

Turning from Sorocold's personal to his professional life, there is no record of where he learnt the skills that made his name. There is no doubt that he did make a name, which impressed Savery and many others. Thomas Savery was the inventor of an early precursor of the steam engine, designed for pumping out mines. His book *The Miner's Friend* was published in 1702 and when dealing with machinery for supplying water to towns he wrote:

> '.. in composing such sort of engines I think no person has excelled the ingenious Mr George Sorocold.'

Another commentator was Sir Godfrey Copley, a fellow of the Royal Society and later to be the founder of the Copley medal, the Society's most prestigious award. He saw 'Mr Saracole's' waterwheels at Marchant's waterworks in London in 1696 and described them in a letter as 'I do think the best piece of work I have seen.'[10]

In 1704 Sorocold was granted a patent for what was described as 'machinery for cutting wood or stone and twisting ropes &c', which was powered by a water wheel and was used for boring elm water pipes at Derby.[11] In 1708 Thomas Johnson, a leading citizen of Liverpool, went to London to consult Sorocold about building a dock and wrote back to a friend describing Sorocold as 'a very ingenious man'. The following year Sorocold was made a freeman of Liverpool in recognition of work he had done for the city.

This reputation for skill and ingenuity went down the years and many more examples could be given, such as Robert Bald who wrote in 1812 of

> 'Sorocold, of Derby, one of the two engineers of his age who never failed in what they undertook, because they considered perfection and success of their work first and their profit afterwards.'[12]

Sorocold's pumping systems continued in use long after his death. At Bridgnorth, where his floating water-wheel was designed to cope with the very great seasonal differences in the level of the river Severn, it continued to provide the town's water supply until 1857. Other towns he supplied with water included Macclesfield, Derby, Norwich, Leeds, Great Yarmouth, Bristol, Wirksworth, King's Lynn, and Deal, as well as the garrison and hospital at Portsmouth. He may also have supplied Exeter, Nottingham and Sheffield.

Sorocold in London

Only one address that Sorocold lived at is easy to discover, from a letter he wrote to Thomas Coke in November 1702 headed 'Cecill street'.[13] It turns out that Cecil Street, now long since demolished, was newly built at that time on the site of the Earl of Salisbury's London home, Great Salisbury House. The street led from the Strand down towards the river Thames, where Shell Mex House now stands. It was described as having 'very good houses, fit for persons of repute.'[14]

Westminster City Council records show 'George Sorocoald' as the occupier of one of the houses in Cecil Street. His name is first seen in a rate book between June 1701 and June 1702 and remains until some time in the year ending June 1707, when it was crossed out and replaced by another.

Among the soot-blackened parchment rolls of legal pleadings stored at the Public Record Office is evidence that Sorocold had cause to regret his dealings with Richard Soame. In 1708 a Kentish ironmaster sued Sorocold for the price of iron fittings supplied. In reply Sorocold applied to the Court of Chancery to stop the action, claiming that he had been working for Richard Soame at the time, and it was Soame's debt, not his.[15] He also explained that on 6th June 1701 he had contracted with Soame to be his engineer at the London Bridge Waterworks for six years, in return for a salary of £200 a year and £30 a year for the rent of a house. The contract included a provision that he would not erect any 'wheeles, water engines or waterworks' in or about London during that period which might affect the London Bridge works.

Soame, who became bankrupt in 1704, had then stopped paying him, with the result that Sorocold's household goods had been seized under a court order for rent arrears and he and his family had been evicted from the house. He said that he had nevertheless kept his side of the contract, including the condition not to work for any other waterworks during the six years.

This seems to be why Sorocold, pre-eminent among water engineers at the time, was not with Wren and the others who were asked to advise the New River Company in 1702. He seems to have started work at New River Head almost immediately the contract ended in June 1707, as a deed dated November 1707 refers to the 'windmill worke' as being newly built, and the construction of the tall brick tower must have taken months.

The same letter that gave the Cecil Street address revealed something else. Sorocold wrote that he had been unable to go out for a week because of his 'ague'. This was malaria, an occupational hazard for water engineers. Although not usually fatal, it causes recurrent debilitating fevers. Combined with worry about debts and lawsuits, it may have affected his judgment and the quality of his work – for the

29 One of the sets of water wheels and pumps of London Bridge Waterworks designed by Sorocold. They could raise over 100,000 gallons of water to a height of 120ft in an hour.

horse-windmill can now be seen to be his only known failure.[17]

The last date when Sorocold was certainly alive is 2nd July 1711, when he wrote a business letter to a London baker who owned watermills on the River Lea. It is a hurried scrawl that gives little personal information.[16] After that date, there is silence. It has been suggested that a lease of waterworks in Derby, granted to Sorocold in 1691 and not surrendered until 1738 confirms that he was alive until then. It does not, because he had mortgaged it to Thomas Coke in 1705. A tradition that he built the second silk mill at Derby in 1717-8 does not seem to be supported by any document, and may result from confusion with his other works in that town.

The nature of Sorocold's work always led to documents. There were letters, proposals, plans, minutes of evidence to parliamentary committees, leases, contracts, mortgages and lawsuits, not to mention descriptions in books and journals. If he was still working after 1711 where are the records? More interesting, how did a public figure, whose works had been praised and described by so many of his contemporaries, vanish without a mention?

Whatever became of Sorocold, his memory seems to have slipped from the public mind very quickly. In 1729, a major work on Hydrostatics and Hydraulics was published. It praises the London Bridge Waterworks and compares it favourably with those at Marly which fed the fountains of Versailles, but continues that the works at London Bridge were,

> '.. as I am told, the work of one Mr Sorocold, a very good Engineer, in the Reign of King Charles or King James the II..'[18]

The reigns of the two sovereigns mentioned began in 1660 and ended in 1689. It seems that by 1729 Sorocold was little more than a distant memory, and so the mystery of the manner of his going remains.

CHAPTER THIRTEEN

The First Surveyor 1718 to 1766

The first Surveyor – Springs and a typewriter – Years of stagnation – '... out of his element...' – A belated obituary – The Breamore tablet – An auction of effects

The first Surveyor

Despite his best endeavours, the Reverend Lowthorp never persuaded the New River Company to appoint him as their surveyor. They did eventually appoint one, but not until about 1718. That surveyor was Henry Mill, and according to a monument at Breamore church near Salisbury, where he is buried, he was a relative of Hugh Myddelton. Perhaps that gave him the edge over Lowthorp. The earliest record of Mill among the Company papers refers to a burnt minute of 1718 that ordered paviours 'not to set down any Cocks without Mr Mill's approbation.'[1] This fits his memorial slab which says he was engineer to the company 'above Fifty Years.' The earliest of Mill's letters to the New River Board dates from September 1722, and in it he refers to a plan that he had drawn up for them 'about two years since'.[2] He was well respected and held his post until his death at the age of eighty-seven on Boxing Day 1770, although his successor Robert Mylne began to take over from him in 1767.

Springs and a typewriter

Mill was something of an inventor, having been given a patent in 1706 for improved carriage springs and another in 1714 for what may have been the earliest prototype of a typewriter.[3] The *Dictionary of National Biography* goes no further than saying it is 'probable' that Henry Mill the inventor and Henry Mill the water engineer were the same person. A comparison between the inventor's signature from a deposition to Queen Anne in 1713 and the signature of the New River engineer in 1751, thirty-eight years later, suggests they were one and the same.

30 Two Henry Mill signatures, 1713 and 1751

The 'typewriter' has not survived, and there is no known drawing of it. Despite this native ingenuity, Mill does not seem to have brought much change to the New River. The 'square horse-works' that can be seen in so many prints from that time are usually said to have been built in 1720, though there seems to be no confirmation of that. There is no record or tradition to link Mill with that building or its design, and as already noted Yarnold and Preston had proposed a building of that type some years earlier when the defects in Sorocold's mill had become apparent.

31 View of New River Head from the north c.1730. Sadler's Wells theatre is to the left.

Years of stagnation

As for the company's dividends, they remained almost static for the fifty years when Mill was the surveyor. In the five years from 1721 to 1725 the average annual dividend on a single Adventurer's share was £242, in the five years 1767 to 1770 it was £251 – an increase of less than 4% in 50 years. Of course, the question of profitability was not entirely in the hands of the surveyor – it depended on market forces such as competition, and also on the amount of capital expenditure being made, since that was paid directly from income in those days. On the other hand, the average dividend rose to more than £400 within twenty years after Mill retired, so it does seem that Mill presided over a period of stagnation.

One of the last events to befall the New River Company, almost exactly one year before Mill's death was the fire at Bridewell Precinct that destroyed so many records. For this reason it is difficult to find much detail about his work for the company. In about 1730 the pipes in the cistern at the Water House were elaborately rearranged, and that was presumably his doing (*ill.9, p.50*). In July 1752 the Board approved a new method he had devised for 'driving the pipes and for preventing so frequent changes in the streets' after he demonstrated a working model, and ordered that 'new joints for the future shall have the joints gaged according to Mr Mill's directions, with the Instruments to be by him prepared.'[4]

'... out of his element ...'

One bundle of documents that escaped the fire casts light on the impression Mill made on one group of New River shareholders. In the winter of 1741 he went to Ware to supervise the construction of a new balance engine for controlling the amount of water taken from the River Lea. While he was there, some of the shareholders on the works committee went on one of their periodic surveys to see the works.

32 View of the 'spa' New Tunbridge Wells south east of New River Head, c.1730

On 28 October, they stopped at Hoddesdon on the way to Ware, to collect him from the Bull Inn, but found that Mr Mill was 'not up yet, having sprained his ancle.' Three weeks later on 17 November, they went to Ware having arranged to see him at an inn there, but found that he had moved to a different one at Hertford, 'and was not come from thence during our Stay.' Going to see the work without him, they learnt that when he did turn up, 'he seldom goes before 11 or 12 o'clock to the men, which is about their Dinner time' and they were surprised at his 'indifference'. On 3 December they went back again, but found Mill absent from the site and 'many men was at work to little purpose.' There was a general opinion the work would not stand and that

> 'Mr Mill doth not design it should, but to putt it off till next Summer ... The Smith & Carpenters were so benumm'd as scarce to be able to handle their Tooles... There is a piece of brickwork ...Wee inquired the Use of it, but it a mistery to every one there as well as to Us ... a great number of labourers ... imploy'd to little or no purpose ... at vast expence ... besides the expences of Mr Mill .. and the Losses occasion'd by the Length of the Nights ... nine boards or planks having been lost in one Night.... The Iron work prepared for the Cistern Surprises everyone with its Bulk & some Persons Suppos'd to understand such work are of Opinion that Mr Mill is out of his Element & Knows not what he is about.'

As they left from that visit they met Mill who was just arriving, and scolded him for his

> 'scandalously dilatory method of Acting; but the weather being so severely Cold would not Wait his tedious Apologies.'

On 14 December they were back again, and found the 'Gates and Ironwork done neatly, but in so grand a manner as if for a Cathedral ... the Expence will be monstrously more than such a Bauble of a cistern could in any reason require.'

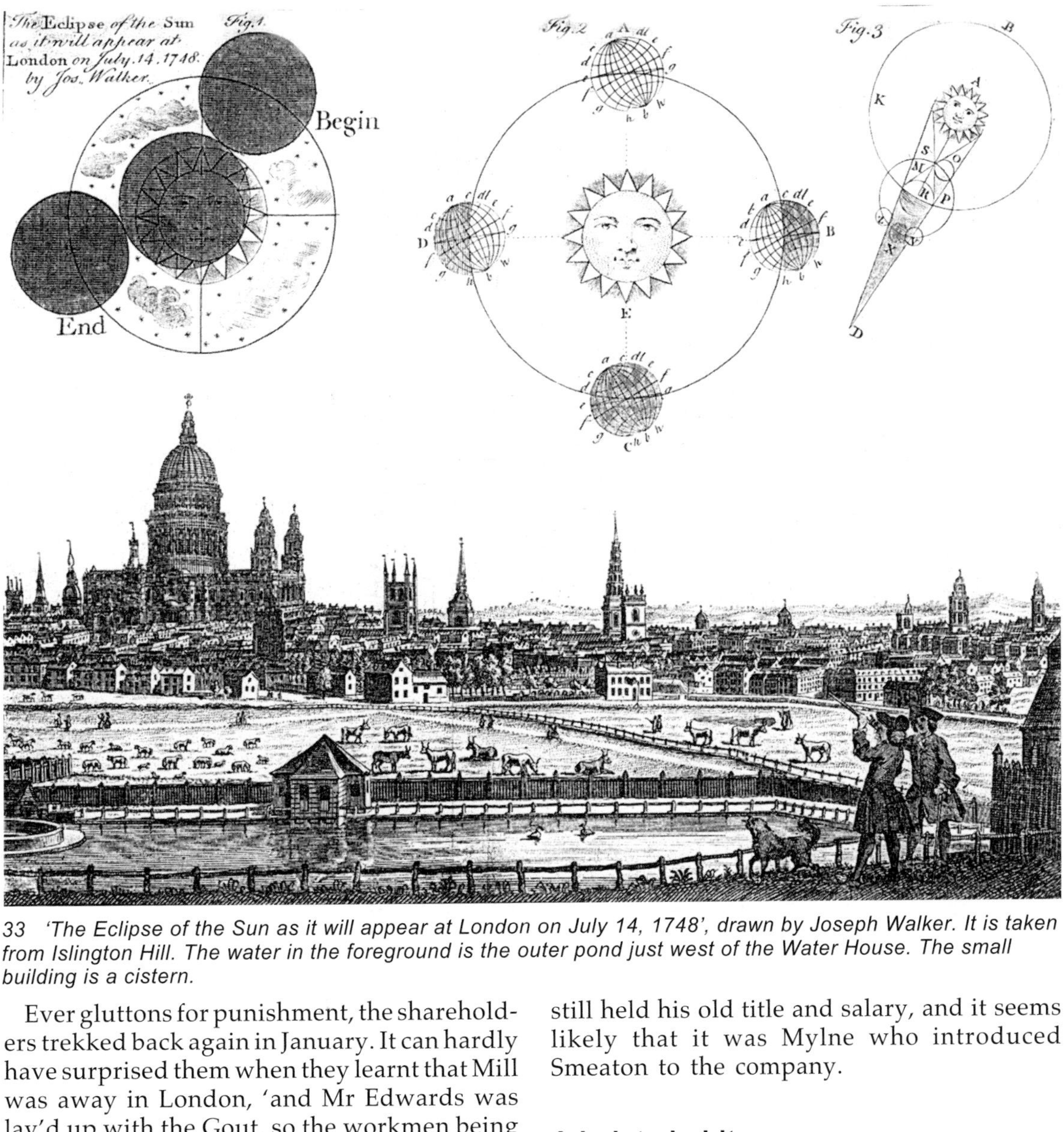

33 'The Eclipse of the Sun as it will appear at London on July 14, 1748', drawn by Joseph Walker. It is taken from Islington Hill. The water in the foreground is the outer pond just west of the Water House. The small building is a cistern.

Ever gluttons for punishment, the shareholders trekked back again in January. It can hardly have surprised them when they learnt that Mill was away in London, 'and Mr Edwards was lay'd up with the Gout, so the workmen being in want of Leaders, their work signify'd little.'[5]

Despite the committee's displeasure, Mill remained in his post until his death almost thirty years later. During that time, there were no major changes to the way water was supplied, and horses still worked the pumps until Smeaton's 'fire-engine' replaced them in 1768. By that time Mill's successor Robert Mylne had been in his post for two years although Mill still held his old title and salary, and it seems likely that it was Mylne who introduced Smeaton to the company.

A belated obituary

Mill's obituary, which appeared in the *Gentleman's Magazine*, first as a very brief notice soon after his death and then much more fully some eight years later, tells us enough about him to make a more appealing picture.[6] The author of the later piece says that he had been moved to write it out of surprise that 'no notice has been taken, or account given to the public, of that most valuable member of society, the late Henry Mill Esq, many years principal engineer to the New-river company; a man to whom the city of London and its environs have many and great obligations'. Mill was said to have had great skill in mechanics from an early age, and to have made improvements in the New River system, probably by extending the network of wooden mains to keep pace with the constant growth of London. He was said to be a man without guile. The obituarist had apparently known him for 'upwards of thirty years' and dwelt on his modesty and other virtues of character but was somewhat vague about the details of his private life. The piece is signed with the initials JN, and something about the almost unctuous style suggests the author was perhaps a churchman.

One revealing fact he mentions is that the New River Company paid the large sum of 60 guineas to have Mill's portrait painted and that it hung in their Bridewell offices, where it was to be seen until it was lost in the 1769 fire. It is a sad loss because apart from showing what he looked like it may well have included attributes like the tools of his trade, the New River as it then was, or even perhaps his typewriter. The fact that the company commissioned it certainly suggests he was well thought of. Unmarried, as a young man Mill had taken lodgings on the upper floors of a house in the Strand 'five or six doors east of Somerset House' so as to be within a short walk of the company's offices. The rooms gave him everything he wanted he said, with a view across the Thames to the Surrey hills from the back windows and a vista up Drury Lane towards Hampstead from the front ones, and there he stayed until he died. He kept two servants, a man and a woman, but apparently made few demands on them. Christmas Day 1770, by which time he was about 87, was to be his last full day and he spent it with his landlady, sharing dinner with her and then talking cheerfully until it was time for bed. The next morning his breakfast cup of cocoa, which the servant left outside his door as usual, was untouched and he was found lying on the floor inside, unconscious and dying.

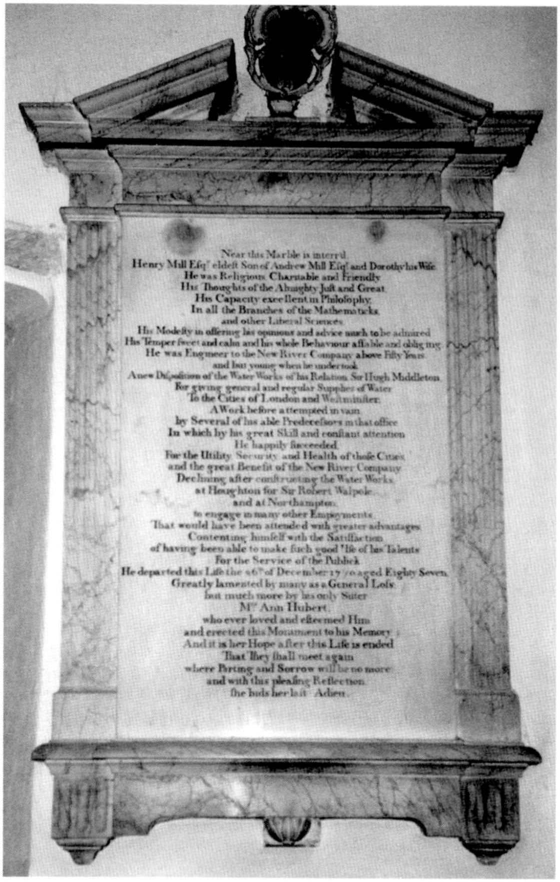

34 The memorial tablet to Henry Mill who was surveyor to the New River Company from about 1718 until Robert Mylne replaced him in 1767. Mill died in London in 1770 but was buried at Breamore, Hampshire as his will requested, and there his sister erected this memorial

The Breamore tablet

When Mill died his sister, who lived at Breamore, near Salisbury, survived him. She arranged for his body to be taken there for burial, as he had asked in his will. There she erected a vast marble wall-tablet to his memory in the Saxon church, setting out in fulsome terms that he was 'but young when he undertook a new Disposition of the Water-Works of his Relation, Sir Hugh Middleton, for giving general and regular Supplies of Water to the Cities of London and Westminster, a Work before attempted in vain by Several of his able

Predecessors.' The inscription gives his age as 87, whereas the burial register shows 88. If this is correct, he was born in 1682 or 1683, and would have been in his mid-thirties at the time of his first known link to the New River Company in the minute of 1718 already mentioned, which does not seem so very young despite his sister's observations. Mill's obituarist in the Gentleman's Magazine wrote that he had discussed Mill's age with the sister, who was in her eighties and only knew that Mill had been either three years older or younger than she was, but had forgotten which. She had perhaps cleared up that doubt by the time she wrote the memorial inscription.

An auction of effects

Almost four months later, on 18 April 1771, Mill's household goods were sold at a two-day auction, and a copy of the sale catalogue happens to survive.[7] The auctioneer was one Samuel Paterson of Essex Street, just yards away from Mill's home. The list of Mill's possessions is intriguing, and in some ways much more revealing than his obituary. It seems from the list that everything apart from clothing was up for sale and the catalogue gives us a rare picture of the lifestyle of a London bachelor. The list includes his general household furnishings and what must have been the contents of his study or library, and shows us the man perhaps more vividly than the missing portrait ever could.

Judging by the catalogue, he had slept in a mahogany four-poster with fluted pillars, a mahogany cornice, blue hangings and a feather mattress with pillows and a bolster. Two plainer bedsteads may have been for the servants. Much of his furniture was mahogany, ranging from chests, escritoires and screens to a dining table, a sideboard and set of leather-seated chairs. There was a wainscot cabinet with folding doors, a falling flap and 'a very singular strong drawer'. There were more than sixty brass candlesticks. There was a silver tea-kettle and lamp, and a brass one on a pillar and claw stand and two hand bells, suggesting cosy firesides in a house with servants. He must sometimes have entertained on a large scale, and his guests could take their wigs off – there were no fewer than 14 wig stands. There were busts of Cicero, Horace, and Milton, Pope, Congreve and Addison, as well as 'a pair of elegant tureen urns and a Bacchanalian vase'.

All the instruments of the surveyor's trade were there and in great variety. There were four large augers – presumably for taking soil samples – a double theodolite in a case, rules, levels, and plungers. There was a telescope, a pocket thermometer, some compass needles and four rules, a four foot telescope, three artificial magnets and something oddly described as a 'large magnet in brass', 'a ring dial and two common ditto', dividers of various kinds, rules, 'a brass plate in a frame to show the earth's motion', 'a Chinese counting table and a pair of pocket globes by Moll', more dividers, a two foot rule with needle, a mathematical dial for taking elevations, a 'compleat universal ring dial in a fish-skin case', a *camera obscura* and a reflecting glass for prints, a double solar microscope, a microscope in a wainscot case, watches and many other instruments. There were two barometers and a thermometer in their cases There were 33 large plans of London and suburbs, as well as Roque's large map of 10 miles round London on a large roller with pulley and brackets and six similar maps, with sundry prints and drawings. There were books on hydrostatics, surveying, arithmetic, air and logarithms as well as Robinson Crusoe and Fanny Hill, alongside general and religious works. There were clocks, watches, dress swords and walking sticks including a gold-mounted cane. There were spectacles, locks, bolts, watch keys, assorted workshop tools a 'large iron melting furnace' and 'two small presses for leather suckers'.

A talented inventor and a 'most worthy member of society' he may have been, but Mill's achievements for the New River Company seem to have been much what might be expected of any waterworks engineer and surveyor at that time. For fifty years he served the company and made some modest improvements to the supply, yet his death found the basic system little changed from what it had been.

As it happens, his successor Robert Mylne was a very different stamp of man.

CHAPTER FOURTEEN

Mylne, Smeaton, Boulton and Watt 1766 to 1799

Mylne's Grand Tour – Surveyor of St Paul's – Mylne and the New River Company – 'A Girl without Money' – Mylne's diaries – A plan for the windmill – Smeaton's report – The Fire Engine – The forgotten waterwheel – An unexpected sequence – Boulton and Watt

Mylne's Grand Tour

The new surveyor was Robert Mylne, and a more different man from Henry Mill would be hard to imagine. He was born in Edinburgh in 1733[1] and came from a line of distinguished forebears who had been master-masons to the Crown of Scotland. They worked with stone but also designed buildings and would probably be called architects today.

At the time when Mylne was growing up, the Grand Tour was very much in vogue. Young men from good families went to Europe for a few months or a couple of years to broaden their education, and this was something Mylne wanted to do. When he was 14, he was apprenticed to a carpenter. His father was not a wealthy man and did not indulge his sons. Robert's younger brother William was allowed to go as far as Paris, to study and when possible to work for his keep. By the time Robert's apprenticeship ended, he had set his heart on a European journey, but his father was less keen, and the son had no funds of his own. It seems that Robert persuaded family friends to wheedle his father and eventually in 1754, when he was 21, he was allowed to join his brother. Paris was never going to be enough for him, as the lure of Italy was too great. He agreed with his brother that they would travel together to Rome, and lacking the money to go by coach they sent their luggage ahead and set out from Paris together in December 1754, travelling as cheaply as they could, often on foot, across pre-revolutionary France. They eventually reached Marseilles in January 1755 and after spending some time there took ship to the ancient port of Civitavecchia on the Italian coast. From there they travelled to Rome where they quickly installed themselves. One of Robert's letters home is dated eight months later, in September 1755. From this it seems that their father had written asking whether they were doing any paid work, and Robert replied that he was far too busy studying architectural drawing, for he had found skills in that subject being taught at Rome far beyond anything known in Scotland.

All this time he was mastering his chosen subject of architecture. He studied in Rome at the Academy of St Luke, where all artistic subjects were taught, Luke being the patron saint of artists, thanks to a tradition that he had made a painting of the Virgin Mary in her lifetime. The academy held a prestigious competition for students, and Robert naturally entered it. The brief was to prepare a design for a public building to provide a gallery for the busts of famous men, and Robert prepared a striking design that owed more to French than to current Roman thinking. In due course he was announced to be the winner. He was the first Briton to win that prize.

By now Robert was building up a network of contacts including Piranesi. He wrote home to say how he was 'teaching architecture to Mr Knight of Kent, worth £7,500 a year, also Mr Milles of a very considerable estate'. He said he was intimate with 'My Lord Archibald Hamilton, brother to the late Duke. He is a nice lad of 19 ... and as all his estate lies in England I expect a great patron in him.' More significantly, he declared that it was now his intention to settle in London rather than Edinburgh.

Mylne had now been away from home for four years and it was time to return. On the way he stayed at Florence long enough to be elected a member of its Academy of Art. The Seven Years War was now under way, having started in August 1756, and Britain was at war with France. Mylne therefore made his way home by going through Switzerland and then down the Rhine to Rotterdam. He stopped for a time in Holland visiting The Hague and Amsterdam to learn something of the skills of Dutch engineers. Once across the channel Mylne's first stop was in London, which he reached in the middle of July 1759 and where he took modest lodgings at Seven Dials. It was his plan to return for a visit to his family in Edinburgh, but then pure chance intervened – there was another public competition being held. Designs were invited for a new bridge over the Thames, to be built at Blackfriars and they had to be submitted by 4 October – little more than two months away.

On the face of it, Mylne was not a strong candidate. He was only twenty six years old and did not have a single building to his credit – how could he expect to be entrusted with what was seen as a speculative undertaking that would take a great deal of the city's money? The competition had already attracted a strong field of candidates, including George Dance the elder (the City's own surveyor), John Smeaton, William Chambers and John Gwynn (whose design was championed in the press by Dr Samuel Johnson). Mylne's design included elliptical arches not previously seen in England, which many thought unsafe. The matter had been referred to a committee of aldermen and common councillors, and no doubt some among them might already have had their own preferred architects. Yet, amazingly, Mylne was able to write to his brother in Edinburgh as early as August 18 saying that he had received encouragement from the secretary of the committee, 'a man of great weight among them, who is very much my friend.' This is a reference to the city solicitor James Paterson and Mylne's speed in recruiting such a powerful ally seems astonishing. The day for the committee's decision finally came on 22 February 1760. Having been 'fully convinced that the form of his arch' was safe, and that his design was 'best adapted to the Navigation at all Times and Tides, without raising the Carriageway to an inconvenient Height' they favoured Robert Mylne.

35 Robert Mylne at the age of 24. A portrait drawn in Rome in 1757, by Brompton.

Mylne's bridge was not finally opened for traffic until 1769. The stone had to be brought by sea from the Dorset coast and this source had its problems, 'sometimes by wind and weather, and several times by Combinations in the Island of Portland' as Mylne later put it. By combinations he meant the early stirrings of organised labour.[2]

Surveyor of St Paul's

By the time Blackfriars Bridge opened in 1769, the outline of Mylne's future career was firmly in place. In October 1766, as his diary records with more than a tinge of smugness, he had been 'appointed surveyor of St Paul's Cathedral by the Archbishop of Canterbury.' The fullness of this entry in contrast to the abbreviated jottings he usually made may indicate his understandable pleasure at this appointment. The part-time post at St Paul's, which made him responsible for approving repairs to the fabric of the building, only brought a salary of £50 a year but obviously carried considerable status. It was a post that he held until his death and it meant that he was involved in any building work and also the arrangements for great state occasions such as funerals and services of thanksgiving. Similar posts at the cathedrals of Canterbury and Rochester followed.

The following year, 1767, he was elected a fellow, or as his diary describes it a member, of the Royal Society, and it seems that he was by then an established figure in what might be called the scientific community.

Mylne and the New River Company

More important for the purposes of this story he had made his first contact with the New River Company. This probably happened because the company's offices were in Bridewell Precinct, just by the northern approach to Blackfriars Bridge and they also had a wharf where timber for water pipes could be landed and stored. His first contact with the company may have been as early as 1762, and on 26 November 1767 they made him their surveyor, jointly with Henry Mill. Mill was by that time some 83 years old and it seems likely that he was allowed to keep his titular post – and salary – until his death in 1770, as a gesture of respect to a loyal servant even though Mylne had taken over his duties.

The New River Company was to be Mylne's chief occupation for the rest of his life though it was by no means his only one. On the contrary he designed bridges, public buildings and houses in England and Scotland, travelled all over the country surveying harbours and rivers, designed fenland drainage schemes and even surveyed the line of a new canal. Yet his first duty seems to have been to the New River and he always asked – and was given – the board's approval if he planned to leave London for more than a week or so.

It would be consistent with Mylne's character if he took up his new appointment with some vigour, and it would be interesting to know if his style was different from Henry Mill's. One document among the company's papers hints at this. Although it is anonymous, there can be little doubt to whom it refers:

> 'Before the scotchman came you were so good as to allow the carpenter and bricklayer 2 pints of beer a day but now they have Lost it – who has found it I cannot tell. Signed, a well wisher to all Honest Englishmen.'[3]

After Mylne's appointment the first major event to befall the New River Company was the disastrous fire of Christmas Eve, 1769. This destroyed their offices at Bridewell Precinct, so that Mylne had to design a new building for the site. He soon produced a design for a neat classical building, and the *Historical Chronicle* records that its foundation stone was laid on 28 July 1770 by the governor of the company, Mr Holford (*ill.19, p.93*).

At first Mylne lived in a house he had built near Blackfriars Bridge, but following Henry Mill's death he was appointed the sole surveyor to the New River Company. He recorded that in his diary for 4 July 1771, with the additional note 'and they granted the use of the house also.'

So it was that Mylne moved up to the Water House at New River Head, an elegant building on the south side of the Round Pond. Effectively it was to be his home for the rest of his life. In the 1780s he enlarged it and it must have been a refuge from the bustle of London.

'...a Girl without Money...'

In 1770, aged 37, Mylne had taken a wife aged 22. Given everything we know about his fierce ambition, and the practice of the times, it would be no surprise to hear that he made what is described as a 'good' marriage. That it was not so can be seen from a letter he wrote to his brother. In it he explained that his bride, Mary Home, was the younger daughter of a London surgeon. He pointed out that as he now had an income of £1,000 a year, a substantial amount,

> 'I have married to please myself. I have ventured to take a Girl without Money. I have married one who is possessed of industry and activity – one who can gild a leisure hour with mirth, as well as make the business one of double value. Her person and her Beauty I say nothing of – I have looked for qualities that suit my inclination.'[4]

Mary Home was to bear him nine children, of whom five survived him. Four girls came first, Maria, Emilia, Harriet and Caroline; all except Harriet dying in their early twenties. Then came a son Robert, who was destined for a military career but died at sea aged 18, on the way to Gibraltar to join his regiment there in 1798. Next was another boy, William Chadwell Mylne, whose middle name commemorated one of the New River's springs. He would eventually succeed his father as surveyor to the New River, and was to write in petulant terms when the company decided in 1859 that the house at New River Head was no longer to be available for his use, '..when for nearly one hundred years my late father and myself have occupied the high position of Engineer to the finest Waterworks in the world'. Another boy Thomas – named for his grandfather – followed, but only survived three months, and then two more girls, Charlotte and Leonora. As for Mary Home she survived only until 1797, when she was forty nine.

Mylne's diaries

What we know of Robert Mylne's work on the New River comes partly from the company archives and partly from his own pocket diaries. These begin in 1760 almost as soon as he arrived in London and continue in unbroken sequence until the end of 1810, just a few months before his death. Sadly he was no Pepys. The diaries he used were early examples of the kind that are still sold today, pre-printed with space allocated for each day of the year, some printed information of a general kind, and columns for entering income and expenses. Mylne used them to record appointments and also brief notes of journeys made and expenses incurred on behalf of his various clients. Very occasionally family matters are mentioned, but only as the briefest jottings. Nowhere does he record his feelings about events; never are the jottings more than perfunctory. As to the New River Company records, these are much fuller and we are more able to assess his contribution to the enterprise.

His duties on the New River meant that he often had to travel its length on horseback checking its condition and seeing to improvements, and he came to love the Hertfordshire countryside of its upper reaches. In later years he bought land at Great Amwell, close to the springs that supplied the New River, and built a house where he and his family lived in the summer. But most of his time was still spent at New River Head, and it was there that he died in 1811, almost fifty years after his first links with the New River Company.

A plan for the windmill

When Mylne first became the surveyor, things at New River Head had changed little for about forty years. The conical tower of Sorocold's windmill still stood to its full height although its useless sails had long gone. We know from one of the papers that survived the 1769 fire that a committee of the company had been grappling with that old problem yet again as late as 1742. 'The committee are of the opinion' they reported 'that the windmill should be repaired and put into a condition of working to raise a greater quantity of water to the Pond with all convenient speed.' It seems that this was never done as there is no further reference to it as a working windmill and none of the many pictures of New River Head from that time on show the windmill except as a bare tower.

Against the windmill's east side from about 1720 stood what was known as the square horse-works – a picturesque single storey building, its pyramidal roof capped by an elegant square ventilator. Inside, a team of horses trudged endlessly round, turning a shaft that worked the pumps that forced water from the Round Pond to the Upper Pond.

Smeaton's report

There is a partial description of the works as they were when Mylne took over, in a report by the engineer John Smeaton. He went to New River Head, because the company had asked him to report on possible methods of improving the way that water was pumped to the Upper Pond. His visit was in 1766, the year before Mylne was formally appointed as surveyor. Smeaton's report was probably destroyed in the 1769 fire – but what appears to be a verbatim copy was sent by Smeaton to Robert Mylne in 1774 and still survives among the records that Thames Water inherited from the Metropolitan Water Board.[5]

Smeaton was one of the foremost engineers of the time and on the face of it, the New River Company could hardly have found someone better qualified to advise them. Just seven years earlier in 1759 Smeaton had been awarded the prestigious Copley medal of the Royal Society for his *Experimental Inquiry concerning the Native Powers of Water and Wind to turn Mills and other Machines depending on a circular Motion.* This enquiry had established, among other things, the relative efficiency of the different kinds of waterwheel. At New River Head when Smeaton went to visit it on 10 March 1766, the 'present horse engine .. was at work with four horses' and his report explains that he had been asked to compare its merits with three alternative power sources – a 'wind engine ... if the present cone is made use of as a base... compared with a Fire Engine properly constructed.. (and) a Water Engine.'

When he spoke of a Fire Engine he was referring to the early precursors of steam engines – atmospheric engines – then in use. So his brief was to compare and advise upon the four 'prime movers' or sources of power then available – muscle, wind, water and steam. The company must have had it in mind that the old windmill tower, the 'cone' Smeaton referred to, was one possible solution.

The upshot was that Smeaton recommended – and the company approved – a fire engine. Despite his expertise, it has to be said that Smeaton was not an entirely impartial expert. His work on waterwheels had been completed and published years before and had brought him the acclaim it undoubtedly merited. By 1766 he was much more interested in developing fire engines, and the wealthy New River Company may have seemed a suitable client to pay the cost of one. Did that influence his conclusions? The report certainly concedes that a waterwheel could be used, but he does not dwell on it beyond observing that there is sufficient slope on the site to allow a 26-foot fall, which would enable the construction of a very large and powerful waterwheel. He suggested that if such a wheel was to raise more water than the existing horse engine it would result in a great quantity of water being run to waste. May he have thought that a fire engine endlessly burning coal, which would have to be brought by sea from Newcastle, would be cheaper than such a waterwheel? He certainly assured the company that he would assemble in such an engine 'all the real improvements that have hitherto been made ... yet I reckon upon Nothing but what I have already seen proved at some place or Other.'

The Fire Engine

What part, if any, Mylne played in these deliberations is unknown. One charred fragment that survived the 1769 fire suggests that the new engine was complete by April 1768. Another fragment tells us that on 14 March 1769 the treasurer was ordered to pay 'to Mr John Smeeton the sum of £50 being for his plans and trouble in the construction of the fire engine at Islington.' This was not, of course, the total cost of the engine – just recompense to Smeaton for his efforts, and by the practice of the time the payment would not have been ordered until after the work was finished. After the fire Mylne was asked to make a valuation of the company's assets so that they could be insured, and he set a value of £1,500 for the 'fire engine at Islington,' presumably meaning the engine and engine-house.

36 John Smeaton's plans for the first 'fire-engine' house, 1766.Smeaton's coal burning Newcomen-type engine proved costly and inefficient. It was assisted by a waterwheel from 1779 and replaced in 1786 by a Boulton & Watt steam engine. The waterwheel continued to be used until the 1840s.

An engine house had to be built at New River Head to house Smeaton's engine, and it was set a few yards to the east of the existing windmill and horse-works. Remarkably, most of its structure survives to this day although the building has been modified and extended several times.

Smeaton's own drawings for that engine survive among his papers. What he had designed was a modified version of the engine invented by Newcomen in 1705. Strictly speaking, it was an atmospheric engine rather than a steam engine, as it did not rely on the expansion of steam but rather on the near-vacuum caused when steam condenses inside a closed cylinder. Newcomen engines had been used at many places, especially for pumping water out of coal mines. At such places they cost little to run, as they could burn low-grade coal that would otherwise go to waste. On the outskirts of London, where coal would have to be brought by sea from Newcastle, the expense would be very different.

Sadly for the shareholders of the New River Company it seems that Smeaton in 1766 – doubtless full of optimism and excellent intentions – led them up the same experimental garden path as Sorocold had done with their predecessors in 1708, and advised the company to put its money into a piece of experimental technology. In Sorocold's case it had been the captivating idea of a windmill with room for horses to work in the base 'when needed' that won the day. Now, with Smeaton, it was to be a Newcomen engine, 'improved' by various ideas Smeaton was keen to try. Was this to be at last the solution the company had been searching for since about 1700?

The answer – a resounding no – is to be gleaned from the copy report Smeaton sent Robert Mylne in July 1774, by which time the Newcomen engine had been belching expensive black smoke into the Islington sky for some five years. This shows that the original report had grossly underestimated the fire engine's consumption of coal. Smeaton gives reasons for his error – he had been relying on some data which he had 'since found to be very much exaggerated'. While accepting the fact he excused himself – he had followed 'the opinion then commonly received, viz. that small Engines perform better in proportion than large ones, whereas from his own Experiments made on purpose since that time he finds that small Engines require considerably more Fire in proportion to the work done than large Engines.' The fire engine continued in use – for a time – but it seems that once again history had repeated itself and the New River Company had plumped for the wrong option.

Modern histories of the New River suggest that Smeaton's engine was eventually replaced by a steam engine provided by Boulton and Watt. They do not mention any intervening method of pumping. In other words, the accepted sequence is from windmill to horsemill to Smeaton to Boulton and Watt – wind, then horse then steam. This sounds plausible enough. As we have already seen it is an over-simplification, because the windmill was actually a dual purpose wind/horse engine. But there was yet another link in the chain, forgotten and waiting to be found.

The forgotten waterwheel

Among the eighteenth-century minutes of the company there are one or two references to something that modern histories largely ignore – a waterwheel. Its starting point seems to be one meeting after which the secretary had recorded

> 'it is the opinion of the meeting that a brick arch be made under ground .. and an overshott Wheel be constructed in the Bottom of the Round Tower so as to work by means of Water let upon it.. and the said Wheel to work the Pump Gear of the present Horse Works which has all the Apparatus fixed for forcing Water up into the High Pond.'[6]

This is intriguing. The 'Round Tower' could only be a reference to the windmill base. Had there really been a waterwheel there once? If so, the site at New River Head would be unusual, as having examples of wind, horse, water, Newcomen and steam engines all performing the same task in unbroken sequence.

The minute book showed that a month later, at a General Court, the whole matter was put back to a committee. Months went by and then years. Had the whole idea been dropped? Then came the answer. According to the minute book

> 'the Surveyor reported that the following works had been done and performed, viz. 1st A hole had been sunk and lined with brickwork where the horseworks formerly stood near the tower at Islington and that a waterwheel on a new construction had been erected in the said hole, which being moved by the waste water, worked the old pumps and forced water to the High Pond.'[7]

This means that the original proposal to put the water wheel in the windmill base had been dropped, and it had been set at the east side of the building instead. This was probably because of the constructional difficulties of excavating inside the mill base.

Another month went by, and then there was a minute ordering 'that a proper roof be made over the waterwheel at New River Head to preserve it from the inclemency of the weather, under the direction of the surveyor.' Still later entries down the years confirmed that the wheel continued to be fully operational until some time after 1842, but it had gone by 1856.[8]

The whole waterwheel project seems to have been efficiently carried out, as might be expected from Mylne. While its pumps filled the Upper Pond, the waste water which had been used to turn it was run down to a new small reservoir, from where pipes dispensed it to more than 700 premises in Clerkenwell which had formerly been served from New River Head. In 1799 it was reconstructed, then set to work again. In 1804 a note of the Engine Worker's duties included attending the 'usual working of the two steam engines and the waterwheel ... to keep the High Pond and its services in a full and complete state .. by night as well as day ... and occasionally on Sundays.' As late as 1833 the yard foreman's duties

37 Smeaton's engine house and the windmill tower, which has lost its cap and was reduced to a nine-foot stump soon after. Drawing dated 1775.

included the injunction to keep a book recording the workings of the steam engines and the waterwheel at New River Head. In 1842 W.C. Mylne, the then surveyor reported that works had been needed to a damaged sewer pipe where 'large quantities of water are discharged … from the waterwheel.'[9]

How could it be that the memory of the waterwheel had been lost? The reason is probably that it was for all practical purposes invisible. An overshot wheel will only work if its top is lower than the source of the water that turns it. This had to be the water level in the Round Pond at New River Head, and it followed that the waterwheel had to be buried out of sight in the 'hole … lined with brickwork' below the general ground level at New River Head. At around this time the yard at New River Head had been enclosed with a high brick wall, so little enough could be seen by passers by in any event. Nor would a waterwheel have had any particular novelty – they had been used to provide power for many centuries.

The water that fed and turned the waterwheel would not of course be wasted – it could still be used to supply customers on lower ground, and would be none the worse in quality or quantity for having tumbled over the waterwheel in the course of its journey. So it was potentially a very efficient system.

Perhaps the most surprising thing of all about the waterwheel is the date when it came into being. That first meeting which had been 'of the opinion .. that an overshott wheel be constructed..' took place as late as May 1774, and the meeting which finally decided the project should proceed was in February 1776. It was not until November 1779 that Robert Mylne finally reported that the work was complete. If we remember that Smeaton's Newcomen engine began working sometime in 1769 it is obvious that approval for the waterwheel came after Smeaton's engine had been running for long enough for the engine's true running costs to be known.

This is confirmed by a resolution passed at one of the company's meetings in March 1780: 'Resolved that the present state of the fire engine be altered and improved so as to perform the whole business when the waterwheel stops.' This suggests two things. The first is that the waterwheel was able to do so much pumping that the fire engine could be taken out of service for a time in order to try and improve it. The second is that without help from the waterwheel, the engine could not pump as much water as was needed.

Here was a case where wind power had failed and been replaced by the muscle power of horses and where the horses had – not surprisingly – in their turn been replaced by an engine fuelled by coal. But only then did water power appear on the scene, and having appeared stayed in use for over sixty years.

38 New River Head from the west in about 1800. the pipes in the foreground are too regular to be elm and are probably cast-iron.

An unexpected sequence

This unexpected sequence raises the question why such an obvious solution as a waterwheel was not built until the late 1770s. It must have been a successful innovation as there are references to its constant use in the decades that followed. It has to be said that the records are few but from them we can infer that the wheel remained quietly and efficiently in use until at least the 1840s – 'at least' because there is no obvious record when it stopped and it may have lasted until the major changes at New River Head in 1856. It needed a little maintenance from time to time but it never seems to have provoked any controversy about its cost or disputes as to how it might be changed. Just

a year after its installation, in 1780, the surveyor reported to a meeting that the sides of the Upper Pond had been built up to allow for 18 inches greater depth of water, so the waterwheel was able to pump even higher than the horses – or the Newcomen engine – had ever previously been asked to do.

Why had the company taken so long to instal a waterwheel? Lowthorp had recommended one in 1704. Perhaps the board had felt that the humble waterwheel, familiar all over England since Anglo Saxon times, was too commonplace to be the right solution for a smart London waterworks. Perhaps they were just carried along by the enthusiasm of Sorocold and Smeaton to test their new ideas.

Boulton and Watt

Mylne's waterwheel was always intended to be backed-up by an engine, and by the 1780s it was clear that Smeaton's was near the end of its life.

Matthew Boulton and James Watt made steam engines at a factory in Soho, Birmingham, from 1773. The engines, designed by Watt, were technically more advanced, and far more efficient, than the Newcomen type engine that Smeaton had designed for New River Head. The New River Company ordered its first engine from Boulton and Watt in February 1785, when Boulton attended a meeting of the board, and it was resolved to erect the engine in an extension to Smeaton's engine house.[10] The new engine began work on 1 December 1786 and seems to have been satisfactory, as the board, never profligate with money otherwise destined for their dividends, ordered a gratuity of 5 guineas to be paid 'to James Law, Mr Boulton's foreman who put the new fire engine together.'[11]

Then, in 1788, an interesting experiment had to be carried out. Watt still held the patent on his steam engines, and in accordance with his usual contract Boulton and Watt were entitled to a royalty of one third of the savings of coal achieved by their machine compared to its predecessor. The Boulton and Watt engine came fitted with a sealed counter that recorded the number of strokes it made, but there still had to be a comparison made with the old machine, in this case Smeaton's. In preparation for this trial, no doubt at Mylne's suggestion, the New River board had ordered that 'the old fire engine be repaired and put into proper working order' so that the trial would be on the 'fairest terms', and the test in due course took place. The two engines were steamed together and it was found that Boulton and Watt's could pump almost three times as much as Smeaton's with the same amount of fuel – 43,000 cubic feet of water compared to 15,000 on 9 bushels of best coal. The counter on the new machine had recorded 3,369,420 strokes in the first 19 months

39 *The windmill base and engine house as they now are. Smeaton's original narrow engine house was widened to accept later engines, by Boulton & Watt, in 1785-6, 1793 and 1818.*

of its use, and at an average of 290 strokes per bushel of coal it had saved 585 chaldrons compared to the old engine. Boulton and Watt were entitled to the value of one third of this, amounting to £306, and this was in due course approved by the board and paid to them.[12]

Whether Smeaton's engine was used again after that seems doubtful. By 1792 John Rowe, the New River Secretary, noted after a row with the engine worker in Mylne's absence 'there is only one fire engine that may properly be worked – the old one, as to the boiler etc. seems to have been for a great length of time totally useless.'[13] In November 1793 the board agreed that it should be replaced with a new one by Boulton and Watt, and the estimate is endorsed with a note that it was to be 'worked occasionally *only,* when any accident may happen in the waterwheel, or to the present fire engine.'[14] The new machine was to cost no more than £2,260 and someone has scribbled on the estimate 'only 7 yrs of the patent to run' – after which time Watt's patent ran out and no further royalties would be payable.

Despite the success of the steam engines, the waterwheel still continued in use until after 1842. From this it seems that it would have been the correct solution back in 1700. The Reverend Lowthorp had deserved a better hearing than he received.

CHAPTER FIFTEEN

Fighting for survival 1800 to 1820

Time for change – The New River in 1800 – Wood gives way to iron – Competition – The new companies – New against old – Fighting back – The effect on the Company – Suing for peace – A dry Christmas – The fall of London Bridge

Time for change

A mood of complacency had settled over the New River Company by 1800. It was almost two centuries old, and a firmly established part of the London scene. It was also immensely profitable. After a slight dip around 1700, dividends had recovered and they continued to grow right through the eighteenth century. The annual dividend on a single share had been £212 in 1700; by 1800 it was £463, equivalent to perhaps £150,000 today. All of the directors owned at least one share, so they were prosperous men, most of whom only attended occasional meetings.

All this was about to change. The nineteenth century was going to be very eventful for the New River Company. There was to be cut-throat competition. Tens of thousands of Londoners were to die in cholera epidemics caused by contaminated water. There was to be mounting public anger with the high cost of such a basic necessity, and a clamour for public ownership. After it all, thanks to a lot of effort and certain natural advantages the Company would reach the end of the nineteenth century wealthier and stronger than ever before, but about to be taken over by the new Metropolitan Water Board in 1904, in return for handsome compensation.

The New River in 1800

By 1800 the New River works had not much altered since 1708. All the water flowed first to New River Head, and most of it was distributed from there by gravity. About a quarter was pumped up to the Upper Pond, though that, as we have seen, was now done by a combination of steam power and a waterwheel. From the Upper Pond, the higher parts of the West End were supplied. Similarly the distribution network, although it had grown much more extensive, was still composed of nine-foot lengths of hollowed elm logs, and no customer had water available for more than a few hours three times a week at best. London was continuing to grow, and its population, which had been 700,000 in 1775, rose to 950,000 by 1800 so there was a continuing demand for new supplies. The same period had also marked the first widespread use of 'water closets' – flushing lavatories – which made extra demands on the supplies.

Wood gives way to iron

Soon after 1805 new water companies provided competition for the New River, and one effect was to focus the minds of the New River board members on modernising their distribution pipework.

Wooden water mains were very bulky and though the largest internal diameter in normal use by the Company was 7 inches, it did not contain much water. Because of this, several such mains had to be laid in places. The main that ran along Goswell Road to the eastern parts of the City consisted of nine lines of pipes laid side by side. The irregular logs from which they were made could be as much as eighteen inches in diameter in places. Thus they took up a great deal of space, and locating a leaking pipe was made more difficult.

Leakage was a constant problem. Wooden pipes could be damaged in a variety of ways, and were all gradually rotting from the moment they were laid, at unpredictable rates depending on the acidity of the soil and variations in the quality of the timber. Wooden pipes were also a great source of public irritation, as streets were being constantly dug up for repairs, while leaks made unpaved streets without drains very muddy.

Cast iron water pipes had been used in France as early as 1682, and the Chelsea Company had used some since 1746, although only from its pumping engine to its reservoir. At first, they were relatively expensive and designed to be bolted together. But, in hot weather, they expanded and then pulled apart at the joints when they cooled. Eventually sliding joints were designed, and these were more durable.

The New River Company had laid an iron main, years before, in 1790. That was a sixteen-inch main from the Upper Pond to a new reservoir near Tottenham Court Road, on the site of what became Tolmers Square. The pipes, bought from a Sheffield ironfounder called Booth, cost £4,157 and the main was over a mile long, with a fall of thirty-six feet, twice as much as the New River fell in forty miles. Robert Mylne described it in a letter he wrote to James Watt about a new engine: 'Our new iron 16" main ... is in full work and blows all our old elm pipes out of the ground in Mary bone.'[1]

The change from wood to iron was a gradual one until 1810. Apart from the main just mentioned, the Company spent an average of only £253 on iron, compared to about £5,000 on timber, each year from 1790 to 1800. From 1801 the spending began to rise, with an average of £1755 a year on iron over the next ten years, but after 1810 there was a major investment and the average spending rose to £17,700 for each of the next four years to 1814, representing an average of eleven miles of pipe laid each year.[2]

Over that period, the Company still continued to lay some wooden mains, although it was ever more obvious that they represented bad value since they had a shorter life and needed more maintenance. As the Company's works committee reported in 1814, they had laid 25.3 miles of wooden mains in 1812. Of this only 5.2 miles was for new mains, while all the rest had gone 'for Changes, or in other words for repairing the unsound and unserviceable Timber in the streets.' In 1813 the proportion was even greater – out of 23 miles laid, only 3 miles were of new mains. It was not just the cost of the pipes, 'to this extravagant consumption of Timber must be added the very heavy expense of labour, and also of repaving the trenches.' During the four years from 1811 to 1814, annual spending on wooden pipes dropped from £7,225 to £524, and thereafter they were hardly used.

The Company was under intense pressure from competitors from about 1810, and this was the driving force behind the decision to replace all the wooden mains with iron. The cost would be enormous. As at 1814, there still remained about £224,000 of work to be done before it would be complete. The change affected the Company at all levels. William Chadwell Mylne designed the new network and devoted much of his time to it so that he was awarded a £1,000 bonus – almost three years' salary – in 1819 'for his exceptional efforts during the preceding seven years of conversion from wood to iron pipes'. Even the yard foreman had his duties increased from 1813:

> 'Mr Hughes to take the management of the Upper Yard, Smith's shop, Steam Engines, Water wheel and Horse Engine, and to pay all the men regularly employed ...every Saturday night... to superintend the laying down of iron pipes, which are to be done by contract, whenever his time can be spared'.[3]

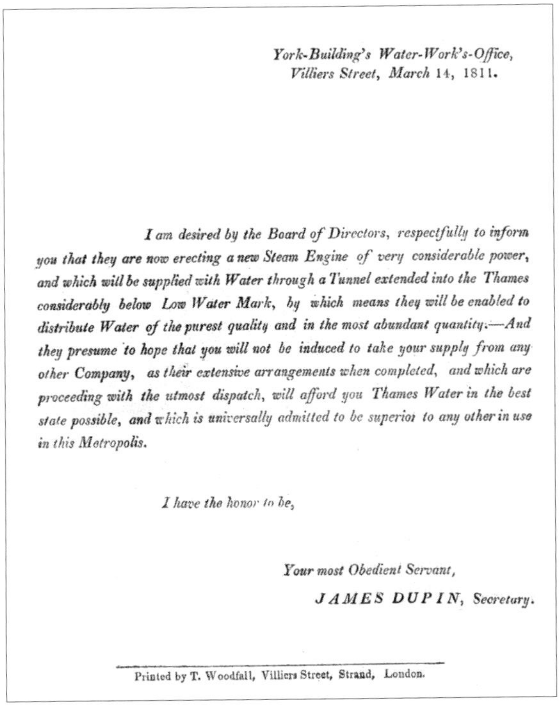

York-Building's Water-Work's-Office,
Villiers Street, March 14, 1811.

I am desired by the Board of Directors, respectfully to inform you that they are now erecting a new Steam Engine of very considerable power, and which will be supplied with Water through a Tunnel extended into the Thames considerably below Low Water Mark, by which means they will be enabled to distribute Water of the purest quality and in the most abundant quantity.—And they presume to hope that you will not be induced to take your supply from any other Company, as their extensive arrangements when completed, and which are proceeding with the utmost dispatch, will afford you Thames Water in the best state possible, and which is universally admitted to be superior to any other in use in this Metropolis.

I have the honor to be,

Your most Obedient Servant,

JAMES DUPIN, Secretary.

Printed by T. Woodfall, Villiers Street, Strand, London.

40 As competition grew stronger in 1811 the York Buildings Waterworks made the bold claim that Thames water was 'universally admitted to be superior to any other in use in this Metropolis.'

There was also a tactical side to pipelaying. Even by 1814 the works committee could foresee some future agreement with the competitors whereby each would cede some of its outlying territory. If so why give competitors good iron pipes? Thus they recommended considering 'the propriety of adopting some boundary line, beyond which Westward, (iron) pipes should not be laid.'

Competition

In 1800, apart from its oldest competitor at London Bridge, there were two other substantial companies supplying central London north of the Thames. The first was the Chelsea Waterworks, formed in 1723, which supplied the City of Westminster and surrounding districts with water pumped from the Thames at Chelsea. The second was the York Buildings Company, which had existed since 1691. It too pumped water from the Thames, and supplied parts of Westminster from a raised cistern at Charing Cross. Two companies supplied areas of east London, the Shadwell Waterworks and the West Ham Waterworks. There was also the Hampstead Water Company, which had since 1692 supplied the distant villages of Hampstead and Highgate from nearby ponds, and which also ran a small supply to the West End.

Of the main four companies, the New River Company was more than twice the size of all the others put together. In 1800 they compared as follows:

COMPANY	Customers	Gallons daily	Annual income
New River	59,000	11 million	£81,000
London Bridge	10,000	4 million	£12,000
Chelsea	9,500	1¼ million	£15,000
York Buildings	2,250	150,000	£3,400

Things were about to change.

The new companies

The legendary profitability of the New River and the continuing growth of London, together with its use of old-fashioned and inefficient wooden pipelines, inevitably attracted others who saw an opportunity for gain. Four new companies were set up, while one of the old ones was taken over and revitalised, all between 1805 and 1811.

The first of these was the South London Waterworks, which began to supply water from Vauxhall Creek in Kennington in 1807. As its name suggests it did not supply north of the Thames, and did not affect the New River.

The next was the West Middlesex Waterworks in 1807, which drew water from the Thames at Hammersmith. Its Act of Parliament authorised it to supply Hammersmith, Chiswick, Brentford and nearby places to the west of London, specifically excluding Westminster and Chelsea after representations by the Chelsea Waterworks. The Company had originally intended to use stone water pipes, but found problems in obtaining sufficient quantities. Instead they decided to lay iron mains, in the hope that the initial high outlay would be recouped by lower maintenance costs.

This was done, and their supply began in 1808.

The third newcomer was the East London Waterworks Company. This was the brainchild of Ralph Dodd, who had also been the original proposer of both the South London and the West Middlesex companies. In every case he seems to have quarrelled with the directors after being accused of some unspecified misconduct, and did not see any of the works through to completion. His plan had been to take water from a tidal stretch of the River Lea at Old Ford and allow it to settle for a while in a reservoir to clarify it. From this he proposed to supply a great swathe of east and north-east London, from Mile End through Hackney to Tottenham including parts of Islington and the City already supplied by the New River Company. Much of this land was still open fields but had great potential for house-building as London continued to spread. His plans were opposed by the owners of the Shadwell and West Ham companies but were authorised by Parliament in 1807. The new company started to construct its works at once, and after some initial indecision accepted the advice of its engineer to lay iron pipes instead of wood.

Last of the incomers was the Grand Junction Waterworks Company. As early as 1798 the proprietors of the Grand Junction canal had obtained power to supply local areas with water from its canal basin at Paddington. In 1810 they deputed these powers to a group who then obtained the necessary Act of Parliament to form the company in 1811. They would have reservoirs at Paddington and proposed to lay their mains as far as Drury Lane in the West End. The result of this would be a four-way competition, since the New River, Chelsea and West Middlesex companies supplied parts of this area. Some dithering with stone pipes, because some of their directors were also involved in a firm making such pipes, delayed the start of their operations. They then decided in favour of iron pipes and began supplying water in 1812.

It was the York Buildings Company that fell first to a takeover. It had been languishing for some time and in 1809 a group that included shareholders from the West Middlesex and East London companies bought it outright. Over the next three years they improved its plant and laid a network of iron mains that extended over a larger area than the Company had previously supplied.

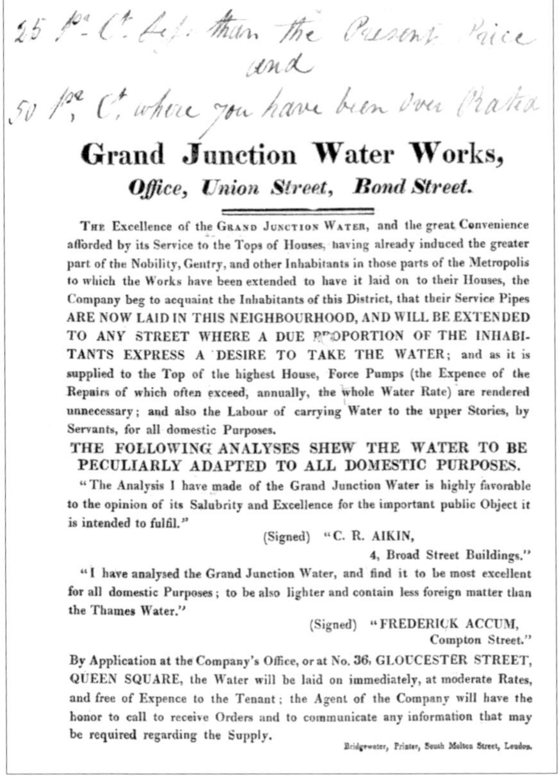

25 Pr Ct Less than the Present Price
and
50 Pr Ct where you have been Over Rated

Grand Junction Water Works,

Office, Union Street, Bond Street.

THE Excellence of the GRAND JUNCTION WATER, and the great Convenience afforded by its Service to the Tops of Houses, having already induced the greater part of the Nobility, Gentry, and other Inhabitants in those parts of the Metropolis to which the Works have been extended to have it laid on to their Houses, the Company beg to acquaint the Inhabitants of this District, that their Service Pipes ARE NOW LAID IN THIS NEIGHBOURHOOD, AND WILL BE EXTENDED TO ANY STREET WHERE A DUE PROPORTION OF THE INHABITANTS EXPRESS A DESIRE TO TAKE THE WATER; and as it is supplied to the Top of the highest House, Force Pumps (the Expence of the Repairs of which often exceed, annually, the whole Water Rate) are rendered unnecessary; and also the Labour of carrying Water to the upper Stories, by Servants, for all domestic Purposes.

THE FOLLOWING ANALYSES SHEW THE WATER TO BE PECULIARLY ADAPTED TO ALL DOMESTIC PURPOSES.

"The Analysis I have made of the Grand Junction Water is highly favorable to the opinion of its Salubrity and Excellence for the important public Object it is intended to fulfil."

(Signed) "C. R. AIKIN,
4, Broad Street Buildings."

"I have analysed the Grand Junction Water, and find it to be most excellent for all domestic Purposes; to be also lighter and contain less foreign matter than the Thames Water."

(Signed) "FREDERICK ACCUM,
Compton Street."

By Application at the Company's Office, or at No. 36, GLOUCESTER STREET, QUEEN SQUARE, the Water will be laid on immediately, at moderate Rates, and free of Expence to the Tenant; the Agent of the Company will have the honor to call to receive Orders and to communicate any information that may be required regarding the Supply.

Bridgewater, Printer, South Molton Street, London.

41 *The Grand Junction Water Works was incorporated in 1811. After a disastrous experiment with stone pipes it used cast iron instead, and began supplying in 1812.*

New against old

Once the new companies were up and running the real competition began. The West Middlesex Company liked the look of Marylebone, which had many good quality houses capable of paying substantial water rates. Until then, the New River and Chelsea companies had supplied the area. Unfortunately, however, Marylebone was almost three miles from Islington, so the flow of New River water was not very good. As for Chelsea water, it came from the Thames and was of poorer quality.

Part of Marylebone was within the liberties of Westminster, and out of the reach of the West Middlesex Company under the Act. Other parts were not, and the Company originally decided just to supply those. It then saw the merits of obtaining a change in the law to remove the restriction on where it could supply, and set about gaining support for an amending Act. Canvassers went from door to door taking signatures to a petition, as they had earlier gone distributing leaflets to advertise the merits of their supply, and found considerable support from disgruntled householders. It seemed that water was often not supplied even three times a week in some areas, and the old companies had been slow to deal with complaints as long as they had near monopolies. The wooden mains of the old companies meant the streets were constantly being dug up, whereas the West Middlesex could lay its iron mains and then forget them. Furthermore, the iron mains could take greater pressure and serve water to the upper floors of houses. The mains would also be of great value in fighting fire.

The Chelsea Company opposed the new Act with much vigour, but it was passed in 1810, and the West Middlesex Company could thereafter supply where it liked in Westminster. One saving clause for the old companies provided that the West Middlesex must not hinder or obstruct their works.

As for the East London Company, one of its first actions was to buy out, in 1808, the Shadwell and West Ham works. It thus had no competitor except the New River Company, and there are strong indications that each company was aware of the risks involved. In June 1808 the New River Company approached its new competitor with a view to seeing if some boundary line between them could be fixed by agreement, but nothing came of this. The East London company also posed a potential threat to the London Bridge works, whose area it overlapped in part.

Although it only joined the fray in 1812, the Grand Junction Company had one ability that none of its competitors possessed. Not only did it supply water at sufficient pressure to reach the tops of houses, but it provided a constant service in all its pipes instead of the usual intermittent three-days-a-week variety. It was far ahead of its time in this respect, as constant supply did not extend to all parts of London until 1904.

Once competition was under way there was a period when the householders of London can hardly have believed their luck. Surly and insolent turncocks and collectors were transformed into courteous callers who popped notes under the door to confirm that this water company or that would meet any other company on its terms. Charges suddenly dropped and supplies became more reliable. Of course it could not last. On the streets, all sorts of stratagems were used. Workmen laying a new main would disconnect householders from their old supplier and join them up without any discussion. Men laying pipes 'inadvertently' damaged those of their rivals in the process. In some districts one street might contain the pipes of three companies, and it would be hard to prove who had done what, especially when so much of it was buried out of sight. There were even reports of open brawling between groups of rival workers.

As the months passed, the competition intensified. The East London Company would not supply water to customers where they were the only supplier if those customers owned property in streets where there was joint supply with the New River Company, unless they would take East London water at all their addresses. A collector reported an example in April 1815. The East London Company had taken away the water from four houses in Dog Row, Bethnal Green (where the New River had no pipes) belonging to Mr Gray of Great Eastern Street, 'in consequence of his having changed fourteen tenements in Whitechapel Road to the New River.'[4]

Fighting back

The minutes of New River board meetings around this time often refer to the problem. In October 1811 the New River Company was still hopeful of gentlemanly behaviour from its competitors. Why else was the secretary instructed to complain to the East London Com-

42 View of part of London from Pentonville, by George Hollis c.1815, shortly before Amwell Street became lined with houses. The stump of the windmill is in the centre, behind the wall.

pany that they 'presume that such conduct must be wholly unknown to the Directors of the East London Waterworks, a proceeding so unjustifiable and unworthy ... can never receive their sanction?'[5]

In November 1811, the Company had adopted their competitors' tactic of direct appeals to customers, with a printed notice:

> 'Sir,
> Being ordered by the New River Company to wait on you to counteract misrepresentations that are industriously circulated to our prejudice, I take the liberty of requesting, you will have the goodness, if any applications should be made to you to induce you to change your supply of Water, not to consent thereto until I have had an opportunity of seeing you: I am directed also to say, that whatever apparent advantages may be held out to you, the New River Company are determined to make a sacrifice, and meet their opponents on any terms they may offer.
> I am, Sir,
> Your obedient humble servant,
> Collector.[6]

Even the Governor of the New River, Robert Smith, had to enter the arena, and he penned a letter to the Company's tenants in February 1812, claiming that in two centuries' service to the metropolis they had at no time received a return of more than $6\frac{1}{4}$ % on their investment. The report that the Company's shares originally cost only £100 each was 'absurd' and 'needed no refutation. The formation of their works at the time of Sir Hugh Myddelton cost, according to the best authorities, £500,000.' As already discussed in Chapter 6, this was quite untrue, yet 5000 copies were immediately printed and distributed, followed by 5000 more the next month, while copies were to be placed in *'The Alfred'*, *The Chronicle*, *The Morning Post*, *The Morning Advertiser* and *Bell's Weekly Dispatch*', in March and April.[7]

It was soon plain that the Company had to fight back. In 1812 a General Court debated the problem, and issued an instruction to Collectors. They were to use their discretion to lower rents, but 'only where the Company is in danger of loss by the new companies laying down their pipes.'[8]

That year there were many cases of special arrangements being made to meet the competition. Mr Lear, a sugar refiner in Great Garden Street would have his rent lowered from £19 to £13. Some new houses in Judd Street off the Euston Road would be charged £1 16s. 0d. a year, instead of £2 as had been intended. The rent of eight tenements in North Street, Pentonville would be reduced from £4 4s.0d. to £3 10s.0d. The collector who covered Pancras Place might use his discretion to reduce rents. Mr Moat, a soap boiler in Bishopsgate Street would be reduced from £9 9s.0d. to £6 6s.0d.[9] Sometimes rents were lowered to match specific offers by the East London Company. Mr Leary's rent for twenty houses in Curtain Road would be lowered from £10 to £8, and twelve houses and cottages in Shoreditch were reduced from £6 14s. 0d. to £4 for that reason. When news came that the East London Company had been soliciting New River tenants in Great Leonard Street the collector was told to use his discretion and lower rents as necessary.

There were even moves towards more subtle forms of marketing. Two house agents were to have a free supply in the hope that they would recommend the Company to tenants. In 1815 it was ordered that 'Mr Eldred the Treasurer of the Middle Temple' should have his supply *gratis*, perhaps for similar reasons.[10]

A typical problem can be seen in February 1812. The Steward of Gray's Inn, a large user, had written inviting the Company to reduce the rates as they had been offered much lower ones by another Company. The board must have known that their reply would become known to the assorted professionals with chambers in Gray's Inn. It was not the occasion for a quiet private arrangement of the kind that a collector might make with an individual householder. The clerk was ordered to reply assuring them 'that the supply of the whole district including the Inn has been calculated at a price which affords a bare compensation to the Company at a rate not exceeding legal interest on their Capital. The Board therefore cannot make any specific offer of abatement, but feeling the necessity of supplying their Tenants at as low a Rate as any other Company, if the Society will state the terms upon which the supply has been offered, the Board will take it into consideration and give an immediate answer.'[11]

The West Middlesex Company was as much of a problem as the East London. On 19 March 1812, the Clerk was ordered to write to the directors of the West Middlesex, 'whose servants frequently break New River Company pipes and leave them unrepaired a fortnight.' In September 1812, he was to write to a plumber for the West Middlesex Company, who had stopped up a New River tenant's supply pipe with clay, demanding repair and threatening prosecution for any repetition. In January 1813 the Clerk was to write to the directors of the West Middlesex to complain that 'more injury is done than the necessary works require and the Board are strongly inclined to suspect that the damage is done in many cases intentionally by the Servants of the West Middlesex Company'.

By January 1813 a collector was reporting that West Middlesex men were canvassing as far east as High Holborn. In June 1815 they had laid pipes in Great Marlborough Street, and were canvassing New River tenants there. There were even allegations of New River staff being suborned. In February 1813 it was noted that 'Thomas the turncock in Somers Town to be immediately discharged,' having 'done the Company great injury with their Tenants in not well supplying them with water' and the Inspector having 'reason to think he had been tampered with by the Servants of the West Middlesex.'[12]

The atmosphere of rivalry of course lent itself to misunderstanding. On 19 December 1811, a street inspector reported that West Middlesex men had changed the supply to the Earl of Peterborough's house in Portman Square, without any direction from his Lordship's agents or servants. It was ordered that a letter be written, setting out the supposed facts and continuing: 'Unwilling as the Board are to trouble your Lordship, they have felt it their duty to make this Communication, and unless there is reason for the contrary, request that permission may be given for the Pipe being re-layed to their works.' Four weeks later the collector had to report that he had called at the Earl's house 'and was informed that the reason of his having changed to the West Middlesex was in consequence of their being able to supply his Water Closet, which would save much trouble.'

The traffic was not all in one direction. In April 1813, a letter came from the West Middlesex, complaining that a New River collector had been telling their customers they were 'in a state of insolvency,' and that those who took their water would only be taken back by the New River on treble rates. Was the collector proceeding under the authority of the board, they enquired? The Clerk was instructed to reply that he was not, with the rider that 'they think that if the origin of these mutual complaints was looked into, it would not appear that the first cause of them was with the servants of the New River.' Nevertheless, the tone of the letter was sufficiently conciliatory to make it clear that the New River Company would not be averse to some kind of mutual agreement.[13]

Similar problems were encountered when the revitalised York Buildings Company began its service. In December 1811 it was reported that a New River turncock had detected two York Buildings men before daylight changing a house in Craven Street, Strand, from the New River water to their own. On enquiry he found that no orders had been given for this either by the present or the former tenant, and he had prevented it being done. Numbers 6 and 7 George Street had been changed in the same way. It was ordered that the clerk should write to York Buildings on the subject to say the George Street premises would be immediately brought back to the Company's service, and 'the Board apprehending that these changes were made without the knowledge of the Company, request that directions may be given to prevent a repetition of such proceedings.' Even this courtesy did not cure the problem, and similar events followed where New River tenants were simply cut off.[14]

Cutting tenants off for non-payment was of course a sanction the New River had included in its water leases since Myddelton's time. In 1815 when a collector reported 'several persons in the limits of the East London Company, who refused payment of their rents and arrears' he was 'directed to select in six or eight streets one or two of them and deprive them of water.' In February 1816 a similar request to disconnect non-payers was approved, but the Company was aware of the risks of seeming high-handed and directed it should be done 'using great caution'.[15]

The effect on the Company

Competition damaged the New River Company in a number of ways. It lost customers and, apart from that loss of revenue, its income was affected by offering lower prices to combat the other companies. But at the same time it had to maintain the lengthy New River and also set about the massive task of replacing wooden mains by cast iron pipes.

In February 1814, a committee was formed to consider the problems. Their report shows that William Chadwell Mylne had provided them with much information. They said that it might be wise to 'retract and draw in, rather than to extend and draw further into the territory of your opponents'. If so a westward boundary line might be chosen, beyond which no iron pipes should be laid. This would reduce their losses if and when such an agreement was reached.

Even the weather was against them – as it happened this was the last winter when the Thames froze sufficiently for there to be a Frost Fair set up on the ice. 'The present unusually long and severe winter, will not only add to your expenses but diminish your revenue from the loss of numerous tenants dissatisfied at not receiving their customary service of water.' This was a reference to the fact that many of the mains simply froze solid at such times.

The committee then turned to 'the state of the contest for public favour and encouragement between yourselves and the New Water Companies.' Successful competition, they said, required an equivalent quality of water, with equal supply at a lower cost. In this regard, the East London could not succeed, for its water was inferior and its reservoir far lower.

The West Middlesex supplied Thames water drawn at Hammersmith, and New River water was at least equal to this in quality. To bring New River water to Islington cost £4,000 a year in maintenance and £350 a year that was paid to the River Lea commissioners for extracting their water. Added to this was £4,500 spent on pumping to the Upper Pond, a total of £8,850 a year to supply 214,000 hogsheads a day – a hogshead was fifty-four gallons. Such a quantity could not possibly be pumped up from the Thames at the same cost. Thus the New River had the advantage over the West Middlesex.

As for the Grand Junction Waterworks, their canal at Paddington was three feet higher than New River Head, giving them a small advantage, but they were further from the centre of the metropolis, which more than redressed the balance. They could only extract 32,971 hogsheads a day, and beyond that had to pay. Here the New River had a vast advantage – the quantity of water it had for £4,000 a year would have cost the Grand Junction Company £20,000. Further, the quality of their water was complained of, particularly in summer. The committee concluded that the New River had advantages over its new competitors, and went on to analyse the problem.

'In the keen and sharply contested competition in which we have been engaged for upwards of two years, a majority of our losses have arisen from the multiplied interests exerted against us. There are not more than 120 persons interested in the New River property and there are only 72 shares.' By contrast the new companies had issued a total of 12,700 shares, 'a large proportion of (which) are held by Tradesmen and Shopkeepers, who are continually canvassing and going from door to door, soliciting your tenants to change, and with a degree of Activity and Perseverance which can alone attach to principals in the concern. Your committee have no hesitation in avowing their opinion that a Board of Gentlemen meeting once a week is perhaps not the best calculated successfully to contend in a Warfare of this description ... and who cannot and will not descend to some of the practices countenanced by their Opponents.'

The committee continued with a collective pat on the back: 'There is no instance of a Monopoly, which has been conducted with a stricter attention to the principles of equity and Justice, while the moderate profits of the Company are the surest proof that when you possessed the power, You never had the inclination to oppress your Tenants by excessive and exorbitant charges.'

Finally, they left it to the meeting to decide how best 'to improve, uphold and maintain this ancient and most useful Establishment, which for two Centuries has so essentially contributed to the health, the comfort and the extension of this great and unrivalled city.'

The solution that was decided on was to press ahead with the money-saving conversion to iron, and to borrow money for that purpose.

Suing for Peace

It must soon have been obvious to all the companies that a struggle had started which would risk hurting them all, and news began to filter in of attempts to reach a compromise.

There was at that time little love lost between the companies. After 1810, the London Bridge works, with its antiquated machinery, had frequent problems, and the New River did not hesitate to poach its tenants. Thus the New River board agreed to supply 'the warm baths at St Mary Axe, previously supplied by the London Bridge Waterworks at the request of the proprietors of the baths.' The application must have aroused some suspicion as the collector was directed to ensure that water was not conveyed surreptitiously from there back into the pipes of the London Bridge Waterworks.[16]

On 3 February 1814, during the great frost on the Thames that year the London Bridge works wrote asking for help: 'From the long continuance and great severity of the frost, four of the wheels of these works on the city side are tied up and that we have but one small wheel at work, and also from the immense collection of ice about these works our Steam Engine cannot work but a few hours in the course of the day.. I am induced to trouble you .. having been told you shut down your mains every night' He was particularly concerned that there would be no water in case of fire. The secretary was directed to reply in somewhat ungracious terms, complaining of standpipes allegedly tapped into the New River mains, and referring to the New River as 'a source that cannot fail'.

As for the directors of the East London Waterworks, one of their resolutions was read at a New River board meeting in May 1813. They were seeking an accommodation, 'since tenants frequently change supply seeking unduly to lower the rates and in many instances evading them altogether.' A solution was needed to 'prevent the growing evils so manifestly to the detriment of both companies.' The secretary was told to reply urging them to adopt 'that principle which used to prevail between water companies', in other words to check first there were no arrears. Two weeks later, the East London Waterworks proposed a meeting, and the offer was accepted.[17]

The first part of the solution came in November 1815, when an agreement was reached with the East London on a demarcation line between the two companies. By it the New River Company lost some territory to the east of the City, but retained the whole of the City itself, along with Islington, Holloway and Stoke Newington as far east as Stamford Hill. Each company lost some pipes in the process, and these were taken over by the other at an agreed valuation. So far as the New River Company was concerned this secured its eastern boundary. There was one problem in Holloway where a local man was trying to set up a water company, but the New River overwhelmed his efforts by laying pipes through his district.

There still remained problems for the New River Company to its west. From what William Chadwell Mylne told a select committee years later, his strategy had been to reduce the area supplied to those central and northern districts most easily served from the New River, and to supply through iron as soon as possible. In that way the New River Company would be strong enough to meet any competition. Furthermore, withdrawal from certain districts would throw increased demand on to the new companies that they would find it hard to supply. When this was done, he said, 'came a truce.'[18]

In April 1813, the chairman of York Buildings asked for a meeting with New River board members on a matter of mutual benefit. Nothing came of this at first, but by February 1816 they wanted to unite with the much larger New River Company. This suggestion was declined, but the New River said it was open to further proposals and by May agreement was reached. The New River Company would buy out the York Buildings Company, taking over their mains from Midsummer 1816, for £250 a year for 96 years, the remaining term of their lease, and also two payments of £5,000. The New River Company would take over the incoming rental, about £3,730, from Midsummer. When the lease expired it was to be renewed to New River every 21 years on payment of £500. The agreement was confirmed at a General Court on 16 July 1816, which also approved taking out a temporary loan for that purpose and for laying iron pipes.[19]

Meanwhile negotiations had continued with the West Middlesex, and by August 1815 were well advanced. The plan was that the two companies would unite from 1 January 1816. Initially the New River would have 80% and the West Middlesex 20%, subject to the New River finishing the conversion of all their wooden mains to iron at their own cost. If after seven years the profits exceeded £600 for each New River share, the proportion would change from 80:20 to 67:33. The New River Company would still be able to agree a line of demarcation with the East London Company, which was nearing agreement. It was provided that certain New River land would be excluded, such as Dorset Yard, the Water House, and the fields around New River Head. A General Court unanimously approved this in principle on 10 August and the following month the West Middlesex wrote to say they too agreed. Eventually, in December 1815 the Company agreed to be united with the West Middlesex as from 1 January 1816, subject to the approval of Parliament.[20] In February 1816 the draft Bill for Parliament was also approved, but then in March was withdrawn following concerted opposition from other water companies and parish representatives.[21]

Despite this setback, the directors of the two companies were well disposed to cooperation by this time, and negotiations with the other central London companies soon followed. The upshot was an agreement, not made public, whereby demarcation lines were agreed and each company then withdrew into its own territory. There were at least two reasons for not making the agreement public. The most important was that the Acts that set up the West Middlesex works contained provisions that specifically forbade the sale or disposal of its powers to any other water company, and arguably prevented the company from making any such agreement. The other was the realisation of the howls of protest that could be expected from Londoners once the anti-competitive elements became clear.

The agreement followed a meeting between four of the five central water companies – the New River, the Chelsea, the West Middlesex and the Grand Junction in July 1817. Between them they agreed where their boundaries would be, and effectively removed competition from the water supply of central London. The small York Buildings Company was not included, but it was then taken over by the New River Company. Even the Hampstead Company reached an agreement as to a demarcation line, on 30 October 1817, as is disclosed by a New River minute over twenty years later when it was varied because of the building development of the Camden estate.[22]

A dry Christmas

This arrangement caused outrage to water consumers. Those whose families had taken New River water in Marylebone for example, perhaps for generations, suddenly discovered at Christmas 1817 that the supply was discontinued. Having cut off the water the New River board did not even discuss the wording of the letter informing customers of the change until 8 January, and the letters were eventually received more than three weeks after the supply had been cut off. The letters said that the Company could no longer afford to supply 'the western quarters of the town, remote from New River Head', and thanked them for their past support. They were then left to make such terms as they could with whichever company now supplied the area, including paying for the costs of the new connection. In some cases the sudden rush of new pipe-laying work for the companies involved was such that it was months before a new supply was connected.

These arrangements came into effect from the end of 1815 for the New River's boundary with the East London, and at Christmas 1817 for the line between the New River and the West Middlesex districts. By 1818 the demarcation agreements with competitors – except the London Bridge works – were all in place and Mylne reported he had 'changed all the Tenants from the wooden services on to the iron pipes lately obtained by exchange from the other companies, as directed by you without putting the tenants to any expense, so that the great object in obtaining such an additional length of iron pipes is now in full operation.'[23]

The fall of London Bridge

The London Bridge Waterworks were also keen to join the general peace-making, and their Secretary wrote in the hope of agreeing where their areas of supply should overlap 'so as to do away entirely with the unpleasant misunderstanding and Warfare which at present subsists to the great detriment of both concerns'. The Clerk was directed to reply that the New River Company would consider any proposals.[24]

Within weeks, the New River Company decided to lay their pipes throughout the City of London, and were able thereby to weaken the London Bridge Waterworks. In June 1816 the Company approved the laying of iron pipes in streets they had not previously supplied including Upper Thames Street, St Clement's Lane, Nicholas Lane, Fenchurch Street, Gracechurch Street, Birchin Lane, Abchurch Lane and Laurence Pountney Lane. They instructed their collectors to 'wait on the inhabitants of the said streets in case they should wish to take the New River in preference to the Thames Water. Within a week the collectors reported back – they had spoken to many of the potential tenants, and there was 'no doubt of the eventual benefit.'[25]

The London Bridge works continued to struggle on with their old technology. In 1817 they sent a circular to their customers asking for patience during times when the supply would be cut off – they had to reconstruct one of their waterwheels. The final straw came in 1821, when after years of discussion, John Rennie's design for a new London Bridge was selected. Fifty years earlier, plans to replace London Bridge had been stalled because they would adversely affect the waterwheels. At that time, the masonry footings or 'starlings' of the bridge piers took up most of the width of the river, so that the water level above the bridge was five feet higher than below, and this was of great assistance to the waterwheels. A new bridge would have fewer arches and cause much less obstruction. There was no future for the waterworks there, and the New River Company agreed to take over its oldest rival in 1822.

The effect of all this was that by about 1820 the New River Company, after twenty years of turmoil, was in a stronger position than before. Its supply network had almost entirely changed from wood to iron, giving a more reliable supply with far lower maintenance costs. It had lost many customers in the West End but was now able to offer its customers a 'high' service. After the period of price-cutting during the competition, it had simply put its prices back to their original levels. The network of iron pipes was now complete, and the Board ordered that 100 guineas should be 'presented to Mr Mylne for his map of the Iron Mains and Pipes.'[26]

The other companies, by contrast, had some difficulties. Where they had reduced their charges to undercut the New River, they now sought to raise them, and unleashed a storm of protest. Marylebone, with its high proportion of well-to-do householders was a particular trouble spot for the Grand Junction Company. One local resident, James Weale, set up the Anti-Water Monopoly Association and published leaflets attacking the companies. The parish vestry even made a series of attempts to obtain an Act for setting up its own waterworks. If this had succeeded it would have destabilised the whole agreement the companies had made, but it was eventually defeated by the combined efforts of the companies.

CHAPTER SIXTEEN

The quest for better water

The 1821 committee – Telford's Commission – Supplying the new suburbs – High Service and Constant Supply – Charles Dickens complains – The problem of waste – Courts and Alleys – Cholera – Cleaner water: The 1852 Metropolis Water Act – The New River in 1853 – The 1856 works – Cutting the loops – Increasing the supply – Constant supply at last – 'An expensive lavatory for pigeons'

The 1821 Committee

What did follow from all this agitation was a Parliamentary Select Committee, set up in 1821 to inquire into the supply of water to the metropolis. This was the first time that London's water supply was considered as a whole, and it was to be the first of a series of parliamentary enquiries that would eventually lead to public ownership of the capital's water in 1904.

The committee heard evidence in February and March 1821, from the water companies as well as from members of the public including James Weale, the Anti-Water Monopolist. The chairman, Michael Angelo Taylor MP had a record of hostility to water companies, but when the committee reported in May 1821, it had not reached many of the conclusions that might have been expected under his chairmanship. It recognised that competition in water supply was very different from competition in other areas, and that companies could not be expected to compete by supplying water in the same streets at ever lower prices until they ruined themselves. As their report put it:

> '... as there can be no great difference in the quality of what they sell, they must vie in lowness of price and will probably be driven to underbid each other down to the point of ruin, because it is better to take anything than to take nothing for that which cannot be carried away: and this must go on until both are worn out, or one has out-lasted the others, and succeeded to a real and effective monopoly, or until by some arrangement between themselves they can put a stop to their mutual destruction.'

Much evidence was heard about how the companies had raised their prices after they had reached their 'General Arrangement,' but it had not been shown that their profits were likely to be excessive. The water supplied to London was provided in far larger quantities than it had been ten years earlier, and this had to be paid for. What did concern the committee was that each company in its own area had the power to fix its own charges for even the most basic level of intermittent supply. In conclusion they proposed an Act to set water charges at no more than 25% above the 1810 level for the 'ordinary service'. The parties concerned could then negotiate the rates for any extra services such as constant supply.

A Bill along the lines suggested was introduced, but by then the fuss had died down and it never passed into law.

Telford's Commission

Allegations about the dreadful quality of Thames water continued to be made, in particular John Wright's 1827 pamphlet, entitled *'The Dolphin, or Grand Junction nuisance proving that several thousand families in Westminster and its Suburbs are supplied with water in a state, offensive to the sight, disgusting to the imagination, and destructive to health.'* This led to the appointment of a Royal Commission in 1827, with the ageing Thomas Telford among its three members. That commission's imaginative but costly proposals were quickly followed by Telford's death in 1834, and were never implemented. In 1840 there was further public outcry, and a Parliamentary Select Committee was appointed, but achieved no practical outcome.

Supplying the new suburbs

The New River Company was being asked to supply newly built districts almost from its beginning. When the Upper Pond was built in 1708, its purpose was to supply the newly built Soho Square and vicinity. At the same time, it also made a supply to the village of Islington possible, and the easy income this provided from a short run of pipes was one of the reasons George Sorocold had used to persuade the Company to build the works he had designed.

By 1765 a pipe ran, not from the Upper Pond but from the New River itself, by what is now Essex Road, to a cistern near the Green Man tavern 'to serve the houses and Cow layer there to take off water.'[1] Other houses in Islington were often supplied as soon as they were built, and bulk discounts existed. In 1776 Francis Carrick agreed to pay ten shillings a year for each of seven new houses built by him 'to be paid whether tenanted or empty,' and this was less than the ordinary rate.

When Hornsey began to be built up there were no New River pipes in the locality. From 1795 it was supplied by water-carts that took water from the New River and supplied seventeen houses there, at the rate of a shilling a cartload.[2] In 1816, the Board declined a request from Hornsey residents who wanted to take a supply of piped water from the river to certain houses. It seemed they had already allowed a Mr Bird to sink a well supplied from the river, and to pump water from it for £10 a year for the same purpose. The latter was written to, telling him to be more attentive to the manner in which he supplied his customers. In 1818 'many respectable inhabitants of Hornsey' were complaining of his exorbitant charges, and he was warned to mend his ways. A few months later, the surveyor was ordered to take possession of the pump Bird used, and it was transferred to a Mr Davison who agreed to pay £20 a year for its use.[3]

By 1808, the extent of new housing in the higher parts of Pentonville and Islington was causing supply difficulties, and Robert Mylne suggested improvements. These seem to have led to the collectors negotiating separate terms with each householder. Standardisation only came after 1816, when the collector suggested that all Islington properties should pay on the same basis as the new houses. This was agreed, and the rates were fixed at £1 a year for a four-roomed house, £1 4s. 0d. for six rooms, £1 10s. 0d. for eight, and £1 16s. 0d. for ten rooms. [4]

The Company was still not prepared to lay pipes until there was sufficient demand. In 1818 a Mr Scott applied to have water in John Street by Islington Workhouse, later Risinghill Street, saying there would eventually be fifty houses in the street. The Company decided that as and when fifteen had actually been built, then they would lay water.

As more building was done in the northern suburbs, water was provided direct from the New River. In 1818 the residents of Highbury Terrace, who had no water supply, asked for one. They were told pipes could be laid from a horse-engine at Highbury Frame, but they would have to meet the cost of £100 for improving the engine and £553 for 860 yards of four-inch pipe with stopcocks. They declined.[5] A horse engine had been installed at Highbury Frame sometime before, and in 1818 some of its parts were stolen. The Company took William Chadwell Mylne's advice and replaced it with a waterwheel, which was working by December 1819.

The Company then built new reservoirs to try and meet the growing demand. The largest were two at Stoke Newington, and in May 1831, Mylne reported that the construction of the western one was well advanced. He said the next difficulty would be 'to obtain at a reasonable price an internal lining for the face of the banks to prevent the effect of the water from washing away the soil in heavy gales of wind which in such large pieces of water will raise waves to a considerable height ...unless proper protection be given to the upper edge, the bank may be in time so diminished as to render it dangerous and perhaps carry it away.'

Old London Bridge had just been demolished, and Mylne negotiated with the contractors 'for so much of the materials of old London Bridge as will be sufficient to face the bank from the upper benching to the top of the bank ... completely round the reservoir.' He went on to reinforce the reservoir with material that may once have underpinned the works of the New River's oldest competitor.[6] The directors seem to have been impressed with Mylne's work, and at one meeting they ordered that a stone should be fixed to the engine house to record that:

> 'These sheets of water, having in many parts a depth of twenty feet, belonging to the New River Company, were suggested and completely formed under the skilful management of their Engineer, William Chadwell Mylne Esquire.'

This initial enthusiasm seems to have worn off a little, and the stone which was put up and still exists on the north end of what remains of the engine house reads:

> 'These reservoirs, the property of the New River Company, were begun in the year 1830 and completed in the year 1833, under the direction of Mr William Chadwell Mylne their Engineer.'

The waterwheel at Highbury was still in use in 1834, when the river was too low to work it because of a drought. Mylne reported that it was a frequent problem. When the waterwheel was new there were few houses in the district, but now there were many more, and they were extending up the hill towards Highgate, thus creating further supply problems. The only solution he could see was a main pipe from the new reservoir at Newington. There was a steam engine there, and it could pump water for the Highbury supply when the river was too low to work the waterwheel. This involved 1660 yards of iron main being laid under the public road at a cost of £1,169, and was done soon after.[7]

The Highbury waterwheel lasted only until 1837, by which time its bearings were worn out. It was removed and re-installed on some adjacent land belonging to the Company for carrying out an experiment in filtration that Mylne wanted to try.[8]

High Service and Constant Supply

The normal water supply provided by the New River and other companies was intermittent, being turned on only at prearranged days and times. It was also a 'low service' in that it was delivered at basement or ground floor level. What was called 'High Service' was then introduced for those customers willing to pay for it. This did not supply a tank in the roof space, as we now expect. The ordinary high service was to a cistern up to thirteen feet above ground level, and was provided for 50% more than the basic charge for a particular size of property. It required special mains and was hardly used. In 1852, less than 3% of the 66,000 customers were on High Service.

One early user was Mr Davis, a surgeon of 35 Great Queen Street. In 1816 he was allowed to have a supply of water to the upper storey of his house from the main at an additional rent of ten shillings a year.[9]

Charles Dickens complains

Another user of the high service was Charles Dickens, and a letter he wrote may sum up what the reality was for many customers.

> 'Tavistock House, Tavistock Square, 8 May 1855
> '... my supply of water is often absurdly insufficient and that although I pay the extra service-rate for a Bath Cistern I am usually left on a Monday morning as dry as if there was no New River Company in existence – which I sometimes devoutly wish were the case ..'[10]

The problem of waste

Waste is a constant problem to water companies, even today. Every extra gallon used increases the pumping bill. In 1814, the New

River Company had temporarily stopped the use of ball-cocks and improved its supply to try and fend off its competitors. This led to a report from the works committee that

> 'the Waste is become so serious, that Your Engine now lifts and forces to the West end of the Town, twice the quantity it did in August 1812 when it was erected. In consequence of this extraordinary and unprecedented Waste, the pipe 16 inches in diameter through which the water is forced is unfortunately become too small, and you are actually consuming to overcome the increase of friction an additional and unnecessary quantity of coals equal to £750 per annum.'

Long into the nineteenth century, water companies were not generally in favour of providing a constant service to households. They feared that it would lead to waste and a lack of control and so the old practice continued, and any given street had its water turned on, usually for a couple of hours three times a week.

The failure to provide a constant supply meant that the mains were left empty at night. In theory, if a fire broke out a message sent to New River Head could get the water turned on, but fire officers complained this could mean a delay of hours. When the Grand Junction Company was set up in 1810 a constant supply was one of its promises, but after the boundary-fixing collusion of 1817 it quietly reverted to an intermittent supply like all the others.

William Chadwell Mylne was not in favour of a constant supply that would in some localities flow into open communal tanks, as appears from a letter he wrote to the sanitary reformer Edwin Chadwick in 1850. 'Among the very poor I disapprove of the use of butts, the occupants too often dip with unclean vessels in them and thus injure the quality of the water... If the water companies were to erect large tanks (at a small additional charge) and take control of them, from which each house should have a pipe, thus the constant means of obtaining water within the premises would be afforded in those miserable localities which are to be met with in a greater or lesser degree in every town in the kingdom.' This suggestion was not adopted.

Courts and Alleys

One particular problem in Victorian Islington, as elsewhere in England at that time, was the growth of housing in courts and alleys. Population pressure had led to the building of low-quality housing in alleyways and in the yards behind older and larger properties. Little rows of ill-ventilated houses clustered around courtyards, and if there was any water supply it was often a single shared pump or tap. Water companies disliked this kind of supply. The tap was nobody's responsibility. It could be left permanently running, and might well be used by outsiders who had no right to it, or so the argument ran.

Sir John Simon was Medical Officer for the City of London, and he described the problem in one of his reports:

> 'In inspecting the courts and alleys of the City, one constantly sees butts for the reception of water, either public, or in the open yards of the houses, or sometimes in their cellars; and these butts, dirty, mouldering and coverless, receiving soot and all other impurities from the air; absorbing stench from the adjacent cesspool; inviting filth from insects, vermin, sparrows, cats and children; their contents often augmented through a rain water pipe by the washings of the roof, and every hour becoming fustier and more offensive. Nothing can be less like what water should be than the fluid obtained under such circumstances.'

In 1849, Islington Vestry's Sanitary Committee ordered a report on the water supply to 'the several Courts and Alleys in the parish.' The report of Thomas Allen, the Inspector, published in March 1850, identified one hundred and two such places. Oddly, the word 'alley' did not appear in any of the addresses, and 'court' in only ten of them; perhaps both had unattractive overtones. Of the rest, 'Place' was the most common suffix, with 40 examples, followed by 11 Streets, 7 Rows, 6 Gardens, 5 Buildings, 5 Cottages, 5 Yards, 3 Groves, 3

43 A water company's emergency standpipe attached to a fire-plug during a prolonged freeze-up in 1861.

Lanes, 2 Rents, 2 Squares (Adelaide and Norfolk) and one each of Mews, Passage and Walk. The report shows that, whatever their names, they had been selected for being the worst housing in the parish, although they were only yards away from smart new terraces and squares.

The water supply to most of these places, with a total population of several thousand, was wholly inadequate. In Caroline Place, forty people shared a single tap that ran three times a week for about an hour. There were two half-barrels into which they could pour water. In Concord Buildings fifty-three people shared a single tap that ran for four hours a week into a water-butt. Five of the houses in Duddies' Rents had no water at all for their thirty-two occupants, just like the twenty-two occupants of five houses in Feston Place. At George Yard, off Islington High Street, 187 people dwelt in twenty-two houses. They shared two taps that ran for an hour and a quarter six times a week: 'It is collected in pails and such like utensils to keep in the various rooms: the inhabitants state that they are often compelled to beg for water in the neighbourhood, or steal it from the courts adjacent.' At Parsley's Court, also off the High Street, 106 people in ten houses shared a single intermittent tap. Not far away, the 239 inhabitants of Smith's Buildings and Smith's Place also shared a single tap, which ran for as much as two hours six times a week. Some of them had barrels into which they could tip any spare water.

In Gifford's Place things sounded better, as each of the five houses had its own service-pipe, but the occupants said that the water was sometimes off for several weeks at a time. In Little Pierrepont Row the inhabitants could pump water from a well into which a pipe ran three times a week, but said they were 'sometimes entirely destitute of water.' At Milton's Yard eighty-three people drew water from a butt into which water ran three times a week, but only after it had filled the cistern of a neighbouring house.

Finally, Wheatsheaf Yard had a house with no water at all, 'the occupiers generally drinking rainwater, or occasionally fetching it from Mr Burt's in the High Street.'

Cholera

In the eighteenth century, the New River was still regarded as a source of cleansing water. Thus a description of London in 1766 noted 'since the city has been well-washed and cleaned by the cocks and plugs of the New River, there have not been so frequent visitations of the plague within the walls and liberties of this metropolis, as in former times.'[11] This reputation did not survive. On 15 November 1849, the Dean of Westminster preached a sermon in Westminster Abbey, in which he said:

> 'Within the Bills of Mortality of this largest and most rich and mighty city upon earth, with a population of 2,206,076 souls, in the three months of July, August and September in the present year more than twelve thousand persons have perished by the pestilence of Cholera; and in all this kingdom more than sixty thousand. Nine tenths of all the London cases have occurred in the poorest and most ill-fed and ill-watered and badly-drained parts of the metropolis.'[12]

Cholera had spread westward from India. It crossed Europe in the late 1820s and reached

England in 1831, when London had its first epidemic. It caused acute diarrhoea, dehydration and kidney failure. It was a disease that killed quickly, and death often ensued on the first day. The first epidemic killed over 6,500 Londoners and caused great alarm. Further outbreaks, in 1848-9, 1853-4 and 1866 killed over 30,000 more. The vestry committees that ran each parish applied to the New River Company for supplies of water to cleanse their streets, and this was indexed in the minute book with entry 'Cholera, extra water to prevent it,' suggesting that some causal link was seen between filth in the streets and the spread of disease.[13] Although it was a very long time before the link between cholera and dirty water was established, it did at least heighten public agitation for better water supplies.

It was a London doctor, John Snow, who at last provided satisfactory evidence of how cholera was spread. In 1854, there was a localised outbreak near Golden Square in the West End, causing many deaths. He took the trouble to map the addresses where deaths had occurred and correlate them with the local water supply. This showed an inescapable link between the outbreak and one particular pump that drew water from a shallow well in Broad Street. Deceptively, the water it drew was clearer than much of that supplied by the water companies, but it was contaminated from nearby cesspits.

Cleaner water – the 1852 Metropolis Water Act

> 'If I would drink water, I must quaff the mawkish contents of an open aqueduct, exposed to all manner of defilement, or swallow that which comes from the River Thames, impregnated with all the filth of London and Westminster. Human excrement is the least offensive part of the concrete which is composed of all the drugs, minerals and poisons used in mechanics and manufactures, enriched with the scourings of all the wash tubs, kennels, and common sewers within the bills of mortality.'

Thus spoke Matthew Bramble, a character in Smollett's *Humphrey Clinker*, published in 1771. The 'open aqueduct ...exposed to defilement' could only refer to the New River, and he makes it sound very slightly preferable to the alternative. It was not until the 1850s that the whole problem of clean water for London began to be solved, and by that time Thames water was far worse even than Smollett had known.

It was the Metropolis Water Act of 1852 that brought about the changes, and it affected the New River Company as well as all the Thames water companies in three important ways. First, domestic water could no longer be taken from the tidal parts of the Thames below Teddington, or the tidal parts of the Lea. Second, all water derived from a non-tidal river or conveyed in an open aqueduct – like the New River – and intended for domestic use had to be filtered. Third all reservoirs of filtered water must be covered if they were within five miles of St Paul's.

The new works involved enormous expenditure, which was inevitably to be recovered by higher charges.

The New River in 1853

In 1853 William Chadwell Mylne provided information as to how the company's supply might be improved to meet the requirements of the 1852 Act.

The Round Pond and Outer Ponds at New River Head could no longer be used in their present form. They could usefully be laid out as filter beds. The Upper Pond in Claremont Square would still be needed, but it would have to be covered over. New filter beds and a pumping station would be needed at Stoke Newington, where he had already established reservoirs in 1830.

The Company supplied 88,000 houses, and 7,000 more would be supplied when the imminent takeover of the Hampstead Water Company was completed. Another 5,000 would be supplied by the time the new works were completed, giving a total of about 100,000 houses and 800,000 people. A further 25% had to be allowed for future growth, giving 125,000 houses and 1 million people.

Mylne set out how much each of the existing sources could supply, giving a total of 33,210,000 gallons a day. It is noteworthy that

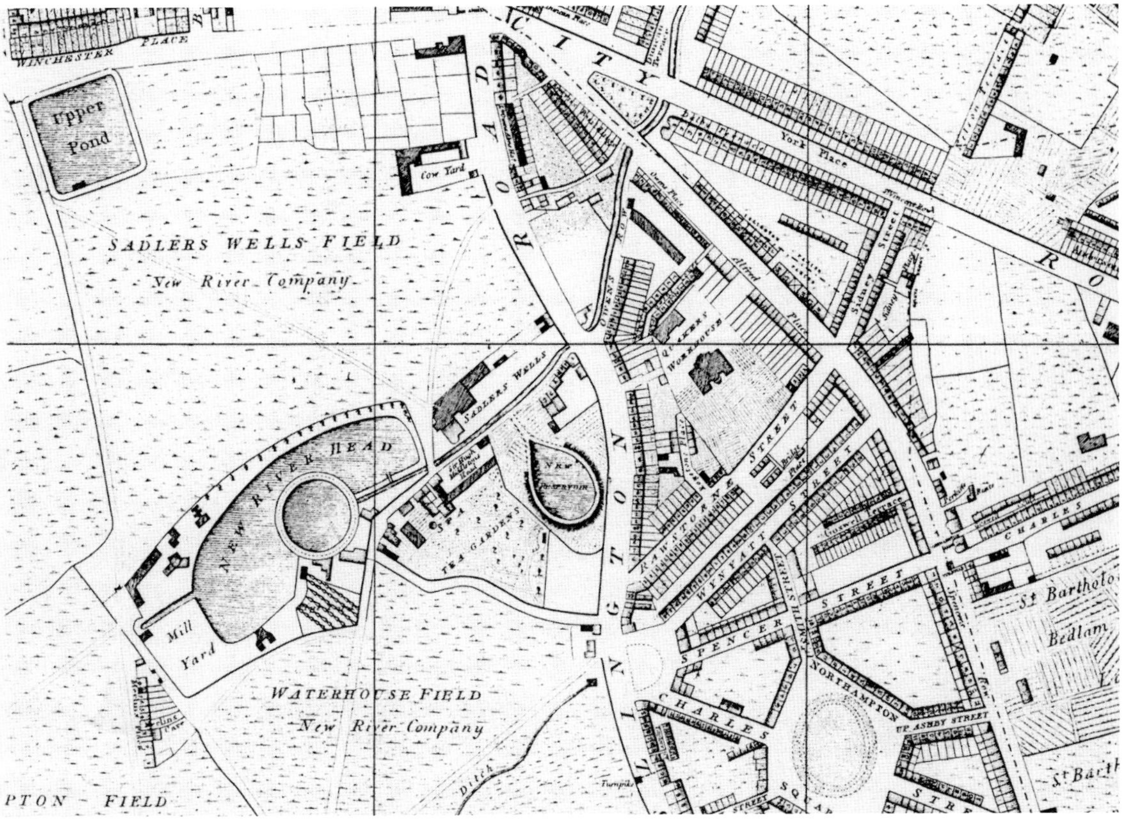

44 *Map of the New River Head area from Horwood's map, early 19th century. The road to the right of the 'New Reservoir' is St John Street. Later that century Rosebery Avenue was constructed between Sadler's Wells and that reservoir. The route of the New River may be seen entering from the north and going beneath City Road, Goswell Road and St John Street.*

by this time Chadwell Spring only provided 2.7 million (8%) of the total in dry weather, and Amwell spring none at all, having long since dried up. The River Lea gave 77% of the total, from the marble gauge at Ware. The rest was pumped up from wells, at Amwell Hill, Amwell End, and Tottenham Court Road. Further supplies could be taken from a well at Cheshunt in an emergency, and about 7 million gallons a day from the River Lea at Tottenham, but this water was of inferior quality.

Mylne recommended that the supply should then be divided 50% to the Stoke Newington reservoirs, 25% to New River Head and 25% to Hornsey. The maximum demand was about 27½ million gallons a day, and the existing pumping engines at New River Head could cope with their share of that.[14]

The 1856 works

At New River Head, the Outer Ponds were converted to filter beds, containing layers of carefully-graded gravel three feet deep, as fine as a pea on top but as large as a swan's egg at the bottom. This gravel was covered with two feet of fine sand from Harwich. The water was allowed to seep up through these layers, leaving most of its impurities behind, and emerging as drinking water of acceptable quality. The Round Pond remained, serving to supply the filter beds. Filtered water could be supplied direct to local mains or pumped to the Upper Pond, which was covered by 1856, becoming the Claremont Square reservoir.

This is still in use. A drawing of the work in progress (*ill.46, p.179*) shows how the acre

45 Changes at New River Head after the 1856 works. The Round Pond has been kept to receive unfiltered water from the New River, while the Outer Pond has been drained and converted into three separate filter beds. This allowed for one to be out of action for cleaning without disrupting the supply. The filter beds are depicted empty, to show how untreated water entered through perforated pipes all over the bottom. The water then percolated upward through a succession of carefully graded gravels and sands, from which the filtered water then flowed.

of ground that comprised the pond was covered by rows of brick arcades inside a perimeter embankment of clay. The opportunity was taken to raise the water level higher than it had been, giving a total depth of twenty-one feet and a capacity of 3½ million gallons. A wide flight of stone steps led from an entrance on the top of the east side to provide easy access when the reservoir was drained for maintenance. The drawing was made from the south-east corner of the square at a time when the work was almost finished. It can be seen that the original railings of 1825 had been largely left in place with only a few sections removed to provide an access route for the workmen. To maintain London's water supply while it was built it was done in stages, with temporary cross dams to keep the water out of the new works. The total cost of the works was £21,000.[15]

It was fortunate that two large reservoirs already existed at Stoke Newington. The major work there involved the erection of an enormous engine house for pumping filtered water, and the building that resulted must rank as one of the oddest industrial buildings in London, ostensibly a castle in the Scottish baronial style, with battlements and towers. This building, traditionally credited to William Chadwell Mylne, seems to have been designed with the assistance of Robert Billings, who exhibited drawings for it at the Society of British Artists in 1856.[16] Its features were all functional except the battlements. The main tower contained a chimney, while other turrets concealed a vast iron standpipe and a spiral staircase giving access to the beams of the enormous engines. Great buttresses, each adorned with the monogram 'MYLNE 1855' in gilt letters

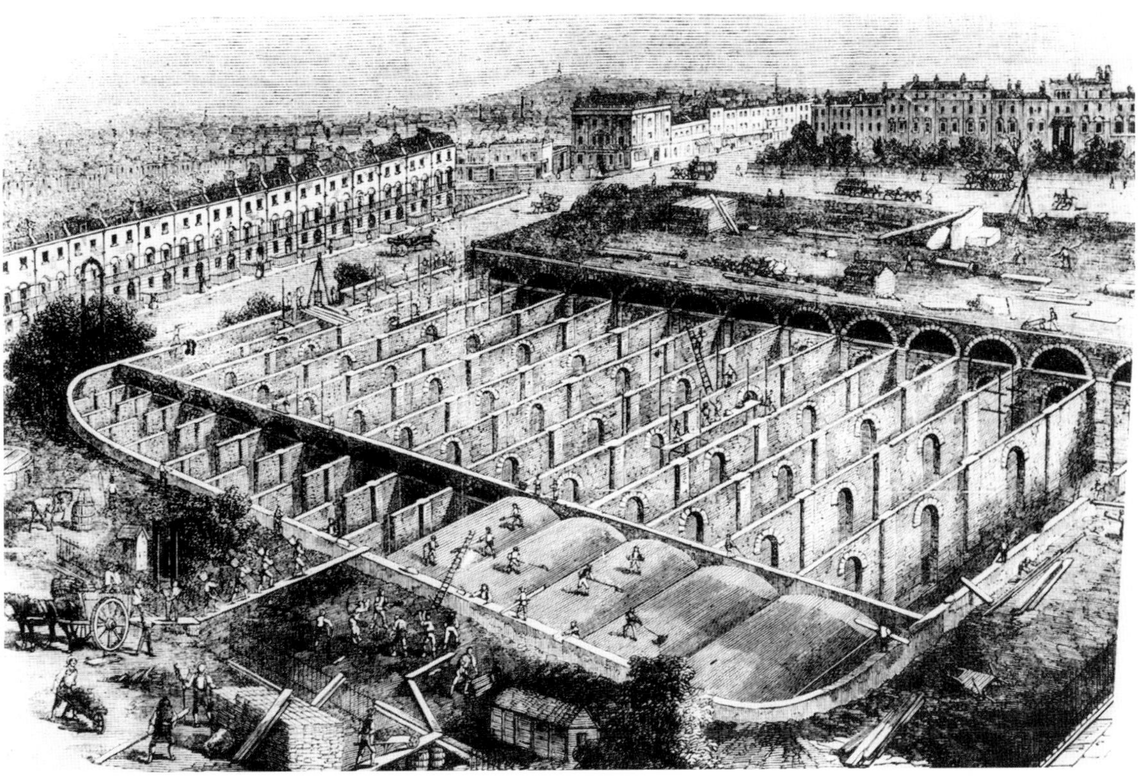

46 Construction of the covered reservoir on the site of the Upper Pond in 1856. This is now the Claremont Square reservoir. The view is from the south-east of the reservoir, with Amwell Street to the left and Pentonville Road at the top. The walls are reinforced by earth banks to help contain 3½ million gallons weighing over 15,000 tons. The depth of the reservoir up to the tops of the crossing walls is 21 feet.

a yard high, stand out from the walls (*ill.54, p.184*). They look as if they are structural, but were built for functional reasons other than support. They are hollow, and provided recessess on the inside of the building into which the three massive flywheels could extend. These were 25 feet in diameter, assembled from ten cast iron segments, and weighed 35 tons.

There were six beam engines inside, working as three pairs with common flywheels. Two of them, by Boulton, Watt & Company, became known as the Lion and Lioness. Their beams were 28 feet long and weighed 22 tons. They had 60-inch diameter cylinders and an 8-foot stroke, each producing 200 horsepower. They were used to pump filtered water up to a raised tank, from where it flowed by gravity through a buried iron pipeline three feet in diameter direct to Claremont Square, without passing New River Head. The route of the pipe took it under the New River at three points but the filtered water in the pipe had to be kept separate from the unfiltered New River water. These engines were modified in the 1880s and thereafter gave almost 70 years of uninterrupted service, sometimes running for months at a time. They were eventually scrapped in 1952-3. As they had been installed before the building was complete, the 28-foot cast iron beams had to be cut into pieces for removal.

The other four engines, from James Simpson & Company were each of 150 horsepower. Their purpose was to pump filtered water to two new covered reservoirs at Maiden Lane, Dartmouth Park (now Dartmouth Park Hill), built to the same plan as the one at Claremont Square, which could contain 7½ million gallons. By the 1890s the Maiden Lane reservoirs had a floating gauge connected to an electric battery that was used to automatically trans-

47 William Chadwell Mylne's New Gauge House of 1856 on the River Lea between Hertford and Ware. This was built to restrict the amount of water flowing from the Lea into the New River to 22½ million gallons a day.

mit the water-level, to the nearest inch, along telegraph wires to the staff at Stoke Newington. A writer noted that 'the electrical arrangements are managed by the General Post Office'.[17]

The total cost of the works completed in 1856 was about £336,000. Of this, £222,000 was spent at Stoke Newington, including £81,500 for the 'engine establishment' there. Converting the pond to filter beds at New River Head cost £32,000, covering the Claremont Square Reservoir £21,000, and the Maiden Lane Reservoirs £61,000.

48 Rye Common pumping station, built in 1883 to pump water up to the New River from a well 200 feet deep. Its steam engine was replaced by electric pumps in the 1930s, and it still contributes to London's water supply.

Cutting the loops

When Mylne reported in 1853, he suggested a number of changes to increase the flow. The dimensions of the New River could be increased to 18 feet wide and 5 feet deep, and many loops of the river could be shortened to reduce the distance between the Marble Gauge and Stoke Newington from 35 to 22 miles. This was done by a combination of embankments (as at Turnford and Hornsey), a fourteen-foot brick tunnel from Myddelton Road to Station Road, Wood Green, and many long runs of buried iron pipes. These were from four to five feet in diameter, and three were usually needed side by side.

Shortening the river had begun as early as 1618, when the length was reduced by 2¾ miles by building the 'Boarded River' in Highbury to replace the loop to Holloway Road, and further savings were made by improvements in Enfield and Hornsey. In 1722, Henry Mill measured the river from Chadwell Spring to New River Head and found it then to be 38¾ miles. It seems from this that the original length of the New River was at least forty-two miles. An old stone still in the wall of the Round Pond in the 1920s bore the figure 42. It had originally been fixed in the arch where the New River entered the Round Pond, and was thought to refer to the distance.[18]

Further savings were made in 1821 with a new flash at Flash Lane, Enfield. In 1854 the contractor Thomas Docwra saved a further 1,370 yards at Wormley with a new aqueduct. In 1859 Mylne was able to report a further reduction of 7¾ miles by virtue of works at Enfield Chase, Southgate, Clay Hill and Edmonton. Another loop remained at Hornsey, but Mylne said that should stay until the newly-built embankment alongside the Great Northern Railway had stabilised, as it had suffered some slips. Thomas Docwra dug a tunnel at Wood Green in 1857-9, mostly by the cut and cover method. It was 1,108 yards long and averaged twenty feet in depth. Another tunnel was built in 1891-2 at Haringey Park. The contractor who began it, Daniel Juett, found it more costly than he had bargained for, and the Company released him from his contract and completed it using its own workforce at a cost of £4,947 – saving £533 on Juett's price.

In 1865 there was a further shortening at Highbury, achieved by laying four-foot diameter iron pipes from Stoke Newington along Green Lanes to Clissold Park. This made Highbury Bank redundant, and it was eventually sold to a Mr Barlow in 1868 for £3,750.

Increasing the supply

Before 1852 the New River Company had never been under any compulsion to lay water pipes in its area merely because the residents wanted a supply. The New River Company's Act of 1852 imposed an obligation to do so, providing that sufficient householders applied whose rents would cover at least 10% of the costs of laying the pipes and who would undertake to remain connected for at least three years, and also provided that no other company already supplied the district. This last provision had the effect of continuing its virtual immunity from competition.

There were always two problems with extending the supply. The first was that the quantity of water in the New River was not unlimited, the second was that much of London's new building was on higher ground where the water would not flow of its own accord.

The first problem – lack of quantity – was solved in two ways. First, from as early as 1620 the Company tapped the River Lea within a few hundred yards of Chadwell Spring. This added millions of gallons a day to the stream, throughout the year. Second, and this came much later in Victorian times, the Company began to sink boreholes by the side of the river. The advantage they had in this respect was that the New River ran through a vast tract of country north of London. The Company could choose a likely spot and buy a piece of adjacent farmland to sink a well. If it was a success, all that was needed was an engine to lift the water to the level of the New River. From there it would reliably make its own way to New River Head by gravity at no further cost to the Company. None of the other London companies had this extended supply route, except to a limited extent the Grand Junction Company, and its water had to be bought from the owners of the Grand Junction canal.

It was for this reason that no less than thirteen engine houses appeared along the banks of the New River between 1846 and 1898. The furthest was at Broadmead, less than a mile from Chadwell Spring, not built until 1880. The nearest was at White Webbs, Enfield, built in 1898. The depth of the wells they pumped varied from 160 feet to 1,010 feet.

Constant supply at last

Predictably, the Metropolis Water Act of 1852 included a requirement for constant, as opposed to intermittent, supply but that was hemmed in with conditions. It need be provided only if four-fifths of the customers on a main asked for it in writing and if at least that number had waste-saving apparatus approved by the water company. Because of this, the New River and other companies got on with the other requirements of the Act, and nothing was done about constant supply.

The next major Act came in 1871. This also provided for constant supply when certain conditions were fulfilled. The New River Company accordingly began the work, but it took thirty years to finish it.

Part of the pressure for completion came from the London County Council, which had powers to require water companies to provide a constant supply in a named area. Thus in 1894

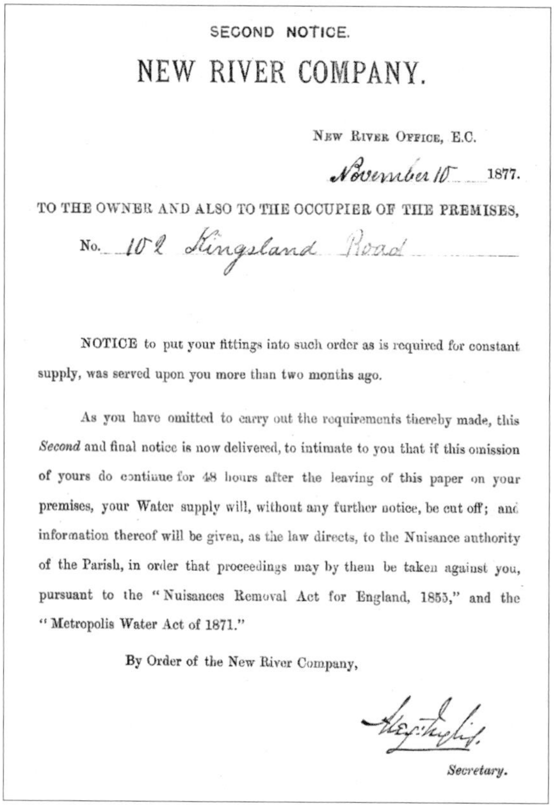

SECOND NOTICE.

NEW RIVER COMPANY.

NEW RIVER OFFICE, E.C.

November 15 1877.

TO THE OWNER AND ALSO TO THE OCCUPIER OF THE PREMISES,

No. 102 Kingsland Road

NOTICE to put your fittings into such order as is required for constant supply, was served upon you more than two months ago.

As you have omitted to carry out the requirements thereby made, this *Second* and final notice is now delivered, to intimate to you that if this omission of yours do continue for 48 hours after the leaving of this paper on your premises, your Water supply will, without any further notice, be cut off; and information thereof will be given, as the law directs, to the Nuisance authority of the Parish, in order that proceedings may by them be taken against you, pursuant to the "Nuisances Removal Act for England, 1855," and the "Metropolis Water Act of 1871."

By Order of the New River Company,

Secretary.

49 The New River company did not provide a constant supply to all its customers until 1904 – the last year of its existence as a water company. Constant supply was only possible if all customers had efficient taps to prevent waste, and this notice shows how that was achieved.

they placed a notice in the *London Gazette* requiring the New River Company to provide such a supply to most of Islington.

The work was not finished until 1904, the very year when the New River Company was about to hand over its waterworks – but not its property company – to the Metropolitan Water Board. The Company's chief engineer, Ernest Collins, gave his directors the details, 'that the whole of the Company's district has now been transferred from the Intermittent to the Constant system of supply.' The first ten years after the Act of 1871 had been spent on extending reservoirs and trunk mains to cope with the increased demand. Then from 1881 the constant supply had been gradually extended. The New River supply area had been divided into 340 districts 'controlled by Waste Meters'. A self-supporting Testing Works had been set up to test and stamp approved water fittings for customers, and it now made a profit of £1,000 a year as well as 'obtaining a stability and excellence in quality of fittings and materials.' This careful control of waste meant that the consumption per head per day, which had been was 23.3 gallons in 1881, was now – with constant supply – reduced to 22.1.

So it was that after almost three hundred years, it was only in the last year of its independent existence that the New River Company provided what we might consider an acceptable supply to its customers.

50 Looking across the Round Pond and filter beds to the engine house, c.1880

51 A stone dated 1818, formerly on the top of the engine house chimney, now lying upside down at New River Head.

52 The yard at New River Head, perhaps c.1880. The windmill base has been roofed and is in use as a store. The engine house has the tapering chimney, which was built in 1818 and remained until 1954. On the far left is a stack of cast-iron pipes, wider at one end to make a socket for the next pipe. Set in the roadway in the foreground is a weighbridge.

53 *William Chadwell Mylne's baronial engine house at Green Lanes, Stoke Newington. It still stands but its interior is now used for training by climbers.*

'An expensive lavatory for pigeons'

By 1972, Mylne's baronial engine house at Stoke Newington was long disused, and there was a proposal to make it a listed building. By then it belonged to the Metropolitan Water Board, and the Clerk, Mr Harry Pitchforth, wrote to the Department of the Environment to express the Board's annoyance. They were particularly irritated that the Board had not been consulted in the matter and only learnt about it from reading *The Times*.

> 'However, on the assumption that it is not yet too late for the defendant to be heard before he is executed, may I say very shortly that this pumping station is completely useless for any purpose connected with the water industry .. the building is an empty shell with no floors .. It constitutes at the moment an expensive lavatory for the local pigeons... the stonework is beginning to show signs of deterioration ...one could not let it become a menace to passing traffic ...we could well use the site for some stores depots..'

He concluded 'I understand the case against us is largely based on representations by an architectural student. How very odd.'[19]

Mylne's whimsical castle was given a starred Grade II listing, all the same. Now, without its great engines, the inside has been fitted out as a centre for indoor climbing, where roped figures inch slowly up immense artificial rockfaces.

54 *The monogram 'MYLNE 1855' emblazoned on the Stoke Newington engine house.*

Chapter Seventeen

Paving the Fields

The Clerkenwell lands – Whitworth's canal – New Inn Farm – The New Cattle Market – Building the estate – Brickmaking – The estate described – St Mark's Church – The man with the pockmarked face – Decline of the inner suburbs – The last of the New River Company

The Clerkenwell lands

William Chadwell Mylne succeeded his father Robert as Surveyor in 1810, at a time when the Company's lands around New River Head stood out like a green oasis amid the encircling streets. On all sides London had encroached, but here there were still over forty acres of open land where cattle grazed and people could stroll. This land had come to the Company after lawsuits in the 1730s, when it was bought to settle a long-standing dispute as to how much rent they should pay for the Upper Pond. After the Earl of Clarendon's death the land on which it stood had changed hands and the new owner had wanted £30 a year for the pond itself and £4 a year for every pipe that ran from it. Eventually, in 1744, the matter was settled when the New River Company bought about 45 acres of land including the Upper Pond and the farm of which it had been a part, for a perpetual annual payment of £362. 10s. 0d. Excluded from the sale were four buildings already used for commercial purposes: 'Sadler's Wells, New Tunbridge Wells, Sir Hugh Myddelton's Head and the Farthing Pye House.' What may have been no more than a convenient way to settle a dispute was to become a valuable asset. The Company first let it as farmland, but gradually found more profitable uses.

The Company seems to have been alert to the potential value of its land and took steps to prevent the public obtaining rights of way across it. In 1781 a row of houses was built on neighbouring land which backed on to the north side of the Hanging Field. When the occupants made back entrances to gain access to the open field the Company sent them notice that unless they blocked them up, their water supply would be cut off.[1] By 1815 there seem to have been footpaths appearing all over, and the Clerk was ordered to write to the tenant Mr Laycock, a prominent Islington dairy farmer, who grazed cattle on the land. He must mend his fences, particularly in the Hanging Field, and if he failed to do so it would be done at his expense, 'to prevent the numerous footpaths'. Public protests followed, from the Reverend Baker and his wife among others, and the Company agreed to reopen a footpath from Sadler's Wells to the Upper Pond 'but on a different track that would conform to the streets in the plan of the intended buildings.' A few months later, the Reverend Baker also persuaded them to reopen a footpath from Sadler's Wells to Merlin's Cave, a public house to the west of New River Head that had existed since early in the eighteenth century.[2] (*ill.58, p.187*)

The main north-south route through the estate, now called Amwell Street, is mentioned in a list of 'Carriage and Footways' made by Robert Mylne in 1798, where it is described as

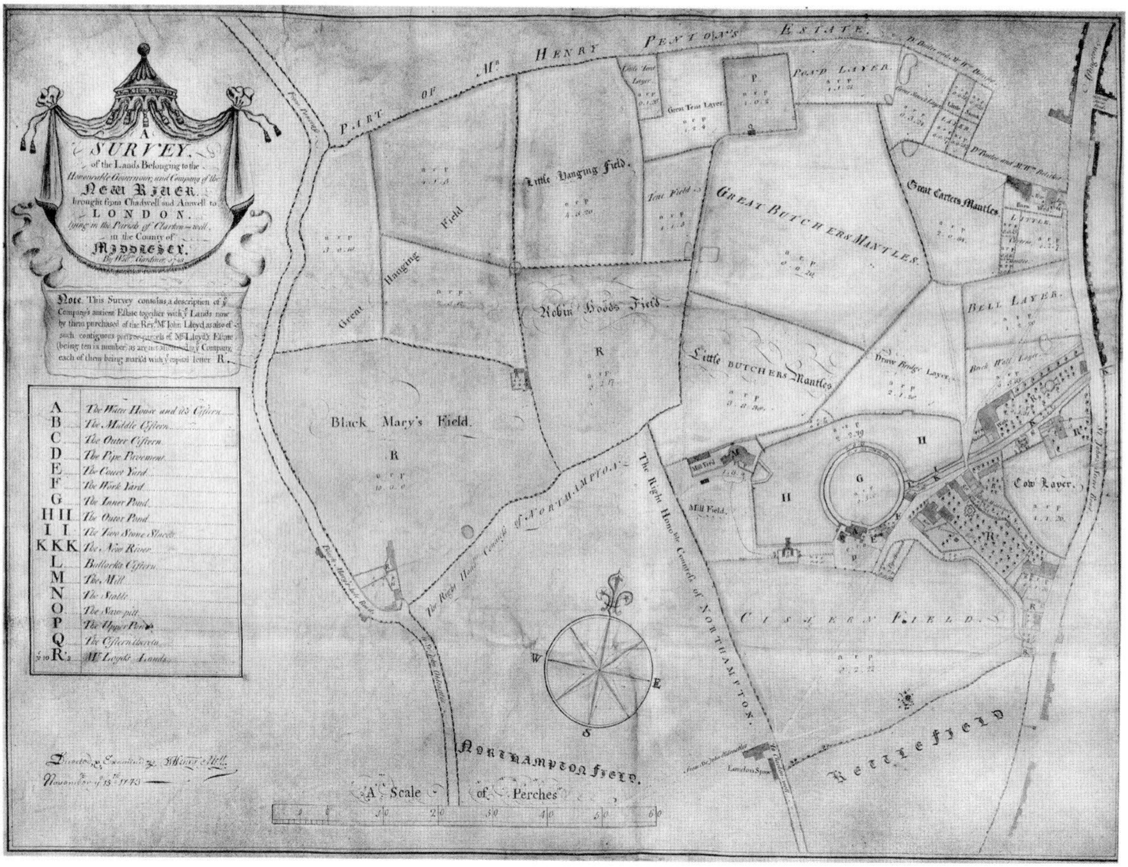

55 Survey of the New River Company's Clerkenwell lands in 1743, following the purchase which settled a lawsuit with the Lloyd family. Areas marked R remained Lloyd's, and include two large fields, Sadler's Wells, and land on the south side of the New River including the Sir Hugh Myddelton's Head and the New Tunbridge Wells.

56 View south down what is now Amwell Street, to the west of the New River Head. The building on the extreme left is Sadler's Wells; the tile kilns on the right were those opposite Bagnigge Wells on the King's Cross Road. Watercolour, c.1815.

57 A view looking north-east from what is now the Mount Pleasant junction where Rosebery Avenue crosses Farringdon Road. This area was often referred to as Spa Fields. Spa Fields Cake House is to the left. The closest building on the hill is the Merlin's Cave. Behind it, the high brick wall encircling New River Head can be seen, but none of the buildings. The wall was completed in 1780.

58 Merlin's Cave, Spa Fields 1840. This public house stood to the west of New River Head from about 1730.

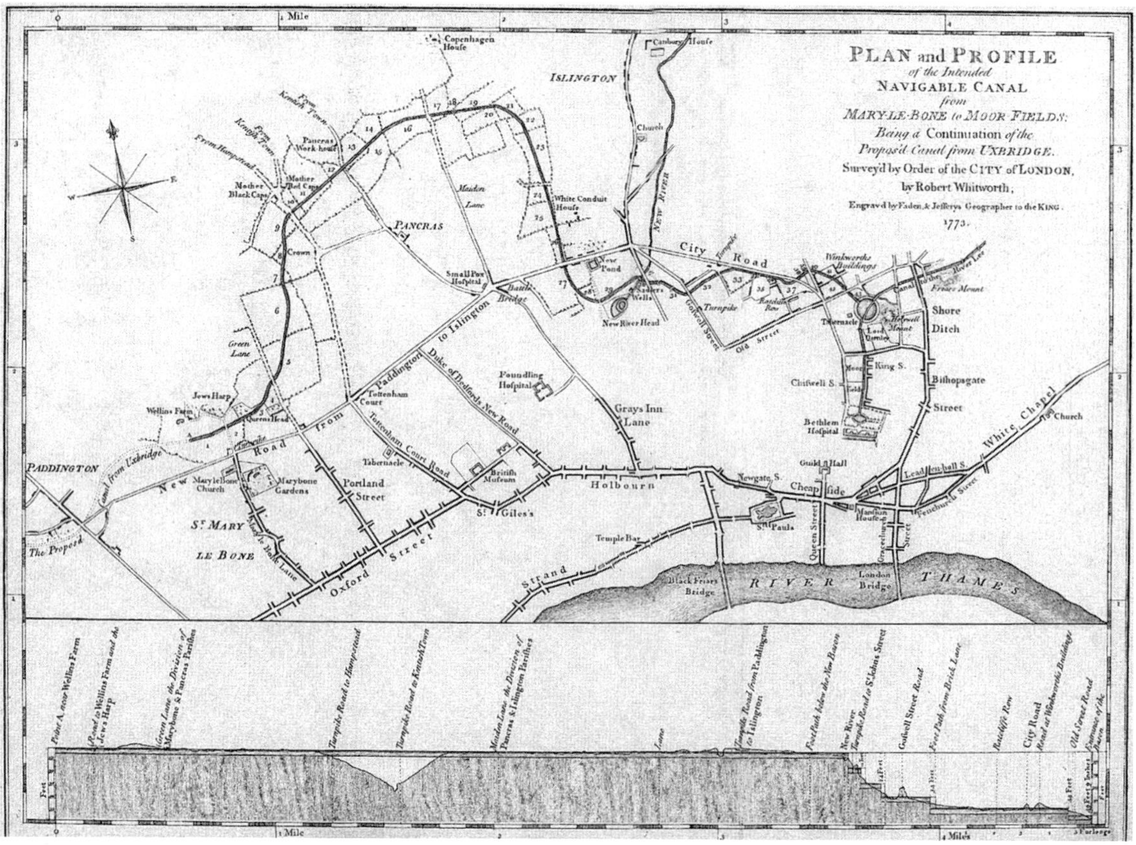

59 *The plan of a canal Robert Whitworth designed in 1773, to give the City of London access to a proposed new canal from Marylebone to Uxbridge where it would join a larger canal network. Whitworth had to plan his route carefully because of the obstacle presented by the New River and its network of wooden mains. His canal was never built.*

'A carriageway from Rosoman Row northward to the back gates of the Engine Yard and from thence to the High Pond and to the Turnpike road leading to Paddington.'[3] By 1817 one of the first building leases refers to it as 'the intended street running from Penton Street to Rosoman Street'.[4]

Whitworth's canal

One early suggestion for using some of the Company's land came from Robert Whitworth, the canal engineer. The City of London had set up a Committee for Canal Navigation, and in June 1773 they instructed him to prepare a report for a canal from Marylebone to Moorfields. The reason for this was that a canal had been proposed from Marylebone to Uxbridge, where it would join the canal network. The City wanted to extend this to Moorfields, on the City's northern boundary. Whitworth's report was ready in October 1773. What he proposed was a canal that would begin at Marylebone, on farmland that is now the site of the boating lake in Regent's Park. From there it would run on the same level, without any locks, north-east to Camden Town and then on towards Highbury. In doing so, it would need a high embankment to cross the valley of the Fleet and the road to Kentish Town. Reaching Islington Hill near present-day Pentonville Prison it would turn south to keep on the same level, and then curve sharply east to pass between New River Head and the Upper Pond.

The New River was a major obstacle, which governed all of Whitworth's planning. He

60 Western entrance to the tunnel on the Regent's Canal that went through Islington from Muriel Street to Colebrooke Row, c.1820.

wanted to keep his canal high enough to go over it. He had considered going just south of New River Head instead of north, and thereby avoiding the New River completely, but that would involve the 'disagreeable Necessity of carrying the Canal upon Arches over all the Pipes that go from the New River Head, which I look upon to be next to impracticable as they lie in almost all manner of Directions.' Between New River Head and the Upper Pond by contrast there were only five parallel pipes, and the canal could pass above them at right angles. He proposed that the canal would cross the New River at the side of Sadler's Wells, then immediately enter a flight of four locks which would take it thirty-four feet lower, passing under new bridges in St John Street and Goswell Road. It would then run along by the south side of City Road, with two more locks before its final basin at Moorfields, making a total drop of forty-nine feet.

Whitworth's canal was never built, and in 1803 Colonel William Tatham published an alternative plan, apparently 'on the invitation of the New River Company,' and based on surveys he had made in 1798. He pointed out that Whitworth's plan was no longer viable because of the growth of new building estates – land that had been 'garden-grounds and pasture' was now all built on, with 'houses and tenements of increased value' by the Duke of Bedford and others. He proposed a canal, linked to some kind of 'railroad' at a lower level than Whitworth's, that would go below the pipes at New River Head. He complained of 'several base and secret attempts to stab my practical reputation in the dark,' apparently because his 'practical' system of engineering was 'dangerous to the arts of jobbing, contracting, peculating, and fleecing both proprietors and workmen.' Sadly he did not name his detractors.[5]

Had it been built this canal would have had considerable effect on the development of adjacent land, attracting industries that used heavy or bulky materials.

The only canal that came close to the New River was the Regent's Canal, which was not completed until 1820, almost fifty years after Whitworth's proposal. That followed a route further out from the centre than Whitworth had planned, and solved the problem of crossing the New River by passing under Islington Hill in a deep tunnel a thousand yards long, passing to the north of the Upper Pond.[6]

New Inn Farm

The first way in which the Company tried to realise profit from its landholding was by letting it for cattle grazing. London's roast beef and mutton arrived in the City on the hoof, driven through the streets to Smithfield Market to be sold and butchered. St John Street, bordering the east side of the Company's land, is less than a mile from Smithfield, so the location was ideal for cattle drovers to stop a day or so, and fatten their beasts for the last time.

The Company also thought that a public house would not go amiss on such a route, and this led to one of their less successful ventures. One Joseph Barron was chosen to run the New Inn, which also included the farmland. In 1744, the year the Company bought the land, he took the lease, and borrowed money from the Company to cover the costs of starting up. By 1746 he was in a debtor's prison, and penned an appeal to his creditors for forbearance, 'by setting me at liberty, which I think will be the only means of putting it in my power to shew what obligations I shall acknowledge to be due to all of you Gentlemen.' The document is fluent, courteous, neatly written, and precisely fills its sheet of paper, suggesting the practised drafting of some prison scribe. Nevertheless, it contains much that is presumably true about the difficulties of attracting passing graziers and drovers to his inn, who already had their own preferred stopping places.[7]

By 1811 the tenant of New Inn Farm was Richard Laycock, and his tenancy came up for renewal that year. By now the Company was well aware of the need to develop the land, and his new lease, at £450 a year, contained provisions that the Company might reclaim parts

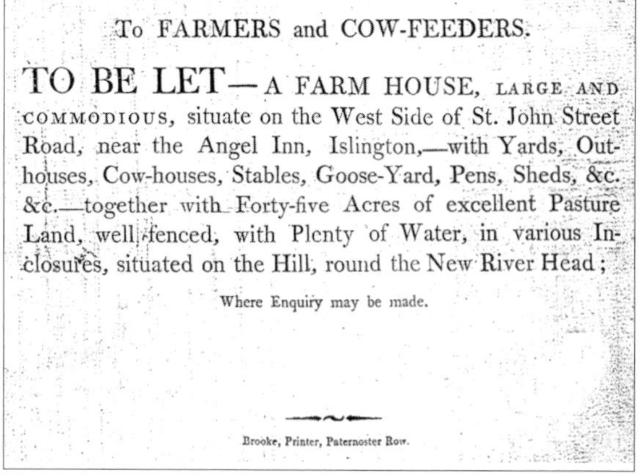
To FARMERS and COW-FEEDERS.

TO BE LET—A FARM HOUSE, LARGE AND COMMODIOUS, situate on the West Side of St. John Street Road, near the Angel Inn, Islington,—with Yards, Outhouses, Cow-houses, Stables, Goose-Yard, Pens, Sheds, &c. &c.—together with Forty-five Acres of excellent Pasture Land, well fenced, with Plenty of Water, in various Inclosures, situated on the Hill, round the New River Head;

Where Enquiry may be made.

Brooke, Printer, Paternoster Row.

61 Until 1810 the New River lands in Clerkenwell were criss-crossed with lines of bulky wooden water mains, and the land could only be used for animal grazing, as this advertisement shows.

of the land on giving three months' notice, in which case the rent would be abated by £10 per acre. This suggests that he had all 45 acres at that time, the full extent of the Company's Clerkenwell lands.

In 1812 the Board ordered their solicitor to give Mr Laycock notice to quit about 1½ acres of land 'on the south side of the Water House Field now staked out for Building purposes,' and that he be given a reduction of £16 12s. 0d. in his rent. By 1816 the lease was up for renewal again, and Laycock agreed to pay £425 a year for the land, to be abated by £15 an acre for any that was taken for building. This suggests that he had only about 30 acres by then, the rest being already taken for building, and that the annual value of grazing land had increased by 50% in five years. He later found in brick-making a more profitable use for some of the land. Laycock was the most substantial farmer in the locality, with a total of over 500 acres of land in different parts of Islington. He also provided overnight lairage for live cattle on their way to Smithfield.[8]

The New Cattle Market

Live cattle driven through London streets to Smithfield Market were becoming an intolerable nuisance by 1800, and the Corporation of

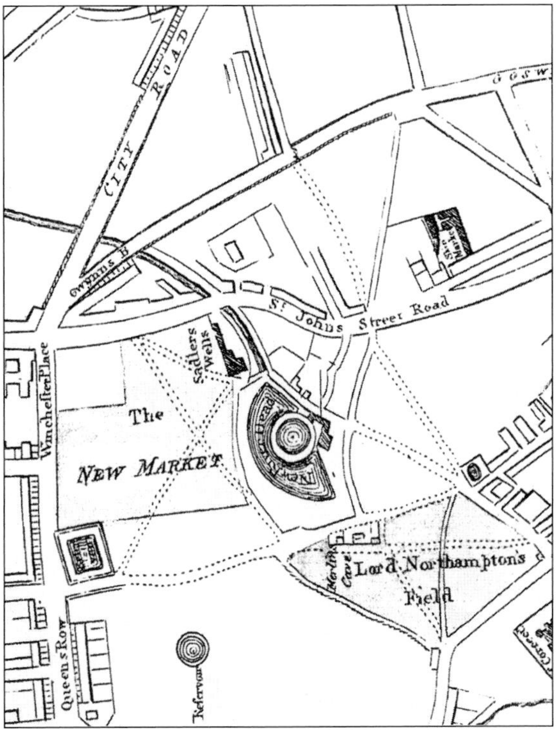

62 Live cattle, pigs and sheep used to be driven through the streets to Smithfield Market, causing congestion and nuisance. In 1810 there was a plan to replace Smithfield with a new market on New River land covering most of the area from Sadler's Wells to the Angel. Although the New River Company shareholders were in favour, the plan was dropped, but not before at least one map had been printed with the New Market shown on it.

London began to consider alternative sites. Supporters of the move set out the problems of keeping the market at Smithfield:

> 'That the Cattle often bruize and lame, and sometimes trample upon and kill each other, by being confined for hours together in a crowded state in the Market; and some of them are maimed or bruized in a shocking manner by the Waggons, Carts and Drays driven through Smithfield during Market Hours. That the Buyers cannot go between or amongst the Beasts .. without danger of sustaining serious bodily Injury.'[9]

One of the sites considered was the New Inn Farm, just southwest of the Angel, still used at that time for grazing cattle. The Company was not averse to a cattle market on its land, perhaps foreseeing it as a large consumer of water. At one point it seemed that the plan would go ahead, and a letter in February 1810 from the Company to the Committee of City Lands proposed that the current grazing tenant of the land could be given notice to quit at Michaelmas that year.[10] Despite the problems at Smithfield the plan then stalled, and it was not until 1855 that the move was finally made to a new Metropolitan Cattle Market at Copenhagen Fields. This was not on New River land, but did at least become a customer for New River water. The Company was in the process of taking over the Hampstead Water Company, and the cattle market became a useful outlet for water now considered unfit for domestic use, derived from the ponds at Hampstead and Highgate.

In the intervening years a new livestock market had been set up by John Perkins on a fifteen acre site to the east of Essex Road in Islington. It had provision for 7,000 cattle, 1500 calves, 4,000 sheep and lambs, and 1,000 pigs. It began in 1836, but was not a success and closed in 1837. Speculators then bought it, and it reopened in 1849 but closed again in about 1850, after which time the land was built on, forming Oakley Road, Englefield Road and Ockendon Road.[11]

Building the estate

The old bowling green just north of the Upper Pond, which dated back at least to Elizabethan times, had never been part of the Company's land. It was built on in the 1790s and was no longer open to the public. It was thereafter only from New River land around the Upper Pond that Londoners and other visitors could see the famous prospect of London spread below and the river glittering beyond. It was not from some altruistic wish to preserve the ancient view that those fields had been left in their verdant state. It was because the New River Company still used wooden pipes.

As supplies were changed and improved over the years new mains were run in all directions and were now strung across all parts of the land, 'like the threads of a garment' as William Chadwell Mylne described them. They had to remain accessible so that they could be dug up and replaced when they started to leak, so there was no question of building houses on top of them. Mylne knew that the only solution was to decide where streets would eventually be needed, and then to replace all the existing wooden pipes with iron ones that followed the lines of those streets, so that they could always be uncovered for repair.

The building of what was to be known as the New River Estate followed a pattern long established in London. The Company laid out the streets, and anyone who wanted could then apply to take a building lease on one or more plots. This required the payment of an annual ground rent and in addition, the leaseholder was required to build a house or houses on the land. Usually the rent was a peppercorn for the first two years to show that the lease existed. This gave the builder time to complete the house before he had to pay any rent to the New River Company. When the house was finished, it could be let to a tenant on a short or long lease at a much higher annual rent than the ground rent. Very often the lease to the builder was not even prepared until the house was built, and was then backdated. The first leases granted on such land could be as short as sixty years, although ninety-nine years was not unusual. The New River Company opted for eighty-four or ninety years in many cases. At the end of that time, the lease would 'fall in' and the land and its buildings would revert to the Company. It was a convenient way for a landowner to develop his estate without investing capital. Its main disadvantage was that builders had no incentive to build structures that would outlast their leases, and the houses had structural weaknesses caused by skimping on materials.

A builder who took such a lease did not have a free hand in designing the building he put on it. The whole area was laid out to contain orderly terraces of matched houses. Some streets would be a little grander than others, but every house built had to fit the master plan for the terrace it was in, as to its height, and the proportions and positions of windows, doors and other conspicuous features. William Chadwell Mylne had drawn the master plans, and the builders followed them. These plans took account of the Building Acts that had applied to houses built in London since the Great Fire. For example, after 1706 all wooden parts such as windows and doors had to be set back four inches into the brickwork – a protection against the spread of fire which also had the pleasing effect of giving house fronts a more solid and three-dimensional appearance.

63 One advantage of terraced housing is that the builders can make some houses larger or smaller than others by varying the width of the frontage, without noticeably spoiling the uniformity of the terrace. This shows an extreme example in River Street, which leads into Myddelton Square. The different upper windows of the right hand house suggest it may have been a piece of subsequent infilling.

The one way in which some individuality was allowed was in the width of the frontage. Some plots were just fifteen feet wide, so that the largest rooms were barely fourteen feet wide after allowing for the thickness of the party walls. Others were eighteen or twenty feet wide, thus enabling larger, grander houses to mingle with more modest ones, though all had the same number of windows. Needless to say, the price to be paid for the lease and the future ground rent were determined by the width of the frontage. Sometimes a builder would buy a single plot to put a house on, sometimes a whole row. In either case, the work would have to receive Mylne's approval.

This method of proceeding allowed the New River Company to develop its land without incurring many capital costs but with the benefit of future ground rents payable every year to add to its income. Mylne was to say afterwards that by putting iron pipes in the land he had increased its income from £500 as grazing land to £4,000 a year as a building estate, an eight-fold increase.

Mylne laid out the grid of streets, and for the most part these were completely new – wide straight roads and squares laid out over the green fields. One of them, Amwell Street, differed in that it followed the line of 'the ancient footpath across the fields, which many readers will remember' as a local historian wrote in 1828. Because of this it is not quite straight, and this troubled one writer who 'regretted that this wide and otherwise handsome street was not planned in a straight line; which would have greatly added to the effect from either end, and have given it an appearance surpassed by few on this side of London.'[12]

One of the first decisions to start building was taken in July 1811, when William Chadwell Mylne who had succeeded his father as surveyor just months earlier, was instructed 'immediately to prepare a plan of Buildings, first rate houses, to extend from the High Pond eastward.' These were the houses that now form a terrace behind long front gardens on the south of Pentonville Road just west of the Angel, originally called Claremont Terrace. Despite this early date, it seems the houses were not built until 1819, and they were built at third, not first, rate. The leases for those plots were at the rate of ten shillings a foot of frontage, and the first six were on plots 18 feet wide, and 180 feet deep, so that each house brought the Company £9 a year in rent.[13]

Another early part of the estate was built around the Upper Pond. At first it was just a terrace of houses on the west side, called Myddelton Terrace, but Mylne then decided to make it part of a square. It was named Claremont Square, after a fashionable country house in Surrey, and had the Upper Pond as its central feature. Some of the leases on the west side ran from Midsummer 1816, and building continued into the 1820s. Since 1757 the pond had been surrounded by a high brick wall, set back 'so as to form spacious walks' around the pond, and these were accessible to residents.[14] One early visitor to the square was Thomas Carlyle, who stayed for about four months in 1824 at the home of his friend Edward Irving, preacher and founder of the Catholic Apostolic Church, who lived at number four. Carlyle later described its pleasant situation;

> 'Our chief prospect from the front was a good space of green ground, and in it ... the big open reservoir of Myddelton's 'New River' ... on the spacious expanse of smooth flags surrounding which it was pleasant on fine mornings to take an early promenade, with the free sky overhead, and the New Road with its lively traffic and vehiculation 7 or 8 yards below our level. I remember several pretty strolls here, ... while breakfast was getting ready close by; and the esplanade, a high little island, lifted free out of the noises and jostlings, was all our own.'[15]

John Scott built several houses on the New River estate, and lived in the best of them in Claremont Square. In July 1825 he wrote to the Company suggesting that the brick wall around the Upper Pond should be taken down and replaced with iron railings.[16] The Company approved of this, other residents agreed to share the cost, the wall came down and the present railings took its place. The opportunity was also taken to align the sides of the enclosure with the new buildings – formerly it had been slightly out of square. There was an odd sequel to this. The north side of the square, formerly the site of the bowling green, was not on New River land and the occupiers of those houses refused to contribute to the cost of the railings. This was discussed at the next New River board meeting, after which the north railings were taken down to be sold, and the brick wall went up again on that side, where it remains to this day, a sooty mass with faded graffiti topped with shards of ancient broken glass set in mortar.

Brickmaking

The use of brick for building in London goes back to Roman times, but it then fell out of favour. In medieval London most buildings were framed in timber and coated in plaster. After the Great Fire of 1666, new Building Acts stipulated the use of brick or stone, under roofs of tile or slate. Good quality building stone cannot be quarried in the London area, though Kentish Ragstone quarried at Maidstone was brought to London by way of the River Medway into the Thames, and better stone by sea from the Isle of Portland. Sir Christopher Wren, for all his use of stone in public buildings, encouraged the use of brick. He pointed out that the earth around London could yield bricks as good as the Romans made, and that such bricks would be more durable in London air than 'any Stone our Island affords.' He left some fine examples to prove the point, such as the finely jointed pillared red brick door surround of 5 King's Bench Walk in the Temple. Brick was soon back in vogue and remained the standard material for houses until the late twentieth century, when it began to be used as a cladding for cheaper materials rather than as the main structural material. Brick earth was dug in Islington and Finsbury from the 1590s. From about 1770 until Islington was completely built up, brick kilns were a common sight as future building plots were first exploited for brick burning, and the fumes of their smouldering fires mixed with the smoke from steam engines and kitchen ranges to begrime the air that Londoners breathed and blacken their buildings, a process that continued until the Clean Air Act of 1956.[17]

The best brick earths around London then became scarce, but methods were found of mixing chalk with London clay to stretch the available brick earth. It became quite usual for the soil excavated from basement foundations to be used for brickmaking. Until 1828 there were tile kilns at Bagnigge Wells in the present-day Kings Cross Road, and it is not surprising that some New River Company land was dug for bricks.[18] Bricks were very cheap to make, but heavy and expensive to transport before the railways came, and much effort was spent to make them as close as possible to the place where they would be used. In 1811 the Board agreed 'that Mr Laycock of Islington be allowed to dig clay from the Company Land, near the Tile Kilns at Bagnigge Wells for the purpose of making One Million of Bricks only, to pay for the same at the rate of 1s 6d per 1000, to do as little damage as possible, and the surface of the Field to be again put in order by him, subject to Mr Mylne's directions.' By January 1813, Laycock had done so, and the board received an account 'signed by the Excise Surveyor & delivered to him by Mr R Laycock of the Quantity of Bricks made on the Company's Land at Islington, viz 1,225,090, which at 1s. 6d. per thousand came to £91 17s.7d.', less a 10% allowance for spoiled bricks.

Some of the builders working on the Company's land tried to exploit this resource. In April 1812 the Board agreed building leases of part of Water House Field to a Mr Richardson of Islington. Two months later Mylne reported that Richardson was using inferior bricks, so the Clerk wrote to him to say that the board would not grant his leases unless he used bricks approved by Mylne. The next month Mr Richardson went to the Board in person to ask to be allowed to make bricks from the clay that he dug out of the foundations of two of the houses he was building. The Board agreed with this but only provided he used in the building such bricks as Mylne approved.[19]

The estate described

The building estate that Mylne set out was on a generous plan by the standards of the time and the streets are noticeably wide. As befitted a development that would provide homes for five thousand people, there was a school and in due course a church, and there were shops and public houses. Apart from Claremont Square and Claremont Terrace, the Company drew on its history when naming streets. Myddelton's name was used for the first street to be developed, at the southern edge of the estate, and also for the principal square, while the west side of Claremont Square was originally called Myddelton Terrace. The springs of Chadwell and Amwell were commemorated as street names. Holford Square, Rydon Crescent, Green Terrace, Hardwick Street, Mylne Street and Garnault Place recalled past officers and servants. Holford Square, which had a bowling green in the centre and also provided an anchorage point for a barrage balloon, was bombed in the Second World War, and Green Terrace was lost to road improvements. There is also an Inglebert Street, commemorating one who had a minor part in helping Hugh Myddelton, but that is a modern re-naming of what was originally Upper Chadwell Street.

In total, there were six hundred houses, most of two or three storeys plus a basement and attic. Most have cast iron balconies, string courses, and a distinctive feature in the form of sunken semi circular 'eyebrow' panels in the brickwork over the first floor windows. The presence of this last feature is not a guarantee that a particular house was built on New River land, as it has been copied for example on some houses built on the west side of Amwell Street which belonged to the adjacent Lloyd Baker estate. This was presumably done to achieve uniformity, and some New River houses were similarly built without the semi-circular panels where they faced existing Lloyd Baker houses, as in Great Percy Street.

The Clerkenwell Parochial School was built in Amwell Street, across the road from the engine house at New River Head. The Company effectively donated the land by giving a 99-year lease at a rent of one shilling a year. By 1934 it had 600 pupils. Just as there are separate entrances labelled 'Boys School' and 'Girls School' there were two head teachers, a man and a woman, as well as twelve other teachers.[20]

64 St Mark's church, Myddelton Square, drawn by Thomas H. Shepherd, c.1829.

In 1934, the whole of the Company's Clerkenwell estate was estimated to be worth £633,305. Other properties belonging to the Company near the line of the New River in Holloway, Upper Holloway, Dartmouth Park Hill, Stroud Green, Winchmore Hill, Enfield, Sewardstone, Cheshunt, Wormley, Broxbourne, Rye House and Wormley Mead were worth £149,160. From these figures, it is plain that the bulk of valuable property was at Clerkenwell.

St Mark's Church

The question of a church for the estate was discussed at a General Court in November

65 A plaque to Sir Hugh Myddelton on the wall behind St Mark's, Myddelton Square. He was buried in his local church, St Matthew in Friday Street in the City. The last church there was demolished in 1883 and when its crypt was excavated, no trace of Sir Hugh's coffin could be found.

1822, after an enquiry from the Church Commissioners. The members asked Mylne to draw a plan for the site of a church in the centre of the 'intended square', the as yet unnamed Myddelton Square. A pious resolution was passed that the Company was 'desirous of furthering the laudable object of the commissioners,' and would grant them free sufficient land for the church. The offer was accompanied by some more business-like conditions.

The church was never to be used for any purpose except worship according to the rites of the Church of England. The building must be completed within six years. There were to be no burials there. The land must be enclosed with iron railings, and the ground within must be kept in perfect order & repair. If any contract or agreement was required by the Commissioners to settle the matter, it must contain such conditions, and must be prepared at no cost to the New River Company.

Finally came a condition pretending to be no such thing. 'The board wish it to be expressly understood that they do not mean to attach any condition whatever to a gift which they offer with the greatest satisfaction, at the same time they beg leave to state that Mr Mylne their Surveyor, an officer long in their employ and in whose skill and integrity they have every reason to confide, has had the planning of the whole of the Company's building estate, and if it were consistent with the views of the commissioners to employ him as their Architect, in the building of the proposed church it would be a great satisfaction to the board to learn that they had done so.'[21]

Two weeks later, a Mr Gilbert attended from the commissioners and asked the Company not to refuse burials in the vaults. He said 'care would be taken to make such arrangements and to put such fees on interments there as would necessarily diminish their frequency.' This seems to have dispelled any fears the board may have had of their fine new square being endlessly congested with paupers' funerals, and they relented. Gilbert also brought news that the commissioners 'were not at liberty to apply funds for railings or laying the ground out ornamentally.' The Board accepted this, but said there would be a railing 'so that persons coming to the church will be prevented from access to the ornamental ground within the railings, which is to be preserved for the use of the inhabitants of the square.' Finally Mr Gilbert confirmed that they would indeed use William Chadwell Mylne as their architect.[22]

The church was built between 1825 and 1827. The parapet of the tower was 94 feet above ground, while the pinnacles reached 106 feet. The vicar in 1921 wrote that it commanded a wonderful panorama of the City and its surroundings, and claimed it to be 'the highest point in London proper'. He may have forgotten the gallery at the top of the dome of St Paul's when he wrote that. The church had seating for 1915, and pew rents brought in £600 in 1850. They then dwindled as the locality became poorer, and amounted to just £12 by the time they were abolished in 1920. The vaults turned out to be useful for more than burials, as 'thousands sought refuge' in the crypt from Zeppelin bombing raids during the First World War, 'when the surrounding district suffered severely'.[23]

The Company's reluctance to allow burials becomes less surprising in view of current conditions. The speed with which London was growing had combined with high levels of mortality, especially among the working classes, to put an impossible strain on London's burial grounds. Within a hundred yards south of the offices at New River Head was the burial ground at Spa Fields, and this was the scene of some of the worst excesses. The details only became known in the 1840s, but had continued for many previous years. It was a privately run burial ground with space for a total of about 2,700 ordinary burials, but the proprietors had allowed about 80,000 burials to take place in fifty years, more than 2000 in one year alone. Coffins were hardly in the ground before they were disinterred and broken up to fuel the stove in the workmen's hut. New graves were dug by cutting down through recent burials, severing arms, legs and heads in the process. A gravedigger gave evidence that he had been 'up to my knees in human flesh by jumping on the bodies, so as to cram them in the least possible space at the bottom of the graves, in which fresh bodies were afterwards placed. These occurrences took place every day.'[24]

That problem was eventually solved, partly thanks to the exertions of such as the Society for the Abolition of Burials in Towns, and the London Cemetery Company, which provided burial grounds out of London at Kensal Green, Highgate and elsewhere in the 1830s.

The man with the pockmarked face

Most of those who took building leases from the New River Company seem to have been respectable small builders, taking between one and six building plots at a time. One who was sufficiently colourful to have achieved notoriety was John Scott. He took building leases from the New River Company for nine houses in Myddelton Street, one of their first developments, and later four others in River Street. Whereas other houses on New River land conform precisely to their neighbours, and vary only in the width of the frontage, Scott somehow managed to put up for his own house in Claremont Square a structure slightly higher that its neighbours and distinguished with a cornice they did not have.

In due course he became a churchwarden, guardian of the poor, treasurer of the parish, trustee of the church, commissioner of sewers, commissioner of King's taxes, and general chairman of the parish workhouse. He thus got his hands on the funds of Clerkenwell's parish charities. These were complex, and Scott seems to have converted a good part of the funds to his own uses. Thanks to the efforts of another trustee, James Pascall, the scandal became known. Scott had no explanation, and he presently fled to France. This led to a wanted notice being published in the press, offering the enormous reward of £500 for his apprehension. It contains a description of him, in suitably Dickensian terms:

> 'ABSCONDED – FIVE HUNDRED POUNDS REWARD – Whereas JOHN SCOTT, late of Claremont Square, Pentonville, stands charged with the EMBEZZLEMENT of large SUMS OF MONEY, raised for the relief of the poor of the parish of Clerkenwell, Notice is hereby given that the abovementioned REWARD of £500 will be paid by the Guardians of the Poor of Clerkenwell to any person or persons who may apprehend the said John Scott, on his being placed in safe custody in the county of Middlesex. –GEO. SELBY, Clerk to the Guardians.
>
> Clerkenwell, 7th Nov. 1834.
>
> The above-named John Scott has been for

many years actively engaged in various parochial offices in this parish, from whence he absconded in April last; is about 48 years of age, five feet nine high, slightly marked with the small pox, has light sandy hair, bald on the top of the head, a florid complexion, rather stout, generally wore black and a white cravat; walks with a short step, and in his conversation uses the W for the V.'

A committee investigated, and eventually concluded that he had probably begun his defalcations with 'an undoubted instance of gross fraud in a Bastardy case' in 1820, and was responsible for a loss of at least £10,487 19s. 6d, most of it destined for the elderly poor. His desk was forced open in the presence of a witness, and contained a sixpenny stamp, some cancelled cheques, and 3s. 6½d. in coppers.

Scott was eventually indicted for his fraud, and his case sent to the Old Bailey for trial. Resourceful as ever, he found a way out. More than anything else, the trustees wanted the money back, and putting Scott in jail would not achieve that. Scott offered to repay everything, if they would just drop the case. The offer was accepted, and the prosecution offered no evidence against him. This was a tactical error, for it meant that he had been found not guilty, and English criminal law does not allow a man to be tried again for an offence of which he had been acquitted. Today it is possible in such circumstances to leave the indictment on the file, not to be proceeded on without leave of the Court, and such leave will not be given unless there is good reason. This is a useful procedure that can sometimes safeguard the public interest in such a case. If any such device existed then, it was not used, and Scott lost any incentive he might have had to keep his word. He thereafter began Chancery proceedings claiming that his agreement had been obtained under duress, and the matter dragged on for years. He was of course disgraced, and eventually made bankrupt, but the poor of Clerkenwell never had their loss made good.[25]

Decline of the inner suburbs

Within about sixty years of its development the New River estate came down in the world, and many of the houses were in multiple occupation. Inner London had become grimier and more congested. Coal fires were universal and their smoke polluted the air and caused incessant smogs. Those who could afford it preferred to move further out, particularly after 1860 when suburban railways and the underground made commuting easy. From about 1900, the original building leases began to reach the end of their terms, at which point house and land reverted to the New River Company. It had once been thought that this time would bring a new prosperity to the Company. Auctioneers selling New River shares in the 1870s enthused that 'on the expiration of the leases in about 26 years, the Rack Rents come into the possession of the Company.'

The reality was very different. Clerkenwell had become a working-class district. The houses were old, unfashionable and black from pollution. Houses were not painted as often as they deserved, and when they were the improvement was soon invisible under fresh sooty deposits. The New River Company stipulated the colours that should be used, and favoured a dispiriting chocolate brown for the stucco that fronted the ground floors of most of the houses.

As time went on, other factors contributed to the same decline. Rent Acts passed after the First World War and intended to give tenants security of tenure and affordable rents had some adverse effects. Landlords allowed houses to become dilapidated or derelict until the tenants left. They were then reconditioned and let 'for business purposes only', thereby obtaining higher rents and less maintenance. It was for reasons such as these that the population of Finsbury plummeted, from 101,000 in 1901 to 76,000 by 1921. This was the impoverished Clerkenwell that Arnold Bennett described in *Riceyman Steps*, published in 1923.

By 1929, one part of the New River estate

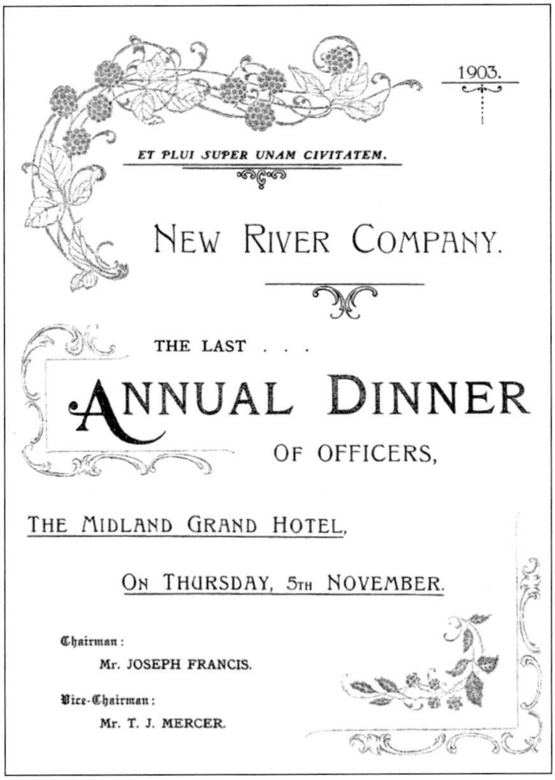

66 The last Annual Dinner of the New River Company in 1903, held at the Midland Grand Hotel, St Pancras.

even found its way into a report on bad housing by the Medical Officer for Health for Finsbury. This was Claremont Mews, originally built to stable horses and carriages for householders in the adjacent square and to provide basic accommodation for the servants who tended them. The Medical Officer reported that it was mostly used for commercial purposes. Out of thirty-seven units, just seven were still lived in. These comprised a total of fifteen rooms, and held thirty-seven residents. In six of them horses were stabled on the ground floor, while the seventh was used for storing potatoes. None had any kind of back yard. They had water closets in dark unventilated understairs cupboards next to the stable area. Some cooked with ovens heated by open fires, others had gas cookers.[26]

From the 1960s there were signs of a revival of interest in housing like that on the New River estate. All over London local councils were still acquiring and demolishing whole streets of brick houses to replace them with soulless blocks and towers of concrete flats, but elsewhere individuals were finding how good the old houses were. Once a century's grime and neglect were stripped away, the plainest house often turned out to have a fine staircase and rooms with good proportions and handsome sash windows. Virtually all of the New River houses that survived the blitz are still intact, and the houses now have a Grade II listing to protect them from any further change.

The last of the New River Company

The 1904 takeover of New River assets by the Metropolitan Water Board did not apply to the Company's properties. These passed to a new limited company, in which the old shareholders received shares in addition to their compensation of Water Board stock. The New River Company Limited continued to operate independently from 1904 until 1974. It had its first offices at 18 Percy Circus, and later at 30 Myddelton Square, both on the Clerkenwell estate, and it continued to collect its rents. While it was at Percy Circus, Lenin and his wife stayed a few yards away at number 16 in 1905. Two more unlikely neighbours than one of London's oldest capitalist corporations and the founder of Soviet Russia would be harder to imagine. By 1974, the Company's properties were worth about £9 million and brought in rents of about £250,000 a year. In that year, there were two major changes. The first was the sale of most of the residential part of the Clerkenwell estate to the London Borough of Islington for more than £4 million, less than £10,000 a house. The second was that the Company was taken over by London Merchant Securities, effectively bringing to an end its independent existence, although it still remains as a separate legal entity within its parent company.

CHAPTER EIGHTEEN

Death and Pleasure; Riot and War

'Found drowned' – The Royal Humane Society – Rescued from drowning – The last of Sir Hugh – The pleasures of Islington Hill – Sadler's Wells – 'Brothels... of the lowest description' – Riots – The Second World War

'Found drowned'

A fast-flowing river that snaked through forty miles of countryside on its way to Islington was obviously a constant source of danger. The first recorded casualty was none other than King James I, perhaps undeservedly given his support for the whole enterprise. Fortunately, in his case the ducking was not fatal. He had been out riding one morning in January 1622 in Theobalds Park, when his mount threw him into the New River. He seems to have gone in head-first, through a thin crust of ice, so that only his boots could be seen. Happily, a courtier was at hand to rescue him, whereupon 'there came much water out of his mouth and body'.[1]

Many others who went into the water were not so lucky. For some it was an accidental stumble or a drunken lurch, for others the New River provided a simple and cost-free exit route from the misery of lives ruined by poverty, despair or the shame of unwanted pregnancy. As Dower wrote in 1739 about the stretch by Sadler's Wells:

> 'The love-sick maid from Death will not refrain,
> Plunges in there, and laughs at future pain.'[2]

Old coroners' records record these deaths, but they were not investigated with the meticulous care of the present day, and some of those who floated down the New River must have been the victims of what used to be called foul play. What the incomplete records show is that death was a regular incident of the New River, so that the total must have run into many thousands. In the two years up to 1783, there were sixteen such deaths in the parishes of Islington and Clerkenwell alone. Of those, ten were women and six men. The identities of four of each sex were never established, and it seems to follow that the circumstances of their deaths were equally obscure.

At the Coroners' Inquests, juries varying in number between eleven and eighteen were sworn to reach a verdict. There is usually no record of the evidence they heard, just their finding as to the cause of death. One of the women was said to have fallen in accidentally, the rest are merely described as 'found drowned.' Often there was simply a standard finding, that the deceased 'had not any marks of violence appearing about him, and how or by what means he became drowned and suffocated no evidence doth appear.'[3]

Other such deaths before and after that time are abundant. A few were of a man or boy who had gone into the New River 'to bath himself'. Children and infants died, but much less often than adults. A child of two and a quarter years fell in near his father's house and 'accidentally, casually and by misfortune came to his death.' One was a newborn male child, 'wilfully murdered' by being cast in the river, while a newborn female child had apparently met a natural death but was found in a coffin floating in the New River in Islington.[4]

The Royal Humane Society

One effect of this steady stream of mortality was, indirectly, the founding of England's oldest lifesaving society. On the banks of the New River where it reached the present Essex Road in Islington stood the Thatched House Tavern, formerly called Job's House. The innkeeper's son, born in 1736, grew up to study medicine and became Dr William Hawes. As a boy he had seen many bodies taken from the New River, and in the 1770s he became very interested in methods of resuscitating the apparently drowned. At that time many doubted that this was possible. Hawes, whose surgery was near the Thames at Blackfriars, placed advertisements offering rewards to anyone who rescued drowning persons from the Thames within two hours of their immersion and notified him at once. He experimented with different methods of reviving them, and was soon able to demonstrate that the apparently lifeless were sometimes within recall.

At first Hawes paid the rewards from his own pocket, but as news spread the work increased beyond his abilities. He then called a meeting of friends and obtained enough support to form what was at first called *The Institution for Affording Immediate Relief to Persons Apparently Dead from Drowning*. It was based on the Dutch Humane Society, founded in Amsterdam in 1767. Its members subscribed to a fund to give rewards and present medals to those who saved others from drowning, and they provided long hooked poles and other rescue equipment at dangerous places, including some on the New River. One of these was near Colebrooke Row in Islington, and when this was to be piped underground in 1861, the Society wrote to say they would remove the 'station for the drags' they had previously maintained there.

The society was prepared to pay 2 guineas for the rescue – dead or alive – of persons who had been in the water for no more than two hours, within thirty miles of London and Westminster. This was doubled to 4 guineas if they were subsequently revived. Publicans were promised a guinea for allowing the bodies into their premises, where a doctor would

67 *Sounding the alarm as a man drowns in the New River.*

attend to revive them, and the society paid for burial expenses if unsuccessful. The society's records show that in the year of its foundation it appointed 'medical assistants' for likely places, and two of these were assigned to the New River – Mr Church, surgeon of Cross Street, and Mr Hole in the High Street opposite Islington Church. The medical assistants were doctors, who gave their services free and were alerted by runners when they were needed. The society was an immediate success. In its first eight years 973 lives were saved, of whom 559 were revived from an apparently dead condition.

Hawes died in 1808 and was buried in Islington parish church, where the Governors of the society he founded placed a tablet in his memory. It praised his achievements, and then advised the reader to 'imitate those virtuous actions which the latest posterity will applaud and venerate, and which the Recording Angel has registered in Heaven'.

Rescued from drowning

Whereas the bald verdicts of inquest juries tell us little or nothing about the motives of those who died or the circumstances of their deaths, the records of the Royal Humane Society are fuller. Sometimes those who were rescued were not only restored to life but also prepared to explain why they had gone into the water. It is sometimes forgotten that suicide was a crime in England until 1961. Obviously those who succeeded were beyond the reach of the courts, but those who tried and failed were often prosecuted. Their actions were regarded as an attempt at self-murder, deserving punishment. For that reason would-be suicides who were saved had a motive to blame chance or an unknown cause.

Some were nevertheless prepared to be frank, at least to those who rescued them. Within a year of the society being founded, its report for 1775 shows just how many people went into the New River. Thus, Mr Bailey of Turnagain Alley was saved from the New River between Islington and Canonbury in March 1775. He told his rescuers that his 'extreme poverty' had caused him to seek death that way. In May a Mr Campbell was rescued near Canonbury House, and in June Thomas Patterson, a boy aged eleven. He was pulled from the river near City Road, and taken to the Coach and Horses public house, where he was 'revived with difficulty.' In September three were saved and revived – an anonymous man, a servant girl who slipped in while filling a pail of water near Camden Street in Islington, and a boy of 3½ who fell in and was revived at the King of Prussia's Head. In October, James Bates of Catherine Wheel Court, Smithfield fell in accidentally by Sadler's Wells and was saved. On the same day an unknown woman threw herself in at the same place, and was rescued by Mr Haynes of the Sir Hugh Myddelton's Head public house, who had gone there for a bucket of water. Once revived, she was taken into the custody of Islington Workhouse. In November Catherine Levidge, described as a young woman, was rescued near the same spot and also revived at the Myddelton's Head. On Boxing Day a German, John Adam Falkenhagen, was rescued near Sadler's Wells and taken to the King of Prussia's Head nearby. The report describes the methods that eventually restored him, including a surprising one that was often used at the time – blowing 'fumes of tobacco' up his anus.[5]

The Last of Sir Hugh

There was a persistent and quite unfounded myth that a vast sum of money was deposited in the Bank of England waiting to be claimed by any descendant of Sir Hugh Myddelton. This was reported in a newspaper in 1838, and resulted in a flood of letters from potential claimants.

A newspaper correspondent suggested in 1794 that the 'inhabitants of London should have raised a statue in gold' to Sir Hugh Myddelton, and regretted that 'there is no memorial of this great and public-spirited citizen except an ale-house sign of his head at Sadler's Wells.' Time was to remedy this with at least three statues, albeit in stone, of which two survive.[6]

One statue can still be seen in the City, facing the Bank of England on the north facade of the Royal Exchange. It dates from 1844-5, when the Exchange was rebuilt after a fire, was commissioned from Samuel Joseph at a cost of £400, and is almost twelve feet high. It shows him holding a scroll in his left hand, and what may be a gauging rod in his right. The right hand is much whiter than the rest of the statue, not for any allegorical reason but because it was replaced in 1999 after its predecessor fell off. The other surviving London statue of Myddelton is on Islington Green, and is described in chapter 20.[7]

Even as late as 1869, Myddelton's reputation was still high. In that year the Corporation of London completed Holborn Viaduct – a massive cast iron bridge that still carries the road from Oxford Street to the City over Farringdon Street in the valley of the River Fleet. Here there were four statues of City benefactors, and the north-east one was of Sir Hugh Myddelton, by Henry Bursill. It is no longer there, as that corner building was badly damaged in the London blitz and demolished in the 1950s, when the statue seems to have been lost. A surviving picture shows him looking morosely at a plan of the New River, one foot supported on a seemingly decayed wooden water pipe.

There may be one other statue or bust of Sir Hugh in existence. It is said that one that was at New River Head was damaged by a lorry, and buried under the floor of the windmill base to conceal the evidence. It may still be there.

Myddelton was buried in his local church, St Matthew's in Friday Street, just to the south-west of St Paul's Churchyard, as directed by his will. He had been a churchwarden, and eleven of his children had been baptised there.

The church was then destroyed in the Great Fire, and rebuilt by Wren. Almost two centuries later, in March 1883 it was about to be demolished, and the churchwarden wrote to tell the New River Company. A facility had been obtained to excavate the crypt, and any remains found would be reinterred at Ilford cemetery 'under the direction of Col Haywood of the Sewers Office.'

The Company quickly decided that a reburial in St Paul's Cathedral would be more seemly if Myddelton's remains were found. As it happened, there was still a Mr Myddelton working in the Company's drawing office, who was one of Hugh's descendants. The Board informed the churchwarden that he would make himself available when the excavations were made, as he would recognise the armorial bearings if a Myddelton coffin were found. Another of Myddelton's descendants also took an interest, Mr W. Cornwallis West, who wrote from Ruthin Castle in Wales and asked to be kept informed. Sadly it all came to nothing. In September the churchwarden wrote again, to say that 'a thorough and exhaustive search of the vaults' had been concluded to an average depth of twenty feet below street level. Many objects of antiquarian interest had been found, but no trace of Sir Hugh.

The pleasures of Islington Hill

Long before Hugh Myddelton's time the fields on Islington Hill around New River Head had been a resort for Londoners wanting an escape from the constraints of the City. The arrival of the New River did nothing to end this, and the waterworks provided an extra feature of interest to the hill, with houses for refreshment such as the 'farthing pye house' and Spencer's Breakfasting Hut on the river bank, whose proprietor warned:

> 'No passage to my hut I have, The river runs before;
> Therefore your care I humbly crave, Pray don't mistake the door.'

Close by, more dubious pleasures soon joined them. There was a pit for bear-baiting and cock-fighting, and prize-fights were staged between women, who had to hold a coin inside their clenched fists to prevent the use of fingernails.

68 Two small pleasure gardens overlooked the Claremont reservoir, on either side of Penton Street. To the east was Dobney's and to the west the Belvidere. Just further up Penton Street was the celebrated White Conduit Street, named after a conduit which had once supplied Charterhouse. This illustration, by Thomas Rowlandson, depicts customers at the White Conduit.

Early maps show there was a bowling green on the top of Islington hill, and it remained long into the eighteenth century until it was eventually built over. The hill was a place where people went for recreation from early times, and it made a pleasant stroll out from the city on a fine day, as Pepys and others have described.

One visitor was the Elizabethan surgeon and herbalist John Gerard. He travelled the country in search of plants he valued for their ability to cure sickness and otherwise affect the body. His 'Herbal', which gave details of these useful plants, and where they could be found, became a standard work of reference. Helpfully the dedication at the start of this work, addressed 'To the courteous and well-wishing reader' ends 'From my house in Holburne within the suburbs of London this first of December 1597', thus giving an address of sorts, as well as a date. Holborn would now be regarded as central rather than suburban, and is within an easy fifteen-minute walk of the hilltop, where Gerard must often have gone. He went there for white saxifrage, and also in search of the plant he calls 'Ladies Traces,' saying that he had found

69 *Sadler's Wells and the New River, from a drawing by R. C. Andrews, 1792.*

it 'growing plentifully in sundry places, as in the fielde by Islington neere London, where there is a bouling place under a fewe old shrubby okes.'[8] His use for Ladies Traces is an interesting one. The roots, boiled in milk and drunk he says, 'provoke venery'. Venery is a rare word now but is defined in an old dictionary as 'sexual indulgence', so the root is an aphrodisiac.

Other local places of entertainments were Sadler's Wells, the London Spa and New Tunbridge Wells. Often they provided more than water. The London Spa, patronised by 'a multitude of people out of the City and other parts' served a dark-coloured mineral water but also used it to brew a beer, worryingly described as 'wholesome and purgative'. One commentator described Sadler's Wells as 'a small theatre for the summer evening exhibition of tumbling, rope-dancing and other drolls, in vulgar style.' According to a 1726 guide-book, it had regular displays and a farce was acted every night 'which anybody may see, drinking and paying for one pint of wine.'

Other places included tea gardens with shaded walks laid out, but they seem to have been less than respectable. In May 1744 the grand jury of Middlesex included Sadler's Wells and the New Wells near the London Spa on a list of six places which,

> 'inviting and seducing not only the inhabitants, but all other persons, to several places kept apart for the encouragement of luxury, extravagance, idleness, and other wicked illegal purposes, which, by such means, go on with impunity, to the destruction of many families, to the great dishonour of the kingdom in general, and this county in particular..'

What 'other wicked illegal purposes' the jury had in mind is not explained, nor is the result of this complaint recorded. Some forty years later in 1786 a writer was more specific, naming four establishments on the flanks of Islington Hill – the Pantheon in Spa-fields, the Bagnigge Wells, the White Conduit House and Sadler's Wells. 'The tendency of these cheap enticing places of pleasure just at the skirts of this vast town is too obvious to need further explanation,' he wrote, then in his next words went on to do just that:

'They swarm with loose women, and with boys whose morals are thus depraved and their constitution ruined, before they arrive at manhood: indeed the licentious resort to the tea drinking gardens was carried to such excess every night, that the magistrates lately thought proper to suppress the organs in their public rooms.'

From a different moral standpoint, a long tedious verse called 'A Walk to Islington' published in 1699 describes how the writer took up 'with a lady of pleasure, who I turned off at will and enjoyed at my leisure' and describes sauntering about with her near New River Head. It may be no coincidence that one of the fields at the top of the hill near the bowling green is marked on one map as 'Whores' Field'. No doubt most of those who visited the hill did so for more innocent purposes, but it seems clear it was a pleasure resort in the fullest sense.

The area was not without its physical dangers, either. On its eastern side, the road from the north ran down from the Angel Inn towards Smithfield Market and St Paul's. A long stretch of this road remained open country until the 1780s and was evidently dangerous at night. In 1828 the Islington historian Thomas Cromwell wrote that until fifty years before,

'..it was customary for travellers approaching London to remain all night at the Angel Inn .. rather than venture after dark to prosecute their journey along ways which were almost equally dangerous from their bad state and their being so greatly infested with thieves. On the other hand persons walking from the City to Islington in the evening, waited near the head of St John's Street, in what is now termed Northampton Street (but was then a rural avenue, planted with trees, called Wood's Close) until a sufficient party had collected, who were then escorted by an armed patrol appointed for that purpose.'

Sadler's Wells

The present Sadler's Wells Theatre, in Rosebery Avenue on the east side of New River Head, is the latest of a series of buildings on that site since about 1683. It is said that they are named after a surveyor called Sadler who happened to excavate an old stone well-head while digging for gravel, and found it to contain a chalybeate spring that tasted nasty enough to have curative properties. Very little is known about Mr Sadler himself, but he may have had a connection with the New River Company. A tantalisingly incomplete fragment of a burnt Board minutes from 1664 or 1665 suggests that Edward Sadler had 'praied to be admitted to Continew and Dwe(ll)' at the Water House, and that this had been granted during the pleasure of the Company.[9]

There is no record of Sadler's Wells as a spa and music house until about twenty years after that date. The founder's first name is variously given as Richard or Thomas, but virtually nothing is known about him. As the surname is unusual, and the Water House was the closest building to the future Sadler's Wells it is possible that Edward Sadler was a river surveyor working for the Company, rather than a road surveyor as he has been described in later texts. It seems more likely that an employee rather than an outsider would have been given the tenancy of the Water House – the next known occupant was the Clerk, John Grene. Unfortunately, most of the Company's records for that period were burnt in 1769.

A number of illustrations exist that show the attractive location of the theatre on the banks of the final stretch of the New River, usually shown lined with anglers. By about 1804, the theatre had taken advantage to its proximity to the New River to become 'The Aquatic Theatre', with a repertoire of watery displays. Charles Dibdin the younger, who ran it at that time, described the New River 'the margin of which young urchins line often throughout the day, catching little fish and great colds…' He went on to explain how in conditions of secrecy, the workmen being 'locked in the theatre while in their occupations', he had arranged the construction of a vast water tank ninety feet long, varying in width from ten to twenty-four feet, and with two branches up to four feet wide extending to the walls of the theatre. This was filled from the New River, first by an Archimedean screw, and later from a piped main. He continued:

> 'Having fixed upon exhibiting the Siege of Gibraltar we procured from the Dockyard at Woolwich, several Shipwrights and Riggers; and immediately set them to work to construct a large number of ships, of all rates, upon a scale of one inch to a foot of those in the Navy; in exact imitation ..brass cannon, cast on purpose and regularly fired, .. the Sails were made to work .. and when they were finished were the most accurate models ever exhibited to the public.. The Expense occasioned by this was enormous, but it was not 'throwing a sprat to catch a herring', it was baiting with a whale to catch a Leviathan.' [10]

In 1823, machinery was installed so that the stage and all its scenery could be raised instantly to the roof of the theatre, revealing the lake of water, something that had previously required a twenty-minute interval. Despite these wonders, the proprietor sometimes failed to settle his water bill. In 1824 the Secretary reported to the New River Board 'that he had made numerous applications to Mr Gilbert the Treasurer of Sadler's Wells Theatre for the Water Rent of £21, which he engaged to pay on the 3rd inst, and that there seemed little probability that it would be paid.' It was ordered that the supply be withdrawn unless the bill was paid by 1pm the next day.

This threat was carried out. Three weeks later it was noted that 'Mr Hughes and Mr Grimaldi this day attended the Board, stating that the management of Sadler's Wells was now changing … and requested the supply to be restored.' To this the Board agreed.[11] 'Mr Grimaldi' was the famous comic actor Jo Grimaldi, 1778-1837, who had first appeared on stage at the age of three, and who lived nearby in what is now Exmouth Market, where a blue plaque marks his home.

'Brothels ... of the lowest description.'

The existence of brothels was widely known in Regency and Victorian London, but polite behaviour precluded their discussion. There were evidently some in Charlotte Street, a curving thoroughfare of terraced cottages that was built in the former garden of the New Tunbridge Wells spa in about 1810. The street subsequently had its name changed twice, first to Thomas Street and later to Sadler Street, perhaps to try and live down an unsavoury reputation. When Charles Booth's researchers were compiling his 'Labour and Life of the People' in the 1890s, they learnt from the local police that it was 'one of the worst streets on the sub-division, the home of ne'er-do-wells, thieves, shoe-blacks.'[12] It survived until the Second World War, by when it was overdue for slum clearance, but German bombing then caused enough damage for it to be pulled down and replaced with post-war council flats. It was surrounded by New River land, but had never belonged to the Company.

The houses on one side of Charlotte Street abutted the St John Street reservoir of the New River Company which had been built in 1805, and in 1831 W.C. Mylne reported to the Board on its state. The fence around the reservoir was decayed, and he suggested it should be replaced with a taller one, 'to exclude the view of the back windows of the Houses, which are all occupied as Brothels of the lowest description'. One in particular, owned by a Mr Duncan, had four windows overlooking the reservoir, all built without the Company's permission. This house, reported Mylne,

> 'being so occupied must certainly be considered a great Nuisance and I recommend your giving Mr Duncan notice to stop up the Windows and in default of his so doing to stop them up by placing Boards against the same.'

This had little effect, and in October the Clerk

gave Mr Duncan notice that 'in consequence of the disreputable manner in which that house is occupied the Board had given directions for the placing of boards against the back Windows overlooking the St John Street Reservoir.

This brought a prompt response in the form of a letter from one Andrew Duncan of South Square, Gray's Inn. Until he received the Board's letter, he wrote, he had not been aware that the house was 'disreputably occupied,' and he continued

> 'I took every precaution I could to prevent it becoming a receptacle for loose characters, for I made Mrs Hamilton, the tenant, sign a paper to that effect. I called at the House yesterday and I confess its general appearance was not satisfactory, and in consequence I gave Mrs Hamilton notice to quit, who promised to leave next Christmas, or before if she could suit herself.'

Why it was such an affront to the Company to have the water in its reservoir overlooked by loose characters is not spelt out. Perhaps they foresaw that one day the land would be built on, and the disreputable back windows would lower its value.[13]

Riots

The anti-Catholic Gordon Riots of 1780 spread great alarm, as riots in London have done more recently. There was no police force at that time, and troops were called in to help maintain order. The rioters burnt a number of houses, and it was said they intended to burn the Bank of England as well as other prominent buildings, and planned to cut off the New River supply to hinder firefighting. This led to troops being stationed at New River Head, at Highbury Frame and at Bush Hill Frame, three places where the supply could most easily have been interrupted.

It is obvious from the Company's letter book that the military overstayed their welcome. The riots were over in June 1780, but Robert Holford, the Secretary, had to write to Lord Amhurst in July and August politely suggesting that the 'Officers of the Cambridge Regiment' on duty at Bush Hill Frame were no longer needed. The Company had a house there, occupied by Cressey the deputy-surveyor, and Holford had earlier written to him about the catering – he was to provide the Officers with a dinner of two dishes, and wine, at his house. This fare seems to have been much appreciated, and by mid October Holford ordered Cressey that there should be no more dinners. Despite this, the letter book shows that the army had not been dislodged from Highbury Frame by 21 December 1780.[14]

The following year the same court ordered that Robert Mylne should receive a gratuity of £100 in addition to his salary 'in consideration of extraordinary services and also for his trouble and expence at the time the Military were stationed at New River Head in consequence of the riots in June 1780'.[15]

It was perhaps because of the riots that in November of that year, the General Court was told that a 'new fence wall of brick' had been made on the west side of the outer ponds 'thereby forming the fences compleat round the ponds &c at the head.' A brick wall was often called a fence at that time, and pictures after that date show how all the ponds and buildings at New River Head were enclosed within a wall that appears to be quite unnecessarily high. There had already been a 'high brick wall' around the Upper Pond for over twenty years; it was built in 1757 and remained until 1825.[16]

The Second World War

By the time of the Second World War, the New River was simply one part of the system administered by the Metropolitan Water Board. There had been much planning for a war that had been foreseen for some time. There were three main worries. First, bombing in built-up areas was likely to breach water mains. This would mean an interruption to a supply that was urgently needed to fight fires started by the same bombs. Second, the same bombing might damage nearby sewers, allowing cross-contamination of water in the mains that could lead to an outbreak of diseases such as typhoid. Third, the Germans might deliberately poison water supplies in open reservoirs.

As it turned out, there were further risks. There were occasions when bombs fell into filter beds, causing damage that allowed untreated water into the public supply. Bomb-damaged sewers also released sewage into rivers that were then being used for water supply.

The danger of poisoned reservoirs was taken seriously. All reservoirs were continuously guarded in the hope of preventing, or at least observing, any such attempt. There was also a procedure for continuous sampling, with laboratory staff working shifts to provide a twenty-four hour testing service. Emergency laboratories were set up at locations outside London in case the main laboratories at New River Head were destroyed. All chlorinating points were provided with duplicates some distance from the originals, and portable chlorinating plants were available, as well as diffusers that allowed for direct chlorination.[17]

One example of bombing damage was potentially very disruptive. At Enfield, a long loop of the New River had been bypassed by channelling the water through three enormous iron mains, each at least four feet in diameter, and the land previously used had been transferred to Enfield District Council in 1938. On the night of 15 October 1940 a bomb that fell in Park Avenue fractured all three pipes, completely cutting off the flow of forty-six million gallons a day to London. Rescuers only realized the New River, and not just a water main, had been breached when they saw dead fish floating in nearby gutters. Water board engineers consulted with London Regional Defence, and decided to try and reinstate the old loop of the river. Fortunately, the ground had not yet been built on although much of it had been filled in, and the Army provided 1200 men to re-cut the old channel, while the Fire Brigade set up emergency pumps to restore some of the supply. As a result, a supply of ten million gallons a day was restored very quickly although it was not until November 1941 that the damaged pipes were replaced, and some New River water flowed through the old loop until 1952. The loop then became a local amenity, as it remains today, and Thames Water supply it with sufficient water to prevent stagnation.[18]

Bombing during the London blitz caused much damage to the Clerkenwell estate. Houses on the north side of Myddelton Square were destroyed, and subsequently replaced with flats by the New River Company Limited, who fortunately chose to match the former facades – an unusual practice at the time. Holford Square was less fortunate, being so badly damaged that it was later demolished and replaced with Bevan Court, a block of Finsbury Borough Council flats designed by Lubetkin, now a listed building but very different from what was there before. Other bombed houses in Great Percy Street were replaced by more modest flats, their vanished predecessors remembered by a wall plaque.

CHAPTER NINETEEN

Private to public and back again

Going public – The last board meeting – Changes to the New River – Thames Water – The London Ring Main – The Artificial Recharge Scheme – The future of the New River

Going public

The question of London's water supply remained under public scrutiny for much of the nineteenth century. Select committees and Royal Commissions made their reports while the competing interests of reformers and water shareholders manoeuvred back and forth.

Some experts thought that London's drinking water should come from distant sources, and not the polluted rivers Thames and Lea. As time went by it was increasingly clear that the epidemics of cholera were no longer the regular threat to London that they had been, and it seemed to follow that the measures for purifying river water by filtration and covered storage, in place since 1856, were enough to make it safe.

The whole question of water supply could not be separated from the question of drainage. Companies such as the New River had never made it a pre-condition of supplying a house that the house should have drains. They were in the business of supply not drainage, and felt it to be no concern of theirs what happened to the water they delivered. As flushing lavatories proliferated, their contents were somehow drained, and generally found their way into sewers that had been designed for no more than rain-water, leading eventually to the Thames. Eventually this problem was solved by the drainage scheme devised by Sir Joseph Bazalgette and built between 1858 and 1875. This received London's liquid waste into lines of intercepting sewers, where its residue flowed eventually into the lower Thames at points where it could do London no harm.

The final Royal Commission, chaired by Viscount Llandaff, was appointed in 1897 and reported in 1900. It concluded that the New River Company was never likely to lower its charges, and that it and the other London companies should be taken over by a new Metropolitan Water Board, rather than the London County Council which was keen to do so.

The Metropolis Water Act of 1902 finally put an end to the New River Company as a water supplier, though not as a landowner, along with London's other private water suppliers. The changeover did not take place until 25 July 1904 in the case of the New River Company, a month later than the other companies. In the meantime, the Metropolitan Water Board was formed and held its first meeting on 2 April 1902. It had sixty-six members, representing all the corporations and local councils in its district, also Thames and Lea river conservancies, and one of its first tasks was to deal with the question of compensation for water company shareholders, as described in chapter six and Appendix 1. It would take over eight companies, the New River, Chelsea, East London, Grand Junction, Kent, Lambeth, Southwark &

Vauxhall and the West Middlesex. Between them, they supplied over a million customers and a population of 6¾ million.

The former territory of the New River Company continued as an entity, under the name of the New River District, until it was merged with the area of the former East London Company to become the Northern District. The 1902 Act had provided that all the old staff of the water companies would keep their employment, and that gave a continuity that may have helped the new enterprise.

The last board meeting

After almost three centuries, the New River and all its waterworks were about to pass out of the ownership of the Company whose only purpose had been to run it and divide its profits. The last meeting of the old board, on 18 July 1904, would surely have been a poignant and self-consciously historical occasion, a time for reflection, reminiscence and a fuller lunch than usual, with speeches and some toasts. What seems clear from the minute book is that nothing of the sort took place. The members, including one of Hugh Myddelton's descendants in the form of an Ellacombe, turned up as usual and presumably collected their attendance money. Then they adjourned, and the Secretary noted that they had agreed to meet the following Thursday as usual. If they did, nobody wrote up the minutes, and the rest of the great brass-clasped minute book is blank, the corporate equivalent of the *Mary Celeste*, sailing on for ever with the cabin table laid for a meal and not a soul on board.

Changes to the New River

London's water supply was greatly changed during the twentieth century yet the New River continues to flow today. The major changes that affected the New River can be briefly described. Some amended its route and others the supply system.

When the Metropolitan Water Board took over the New River Company, some water still flowed all the way from Ware to Islington as it had done since the river was first built, although three-quarters of it was diverted into the filter beds and reservoirs at Hornsey and Stoke Newington. The rest went to New River Head where it was filtered, and either supplied directly into local mains or pumped up to Claremont Square. Hugh Myddelton's Round Pond survived at New River Head until 1914, when it was taken out of commission because part of the land it was on was needed for the Board's new headquarters building. The New River still flowed there, to feed the remaining three filter beds. The most easterly of those disappeared in 1936 to make way for a new Laboratory building, while the other two continued until 1946 when they were taken out of service. The iron pipes that had conveyed the New River from Stoke Newington since about 1850 were then removed in 1950, and some were still good enough to be reused elsewhere.

The Claremont Square reservoir received filtered water direct from Stoke Newington from 1856 until 1946, as well as some filtered water pumped up from New River Head. After 1946, it continued to receive water pumped from New River Head, but from 1950 that water originated from Walton on Thames and not the New River. Until 1950, steam engines were still in occasional use for pumping, but they were then replaced with much smaller electric pumps. The flow of the New River is now all diverted at Stoke Newington to a treatment works at Coppermills, near Walthamstow, which is linked to the London Ring Main.

In December 1956 there was a proposal to make the engine house at New River Head a listed building, and the chief engineer of the Metropolitan Water Board wrote to the Ministry of Housing and Local Government to disagree. He wanted to demolish the engine house down to a single storey, raise the floor three feet with concrete, re-roof the building and use it for storing vehicles. The Ministry wrote back in January 1957, agreeing that this could be done and that the engine house would not be listed. For some reason the demolition never took place. Then, in 1972, the Greater London Council took an interest in the building. After a meeting with them, the Chief

Engineer wrote a despairing internal memo on 24 May 1972:

> 'As far as can be ascertained (it) dates from 1789, but apart from its age it has no virtue whatsoever. It is ugly, outdated, and a serious obstacle to redevelopment. It is to be hoped there will be no serious attempt to preserve this building.'

He followed that up with a letter saying that he was 'horrified' that it might be preserved,

> 'not only because it is so ugly, useless and costly to maintain ... but a serious obstacle to redevelopment.'

On 5 June 1972 he wrote to the GLC saying that he intended to demolish it, but was informed on 5 July that it, together with the windmill base, the oak-panelled boardroom, an old conduit head and some remains of the old inner and outer ponds were all listed as Grade II structures. The Board had intended to build a large extension with 60,000 square feet of offices, which would have a new pumping station underneath its basement car park, but this plan never went ahead.

Thames Water

Less than seventy years after its creation, the Metropolitan Water Board was abolished. A Conservative government under Edward Heath decided to reorganise the whole water industry of England and Wales, as to water supply, drainage and river conservation. The result, in 1973, was a series of ten Regional Water Authorities, of which Thames Water was one. This body had responsibility for a far larger area than London, extending right up the Thames valley to Gloucestershire. Its board was composed of the representatives of local authorities and undertakings in its area, much as the Metropolitan Water Board had been.

As the years passed Parliament changed this structure, so that Thames Water had fewer members and they were differently appointed. This seems to have been done in preparation for privatisation, which was put through by Margaret Thatcher's Conservative government in 1989. Thames Water then became Thames Water Plc and the New River, like all its other components, was once more back in private ownership. Its new owners seem to have given the assets a fresh look, and decided to develop and sell surplus land and properties. Thames Water in its turn was taken over, and became a member of the Frankfurt based RWE Group in 2000.

By 1986, changes in London's water needs had made it seem possible that the New River would cease to exist south of Cheshunt. Then rescue came, because of a number of factors including the London Docklands Development Scheme, which proposed large areas of new housing and commerce on derelict industrial land in east London. This meant that London would need more water.

The London Ring Main

The London Ring Main, in use by 1994, used modern tunnelling techniques to build the liquid equivalent of the M25 motorway. Unseen and largely unknown, the fifty-mile long concrete-lined tunnels stretch from Coppermills, near Walthamstow in the east, south to Streatham, west to Walton on Thames and Ashford, and back to Coppermills by way of Hampstead in the north. The ring main is about 130 feet deep, has a diameter of 7 feet 6 inches, and can hold 250 million gallons. From it, seventeen shafts come up to the surface where they join reservoirs or the public mains. One of these is at New River Head. The result is a flexible and cheaply run distribution network that avoids many duplications of pumping that were previously needed.

The Artificial Recharge Scheme

Continuing concern about water supplies brought about the Artificial Recharge Scheme, which began in 1991 and was operational by 1995. This makes ingenious use of the channel of the New River as a means of conveying water to and from deep boreholes. The Victorian pumping stations along the line of the New River were simply designed to extract water from deep, water-bearing strata. The recharge system adds an element of sustainability to this concept. In times of drought, water can be extracted as it previously was, to flow down the New River to London. When supplies are plentiful, the new pumping stations divert surplus treated water from the mains down into the aquifers, where the water stays until the next drought.

The system consists of a network of twenty-one pumping stations all along the New River, some newly built and some inside the former Victorian engine houses.

The future of the New River

Thanks to the Artificial Recharge Scheme, any doubts about the future of the New River seem to have been dispelled. It is still a supply route for a significant proportion of London's water supply, and will so remain. It is also now recognised as having amenity value both for walkers and as a wildlife corridor, and this value can only increase if the population of the region continues to grow as predicted.

At New River Head, Sorocold's windmill base and the engine house linked to Smeaton, Boulton & Watt, and two generations of Mylne seem safe now that they are listed buildings, and suitable uses may be found for them. Even Claremont Square reservoir has a future. In the 1990s it became disused, but its value as a reservoir has now been recognised again. In 2003 it received its first major refurbishment after 147 years of service. This involved treatment to cure some leaks. The top covering had become permeable to rainwater, and the turf was removed so that a waterproof membrane could be applied. The earth was then replaced and returfed, so that the reservoir could be connected to the London Ring Main. It purpose now is as a balancing reservoir to even out fluctuations in demand, filling at night and emptying in the day.

George Sorocold's Upper Pond of 1708, built on the site of a Civil War fort, thus remains a permanent part of London's water supply, and a small part of the Ring Main water it receives comes down the New River from Chadwell Spring. Four centuries after Captain Edmund Colthurst went to look at Chadwell Spring and then told Queen Elizabeth about his plan, his New River continues to flow from Londoners' taps.

CHAPTER TWENTY

Walking the river

The New River Today – The Angel and the Upper Pond – New River Head – The course through Islington to Hornsey – Wood Green to Enfield – Chadwell Spring and the intake from the Lea

The New River today

From the earliest days of the New River Company, the Governor's River Survey was an annual ritual. Those surveys always began at Islington, as will this description, following the river upstream against the current. A footpath now follows the whole route, and leaflets are available from local information centres, though some stretches are less interesting or accessible than others. A detailed guide exists that describes almost every feature along the route, Dr Essex-Lopresti's *Exploring the New River*. Some of the more interesting sections are described below.

The Angel and the Upper Pond

The crossroads at Angel, Islington makes a convenient starting point, having many bus routes and an underground station. The Co-operative Bank on the northwest corner marks the site of the Angel Inn, which dated from pre-Reformation times. Walking west from here along Pentonville Road, the terrace of old houses on the left is one the earliest building developments on the New River estate, planned in 1811 but built in 1819 by speculative builders, to a standard design by the company's engineer William Chadwell Mylne. The semi-circular brick recesses over the first floor windows are a feature of his design, which otherwise resembles many other terraces from that time. Many of the houses still have original fanlights over the front doors, and these vary according to the taste of the builder.

As the road approaches the covered reservoir at Claremont Square, on the left, it can be seen how the ground continues to rise until the midpoint of the reservoir, and then falls steeply away towards King's Cross and the valley of the now covered River Fleet. The reservoir is on the top of Islington Hill. Continue to the end of the reservoir, then turn left at the traffic lights.

There has been a reservoir here since the Upper Pond was built in 1708, in accordance with George Sorocold's plan to store a head of water for supplying the higher parts of the West End around Soho Square. In 1856 it was covered over with rows of brick arches topped with earth to raise the water level, increase the capacity and protect the filtered water it by then contained from airborne pollution. Once that was done, it contained water twenty-one feet deep, with a total capacity of 3½ million gallons. It is still in use, having been refurbished in 2003, and provides a buffer of water to even out fluctuations between supply and demand.

This was the site of the so-called Fort Royal in the 1640s, one of the ring of earth fortifications built by the citizens of London to protect the City from Royalist forces as described in Chapter 9. The western half of the present reservoir and the terrace of houses numbered 2 to 17 Claremont Square cover the site of the fort.

70 The Angel, Islington, 1895. This was then demolished to make way for a hotel which itself became a Lyons Corner House. Of late it has been a Co-operative Bank.

Walking south along the west side of the reservoir and straight on down hill, the road becomes Amwell Street, named after one of the Hertfordshire springs that fed the New River. Side streets to the right show how steeply the ground falls away into the valley of the River Fleet, and give views west over London. Inglebert Street, to the left, provides a vista to St Mark's Church of 1825-7, designed by William Chadwell Mylne, who also designed the surrounding terraces of houses that form the New River Clerkenwell estate.

Further down Amwell Street is Lloyd's Dairy, an early corner shop that was run by members of the Lloyd family until after 2000. Just past it on the right is Clerkenwell Parochial School built on New River land.

New River Head

Opposite the school are the gates to the yard of New River Head, where the Round Pond was built in 1613 to receive the water of the New River. The round brick structure with a tiled roof is the base of George Sorocold's windmill of 1707-8. This was designed to pump water from the ponds here up to what is now the Claremont Square reservoir – the only pumping that was done on the entire New River system at that time. Everything else flowed by gravity and this was the key to the New River's profitability: it was cheaper in the long run to dig a forty-mile channel and let the water flow gently downhill to London than to pump every gallon twenty or thirty feet up from the Thames. The windmill did not operate after 1730 because of storm damage. It always had provision for horse-driven pumps in its base for use in calm weather, and these were supplemented from about 1720 by another horse-engine in the 'square horse-works', a small building on the east side of the mill that was demolished in about 1770. An overshot waterwheel, turned by water from the New

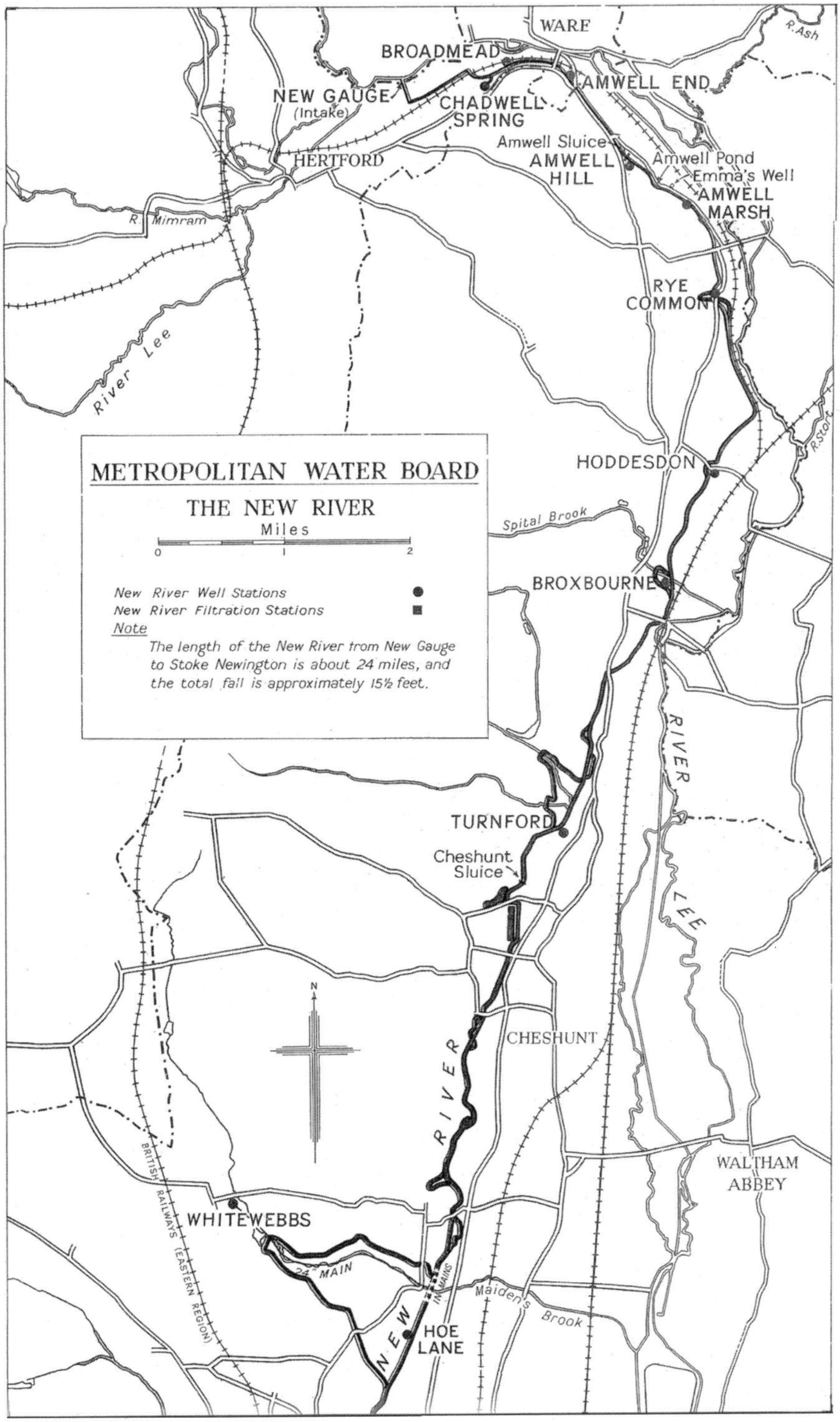

71 The upper course of the New River, from the New Gauge on the River Lea, past Chadwell and Amwell to Hoe Lane, showing abandoned loops as well as the newer sections.

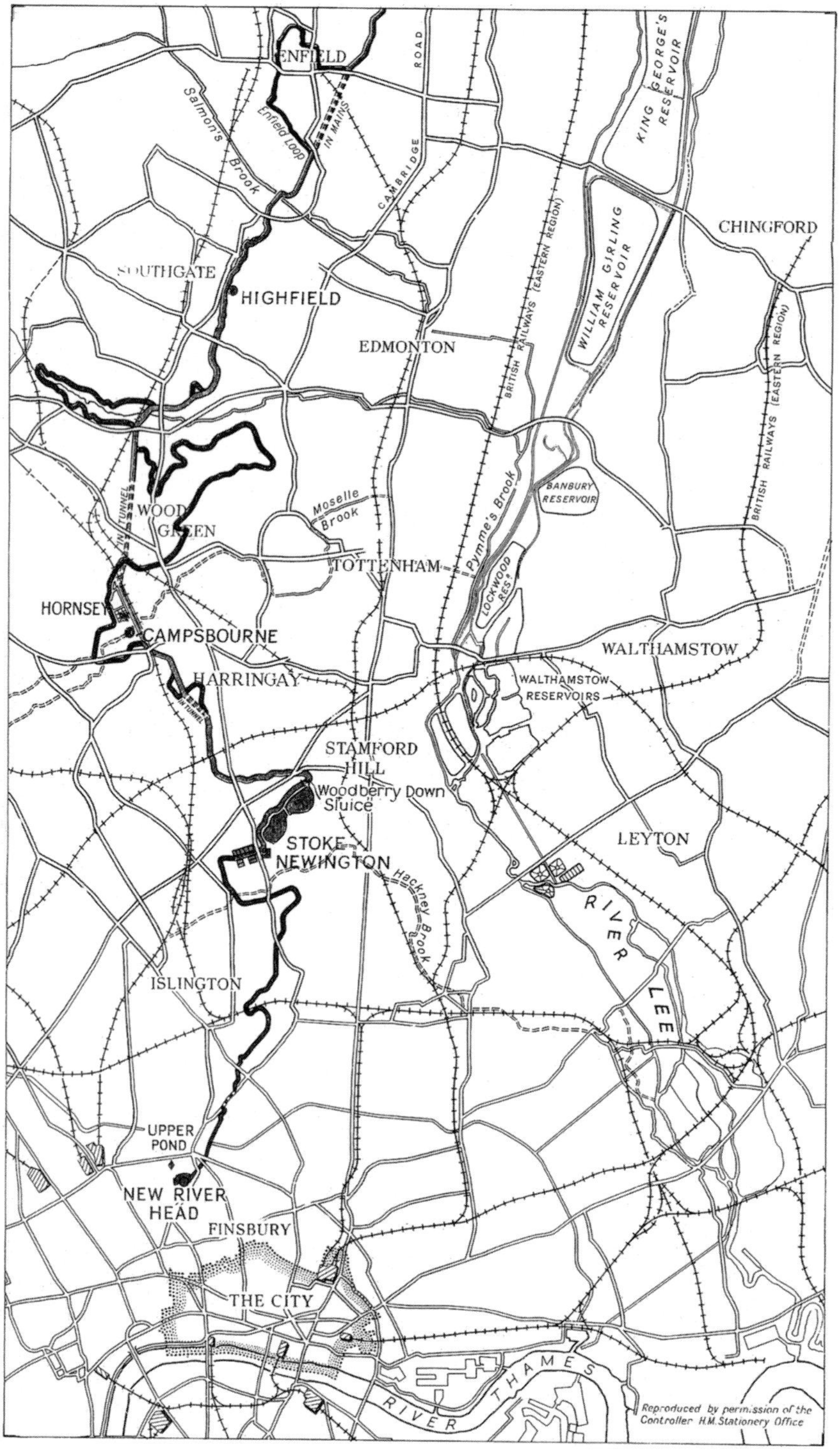

72 *The course of the New River through Southgate, Haringey and Stoke Newington, to the New River Head. The Islington loop abandoned in 1618 is not shown, but can be seen in ill.73, p.217.*

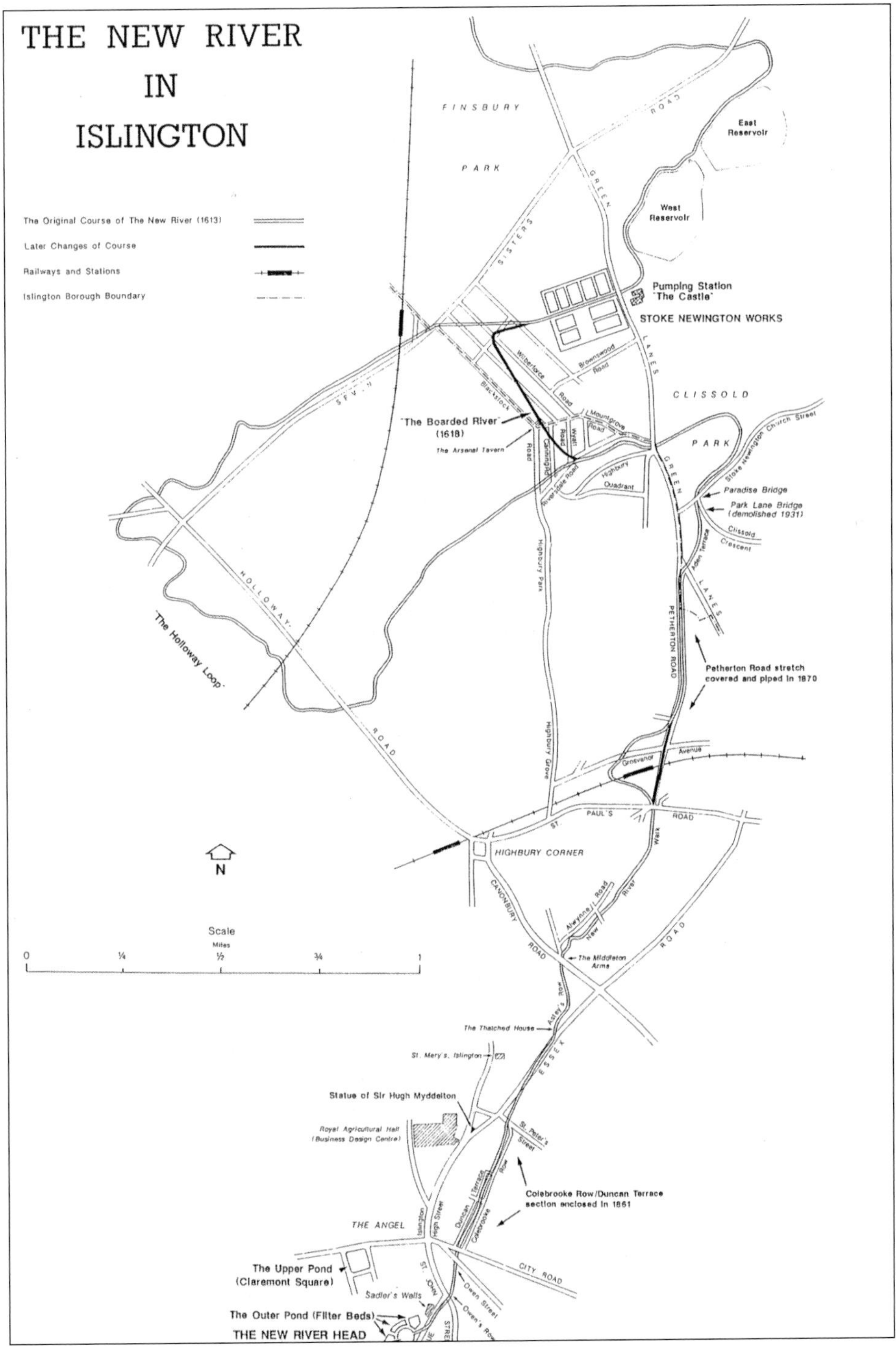

73 The course of the New River through Islington, showing how the 'Boarded River' at Highbury replaced a long loop that went west of Holloway Road. The 'Boarded River' was the first major change to the New River and was built in 1618.

River, was placed in a brick-lined pit on the site of the square horse-works in 1779 and was used to supplement the steam engines pumping water to the Upper Pond until after 1842. No visible traces of the waterwheel or its pit remain.

Beyond the windmill stump is a tall brick engine house. What can be seen today is the building in its final form of 1818, apart from a tall, tapering square chimney that was demolished in 1954. The last steam pumping was done in about 1950, and the engines were then removed. Within the structure is the smaller engine house built by John Smeaton in 1767-9 for his 'fire-engine', later extended to house steam engines by Boulton and Watt that were more efficient than Smeaton's, and later still by other engines. Walking on down Amwell Street, there is a brief glimpse of the dome of St Paul's Cathedral straight ahead, a reminder that until the building development after 1815 the hillside gave extensive views over London.

Turning left along Hardwick Street, named after a Governor of the New River Company, the road joins Rosebery Avenue. The large building of red brick and white stone on the left is the former home of the Metropolitan Water Board, designed in 1913 but delayed by the First World War and not completed until 1920. The top storey was added in 1935. Above two first floor windows on the west side, visible from Hardwick Street, can be seen two semicircular inset stones. These were taken from the old Water House building and record restoration there by Robert Mylne in 1782. Behind those windows is the Oak Room, dating from about 1690 when it was added to the 1613 Water House. The Oak Room (*ill.74*) was retained when the 1613 building was replaced in 1819, and moved a few yards to its present position a hundred years later when the present building was put up. It contains elaborate carving, much of it on watery themes, possibly by Grinling Gibbons, and an elaborate plaster ceiling with a painted panel of King William III in armour.

The building is now converted into residential apartments. If access can be gained to the front hall the arms of the New River Company and the other London water companies taken over by the Metropolitan Water Board in 1904 can be seen.

74 The Oak Room of 1693 at New River Head, with carving attributed to Grinling Gibbons.

Continuing up Rosebery Avenue, a rose garden behind railings on the left marks the approximate position of the original Round Pond to which the New River first ran on 29 September 1613. Behind it is the former water-testing laboratory of 1936, now also turned into apartments and flanked by a block of new apartments built to a similar design.

The course through Islington to Hornsey

Walking up Rosebery Avenue, the pavement in front of Sadler's Wells Theatre follows the former course of the New River. The water ran here in an open channel until 1891 when Rosebery Avenue was constructed and the channel was replaced with an iron pipe. The last time New River water flowed to New River Head was 1945, and the pipe was removed in 1950.

At the junction with St John Street a low brick

75 The statue of Sir Hugh Myddelton on Islington Green. The sculptor was John Thomas. Costing £900, it was paid for by local subscription and by the railway entrepreneur Sir Morton Peto. It was unveiled by Gladstone on 26 July 1862. The chain around Myddelton's neck is a reward given to him in 1623 by the City of London after water from the New river had been used to put out a dangerous warehouse fire.

wall topped with railings is straight ahead, and marks the point where the river used to cross.

The route can be followed from here along an alleyway, across City Road and into Colebrooke Row. Here the river ran as an open channel until 1861, and the Royal Humane Society formerly provided lifesaving equipment here and at other points along the route. The route is marked by public gardens. 64 Duncan Terrace has a plaque to show it was the home of the essayist Charles Lamb. It was here in 1823 that he had the memorable experience of seeing an absent-minded departing guest walk straight into the New River, 'instead of turning down the right-hand path by which he had entered – with staff in hand, and at noonday, deliberately march right forward into the midst of the stream that runs by us, and totally disappear.'[1]

The gardens finish close to Lamb's former house. Here the New River emerged from a brick-built underground channel, known as the Dark Arch, which carried it underneath what is now Essex Road for a distance of about 400 yards from 1649 until 1851, when it was replaced by iron pipes.

A short detour south along Essex Road at this point will lead to the statue of Sir Hugh Myddelton on the southern tip of Islington Green. The monument, with a total height of 21 feet, includes Myddelton's figure in Sicilian marble on a pedestal of grey Devonshire granite, all on a base of Portland stone and provided with a public drinking fountain. The sculptor was John Thomas, and William Gladstone unveiled the monument in 1862.

Walking north along Essex Road, there is a public library on the left just after the junction with Cross Street. Just past the library, a footpath leads into New River Walk, another long garden that marks the former route of the river. The watercourse that shows here in places has little resemblance to the former watercourse. Parts are provided with water via an ordinary supply from the mains.

The route crosses Canonbury Road, and continues on the left side of Canonbury Grove where a section of the original watercourse can be seen in a more authentic form, and leads to New River Walk, and north to the point where it reaches St Paul's Road. Here the water disappears. Its former route is marked by curving Petherton Road, with its central grass reservation where the open river ran until it was piped underground in 1870. Its appearance in the 1860s was 'trimly kept ... running between rows of villas and neat residences (it) skirts their gardens, expanding and curving gracefully.' At the end of Petherton Road the route crossed into Aden Terrace, and on into and round Clissold Park, where a small section is preserved to the west of Stoke Newington church. Today there are deer in the park, making a fitting foreground for Mylne's Scottish baronial pumping house whose outline can be seen through trees to the north.

To the west of here was one of the earliest changes in the route of the New River, when a long loop that ran west as far as Holloway Road was short-circuited in 1619 by an embankment topped with a wooden trough for the water, 420 feet long. Known as the Boarded River, this was occasionally improved and survived until about 1866, when it was piped underground.

After this, the final route of the river disappears underground along the line of Green Lanes, re-emerging by William Chadwell Mylne's Scottish baronial pumping house just north of Lordship Park. The buttresses bear an elaborate monogram – 'Mylne, 1855' (*ill.54, p.184*).

The route passes along the north side of the two reservoirs, crossing Lordship Road in the process, heads east as far as New River Close and then turns west, until it enters Finsbury Park and then heads north again through Haringey until it passes a water-treatment works in Hornsey and then enters the Wood Green tunnel, built in 1859 to replace a long loop of the river that led a mile and a half to the northeast towards Edmonton, as far as Empire Avenue and back again. The tunnel is too small for pedestrian access.

Wood Green to Enfield

The northern end of the brick tunnel is at Myddelton Road, left of the High Road about two thirds of a mile north of Wood Green tube station. From here the route can be followed

76 The New River at Douglas Road, Canonbury c.1904

to Enfield, passing on the way the embankment at Bush Hill that marks the site of the Bush Hill Frame – the only significant aqueduct on the original course of the New River, built to avoid a long detour up the valley of Salmon's Brook (*ill.79*). An arch reconstructed in 1682 and bearing a commemorative plaque marks the point in Bush Hill where the New River crosses the Brook, but access is down a flight of steps with a gate that is often locked. The course of the New River can be followed along the top of the embankment as far as Bush Hill Road.

North of here, a very attractive stretch of the New River makes a pleasant walk at Enfield. There was a long loop of the river here, which was bypassed with a run of iron pipes about ¾ mile long in 1938. The new pipes were then damaged by bombing in October 1940, with the result that the old loop was reinstated and used until 1950. It then became a local amenity, and is maintained in something close to its original appearance although no longer used for water supply. It is best approached by entering Enfield Town Park by the entrance in Uvedale Road. From here, a short walk uphill to the left leads to the banks of the New River, which runs between the park and a golf course. Turning right, the river can be followed for about 1½ miles. After circling the park it passes under Church Street close to Enfield Parish Church, and then on past the waterside gardens of houses in Gentleman's Row along a footpath called River View that crosses and recrosses the water. There are several cast iron bridges, bearing dates from the 1820s, and the whole route gives a pleasing impression of the way the New River must have appeared in earlier centuries.

North of the M25, whose route was lowered so that the New River could pass over it in an aqueduct just west of the A10 interchange, the route can be followed through Theobalds Park and then northwards.

Chadwell Spring and the intake from the Lea

The source of the New River at Chadwell Spring, with its nearby relics of New River

77 Highbury Sluice House Tavern c1863. This stood to the east of Blackstock Road.

history, is well worth a visit. It lies in the flat-bottomed, steep-sided valley of the River Lea between Hertford and Ware. Southbound cyclists can obtain an excellent overview of the whole area from the A10 Ware by-pass, as it sweeps across the valley on a high viaduct, but it has no stopping place of any kind for cars. In any event, the spring can only be visited on foot. This is most easily done by parking at Chadwell Spring Golf Club on the A119 between Hertford and Ware, just east of the A10 viaduct. Chadwell Spring is on the valley floor immediately adjacent, and can be reached by a footpath that begins directly across the road from the golf club car park.

Chadwell Spring flows up into a stone-rimmed circular pond, and from it the channel of the New River begins. The combination of round pond and straight channel caused it to be known locally as the banjo. On its banks, a stone records that it was opened in 1608 and 'repaird' in 1728. This was at a time when Henry Mill was the Company's Surveyor. The stone also lists the extent of the Company's surrounding land, and inscribed marker stones around the boundaries confirm this. Where the water leaves the pond there is a stone threshold, designed to prevent backflow in times of drought, and this allows the rate of flow to be judged. Standing at this point and watching the clear spring water streaming over the threshold slab, it is tempting to cup a hand into the stream and taste the water that Colthurst and Myddelton knew.

From the Spring, the channel heads south-east, but is soon joined on its left by a tributary channel coming from the River Lea. Three structures can be seen if this channel is followed upstream, all connected with the need to control the amount of water taken from the Lea. The first is a large stone box surrounded by iron railings. It bears no inscription, but was known as the marble gauge and was built in 1770 to replace the 1740 structure built under Mill's occasional supervision as described in chapter 13, and which no longer exists. The marble gauge is now bypassed by the stream, but formerly admitted water through a fixed gauge to control the quantity. Next is a white wooden building dating from 1746 that con-

78 View of the New River north from Aden Terrace. Watercolour by E. Carswell, c.1900

79 This arch, which still exists, carries the New River over Salmon's Brook, a tributary of the River Lea, at Bush Hill, Enfield. What looks like a close-boarded fence on top is the side of a wooden trough containing the New River. It was originally built in 1613, was 660 feet long and had joints caulked by shipwrights. For most of its length it was supported on a wooden frame. Much water escaped through leaks, and it was then lined with sheets of lead. In 1786 the embankment was built up and raised and the water then ran in a channel cut into the top, as it does today.

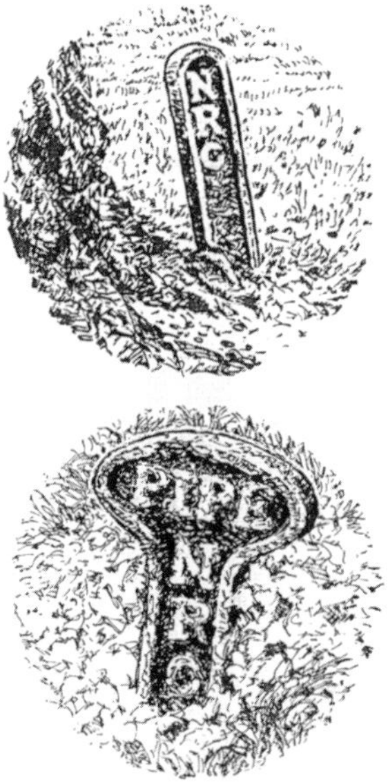

80 New River Company boundary and tunnel markers, still in Avenue Gardens opposite Alexandra Park railway station. Drawings by Peter Garland.

81 Notice board to discourage fishing and the throwing of stones. To the left is a monument by the side of Chadwell Spring.

82 A restored loop of the New River close to Enfield church. Having been bypassed with iron pipes in 1938 it was already being filled up when it was pressed back into service after German bombs destroyed the new pipes in 1940. It remained in active service until 1952, and is now kept in water for its amenity value.

83 Restored section of New River, in Enfield Town Park

84 New River, Enfield. The cast iron footbridge is dated 1841

85 Monument by the New River at Great Amwell, dedicated in 1800 by 'Robert Mylne, Architect, Engineer & ca', whose 'humble tribute' to Myddelton shows his own name in rather larger letters than Myddelton's.

86 The Mylne family mausoleum in Great Amwell churchyard. Robert Mylne built it, and his wife is buried there, but he preferred St Paul's Cathedral for himself.

tained a sluice to divert muddy water from the Lea away from the New River in times of flood. Finally, as the stream reaches the River Lea is a substantial brick-built Gauge House of 1856. The water can be seen flowing into and through it. As described in 1899, there was a floating boom inside, attached to a bronze plate that could rise or fall across the channel. This worked so that a constant amount of water was admitted from the Lea into the New River, whether the Lea is high or low. Other plates could be added to regulate this more precisely, or to shut off the flow completely to keep turbid water out of the New River or for maintenance.[2]

From this point the riverbank can be followed upstream for about 1½ miles to Hertford, and Hertford East station makes an alternative starting point for the walk. Another very pleasant walk is from Chadwell Spring to and beyond Great Amwell, the section Edmund Colthurst began in 1604. It is easy to see here the way the New River was cut into the slope of the valley side, and why the Walksman kept the right bank for himself while leaving the more troublesome left to his labourer. The spring at Amwell dried up in the 1830s, but there is an attractive pool there with a monument on an easily accessible little island. Robert Mylne bought himself a small estate and built a house at Amwell, *The Grove*, which still stands but has been altered. Here on the island he erected a monument to praise Sir Hugh Myddelton's achievements. Above the pool is Great Amwell church, to which Hugh Myddelton presented a copy of the new King James bible, although it has not survived. In the churchyard is the classical mausoleum Robert Mylne built for his family, though when his own death came his wish to be buried in St Paul's Cathedral was granted, so his wife and some of his children rest here without him.

Appendix One

The best shares in the World

The best shares in the world

In 1888 Edwin Fox and Bousfield, City of London auctioneers, were about to sell a half of one share in the New River, and wrote in the sales particulars that the New River Company 'may safely be pronounced the most remunerative and successful of all the trading corporations of the world', and it follows that the shares must equally have been the best. They do not explain how the calculation was done, but the fact that such a statement could go unchallenged is itself revealing. This appendix will look at the classes of shares, the benefits they conferred by way of dividends and otherwise, and the way shares came to be sold.

Three kinds of share

When the New River Company was first incorporated in 1619, half of its ownership, costs and profits were split among thirty-six Adventurers' shares, as described in Chapter 4. The other half was reserved for the King under an agreement made in 1612, and was known as the King's moiety. In 1631 the King, by then Charles I, sold his moiety back to Myddelton in person. Myddelton then decided that half should also be divided into thirty-six shares, thereafter known as King's shares. The seventy-two resulting Adventurers' and King's shares were thereafter the only shares in the Company until 1866, when some New shares were issued to raise capital.

Adventurers' shares

Hugh Myddelton persuaded others to share with him in the costs of building the New River. He originally intended that there should be thirty-six equal shares, but they were shares in his personal venture – there was no formal company or corporation until 1619, years after the money had been invested and spent. We know a little about the nature of these shares from documents that survive, such as the deed that sets out the agreement between Myddelton and Sir Henry Neville already discussed in Chapter Five.

The main benefits of each Adventurer's share were that it gave a share of the profits and also made the holder eligible to sit on the Board and stand for office.

King's shares

The thirty-six King's shares differed in two important respects from Adventurers' shares. First, they gave the holder no right to stand for a seat on the board – potentially a lucrative activity – and no right to take any other part in the management of the company. Second, the so-called Crown Clog, the annual payment of £500 to the Crown or its nominee, was divided among the holders of King's shares. That meant that each King's share would receive an annual dividend that was about £14 less than the amount paid on an Adventurer's share. In the 1630s when dividends only averaged about £18 this was a major reduction. By the 1690s when dividends had reached £200, it was much less so, and the distinction was eventually meaningless in terms of the dividend yield. Nevertheless, Adventurers' shares seem to have commanded a premium of as much as 10% right up to the 1900s, perhaps because of the perceived status of a seat on the New River Board.

New shares

Finally in 1866 the company obtained an Act of Parliament that allowed it to raise half a million pounds for its needs by issuing 5000 shares of £100 each. These were to be offered first to existing shareholders and then to the public. Perhaps to avoid the expense incurred in transferring the King's and Adventurers' shares they were stated to be 'personalty', in other words ordinary personal property rather than real property. They did not carry any voting rights.[1]

The Act recognised that the pre-existing shares were deemed to have a total value of £1,519, 958, which divided by 72 gives about £21,110 per share The new shares, with a nominal value of £100 would receive a proportionate share of all dividends.

In 1883, some New shares, which had paid a dividend of £11 17s. 4d. the previous year, sold at auction for £380 each.

The nature of the shares

It may seem strange that a single share in a waterworks company should have come to be regarded as equivalent to freehold land. It may be that neither Myddelton nor any of the Adventurers intended this result. The wording of the deed that records an Adventurer's interest in the business suggests that he was simply acquiring a share in the business. The whole question of why the shares came to be regarded as real property has been elegantly analysed by Professor Rudden in his book on the legal history of the New River.[2]

His view was that 'put at its simplest', a share was treated 'as if it were the interest of a tenant in common in fee simple absolute in possession of a corporeal hereditament'. This string of complex legal concepts means, roughly, what most people would call jointly-owned freehold land. For present purposes, it may suffice just to note that they were so regarded, and this was recognised by the Act of Parliament whereby the company was taken over by the Metropolitan Water Board in 1904.

Shareholders' perks

Ownership of any of the original shares, or even a fractional part of one of them was regard as equivalent to freehold property, and this was assumed to be the position from the earliest dealings. It meant that any shareholder was regarded as owning land in the counties through which the New River flowed. The law governing elections provided that ownership of land above a certain annual value in a county carried with it the right to vote, even if the owner was not resident in the county. Male shareholders therefore gained the right to be registered as voters in Hertfordshire and Middlesex, and this was a more valuable right at a time when it was only males with substantial property interests who had any right to vote in Parliamentary elections.

The second useful perquisite only applied to a holder of at least one full Adventurer's share. This was the right to stand for election to the board of the company, limited by the 1619 charter to twenty-nine members. Some of the elected members could hold office and thereby gain large salaries; others received payment for their attendance at meetings. It did not apply to holders of King's shares, because the charter had specifically excluded the King from any part in the running of the company.

Edwin Fox & Bousfield, who occasionally sold New River shares in Victorian times, knew how to make this distinction in terms that showed whichever kind of share they were selling in its best light. In 1890 when a King's share came up for sale they wrote that the only way in which it differed from an Adventurer's share was that its holder would be 'relieved of all trouble, labour, anxiety and responsibility of management. The holders enjoy their happy and untrammelled privilege – occupying the proud position King James secured for himself, of profiting by the labours of others.'

Just ten years later the same firm had an Adventurer's share for sale, formerly owned by the Governor of the Company, and the half-empty glass suddenly became half-full: 'The possession of an Adventurer's share qualifies the holder – or his nominee – for a seat at the Board; the acquisition of the Share now offered for sale will enable the purchaser to aspire to the honour and emolument of the distinguished position vacated by the vendor'[3]

Transferring shares

Because of the nature of the shares, they could only be transferred from one person to another as though they were transfers of land. Because of this anyone claiming to be the new owner of a share had to satisfy the company of his good title to it, as has to be done with unregistered freehold land. This could be an expensive process and made share transfer inconvenient. Frequently shares were mortgaged in whole or in part just like any other real property.

An early description of the shares comes in a letter the Earl of Clarendon wrote in 1685, to his brother Lord Rochester who had proposed that he should sell six shares in the King's moiety. Clarendon's shares evidently represented a major part of his wealth, and he was trying to arrange a marriage settlement for his son Lord Cornbury. His wife did not want them to be sold, he explained 'and in truth I cannot blame her, for it is visible that revenue does daily more increase than land can do; and by some new rules which we have lately made, a very considerable improvement will appear within a year.' Rochester evidently knew of someone who had offered £21,000 for the six shares, and Clarendon conceded that he would part with them at that price, but only on condition that they could be bought back at the same price three years later if he chose, the purchaser to receive all the income from the shares in the meantime. He also mentioned that he owned eight Adventurers' shares, and said they were worth 'much more' than those in the King's moiety.

Complications arose when shares became divided, usually under the terms of a series of wills, or sometimes at auction. An auction in 1883 divided a half King's share into 50 separate lots and one sixteenth of a King's share into ten separate lots. Two further lots were a one-hundred-and-ninety-second part of a King's share and two one-hundred and twentieth parts of a King's share. One fractional Adventurer's share had reduced to 841/3360 by the time the Metropolitan Water Board took over in 1904, while there were fractional King's shares of 1183/1920 and 17/2400.[4]

Most owners of shares had managed to keep them intact. In 1810, thirty Adventurers' and twenty-seven King's were still undivided, making 80% of the total shareholding of the company.

Dividends

Dividends were paid twice yearly. Their growth can be seen from the following table, which shows the average annual earnings of one share, fifty years apart.

1630s	£13
1680s	£193
1730s	£206
1780s	£370
1830s	£630
1880s	£2526
1903	£2704

This rate of growth can usefully be compared with a labourer's wage. In 1630 this was about 5s. 0d. a week, or £13 a year. By 1903, it was about four times that amount, or £52 a year. So over a period when wages rose about four times, the earning on one New River share rose about two hundred times.

The value of the shares

Shares were sold publicly as well as privately. In 1766 a King's share was 'sold at the Senegal coffee house, St Michael's Alley', and fetched £4,400. Other King's shares sold for £500 in 1657, £7,000 in 1770, £8,740 in 1821, £81,000 in 1888 and £115,000 in 1898.

Adventurers' shares were sold for £3,900 in 1707, £5,000 in 1732, £15,200 in 1827, £95,000 in 1883, £122,800 in 1889 and £125,500 in 1897.[5]

Share auctions

One auction of New River shares took place at Tokenhouse Yard next to the Bank of England on 19 March 1879, and the hyperbole of the auctioneer's catalogue is remarkable. Forty-six lots were to be sold, but none was a complete share. In total, they amounted to about one fifth of a King's share and one twenty-fourth of an Adventurer's share. Twelve of the lots were for a one-hundred-and-ninetieth part of a King's share, each then yielding £11 11s. 7d. a year, while others were for one ninety-fifth or one ninety-sixth. The catalogue devotes twelve pages to 'Introductory Remarks' praising the New River Company. It begins with a history of London's water supply and that of the New River in particular before turning to financial matters. It claims – quite wrongly – that the dividends of the company have never fallen 'each year showing a large advance on its predecessor'. This may have been true for many years prior to the auction, but was certainly not the case between 1695 and 1710, or between 1810 and 1820, when dividends fell sharply.

The catalogue explains how the New River Company had the exclusive right of supplying water to the entire City of London together with a large part of the City of Westminster, including 'some of the wealthy districts of the West End, the populous localities north, north-west and north-east of London, and the increasingly important residential districts in Middlesex and Hertfordshire.' Into this district, it boldly claims, 'no competition can by any possibility intrude; and the danger of opposition, which always threatens the main trunk lines of railways, has ruined branch lines, and annihilated canals and other useful works, can never arise.'

Having thus dismissed the comparative worth of railway shares, the catalogue then belittles shares in another nineteenth-century boom industry, the gasworks, by pointing out that users of gas only pay for the quantity consumed, whereas a fixed charge can be made for water irrespective of usage. Thus the poor must pay their water rates and that system was unlikely to change – 'It is imperative for the health of towns that water should not be an object of economy in poor districts, as would be the case if the amount of the consumption were governed by the payment.' Even better it continues – far-sightedly for 1879 – 'While gas may be superseded by electricity or other modes of illumination, the demand for water cannot be affected by any change in the habits of man, or by any advance in scientific discovery.... a shareholder in a water company can contemplate his position with calm satisfaction.'

The catalogue then turns to the company's other great asset – land. 'These Estates include not only the Watercourse of the River itself, with frontages, extensive reservoirs, wharfs &c ... but more than seventy acres in the heart of the Metropolis ... for the most part covered with buildings, and now producing annual ground-rents to a considerable amount. On the expiration of the leases in about 26 years, the Rack Rents come into the possession of the Company.'

The purity of the product is then extolled ('the superiority of the water ... purer than any other of the Metropolitan water companies') before the catalogue reaches new heights of ecstasy at what the future may hold:

'Wonderful as has been the advance of the New River, large as is its present revenue .. it may unhesitatingly be asserted that its brightest days are yet to come. The transition which the City of London has undergone of late years – crowds of small houses giving place to palatial buildings – is but the prelude to similar changes in Westminster and the West End, and the yearly increase in the rating value of property in these districts is no small consideration .... For years past the chief extension of London has been on the South side: now, however, that the North enjoys equal facilities of railway transit, it is rapidly advancing in public esteem, and building operations are proceeding with vigour. As the heights of Highgate, the undulating pastures of Hampstead, the rural vales of Hornsey, and the picturesque districts of Edmonton, Enfield, Cheshunt, and other points are rendered easily accessible by the Great Northern, Great Eastern, and Midland Railways, they are rapidly becoming centres of population and consequent sources of income to the New River Proprietors.'

Nor were the benefits only financial, the catalogue continued. Even a fractional holder of a share – provided it was worth more than £2 a year - would be entitled to vote in Parliamentary elections in all constituencies where the company held land, 'and also renders the holder eligible for the Magistracy and other appointments requiring a landed qualification.'

In 1889 there was an auction of a single Adventurer's share, and a newspaper report gives the flavour of the proceedings. After a short introduction, bidding started at £80,000, reached £95,000 – many millions at today's prices - and then paused. The auctioneer spoke again. 'Gentlemen, I do not want to suggest such a thing for a single moment, but I think you are making a mistake in your calculations ... you must not ignore the future profits – the income doubling, the estates falling in, the monopoly of the supply. Think how fast the green fields are being covered with houses, and you will have the monopoly of the supply. Then there are the estates in Hertfordshire, in Middlesex, and in Clerkenwell – 50 acres – within a mile of where we are, that land worth £2 a foot. Think, gentlemen, only think of these things. (A Voice: £96,000. Then other voices: £97,000, £98,000 (in two places), £99,000, £100,000.) Thank you gentlemen; I am waiting. We do not sell you a seat at the board but you will get it. You have only to knock at the door and say 'Please show me my chair', and instantly it will be shown you, because you will be regarded as a man of superlative wisdom by having bought this share, (laughter.)' The bidding started again, and the share was eventually knocked down for £122,800, to the Secretary of the Prudential Assurance Company.

In 1890 another share was sold, and the auctioneers did not shrink from mentioning the possibility of a public takeover and the compensation shareholders would be paid if that happened. In such a case, 'not only must the present bounding income be paid for, but also the prospective increase therein, and the company must still be left in possession of its landed and other properties, sufficient to entitle it then to rank among the large corporate holders of Real Estate in the Kingdom'[6]

As it turned out, the wisest shareholders were those who sold their shares before the Metropolitan Water Board takeover in 1904. Adventurers' shares had raised £125,000, and King's shares about £115,000 in the last few years of the Company's existence, and the compensation claimed by the Company in 1904 would have been worth about £150,000 per share if granted. Sadly for shareholders, the compensation issue was argued and appealed as far as the House of Lords, where the Company lost. As a result, its claim for over £13 million was reduced to about £6 million. When divided among Adventurers', King's and New shareholders this meant that the holder of one of the old shares received compensation worth about £69,000.

Appendix Two

Swallowing Minnows

During its existence, the New River Company took over several rival companies and forced others out of business.

Fogwell Spring

The first to succumb to the New River was Mr John Darge who ran a small waterworks in the City of London supplied from Fogwell Spring. It was said that he made an annual profit of £60, but when New River water was piped into the City he chose to sell his works to Myddelton. The accounts show that on 2 July 1614 he was paid £25 11s. 0d., in return for which he agreed to surrender all his tenants to Myddelton and 'shall serve noe more water from Fogwell springe.' Myddelton also purchased his lead pipes, 490 yards in length, for which he was paid £74. Whether he owned any wooden mains is not recorded.

Sir Edward Ford's Waterworks

There was a waterworks in the grounds of Somerset House during the 1660s. Sir Edward Ford erected these under a patent granted to him by Oliver Cromwell the Lord Protector in 1655. It was located near what is now the bottom of Surrey Street, and raised river water by animal power into a tapering wooden tower to obtain a sufficient head of water to supply the locality. Unfortunately, it overlooked the gardens of Somerset House and thereby irritated Charles II's mother Queen Henrietta Maria, who lived there. The King ordered Ford to remove it, and this was done despite Ford's petition that hundreds of tenants had laid in the water to their houses. The upshot was that Ford was licensed to put up new waterworks at 'Wapping, Marybone and one between Temple Bar and Charing Cross'. He built the first of these at Wapping Wall, and the third, at Durham Yard, near the present Adelphi. The site of his Marylebone works is unknown, but when he sold it the indenture of sale places it at 'the slip neere the highway from Tyburn to S Gyles in the fields', i.e. somewhere off Oxford Street. On 13 August 1667 it was said there were six horses at work at 'Durram yard', four horses with two pumps and capstans at 'Marybone' and three horses at Wapping.[1] Ford's works then passed to Sir Robert Vyner and others, and were sold to the New River Company in December 1667 for £6,100.

In July 1950 a document turned up that reveals something about the negotiations before that sale. Its existence was revealed in a letter to the Metropolitan Water Board from C.C. Chamberlain, a Chelmsford book dealer, who was happy to accept the £1 10s. 0d. they offered for it. It is undated, but includes a reference to 'when London is rebuilt' putting it somewhere in the fifteen months between the Great Fire of September 1666 and the completion of the sale in December 1667.

It is headed 'Instructions for proposalls in our treaty with the New River', and begins 'Demand 20 yrs purchase – £14,000.' It then details the arguments to justify the price. First, the New River Company would gain a monopoly in the western parts of town. Second, they would gain 3000 yards of pipes. Thirdly, 'that when London is rebuilt it may be very consistent with their interest to invade all that part of the Towne which was served by the Thames water, between the (London) bridge and Bridewell dock, to which end nothing can be more expedient than to have greate quantityes of pipes ready, and the 3000 yds of pipes which may be here spared if the bargaine proposed doe proceed being sufficient for all their purposes for Pipe at this end of the Towne, theire Stores of new pipe will thereby be preserved to be ready for the speedy execucon of that Designe when the Tyme shall come, and this being a matter of surprise, and requiring such speed ...'

Thirdly, '...Our revenue notwithstanding all the craft and opposition of the new-river doth every day increase ... But admitting that in tyme, in Spight of all the foresaid Argum'ts they might destroy us, yet considering what persons are ingaged in our works, and what meanes to supply our Tenants plentifully with Thames water, as alsoe to abridge the charges, .. they cannot hope to determine us in a few yeares. Now the benefit of the Encrease of their Revenue by this bargaine in fewer yeares than is imaginable can destroy us, being added to the sum which they must necessarily expend in laying of Pipes throughout our quarters will make up a greater Sume than wee demanded.'[2]

The reference to £14,000 as 'twenty years purchase' suggests that Ford's works had an annual profit of £700, and by inference served perhaps 1400 houses. The actual sale price of £6,100 shows that the New River Company thought the deal worthwhile, whether for the value of the works or for disposing of a competitor. The New River Company would have needed no prompting to realise the opportunities for expansion into London Bridge territory after the Great Fire destroyed the London Bridge Waterworks, and there was to be a later complaint to the Privy Council that they had done so. This they piously denied.

London Bridge Waterworks

The waterworks at London Bridge had existed from 1582. The New River was its principal rival, always ready to supply disgruntled customers. The London Bridge manager Samuel Hearn described the problems that afflicted his works in 1745:

'Although the Service from these works in General is very large and constant, yet there are times and seasons of great grievance, as Low Neep Tides, Dry Seasons and in times when Repairs are necessary. Though these things are absolutely unavoidable and happen but seldom, yet the greater part of mankind do not or will not consider it, but Murmer and Complain and refuse to pay their Rent, and many will change to the water of the New River at those seasons; this is not only decreasing the Company's Interest but the Credit of their Water also.'[3]

Documents show that in 1738 there was an agreement between 'the gentleman managers' of London Bridge and the Governor of the New River to regulate the conduct of their 'respective Collectors and other inferior officers.' What they agreed not to do illuminates what must previously have happened on occasion. They would not change the pipes of vacant houses from their competitor's supply to their own without instructions from the owners. They would not take on new tenants who owed arrears to their rival. Above all 'No false pretences or clandestine means to be used to gain or Perswade any to become Tenants for the Water, by underletting or otherwise.' Underletting was perhaps some form of price cutting. This agreement was ratified again more than forty years later, in 1784.[4] Despite the agreement, the New River Company had to lodge a complaint in 1746 – the London Bridge paviours had been switching New River tenants over to London Bridge water again.[5]

This kind of arrangement was not unique. In 1667, there was a proposed agreement with Sir William Smith, who conveyed water from Marylebone to the district around Covent Garden. This stipulated that neither party would serve any ten-roomed house for less that £1 1s. 0d. a year, 'nor sell water by their standcocks cheaper than two firkins, containing 14 gallons, for a Peny.'

By about 1815, the London Bridge works was failing. A new Paving Act meant that its wooden mains would eventually have to be replaced by iron, and the revenue barely justified the expense. The quality of the Thames water had also deteriorated with the increase of industrial pollution and the vast numbers of water closets whose contents were now flushed and found their way through sewers into the Thames.

After the New River had fought off competition from the new water companies by the agreement of 1817, it became increasingly predatory towards its old rival. By 1818 there were for the first time New River pipes in every street of the City, and they were iron pipes able to take the pressure needed for supplying a 'high service' to upper floors. Finally came news that London Bridge itself was to be demolished and replaced. An agreement was eventually brokered by the City, by which the New River Company took over its rival. This was provided for in the 'Act for removing the waterworks at London Bridge' of 1822.

At that time 260 years of Peter Morice's original 500-year lease from the City still remained. The agreement was that the New River Company would pay £3,750 a year (calculated at the rate of £2 10s. 0d. for each of the 1500 London Bridge Waterworks shares) until the expiry in 2082. In addition, the Corporation of London paid £10,000 compensation to the London Bridge Waterworks. The Corporation also provided the New River Company with a riverside site close by, so that water could be pumped from the Thames if necessary. This was at Broken Wharf, on the north bank to the west of London Bridge.

Broken Wharf, also known as Poore's wharf, already had a history as a source of water supply. In about 1595, one Bevis Bulmer of Sutton had erected a waterworks there. This was taken over by the London Bridge Waterworks by 1733, and the site was then transferred to the New River Company. Here the Company erected a steam engine (supplied by Boulton & Watt in 1824) and pumps linked to their Cheapside main for emergency use. Because of the bad quality of Thames water by that time, the engine was hardly ever used. The last occasion is said to have been in 1850, when the New River froze in a severe winter.

Changes to the law then provided that unfiltered river water could not be supplied for domestic use after 1856 and, in anticipation of this, the Broken Wharf engine was moved to a pumping station at Tottenham in 1851. The site at Broken Wharf, being part of the New River water undertaking rather than their landed estate, passed to the Metropolitan Water Board in 1904. It was valuable, as the lease ran until 2093. There were some restrictions on its sale, the Corporation of London having a first refusal and any purchaser having to be a free citizen of London, but these were overcome by substituting a fresh lease after negotiations with the Corporation. The site was then sold by auction in 1927, and realized £3,000.

York Buildings Waterworks

The York Buildings Company had its origins in 1675, when Bucknall and Wayne obtained a patent to erect a waterworks near the Thames in the gardens of York House and to supply houses in Piccadilly and St James's Fields. Horse-power raised the water to the top of a tower, from where it was piped. This supply lasted until 1684, when the works burnt down. To replace it, a new company was formed by Act of Parliament in 1691, known as 'The Governor and Company of Undertakers for raising the Thames Water in York Buildings.' Bucknall was one of the proprietors, and it supplied water to about 2,700 premises in Piccadilly, Whitehall and Covent Garden, probably using horse power to work the pumps. Later the works used one of Thomas Savery's atmospheric engines, installed in about 1713 and evidently found to be more trouble than it was worth. As described in Chapter 15, the York Buildings Company was taken over in 1809 and its network upgraded. Despite this, it could not meet the intense competition from the New River and Chelsea companies, and the New River Company bought its works and new iron mains in 1816, by an agreement that was not finalised until 1818. The price was an annual payment of £250 18s. 6d. This left the York Buildings Company, which had other trading interests, in existence; but it agreed never to supply water to the public again.

The site of the works is now covered by Charing Cross railway station, and is not the turning off John Adam Street called York Buildings.

Hampstead Waterworks Company

In 1544, the Corporation of London obtained an Act entitling them to draw water from springs in the parishes of St Pancras, Hampstead and Hornsey.

These powers were exercised in 1590, and by chance John Gerard the herbalist was present when the first work was done, and made a note of a previously-unknown plant he had seen there, Broad-leaved hedge hyssop (*Gratiola latifolia*).

' I found it growing upon the bog or marsh ground at the further end of Hampstead Heath; and upon the same heath towards London neere unto the head of the springs that were digged for water to be conveied to London, 1590, attempted by that careful citizen John Hart, Knight, Lord Mayor of the city of London, at which time myself was in his lordship's company; and viewing for pleasure the same goodly springs, I found the said plant, not heretofore remembered.'[6]

In 1692 the City leased the right to use these springs

to a group including William Patterson, better known as the founder of the Bank of England, on a lease for 31 years, and this was thereafter renewed at intervals. The proprietors were known as the Society of Hampstead Aqueducts, but their venture ran into financial difficulties. The springs that could be tapped under the City's Act were insufficient for a constant supply, so they took a lease on ponds at Kenwood belonging to the Earl of Bute. In 1735 the proprietors appeared before the City Lands Committee saying they were 'great loosers' in running the waterworks, and were allowed to renew their lease although there were rent arrears. By 1758 they owed £340 to the City but petitioned to have their lease renewed again. Caleb Jeacocke and other proprietors said that their debt had not increased for twenty years past, for although they were unable to pay the arrears they had managed each year to pay the current rent 'though with great difficulty'. They asked to be allowed to renew their lease despite the arrears, so that they could continue with 'an Undertaking so useful and Beneficial to the Publick in General and the City of London in particular.'

The committee questioned two of the proprietors, and ascertained that the venture was not profitable. Laying pipes had been very costly and they had also had to rent springs and reservoirs on private land 'in Aid of those belonging to the City which in dry seasons were sometimes almost destitute of Water.' They were in arrears of rent to their private landlords as well, but one of them, Lord Mansfield who now owned Kenwood, had remitted the debt and the other, Sir John Cross, was not pressing for payment 'being well satisfied that it was not in their Power to discharge the same.' Despite the expense, they had never received a shilling benefit. They asked to be allowed to continue and for the arrears to be remitted so that they could 'proceed in their Undertaking with Cheerfullness and in Hopes of reaping some tolerable Advantage therefrom in times to come', failing which they were likely to abandon the scheme.

The committee concluded that these claims were true, and that if renewal was refused it was very doubtful anyone else would take up the lease. People would know how many attempts had been made in years past by 'persons of Substance and Capacity fit for such an Undertaking' with little or no benefit. The City would then lose even the current £80 a year, which went to the benefit of the orphans of the City.

Worst of all, they pointed out, 'that Powerfull body the New River Company' would take over those parts of town formerly supplied from Hampstead, and 'would be at Liberty to extract of the Inhabitants what Rates they should think proper when there was no other to oppose them.' Having heard this, the City agreed to write off the arrears, and the lease was renewed for another 31 years from Michaelmas 1757 at £80 a year.[7]

In 1763 the company suffered a fire that destroyed their early records. As time went on the difficulties continued even though the company was able to supply some of the new residential districts. In June 1815, they agreed to relinquish some of their tenants in Frances Street, Upper Thornhaugh Street and Tottenham Court Road to the New River Company.

Then, in March 1816 Thomas Collings chairman of Hampstead Waterworks wrote to the New River Company. In consequence of unusual dry weather for several months past, they would not have sufficient water to serve their tenants during the ensuing summer. He asked the New River Company to assist in supplying certain parts of their service, on the basis that the Hampstead company would pay over the rent received from those houses, only deducting the collectors' poundage. He continued 'these were the same terms on which the New River Company was so kind as to assist the Hampstead Water Company in the year 1803'. The New River Company agreed to this, and it was effected by Mylne arranging a 4" branch from Hampstead Road to join up with their wooden mains.[8]

In October 1817 an agreement was reached with the New River Company as to a mutual boundary line. The Hampstead works agreed to give up their tenants 'on the south side of Fig Lane leading to St Pancras poor-house', while the New River undertook not to extend their service to any houses in Camden Town or Kentish Town or along Hampstead Road to the north of Fig Lane. Years later, in the summer of 1839 William Chadwell Mylne had a meeting with Mr Hakewill of the Hampstead Company to amend this, as many new houses were now being built on the old farmland of the Camden estate and a new boundary was agreed.[9]

The company made one last effort in the 1850s, sinking a well near Camden Town. The deeper it went without finding water, the more despondent the directors must have become. Eventually in 1854, they appealed to the New River Company for some water from their mains. William Chadwell Mylne reported to his Board:

'The Hampstead Company's well is now 1,120 feet deep and no water. The water from the ponds has been so filthy of late that it was unfit to be delivered to their tenants yet it has all been disposed of for the general supply of Camden Town.'

He went on to predict that they might soon be asked to take on the whole district. The Board resolved they would 'supply to the Hampstead Company for the present.' The following April the New River Company was still supplying water to the Hampstead works, and the engines at New River Head were put to work all night, because their new engines at Stoke Newington were having to work 'for the supply of Hampstead, Highgate and the New Cattle Market the whole 24 hours.'[10]

The 1852 Act had made it impossible for the Hampstead works to survive unless new supplies were found, and in this they failed. The Act required all water for domestic purposes to be filtered before use, and all reservoirs of filtered water within five miles of St Paul's to be covered. The company knew how short its supplies were in dry weather and could not contemplate the necessary expense. It was eventually taken over by the New River Company in 1856, though the formalities dragged on until 1861.

By taking over the Hampstead Company, the New River Company gained not only some customers, but also the reservoirs. These were in a series of linked ponds on Hampstead Heath and at Highgate. Even if the water was seasonal and not suitable for domestic supply, it could be used for other purposes. There was also a storage reservoir at Camden Park Road.

William Chadwell Mylne looked into the cost of covering the Camden reservoir with canvas, to make it legal for storing domestic water, but the cost of £560 was uneconomical. It was then agreed that the Hampstead tenants should be supplied by steam pumping all the way from New River Head.[11]

The New River Company therefore began to supply the unfiltered water from the Hampstead and Highgate ponds to the two railway companies that had just brought their termini to North London – the London North Eastern at King's Cross in 1852, soon followed by the London, Midland & Scottish at St Pancras. The railways were happy with cheap unfiltered water for the boilers of their locomotives. It also provided a supply to the Metropolitan Cattle Market, in Copenhagen Fields to the north of King's Cross. This had just opened, in 1855.

The Hampstead waterworks remained an identifiable entity within the New River Company, even when that company was taken over by the Metropolitan Water Board in 1904. The lease of the Hampstead and Highgate Ponds from the Corporation still had to be renewed from time to time, and the Metropolitan Water Board renewed it for the last time in 1927, at the usual rent of £80 a year. At Midsummer 1936 it was due for renewal again, and in March of that year the Board's district engineer at New River Head advised against renewal. In the past it had been profitable, he noted, but seven drought years from 1929 to 1935 had resulted in a loss. Moreover, the two railway companies, who had been the largest customers for unfiltered water had given notice that they no longer wished to use it. The only remaining customers would be St Pancras Borough Council, for its gardens and lavatories, and the cattle market. Further, the lease of the open reservoir at Camden Park Road would expire in 1939. The New River Company had been able to take a long lease from the Marquess of Camden for £10 a year in 1848 but it seemed unlikely to be renewed on those terms in 1939. Finally, the cast iron mains dated back to 1829 and were nearing the end of their life.

The engineer advised that although it might seem 'a pity to abandon a supply that has been in existence for such a long time' he saw no useful purpose or financial advantage in doing otherwise. The lease from the Corporation of London should not be renewed. Existing customers could be supplied from the Board's filtered water system.

By an odd chance, the engineer's letter, which passed an effective death sentence on the Hampstead Water Company, was typed on paper edged with a thick black border, the Metropolitan Water Board's mark of respect for the recently dead King George V.

North Middlesex Waterworks

From about 1851 there was a well, 142 feet deep into the chalk, with a pumping station at Betstile, Colney Hatch, near the present New Southgate Railway Station. In 1867 its then owner William Bull formed it into the North Middlesex Water Works Company Limited, though it was also known as the Colney Hatch Water Works. It was used to supply local houses but was never a financial success. In 1871, by which time it only had 250 customers, it was sold to the New River Company for £4,500. The well became disused, but the engine was used for some years to pump water to Southgate Reservoir.[12]

Bush Hill Park Company

A substantial mansion known as Bush Hill Park used to stand by the New River on the southern edge of Enfield parish. In 1872 some 373 acres of its parkland were sold to the Bush Hill Park Estates Company for house building, and they sank a well and made a small reservoir to supply the new estate. The well proved inadequate, probably because both a neighbouring asylum and the Barnet District Gas and Water Company were extracting water close by. Then, in 1887, the New River Company took over the whole supply at a price of £2,500. The site of the well passed to the Metropolitan Water Board in 1904 and was sold by them in 1925.

Holloway Waterworks Company

The story of the Holloway Waterworks shows how the New River Company could crush a small rival. Soon after 1800, George Pocock was a builder of new houses in the then rural district of Holloway. The New River Company was not inclined to lay pipes there at that time, though householders could obtain supplies at a halfpenny a bucket from water carriers. Pocock expended almost £2,000 to dig a well 172 feet deep at Cornwall Place, now Eden Grove just south of Holloway Road underground station. The well was a success and he then obtained a steam engine and the necessary plant to supply the neighbourhood. To raise sufficient capital he obtained a private Act of Parliament, the Holloway Waterworks Act of 1810, to supply water to 'Upper and Lower Holloway, Highbury, Canonbury, Upper Islington and their respective vicinities.' The Act did not contain any prohibition from interfering with the New River Company's activities.

Until that time the New River Company had always declined to lay pipes in the area, despite many requests from the new residents. As a cheaper alternative the company had installed a pump connected to the New River at the bottom of Hopping Lane. Proprietors of water carts were allowed to fill their barrels from this – for an annual charge - and then peddled the water from house to house by the bucketful. As soon as it was clear that Pocock's Act was likely to be passed, the New River Company began an energetic programme of pipe-laying throughout Pocock's district.

In May 1815 the collector reported to the New River board that the Holloway Company was unable to continue with its works, and that most of the tenants had changed over to New River water.

The Holloway Company then went into liquidation. Its liquidators in due course wrote to the New River Company asking whether it would be good enough to buy the wooden mains and lead supply pipes, all still in the ground. No, they were told. The wooden mains were of no value to the New River Company as it was changing its system to iron. As to the lead ones, which had long since been reconnected to the New River mains, they assumed them to be the property of the householders and not of the Holloway Company.[13]

Appendix Three

Extract from *The Gentleman's Magazine*, 1753 pp. 114-6. (Although not published until 30 years after Wren's death in 1723, this paper seems to have been written in 1702: see Chapter 11, p. 122.)

Thoughts of Sir CHRISTOPHER WREN concerning the distribution of the New River Water; not published in his Works or elsewhere.

BEING desired by some persons of honour concerned in the New River water, to give them my thoughts about the most profitable distribution of the water; and particularly how the high parts about *Soho square* might be supplied; I have, as well as my age and the continual avocations of publick business would permit, applied myself to make the best inquiries I could, about the present state of the water: but the more I looked into this affair, the more I found myself unequal to give a pertinent opinion how it might be meliorated to the best advantage of the company. For the mistakes are fundamental in laying down the contrivances, and every day since new errors have been added, which are now inveterate; tho' I hope a right method for the future may cure many of them with time. But as a physician being called for to amend the distempers in a morbid body, must know what is naturally the anatomy and constitution of a sound body, I shall crave leave, as a naturalist, and somewhat versed in geometry, to begin from the first projection of this work, and consider as if there were not yet one pipe laid, what methods should have been taken from the beginning for the best and most equal distribution of the water brought to *Islington*; and when the right way is known it is easy to judge and amend what is wrong.

Suppose, then, that the founder, at the beginning, had asked the advice of an able mathematician, what he would have done? – I think thus.

1. Let there be an exact map drawn of the streets, and a level taken from the pond to the *Thames*: Then consider the hills and highest grounds, and take the level of such eminencies from the pond.

2. Divide the whole perpendicular of the pond above the *Thames*, which, for examples sake, may be 60 feet into 4 parts, that is 15, 30, 45, 60 feet, and draw a crooked line over the streets for a level of 15 feet below the pond, without this, another of 30, and the like for 45, the shore of the *Thames* representing 60 feet. Thus the whole map will be divided by levels, and according to this, the distribution of the water must be regulated, that every region of the town may be equally supply'd, or at least without a remarkable inequality, by the following direction.

3. It is vulgarly known that the descents of bodies are by nature performed according to a series of square numbers, and water observes the like proportions: To make this the better understood,

Let AB be a vessel of any height and capacity, into which flows a constant stream of water to keep the vessel full. Divide the whole height into 4 equal parts, as D, E, F, G, and put there so many cocks of the same orifice. It will be found by experiment that the cocks, as they are situated one lower than another, do run with abundantly more velocity one than another, and consequently yield more water in the same time, according to the proportion which shall hereafter be set down in a table calculated for that purpose, and ascertained by true geometrical principles, and approved by undoubted experiments.

Since 'tis plain that the lower cocks run more water than the upper, they must have less and less orifices respectively, that the several regions of the town may be equally supply'd, as they are described in the map, and an exact table must also be calculated of the diameters of the orifices proper to each region, which must be inviolably observed by the proper officers, by which means all the inhabitants will be equally supply'd, without waste.

But this caution alone (tho' twill generally hold) is not sufficient where the pipes run a great way from the sources, because 'tis found that the velocity of the water is considerably abated in a long pipe (suppose of 1000 yards) by a natural cause which may be hereafter explained, and confirmed by good experiments, and a table made also of the proportions of this anomaly. Therefore 'twill be convenient to avoid the extraordinary length of the mains as much as may be, and not always to trust to one source, but to have upon any considerable eminence remote from the pond, a particular cistern to be filled by a large main from the pond first, and from thence derived by branches lying always, if possible, in a declivity, otherwise the air will gather and be apt to stop where they bend upward, and filth will gather where they bend downward.

Because there is one remarkable eminency at *Soho square*, 9 foot lower than the pond, and some thousand yards remote from the pond, it seems very requisite that should be a place for a proper cistern to begin again the several branches that should be divided to the neighbouring parts.

These, I think, are the most pertinent directions that should at first have been observed more regularly: But as all cities are built by time and chance, and not by mathematical designs; so the distribution of this noble aqueduct hath fallen by chance into the present economy, which altho' it serves pretty well the turn, is capable of improvement in time; and the more, by how much nearer it can be brought to such a primitive state, as is here rather wished for than advised; for an inveterate evil is often better tolerated than changed: Yet much may be done by time; and a steady application to what is a truth; and in order to this, it will not be amiss to recite the principal faults that in my small observation have occurred to me.

1. There seem to have been more mains laid at first than are necessary; for the old undertakers, having expended much money in bringing the river to the pond, were in haste to be reimbursed by taking in tenants (and so the first mains were irregularly carried) as they offered; and as the city increased, they increased the branches, and lengthened the mains, carrying them down, and up, and down again, until the mains failed of carrying the quantity desired, being obstructed by air, or filth, or too long a run.

2. There was little care taken of levels, and so the lower parts of the town have too much by a great proportion, and great wastes are there made and accidental branches (sic.- breaches?) and leakages soon exhaust a whole main, whereas the upper parts and the most remote were too scantily supply'd; for the water will ascend up the hill very weakly, if drawn off all the way, by branches being laid upon the main, before it gain the level where it should spread into particular cocks.

3. The ferrils which are put into the pipes, seem all of a size; which should be regulated according to the levels; every region having its peculiar size, to bring the force of the water to an equality.

Tho' the officers seem men of integrity and industry, yet they cannot look into houses; and when men have got a cock into their houses, who can hinder them from putting on more? unless their pipes be gauged with brass plates without doors; and without a comptroller, who may make it his whole business to see the company suffer no damage, I cannot see how they can be secure.

I don't find a superior plumber, who may see that orders be impartially observed, and hinder interlopers from medling with the company's pipes.

Having touch'd, in short, what mistakes occur to me in the management, I shall need say no more, but that they may, in a great measure be amended, if respect be had to the natural method before laid down. But being particularly requested to tell my thoughts about bringing the water to *Soho*, and the higher parts of the neighbourhood, to which it comes but weakly; and some remedies being suggested ; the chief most insisted on by the officers of the company, was to have a pump engine set at the pond, wrought by 3 horses, which by cranks dipping 16 inches, and working in 6 eight-inch barrels of brass, each playing 8 times in a minute, which engine, the undertaker asserts, will deliver 60 tuns in an hour, and the charge of the same to be under 300*l*. and the charge of the horses 150*l*. *per ann*. My opinion of this proposition was desired. I think such an engine will cost very much more than 300*l*. and if these 60 tuns an hour be raised 30 feet high, to fall again into the main, (which is proposed) I am certain this is not to be done by 3 horses; which, if they are strong enough to work it, yet 9 horses are requisite for change, and 2 men to look after the horses. The engine itself, will spend, in brass, iron, wood, leather, and oil, more than the feeding of another horse. If the engine breaks, the repair is chargeable, and the while the tenants want water. A Tower must be raised for the water to rise, and stabling built for the horses. Upon the whole Matter, I think an engine is not adviseable, if the place can be supplied without one, as I think it may.

I went lately with some friends of the company, and the officers, to *Soho Square*; and opening the main, and causing all branches and cocks to be stop'd upon the 6 inch main (tho' it was not sincerely done) it filled a hogshead in 38 seconds; if all had been stopped it would have run in 30 seconds, that is a tun in 2 minutes, which is 30 tuns an hour, naturally with one 6 inch main: but it is remarkable that at a long run, a larger pipe doth not only run more water than the lesser, according to the square inches of the bore, but is less subject to the impediments caused by the streightness of the pipes, which I mentioned before by the name of Anomaly. So that I am confident a 7 inch main, running into a cistern day and night, built properly at *Soho* and thereabouts, would be more useful than an engine; which is submitted to better judgement.

CHR. WREN.

Appendix Four

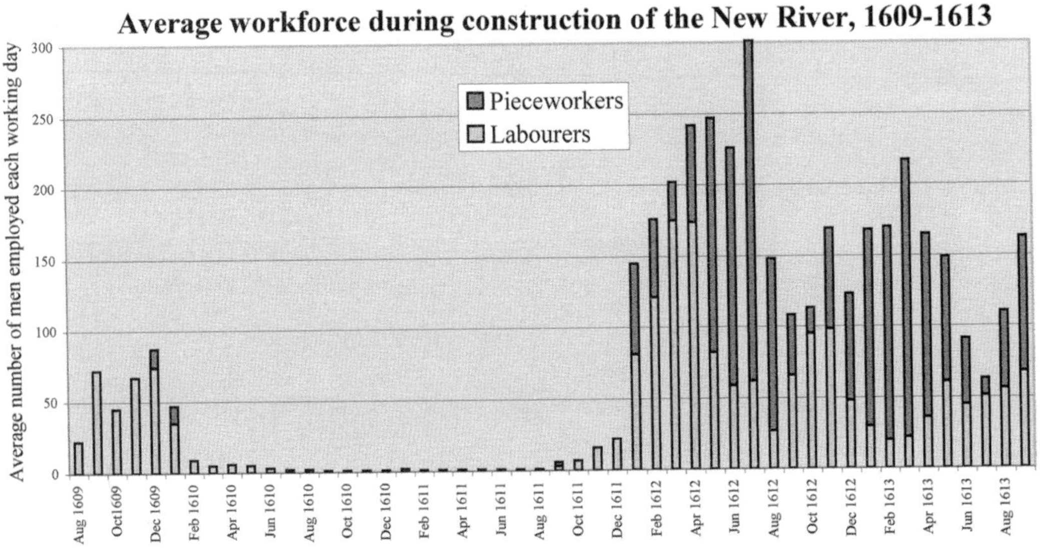

Principal dates in the history of the New River

c1600 Capt. Edmund Colthurst seeks Queen Elizabeth's approval to build New River.

1603 Death of Queen Elizabeth I before consent given.

1604 King James I grants charter to Colthurst to dig New River. Colthurst begins work.

1605-6 City of London obtains two Acts of Parliament to dig similar water supply. Colthurst stops work.

1609 Hugh Myddelton reaches agreement with Colthurst to complete project with his help, and City of London transfers its powers under the Acts to Myddelton. Digging resumes May 1609.

1610 Digging stops after opposition from some landowners, who seek to have the Acts repealed.

1611 King James dissolves Parliament, which is not recalled until 1614. Digging resumes.

1612 Myddelton sells 1/36 shares in the enterprise to 'Adventurers', and gives Colthurst 4 free shares. Shares cost £100 with liability to make further contributions as needed. Total cost approximately £300 per share.

1612 King James I agrees to contribute half of costs in return for half of profits. Adventurers will share the other half of costs and profits.

1613 New River completed, with spring water from Chadwell and Amwell flowing 42 miles to round pond at New River Head, Islington. (Later embankments and tunnels between 1618 and 1892 halved this distance.)

1613 Water House built on south side of Round Pond. Wooden pipelines distribute water to City.

1616 Only 400 households taking water supply. King, through Privy Council, directs Lord Mayor to increase number.

1619 Over 1500 households supplied. Company authorised to extract water from River Lea near Chadwell Spring to increase flow.

1619 King James I grants charter incorporating the New River Company.

1622 King seeks to buy out the Adventurers, but is refused.

1622 King grants baronetcy to Myddelton, waiving the usual fee.

1625 Severe outbreak of plague kills c. 35,000 Londoners, reducing potential customers and income.

1625 Death of King James I, who is succeeded by Charles I.

1630 Rival water scheme proposed by Sir Walter Roberts and others, offers to pay King Charles £4,000 a year just for approving it, which he does. (In the event it was never built, and no such payments were made.)

1631 King Charles I sells his half share in the New River to Sir Hugh Myddelton on 18 November, for £500 down and £500 a year in perpetuity. Myddelton splits it into 36 'King's' shares which he keeps. Unlike the 36 Adventurers' shares, they are non-voting.

1631 Death of Sir Hugh Myddelton on 7 December.

1640s English Civil War. Parliamentary 'Fort Royal' on Islington Hill, later to be site of Upper Pond. Some New River shareholders fight on Royalist side, some for Parliament.

1649 Execution of Charles I.

1660 Restoration of monarchy.

1693 Oak Room built in Water House at New River Head.

1696 Bankruptcy of Thomas Darwin, Treasurer of New River Company. Loss includes company money.

1701 'Water plot' by speculators to take over London Bridge Waterworks, (founded by Peter Morice in 1582) and Marylebone conduit supply. George Sorocold builds much-improved waterwheels for London Bridge.

1702 New River Company seek advice from Wren and others how to increase water pressure.

1707-8 George Sorocold builds combined horse mill / windmill tower to pump from Round Pond to a new Upper Pond on summit of Islington Hill, now Claremont Square reservoir. (Base of mill still at New River Head.)

1717 Company moves offices from Puddle Dock to Thames-side house and wharf at Bridewell precinct.

c1720 'Square horse-works' built at New River Head worked by four horses, which supersedes pumping from windmill tower

1769 John Smeaton's coal-burning Newcomen type 'fire engine' supersedes horse-pumping at New River Head.
1769 Christmas Eve fire at Bridewell offices destroys most early records, though charters survive.
1770 New offices and pipe wharf by Thames at Dorset Garden, just west of Bridewell site, to a design by Robert Mylne.
1779 Waterwheel by Robert Mylne at New River Head to supplement Smeaton's engine pumping water to Upper Pond.
1786 First Boulton & Watt steam engine at New River Head.
1800-17 Period of intense competition with newly formed water companies.
1810-18 W.C. Mylne, engineer, replaces all wooden water mains with iron.
1818 With wooden pipelines gone, Clerkenwell lands free for building New River estate, designed by W.C. Mylne.
1819 New River Company moves offices from Dorset Garden to new building at New River Head, which incorporates parts of Water House including Oak Room.
1822 New River Company takes over London Bridge Waterworks
1831 London's first cholera outbreak.
1842 Waterwheel still pumping from New River Head to Claremont Square Upper Pond.
1852 Metropolis Water Act requires improvements to source, storage and distribution of London water.
1856 Completion of New River Company's works to improve quality of supply. Claremont Square Upper Pond becomes covered reservoir.
1904 Constant, rather than intermittent, water supply to all New River customers finally achieved.
1904 New River Company taken over by Metropolitan Water Board. 'New River Company Limited' formed to hold the landed estate of the old company, which was excluded from the takeover. Shareholders received £6,000,000 compensation (£67,800 for each Adventurers' or King's share, and £1,365 of shares in new property company. By contrast, labourers earned about £65 a year.)
1920 Completion of new offices for M.W.B. at New River Head on site of Water House, incorporating Oak Room.
1973 Thames Water Authority takes over from Metropolitan Water Board
1989 Thames Water privatised.
2003 Footpath along course of New River from Islington to Chadwell Spring. Claremont Square reservoir refurbished and linked to Thames Water London Ring Main.

Notes and Sources

NOTES TO THE TEXT

Abbreviations: **BL** British Library, **CSP Dom. / Treas / Ven.** Calendar of State Papers, Domestic / Treasury / Venetian **G** Guildhall library, **CLRO** City of London Records Office, **GM** Gentleman's Magazine, **HMC** Historical Manuscripts Commission, **Jo** City of London Journal of Common Council ,**LMA** London Metropolitan Archive, **LSE** British Library of Political and Economic Science, London School of Economics, **M** Minutes of New River Company meetings, in series ACC 2558/ NR1/1-45 at LMA. From 13 March 1817 the minutes of General Meetings were kept in different books from those of Weekly Meetings i.e. NR/1/39-45. **Nott. UL** Nottingham University Library, Portland collection, **PC** Privy Council, **PP** Parliamentary Papers, **PRO** Public Record Office, **Rem.** Remembrancia, City of London, **Rep.** Repertory of Court of Aldermen, City of London, **SM** Science Museum Library, **RIBA** Library of the Royal Institute of British Architects, **SRO** Suffolk Record Office, Bury St Edmund's.

Chapter One: On Islington Hill

1. Christopher Thomas, *The Archaeology of Medieval London*, 2002.
2. Walter Harrison, *New & Universal History Description and Survey of the Cities of London & Westminster etc* 1775, p338.
3. Rem. (1878) I.656.554, 23.4.1592 and II.32.554, 30.9.1594, II.321.554, 8.6.1608; III.100 p555, 9.6.1613. Henry Berry, MIMechE etc, Chairman MWB, *London's Water Supply*, 1943, p3.
4. HMC Cecil Mss xiv.157
5. HMC, pt 13, 1910, p242
6. CSP Dom. 1603-10 p181.
7. LMA ACC 2558/ MW/C/15/017; Patent Roll 2 James 1 part 25; HMC Cecil Mss 17.181; CSP Dom 1603-10 p.93.
8. CSP Dom., 1603-10, 189, 92-4. (Colthurst mentions in 189.94 that he was currently 'at Cambridge, bringing a river there.' From the date, 1604-5, it seems this must have been the conduit from Great Shelford, built at that time, still flowing, and now called Hobson's Conduit. Colthurst never seems to have been credited with this work - see e.g. C.H. Cooper, *Annals of Cambridge*, 1845, p36-7.)
9. Rep 26/2 514b.
10. Wilson, D.H. ed., *The Parliamentary Diary of Robert Bowyer 1606-7*, 1931, p12, 177.
11. 3 Jas. I c.18 (1605)
12. 4 Jas. I c12 (1606)
13. Fuller's *Worthies*, p.152.
14. 9 September 1606, Rep 27/263; HMC pt 13, 1910, 26 June 1606, Rep 27/227b
15. 11 September 1606 Rep 27/265
16. 14 October 1606, Rep 27/89
17. 4 December 1606, Rep 27/412
18. 28 October 1608 Rep 28/288
19. 14 March 1609, Rep. 29/3.
20. Jo. 27/377-8.
21. Aubrey, *Brief Lives*, ed. Clark 1898.
22. CSP Dom. 1603-10, p.187.

Chapter Two: The first ten miles – 1604 to 1609

1. PRO LR2/27-35.
2. LMA ACC 2558/ NR 13/7 folder 1
3. BL Mss Lansdowne 92 f 113
4. CSP Dom. 1603-10, 189, 91-4
5. 11 Sep 1606 Rep 27/265
6. E.G.R. Taylor *History of Technology* vol. 3 p543.
7. Hutton, C. *Mathematical Tables* 1785, p28n
8. 21 Mar 1612,
9. Aubrey, John *Brief Lives* ed. O.L. Dick, 1949 p198
10. M, 7 Nov 1782
11. E. Howes, *Annales or a Generall Chronicle of England begun by John Stow*, 1631, p1015.
12. *Gentleman's Magazine* vol. 58 pt I, p.460.
13. LMA ACC2558 MW/C/15/65
14. 14 & 21 Sep 1611

Chapter Three: Completing the New River – 1610 to 1613

1. Bodleian Mss Tanner 98, fo. 113.
2. Sir R. Winwood, *Memorials of Affairs of State in the Reigns of Queen Elizabeth and King James I* , 1725, iii, 160, Mr Beaulieu to Mr Trumbull .
3. CSP Dom. 1611-18, vol 78 no 106; Bodleian, Tanner Ms 98, f 113
4. Gough 45
5. Rep HMC iii (1872) App. p58, (Duke of Northumberland's MSS)
6. 28 & 21 Aug 1613

6a. BL Add. Ms. 70341/29/2.

7. HMC Cecil Mss 12. 370, 16. 55, 17. 181.
8. HMC, pt 13, 1910, p242
9. CSP Dom 1611-18, SP14 vol 78 no 106; Bodleian.Tanner Ms 98, f 47-9, 113.
10. 15 May 1613
11. 28 & 21 August 1613

Chapter Four: Source, storage and supply

1. HMC, Pt 13, 1910, p242

2. 15 May 1613
3. 10 October 1618
4. 7 November 1618.
5. 5 September 1619
6. 17 June 1620
7. LMA ACC 2558/ NR13/7 p.199
8. Acounts, 27 December 1617
9. LMA ACC 2558/ NR13/7/ Folder 3, 177
10. Accounts, 24 December 1614 & 30 December 1615 etc.
11. Robert Seymour, *Survey of London & Westminster &c*, updating Stow, 1734, p.26
12. M, 6 November 1781.
13. M, 23 May 1805, 26 May 1857
14. F.W. Drake, op. cit. p.442
15. Times 1 July 1930, BWA 1930/541.
16. M, 19 September 1779, 27 June 1771, 5 October 1693, 19 August 1770, 30 June 1714, F.W. Drake, op. cit. p.441.
17. J.T.Smith, '*Book for a Rainy Day*', F.W. Drake, op. cit. p. 441
18. 20 November 1613
19. PRO LR2/43
20. LMA ACC 2558/ MW/C/15/284
21. CSP Treas 1720-8, p339, vol.252 no 64.
22. PRO, LR2/35; LMA ACC 2558/ NR 13/304 p34-6.
23. PRO LR 2/35.
24. PRO LR 2/43.

Chapter Five: More help from the King – 1616 to 1631

1. City Remembrancia 1878. 23 Dec1616 4.46.p556.
2. ditto January 1617, 4.96.p557
3. ditto 27 February 1617, 4.101.p558, Accounts 4 April 1618
4. GL, Ms 3505, fo. 13.
5. M.S.R.Jenner, 'From conduit community to commercial network? - Water in London 1500-1725' *Londinopolis, Essays in the cultural and social history of early modern London*, Manchester, 2000, p.250.

5a. "... as of our manor of East Greenwich... in free and common socage by fealty only and not in chiefe nor by knight's service."

6. Sackville MSS (HMC) no 505 (M 1008); Acts PC Jan 1618- June 1619, vol 36, pp 404,157, 158.
7. BL Harleian Mss, no.1507 art. 40 (Cat ii 84b)
8. E. Howes, *Annales or a Generall Chronicle of England begun by John Stow*, 1631, p.1041 b.
9. LMA ACC 2558/ NR 13/304, p.34-6.
10. Roberts, Sir W., *A Proposition for the serving and supplying of London, Westminster and other places adjoining*. 1641.

Chapter Six: Cost and Concealment

1. PRO, LR 2/27-44.
2. Gough p36
3. LMA ACC 2558 NR 1/40
4. LMA ACC 2558/ NR13/304. The late Mr G.C. Berry, M.W.B. Archivist, deserves the credit for realising the significance of Wilkinson's manuscript.
5. *Archaeologia*, in 'London Water', MWB 1934, p550; see also chapter 16, note 10.
6. M, 5 March 1812.
7. PP 1828, viii, App 4, pp314-5
8. PP 1851 xv, Q 11708-16, pp661-3
9. PP 1852, xii, Q 8212, p507
10. PP1900, vol 38, Pt2, Q22, 330-2: 22, 612

Chapter Seven: New River People

1. LMA ACC 2558/ NR13/7
2. LMA ACC 2558/ NR 13/7, F.W. Drake, op. cit. p. 393
3. London & Its Environs Described, 1761, vol. 5, p37-42, BL 577.d.5-7.
4. LMA ACC 2558/ NR13/15/6; and Board papers 7 Nov 1792.
5. LMA ACC 2558/ NR 13/7, folder 3.
6. CSP Dom 29/117/103.
7. LMA ACC 2558/, NR13/7, folder 3, April 1665
8. BL Portland 70341 29/2; Nott. U.L. – Pw 2 Hy/ 895
9. F.W. Drake, op. cit. p. 392.
10. F.W. Drake, op. cit. p.392
11. F.W. Drake, op. cit. p.392
12. GM v52 1782 p74
13. LMA ACC 2558/ NR 13/12,
14. LMA ACC 2558/ NR 13/10/1.
15. LMA ACC 2558/ NR 13/7 folder 1
16. LMA, ACC 2558/ NR13/9, NR13/188.
17. BL Ms Add 70341
18. BL Ms Harleian 3604
19. LMA, ACC 2558/ NR13/9
20. Rev. J. Nightingale, *Beauties of England & Wales*, vol. 3, 1815.
21. M, 13 Oct 1859
22. LMA ACC 2558/ NR 13/12
23. M, 14 July 1785
24. M, 13 Jan 1803.
25. Maitland, *History of London*, 1756, vol. 2, p.1269
26. LMA ACC 2558/ NR 1/5 p.173; MW/C/15/ 253/1; NR 1/7 p.80; NR 1/9 p.171
27. LMA ACC 2558/ NR13/314/9; NR 1/5 p151;NR 1/7, p.307.
28. LMA ACC 2558/ NR 1/8 p.108, 113.
29. LMA ACC 2558/ NR 1/10 p.183, 188.
30. LMA ACC 2558/ NR 1/8 p.202.
31. LMA ACC 2558/ NR 1/19 p.31, 33.
32. LMA ACC 2558/ NR 1/17 p.135, 164.
33. M, 11 Dec 1800, 12 Feb 1801, 13 Jul 1801.
34. LMA ACC 2558/ MW/C 15/ 261/1
35. M, 14 Jun 1804, 21 Apr 1803, 31 May 1804, 26 Jul 1804
36. LMA ACC 2558/ MW/C/15/197/3.

Chapter Eight: Premises and Problems

1. Rev. J. Nightingale, *Beauties of England & Wales*, vol. 3, 1815.
2. LMA ACC 2558/ MW/C/15/364
3. BL Add Ms 23071, cited in Walpole Society edition of George Vertue's notebks, vol. 4, p65.
4. M, 7 Nov 1782.
5. David Green, *The Oak Room,* p.138
6. Letter 4 Mar 1886, referring to work in 1868.
7. Letter, Metropolitan Water Board Statistics section, 2 April 1951
8. LMA ACC 2558/ NR 13/13/1
9. LMA ACC 2558/ NR 13/54/1-6
10. LMA ACC 2558/ MW C/46/ 26(2)
11. LMA ACC 2558/ NR 13/53/1-10.
12. Hugh Phillips, *The Thames About 1750*, 1951.
13. M, 5 Feb, 5 Nov & 14 Nov 1771; John Noorthouck, *A New History of London,* 1773
14. LMA, ACC 2558/ MW C /15/364,
15. F.W. Drake, op. cit. p. 416.
16. *Fifty Years Review 1903-53,* Metropolitan Water Board pp.25-6, 30, 71.
17. PRO, LR 2/28-29; 18 Jun, 2 Jul 1614
18. LMA ACC2558 NR 13/7, 4/36a.
19. BL Ms Harleian 3604
20. PC 23 Jun 1669.
21. PC 21 July 1669.
22. LMA ACC 2558/ NR13/10/1
23. PRO LR/2/27-33, Jun 1614, 30 Mar 1616
24. LMA ACC 2558/ NR2/2.
25. LMA ACC 2558/ MW C/15/105; BL Add. Ms. 48904, f.18.
26. M, 17 Jul 1783.
27. LMA ACC 2558/ MW/C/15/142-8.
28. LMA ACC 2558/ MW/C/15/105/1
29. *Diary of Joseph Farington, 8 December 1809,* ed K. Cave, Yale, 1982.
30. LMA ACC 2558/ NR13/10/13.
31. LMA ACC 2558/ NR13/7 folder 4
32. M, 11 Feb 1813

Chapter Nine: A Lost Fort in London – 1642

1. CSP Dom. vol 539 pt II no 169.
2. 2.BL, Thomason Tracts E.92.11.
3. CSP Ven, vol 26, 1642-3, 24 October 1642.
4. BL, Thomason Tracts, E.124.25 and 27.
5. CSP Ven, vol 26 p.192, 7 November 1642.
6. CSP Ven, vol 26. p.198
7. CSP Ven, vol 26. p.256
8. CSP Ven. vol. 26, p.273, 15 May 1643.
9. CSP Ven, vol 26. p.273
10. McColvin, H, Ransome, D.R. & Summerson, J. *History of the King's Works, vol 3, part 1.* 1975; p.158.
11. See Smith, V. and Kelsey, P. 'The Lines of Communication: the Civil War Defences of London' in Porter, S. ed. *London and the Civil War,* 1996, pp 117-48.
12. William Lithgow, *The Present Surveigh of London and England's State,* 1643
13. BL, Thomason Tracts, E.49.25; Raikes, G.A., *History of the Honourable Artillery Company,* 1878; Raikes, G.A., *The ancient vellum book of the Honourable Artillery Company,* 1890.
14. CSP Ven, vol 26 p.257, 27 March 1643.
15. Maitland, W. *History of London,* 1756 ed. p.1365.
16. See map at BL K.Top. 20.16, and Bowles, *New and Exact Prospect from the North Side of London,* 1730.
17. G.Vertue, *Descripton of the works of Wenceslaus Hollar with some account of his Life,*1745.

Chapter Ten: The water plot – 1701

1. PRO SPD Charles II, 229, No 162.
2. HMC, BL at HLR 941, MC29 vol 6.
3. PRO C9 158/36, *Taylor v Darwin,* 1700.
4. Glasgow UL, Ms Hunter 73 (T.3.11) ff 33-34.
5. S.W.Singer, *Correspondence of the Earls of Clarendon and Rochester,* 1844, vol.1, 198-200.
6. Nott. U.L., Pw2 Hy 336.
7. W. Maitland, History of London, 1756
8. SRO, HAS40/3/11/1
9. PRO C5/257/19, Morris v Soame, 1705.
10. G, Cl.ACC. fo. Pam. 56
11. SRO, HA 540/3/11/2
12. HMC Portland Papers vol. 4, p. 51, 20 Nov 1702.
13. CLRO Misc. Mss. 356/22
14. BL 19.h.1 (140), March 1719.
15. BL 19.h.1 (140)
16. PRO, C9/467/164, Sorocold v Newsham
17. PRO, C5/216/1, Almanza v Soame 1701, C5/328/40, Seignoret v Soame 1704.
18. Suffolk Record Office, HA 540/3/11/3
19. Nott. U. L. Pw2 Hy 362.

Chapter Eleven: Wind, horse or water? – 1702 to 1705

1. BL HMC at HLR941 MC29, vol 6 (see p.109 above)
2. LMA ACC 2558/ NR14/01(5).
3. BL Add Ms 70341 /29/2.
4. Gentleman's Magazine, vol 23, 1753, pp114-6.
5. LMA ACC 2558/ NR13/188.
6. Nott. UL, Pw 2 Hy 305.
7. Nott. UL, Pw 2 Hy 336.
8. BL Add Ms 70341/29/2.
9. LMA ACC 2558/ NR 14/01.
10. BL Add Ms 70341/29/2.

Chapter Twelve: Sorocold's Solution – 1707 to 1711

1. LMA ACC 2558/ MW/C/15/199.
2. LMA ACC 2558: NR 13/314/6; NR 13/37/ 1-14; NR 13/285; MW/C/15/72.
3. BL Add Ms 70341/29/2.
4. LMA ACC 2558/ NR 14/01(15).

5. LMA ACC 2558/ NR 13/7 folder 4, p266.
6. J.T. Desagulier, *A course of Experimental Philosophy,* 1734.
7. M, 6 November 1779.
8. J. Warner, BL Ms Lansdowne 841 f113-4
9. R. Thoresby, *Ducatus Leodiensis, Topography of Leeds,* 1715, p607.
10. BL Mss, Stowe 747, vol V, f 63, 66
11. Patent 369 of 1704; Extract from Wolley, 1711, quoted in Simpson's *History of Derby.*
12. R. Bald, *General View of the History of the Coal Trade of Scotland,* Edinburgh, 1812.
13. BL Add. Ms. 69947, fo. 89, 17 Nov 1702, with Sorocold's signature
14. Survey of London, vol. 17, The Strand.
15. PRO, C9/467/164, Sorocold v Newsham
16. CLRO, Reports & Papers of the Bridge House Committee 1710-14, and see Guildhall Ms 2194.
17. BL, Add. Ms. 69949.
18. S. Switzer, *An Introduction to a General System of Hydrostaticks and Hydraulicks,* 1729, p.319

Chapter Thirteen: The First Surveyor – 1718 to 1766

1. LMA, ACC 2558/ NR 1/1.
2. LMA ACC 2558/ NR 13/188.
3. Patent 395 of 1714.
4. LMA ACC 2558/ NR13/7, Folder 4
5. LMA ACC 2558/ NR13/10/6-9
6. GM, 1771 p.46; 1779 p.537-9.
7. BL C.131.ff20.(18).

Chapter Fourteen: Mylne, Smeaton, Boulton and Watt – 1766 to 1799

1. Mylne's year of birth is sometimes given as 1734 but he believed it to be 1733, as shown by a note in his diary in January 1801 that it was his 68th birthday.
2. Guildhall, A.8.5 (35)
3. LMA ACC 2558/ MW/C/15/243/3.
4. RIBA, MyFam 5/6 13 September 1770, RM to WM.
5. LMA ACC 2558/MW/C/15/41
6. M, 11 May 1774.
7. M 6 November 1779.
9. M, December 1842, LMA ACC 2558/ NR1/15/1 p.186.
9. M, 6 November 1781, 4 July 1799, 22 November 1804; LMA ACC 2558/ NR11/ 155/1; M, 22 Dec 1842.
10. M, 24 February 1785.
11.M, 23 November 1786.
12. LMA ACC 2558/MW/C/15/283/5.
13. LMA ACC 2558/ NR13/314/9.
14. LMA ACC 2558/ MW/C/15/68/05.

Chapter Fifteen: Fighting for survival – 1800 to 1820

1. LMA, ACC 2558/ MW/C/15/68/1
2. Report of New River Company Works Committee, 1814.
3. M, 5 August 1819, 4 March 1813.
4. M, 20 April 1815
5. M, 31 October 1811
6. M, 7 November 1811
7. M, 5 March, 19 March, 16 April 1812.
8. M, 30 July 1812
9. M, 19 December 1811, 13 February 1812, 27 February 1812,12 March 1812, 19 March 1812
10. M, 29 July 1813 and 15 June 1815
11. M, 13 February 1812
12. M, 19 March, 10 September 1812, 21 & 28 January, 11 February 1813
13. M, 15 April 1813
14. M, 19 December 1811, 27 August 1812.
15. M 5 October 1815, 15 February 1816
16. M, 14 May 1812
17. M, 6 May, 20 May 1813
18. PP 1851 xv Qs 11766, 11776, 11790-2.
19. M, 15 April 1813, 21 May 1816
20. M, 10 August, 7 September, 14 December 1815
21. M, 28 September, 9 November 1815, 22 February 1816.
22. M, July-August 1839.
23. M, 26 January 1818.
24. M, 19 March 1816
25. M, 11 June, 18 June, 25 June 1816.
26. M, 10 August 1820.

Chapter Sixteen: The quest for better water

1. M, 16 May 1765.
2. M, 4 November 1795
3. M 23 March 1815, 28 February 1816, 6 August, 24 September, 1 October 1818.
4. M, 5 May, 12 May 1808; 2 July 1816.
5. M, 6 August, 13 August 1818.
6. M, 26 May 1831
7. M, 25 September, 16 December 1819, 3 July, 10 July 1834
8. M, 25 May 1837
9. M 5 March 1816
10. *Archaeologia,* in 'London Water', MWB, 1934, p550. (Photograph of original holograph letter, said to be the property of Miller & Co., Mechanical Engineers, Heneage St., London E.)
11. Entick, *History & Survey of London,* 1766, vol. ii p.114.
12. LMA ACC 2558/ MW/C/15/166
13. LMA ACC 2558/ NR1/12, pp. 462, 464
14. LMA ACC 2558/ MW/C/15/217/3
15. Illustrated London News, July – December 1856, p521-3.
16. Pevsner, *Buildings of England, London North.*

17. Richard Sisley, *The London Water Supply,* 1899, p.43.
18. F. W. Drake op. cit. p.439, and see John Noorthouck, *A New History of London,* 1773, p.149, N. Salmon, *History of Hertfordshire,* 1728;
19. LMA, ACC 2558/ MW/C P/090, 24 January 1972.

Chapter Seventeen: Paving the Fields

1. LMA ACC 2558/ NR13/11/12 15 May1781.
2. M, 9 & 16 November 1815, 9 April 1816.
3. M, 26 April 1798.
4. LMA ACC 1953/ C/1322, 27 February 1817.
5. William Tatham, *London Canal and Rail Road – Explanatory Remarks,* London, 1803 (Royal Society of Arts) Col. Tatham later took his own life by throwing himself in front of a cannon just as it was fired.
6. LMA ACC 2558/ MW/C/15/150.
7. LMA ACC 2558/MW/C/15/179/01-08.
8. M, 28 February 1811, 16 April 1812, 7 May 1816; VCH Middlesex, vol 8, p.71.
9. LMA, ACC 2558/ NR 13/20/2.
10. M, 15 February 1810
11. W.J. Passingham, London's Markets, 1934; VCH Middlesex, vol. 8, 1985, p.73.
12. Storer, J. & H. S., with T. Cromwell, *History & Description of the Parish of Clerkenwell,* p332
13. M, 25 July 1811, 1 October 1818, 10 February 1820
14. *Public Advertiser,* 27 May 1757.
15. Thomas Carlyle, *Reminiscences,* 1887, vol.2, p.116.
16. M, 21 July 1825.
17. Nelson, *History of Islington* (1829) p.112.
18. Storer, J. & H. S., with T. Cromwell, *History & Description of the Parish of Clerkenwell,* p.153.
19. M, 28 November 1811, 16 April & 11 June & 2 July 1812, 21 January 1813
20. LMA ACC 1953/C/1296
21. M, 21 November 1822
22. M, 5 December 1822.
23. *History of St Mark's,* Rev. H.L.L. Denny, 1921; *Records of the Raids,* Bishop Rt Rev. H.L. Paget, 1918.
24. *The Times,* 5 March 1843, Pinks 150-1
25. *'Weekly Dispatch',* 27 April 1834; Pinks; *'The Times'* passim, PRO C/107/127.
26. LMA ACC 1953/C/1337

Chapter Eighteen: Death and Pleasure; Riot and War

1. J. Nichols, *The Progresses .. of King James I,* (1828) iv. 749.
2. E. Dower *New River Head,* annexed to The Salopian Esquire, 1739.
3. LMA MJ/SPC/W/0007
4. LMA MJ/SPC/W/1814
5. Royal Humane Society, Reports for 1775, BL.
6. *Morning Post,* 19 July 1794; Pinks p.465.
7. Philip Ward-Jackson, *Public Sculpture in the City of London,* Liverpool 2003.
8. John Gerard, *Herbal,* 1597; BL 449.k.4, vol.1 p.168.
9. LMA, ACC 2558/ NR13/7 folder 3, fo.181a
10. *Memoirs of Charles Dibdin the younger,* ed. George Speaight 1956, p.59
11. M, 24 June, 15 July 1824.
12. LSE, Booth notebooks, 353, p.128-9.
13. M, 25 May 1831, 13 October 1831, 20 October 1831.
14. M, July 1780, 17 August, 19 October, 21 December 1780.
15. M, 6 November 1781.
16. *Public Advertiser,* 27 May 1757, in BL 10349.h.14, Pinks, 1881
17. LMA ACC 2558/ MW C/48/056.
18. LMA ACC 2558/ MW/C/05/5.

Chapter Twenty: Walking the river

1. Charles Lamb, *Essays of Elia – Amicus Redivivus,* 1823.
2. Richard Sisley, *The London Water Supply,* 1899, p.28.

Appendix One: The best shares in the world

1. New River Company's Act (1866), 29 & 30 Vict. c.230
2. Rudden, *The New River, a legal history,* Oxford, 1985, pp. 43-71
3. LMA ACC 1953/ A/251
4. F.W. Drake, op. cit. p. 358
5. Annual Register 1766, F.W. Drake, op. cit. p. 359; RIBA, Robert Mylne's diary 1765,
6. LMA ACC 1953/A/251; GL, Cl. Acc. Pam. 1410.

Appendix Two: Swallowing minnows

1. CSP Dom 1663-4 p655, 1664-5 p230; Dickinson p.19
2. SM Arch:Berry 3/3/1
3. LMA ACC 2558/ MW/C/15/102.
4. LMA ACC 2558/ MW/C/15/291/01
5. LMA ACC 2558/ MW C/15/290.
6. John James Park, *Natural History & Topography of Hampstead,* reprinted 1818, p. 26
7. LMA ACC 2558/ C/46/24/2, City Lands Committee 57/344, 61/140, 61/215b, 61/229;
8. M, 8 June 1815, 19 March, 26 March1816
9. M, 30 October 1817
10. M, 16 November 1854, 5 April 1855
11. M, 23 August 1855
12. F.W. Drake, op. cit. p. 617, Dickinson 76
13. M, 4 May 1815; Nelson 1811, p105; Rudden p.138 n.10. F.W. Drake, op. cit. p. 617.

PRIMARY SOURCES

The main source of original New River Company documents is London Metropolitan Archives, where Thames Water deposited the vast quantity of material inherited from the Metropolitan Water Board, which had the archives of all the companies it had taken over. The papers of the late Mr G.C. Berry at the Science Museum Library also contain useful material. Other documents are to be found at the institutions listed in the preface.

PRINTED SOURCES

Anon. *Letters from a Moor at London to his friend at Tunis containing an account of his journey through England*, 1736.

Anon. *An echo from Heaven*, 1652.

Bailey, N., *The Antiquities of London & Westminster*, 1734

Barton, N., *The Lost Rivers of London* 1962, reprinted 1992.

Berry, G.C., 'Sir Hugh Myddelton and the New River' (in *Transactions of the Honourable Society of Cymmrodorion* for 1956, published 1957, pp 17-46.)

Berry, C.G. *London's Water Supply 1903-1953*.

Besant, W., *Clerkenwell*, 1906

Colburn, Z., *The Waterworks of London*, 1867.,

Cosh, Mary, *An historical walk along the New River*, 1988

Cosh, Mary, *The Squares of Islington, Pt 1*, 1990.

Desaguliers, *Course of Experimental Philosophy*, 1734

Dickinson, H.W., *Water Supply of Greater London*, 1954

Drake, F. W., *Sir Hugh Myddelton and the New River Company*, Aquarius magazine (MWB), passim, 1923-6.

Entick, J., *New & Accurate History & Survey &c.*, 1766

Essex-Lopresti, M. *Exploring the New River*, 1986, third edition 1997.

Garbott, W., *New River – a Poem*, 1750

Gerard, J., *The Herball or General Historie of Plantes*, 1597 and 1633,

Gough, J.W., *Sir Hugh Myddelton, Entrepreneur and Engineer*, Oxford, 1964.

Graham-Leigh, J. *London's Water Wars*, 2000

Green, E., *The Case of Ephraim Green, late Clerk to the New River Company*, 1717.

Griffiths, P. & Jenner, M.S.R., (eds), 'Londinopolis: Essays in the cultural and social history of early modern London', 2000.

Halliday, S., *The Great Stink of London*, 1999

Harrison, W., *New & Universal History, Description & Survey of the Cities of London & Westminster*, 1775

Hatton, E., *New View of London*, 1708

Jenkins, Rhys, 'George Sorocold: a chapter in the history of public water supply', in *Collected Papers of Rhys Jenkins*, Newcomen Society, Cambridge, 1936.

Maitland, W., *History of London*, 1756

Matthews, W., *Hydraulia*, 1835

McKellar, Elizabeth, *The Birth of Modern London*, Manchester 1999.

Morris, Christopher, ed., *The Illustrated Journeys of Celia Fiennes 1685-1712*, 1982

Mylne, R.W., *The master masons to the Crown of Scotland and their works*, Edinburgh, 1893.

Nelson, J., *History of Islington*, 1811, reprinted 1980.

Noorthouck, J., *A new History of London*, 1773

Phillips, Hugh, *The Thames About 1750*, 1951.

Pinks, W. J., *The History of Clerkenwell*, 1881 (reprinted 2001).

Porter, S. ed., *London and the Civil War*, 1996.

Pugin, A.C., *Series of views in Islington & Pentonville*, 1819.

Richardson, Sir A.W., *Robert Mylne, Architect and Engineer*, 1955

Richardson, J., *London and its People*, 1995

Richardson, J., *Islington Past*, 2000.

Roberts, K., *London & Liberty – Ensigns of the Trained Bands*, 1987.

Roberts, Sir W., *A proposition for the serving & supplying of London, Westminster &c.*, 1641

Rudden, B. *The New River, a legal history*, Oxford, 1985

Sisley, R. *The London Water Supply*, 1899

Smeaton, J., *Reports of the late John Smeaton*, 1797

Smeaton J., *An experimental enquiry..*, 1760.

Smiles, Samuel *Lives of the Engineers*, vol I, 1862.

Smith, Denis *Civil Engineering Heritage: London and the Thames Valley*, 2000.

Storer, J. & H.S., with Cromwell, T., *History & description of the Parish of Clerkenwell*, 1828

Stringer, G.F., *Some Descriptive Notes on the New River Head*, 1927.

Stringer, G.F., *The Water Supply of London*, 1949

Switzer, S., *Introduction to a General System of Hydrostaticks & Hydraulics*, 1729

Tames, R., *Clerkenwell and Finsbury Past*, 1999.

Thoresby, Ralph, *Ducatus Leodiensis – Topography of Leeds*, 1715

Thornton, W., *New Complete & Universal History .. of London & Westminster*, 1784

Tomkins, T. E., *Perambulation of Islington*, 1858.

Trench, R. & Hillman, E. *London under London*, 1993.

Ward, R., *Animadversions of Warre*, 1639.

Ward-Jackson, Philip, *Public Sculpture in London*, Liverpool, 2003.

Williamson, F., 'George Sorocold of Derby', *Journal of the Derbyshire Archaeological & Natural History Society*, (1936, published 1937) pp 49-93.

INDEX

There are main entries for **City of London, New River, New River Company, New River Head, Parliament, Pipes,** and **Pumping methods.**
For **Architects, Engineers and Surveyors** see individual entries for Aldersey, Ball, Bazalgette, Beckingham, Billings, Blagrave, Boulton & Watt, Dodd, Genebelli, Grace, Grant, Hearn, Evan Jones, Inigo Jones, Mill, Morice, Mylne family, Lowthorp, Pond, Rennie, Ruddell, Savery, Smeaton, Sorocold, Staper, Tatham, Telford, Vanbrugh, White, Whitworth, Wren, Wright, Yarnold.
For **Artists, writers and craftsmen** see individual entries for Aubrey, Bennett, Bursill, Canaletto, Carlyle, Cooke, Cruikshank, Defoe, Dibdin, Dickens, Evelyn, Gerard, Gibbons, Hollar, Joseph, Lamb, Thomas Middleton, Nicholls, Scott, Smollett, Thoresby, Ward.
Pages with illustrations are starred *

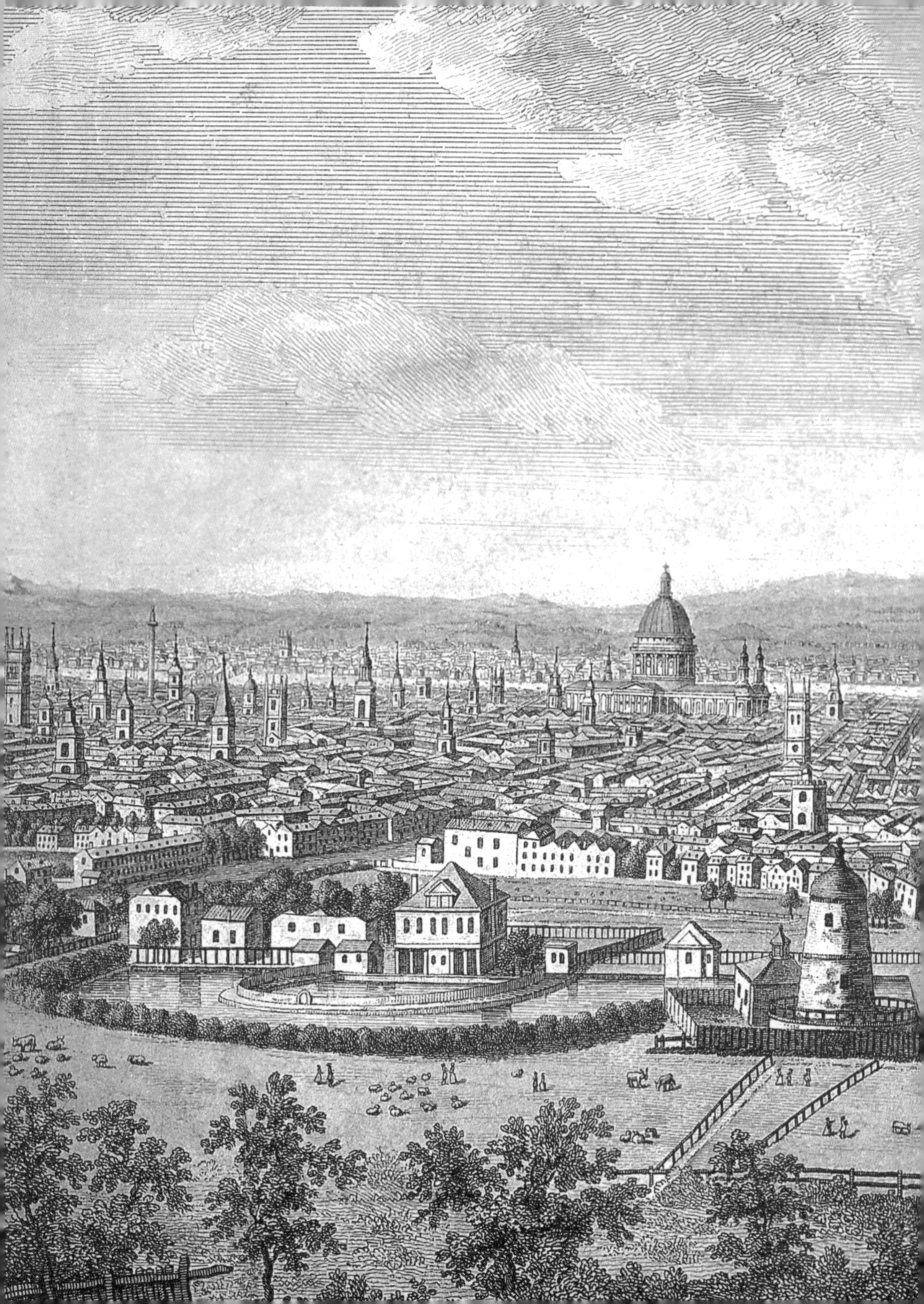